BRIG.-GENERAL G. N. JOHNSTON, C.M.G., D.S.O., (d). (F).
who commanded the New Zealand Artillery in the Field during the whole period of the war

New Zealand Artillery in the Field

1914-18

BY

LIEUT. J. R. BYRNE, N.Z.F.A.

ERRATA.

Page	6,	Line 9	"On Sept. 29th"—to be deleted.
,,	6	,, 10	"shortly after mid-day"—to be deleted.
,,	6	,, 5	from bottom, for "Lieutenant E. Gardner" read "Lieutenant D. E. Gardner"
,,	12	,, 16	from bottom, for "Empress of Asia" read "Empress of Russia"
,,	13	,, 9	for "Empress of Asia" read "Empress of Russia"
,,	48	,, 18	for "untrained" read "trained"
,,	48	,, 27	for "of the left" read "on the left"
,,	82	,, 4	for "Lieutenant" read "Captain"
,,	84	,, 16	from bottom, for "Lancastrians" read "Lancashires"
,,	87	,, 12	for "Colonel Johnstone" read "Colonel Johnston"
,,	91	,, 18	for "Mounted Artillery" read "Mountain Artillery"
,,	125	,, 17	for "Divisions" read "Division"
,,	179	,, 15	for "for the 11th Battery" read "from the 11th Battery"
,,	254	,, 6	from bottom, after "(Rifle) Brigade" insert "with the 1st Infantry Brigade"
,,	289	,, 7	for "defensive" read "offensive"
,,	295	,, 17	for "battle" read "attack"
,,	295	,, 24	for "preceded" read "proceeded"
,,	306	,, 13	for "Brigade" read "English"

Page 101 Line 22 for "Captain Beattie" read "Major Beattie."

CONTENTS

Foreword vii
From the C.R.A. xi

PART I.
THE GALLIPOLI CAMPAIGN

CHAPTER		PAGE
I.	The Outbreak of War	1
II.	The Landing at Anzac	24
III.	The Isolation of Anzac	41
IV.	How the Guns were Starved	55
V.	The 3rd Battery at Helles	61
VI.	The August Offensive	67
VII.	Nearing the End	90

PART II.
THE WESTERN FRONT

I.	The Division Sails for France	100
II.	The Battle of the Somme	121
III.	Fleurbaix	152
IV.	The Battle of Messines	161
V.	Passchendaele	184
VI.	Wintering in the Salient	205
VII.	The German Bid for Amiens	218
VIII.	The Retreat from Messines	237
IX.	The Turning Point	250
X.	The Enemy in Retreat	264
XI.	Breaking the Hindenburg Line	268
XII.	Le Quesnoy	289
	Appendix—Honours and Awards	309

LIST OF ILLUSTRATIONS

Brigadier-General G. N. Johnston, C.M.G., D.S.O. ...	Frontispiece
The First Battery in action	Facing page 24
One of the 3rd Battery guns at Cape Helles	33
The "water queue" on the beach at Anzac	48
Lieut.-Colonel F. B. Sykes, D.S.O., (d) R.A.	65
The 18 pr. Q. F. Gun	80
The Tragedy of Ypres	96
One of the massive German "pill boxes" wrecked by heavy artillery fire	112
The 4·5 in. Howitzer	113
Lieut.-Colonel I. T. Standish, C.M.G., D.S.O.	128
Lieut.-Colonel N. S. Falla, C.M.G., D.S.O.	129
A pack column going forward to the guns at Passchendaele ...	144
Lieut.-Colonel R. S. McQuarrie, D.S.O., M.C.	145
A New Zealand battery in action near Kansas Farm ...	160
Wintry conditions in the Ypres Salient	161
Extracting a pack mule from a shell-hole	177
"On trek"	192
A British tank going into action	192
A depressing prospect: the Ypres Salient under snow ...	208
A watering point at Louvencourt	209
A British heavy gun in action	224
Well concealed: a 4·5 in. Howitzer	225
A captured German Tank	225
A 6 in. Trench Mortar in action	241
Peaceful surroundings	257
New Zealand Artillery crossing the River Selle	272
The guns going forward	289
Open Fighting	296
One of the mobile mortars designed by the Divisional Trench Mortars	304
A New Zealand Battery coming into action	304

LIST OF MAPS

Gallipoli Peninsula	Facing page 28
Anzac	66
Armentieres	106
Somme	136
Messines	168
Passchendaele	200
Ypres	212
Somme, 1918	222
Final Offensive	252
Road of Artillery to Cologne	306

FOREWORD

I have been asked to write a few words as a foreword to the Regimental History of the N.Z.F.A. I am naturally glad to do this, though I do so with the greatest diffidence, owing to the fact that my close personal relationship with the New Zealand Field Artillery ceased in July, 1916, when to my very great regret the New Zealand Division left my command. I can, therefore, write only about the early period of the war, though I need hardly say that I never failed to take the greatest interest and real pride in the achievements of the New Zealand Forces.

It was in December, 1914, that I first made acquaintance with the New Zealand gunners, when the artillery sent from the Dominion consisted of one brigade of field artillery, viz., three four-gun batteries. This force was under the command of Lieutenant-Colonel G. Napier Johnston, R.A., a Canadian by birth, who, after graduating at the Kingston Military College, had entered the Royal Artillery, and whose services had been placed at the disposal of the New Zealand Government. Colonel Johnston had as his battery commanders Majors Symon, Sykes, R.A., and Standish. During the breathing space given us in Egypt in the early months of 1915, no time was lost by Colonel Johnston in bringing his brigade to a high stage of efficiency; and in this work he was most ably seconded by his battery commanders.

Later on, and shortly before leaving Egypt, the brigade received a most welcome addition in the form of the 4th (four-gun) Howitzer Battery, under the command of Major Falla. It was this battery which had the honour of being the first to land at Gallipoli, as it did on the morning of 26th April, 1915. It will, I am sure, be readily realized what immense importance I, together with all my comrades on the Anzac position, attached to this particular battery, when I say that for a considerable time these four little 4.5 in. howitzers were the only howitzers of any description on the whole of the front held by my army corps— and real stout and yeoman work they did for us.

Later in the same month, the 2nd and 1st Batteries joined the 4th Howitzer Battery at Anzac, while early in May the 3rd Battery was landed at Cape Helles, but rejoined the rest of the brigade at Anzac in the middle of August. In the same month the 5th Battery arrived at Anzac from New Zealand, to be followed in October by the 6th Howitzer Battery.

Only those who served throughout those weary months at Gallipoli can fully realize the strenuous times which all the gunners went through; and only those who were able continuously to visit the gun positions will ever know the magnificent work done night and day, for weeks, and even months, without relief, by all ranks of the batteries. The great spirit shown by all, and their determination not to be daunted by any difficulties or discomfort, or by the heavy enemy artillery which was constantly shelling our positions, are qualities which will ever live in my memory; and I shall always have a feeling of the greatest admiration, and, indeed, I might say affection, for the New Zealand Artilleryman. His Australian brother well knew his value, for Australia and New Zealand were there fighting shoulder to shoulder, realizing how the safety and honour of the one depended equally on the staunchness and courage of the other—and neither ever failed. I cannot think of gunners ever having had to work over more difficult ground than they were called on to do at Gallipoli. They always rose to the occasion, and well lived up to that proud regimental motto of "Ubique."

The day came, however, when the Gallipoli Peninsula had to be evacuated. On our withdrawal to Egypt in the spring of 1916, the New Zealand Forces were reorganized and expanded to a complete division, which included the formation of the artillery into the normal divisional organization of three brigades, and as such it proceeded to France in March, 1916.

On arrival in France, the Anzac Corps was called upon to occupy that portion of the front of the British lines in the immediate vicinity of Armentières; and so well do I remember with what real goodwill the New Zealand gunners first established themselves on the outskirts of that town. Here it was, I think, that the infantry began to realize to the fullest extent how much their whole existence in the line and eventual success must depend upon the work done by the artillery; and how no army could hope to win battles unless infantry and artillery had complete confidence in each other. That the infantry did possess this complete confidence in the accurate shooting of their batteries speaks for itself; for, having acquired this, the infantry realized that they could carry out an attack and advance under the closest covering fire from their own guns with as much immunity as it is possible for infantry ever to have in a modern battle—and this must always be the greatest glory which gunners can achieve.

The part taken by the New Zealand Artillery during the latter period of the war must be described by others who know it better than I do. I will conclude by saying what a real privilege I have always considered it to be the commander and comrade of these brave and true men for the many months we served together, and I most heartily wish them all happiness and prosperity for many years to come in this beautiful land of New Zealand.

W. R. BIRDWOOD,
General.

22nd July, 1920.

FROM THE C.R.A.

I have been asked to write an introduction to the History of the New Zealand Field Artillery in the Great War, now being prepared in New Zealand. That History will contain all details regarding the New Zealand Field Artillery in the war, so that I may only be expected to make some general observations. From the formation of the original Brigade in New Zealand, the Artillery was always animated by a spirit of self-sacrifice and a desire to fulfil to the very limit of its ability its function of protecting and supporting its own infantry. How well it succeeded in accomplishing this task at Anzac, and in all the hard-fought battles on the Western Front may be gauged from the regard in which the New Zealand infantrymen held their own gunners.

After the Armistice the Artillery marched to Cologne, through an interesting country, passing by many of the old historic battlefields of the Netherlands—Malplaquet, Ramillies, Oudenarde, Waterloo, etc. One could not help thinking how surprised some of those old warriors of the past would have been could they but have seen a Division of their descendants from far-off New Zealand march past—a Division that had fully maintained the high fighting reputation of their forebears. The Artillery journeyed past Maubeuge, Mons, Charleroi, Namur, Liege, and so into Germany, arriving at Cologne shortly after Christmas, 1918. After a pleasant and interesting experience at Cologne, the Artillery, in common with the rest of the Division, was demobilised, and within a month or two had ceased to exist.

The New Zealand Divisional Artillery is now a thing of the past; its guns are silent and many of its members lie buried on the battlefields of Gallipoli, of Flanders, and of France. Those who came safely through have settled down again to their normal occupations; the survivors will, I feel sure, look back with a feeling of growing satisfaction when they think of the Great War, and what they did to help it along. Their memories will be varied; many will recall when they stood in the presence of what makes all men equal; they will recall in those moments of shining remembrance the wonderful spirit which animated every man in the Division; part of it was the consciousness of the single purpose which inspired the whole Division, and the obedience to it of men who trusted one another.

All who had the honour of belonging to the New Zealand Field Artillery will, I feel sure, cherish the memory of their association with that Force as time goes by; forgetting the hardships of the war, they will remember only the spirit of good feeling and friendliness that animated all ranks in every phase of the conflict. Their varied experiences and journeyings in foreign lands will be pleasant to look back upon as the years roll by; and above all they will always cherish an increasing feeling of satisfaction at the thought of duty well done in the greatest war known to history.

It only remains for me, as the old C.R.A. of the New Zealand Division, to thank all ranks of the Artillery for their loyal co-operation throughout. I shall always look back on my command as the highest honour which could have befallen me, and I count myself fortunate in having been so long associated with such men.

G. N. JOHNSTON,
Brig.-General,
C.R.A. N.Z. Division, 1914-19.

New Zealand Artillery in the Field
1914-1918

PART I.—THE GALLIPOLI CAMPAIGN.

CHAPTER I.

THE OUTBREAK OF WAR.

A distinguished writer of another generation has described history as being mainly a register of the crimes of rulers and the sufferings of the people. This statement, no doubt, had its origin in a long and unbroken succession of wars—dynastic wars, racial wars, and wars of conquest—all of which down through the ages, from the campaigns of Cæsar to the Napoleonic wars, and the most frightful war of all the centuries in our own most recent day, have formed the staple subject of history. The general truth of the statement is incontestable; but never from the beginning of recorded time has it been pregnant with such terrible meaning, or exemplified in a form so appalling in its consequences to the world, as in its relation to the Great War that raged for nearly five years, from August, 1914, onwards, with a violence and on a scale of destruction and suffering and loss of human life without parallel in the history of the world.

The clear and instant comprehension of one outstanding fact —the peril that menaced the Empire—was the clarion call that roused the young nations in the outer seas of the world to a sense of the danger that threatened the Motherland, under whose protecting hand they were able to follow unmolested in their removed isolation, the peaceful way that led to growth and nationhood. The people of New Zealand clearly, and at once, recognized that a struggle was being forced upon them as a member of the household of British Nations, and by an enemy bearing already a record of infamous crime, and that the issue plainly resolved itself into a fight not only for their country, but for their hearths and homes; for the future and for the nationality of their children. But, perhaps more powerful than all else, was the surging force of loyalty to blood and kindred, and the appeal of great and moving traditions, immemorial and imperishable, which in times of stress and danger are the real links of Empire; the indissoluble ties that bind and hold together the scattered members of the great family of nations; the sublime inspiration that rises above every new call for sacrifice, that gathers fresh strength and greater daring from reverses, and sees in the darkest hour only the light that leads to victory.

Overshadowed somewhat by the vastness of the armaments on land and sea, which the Great Powers of the world had launched against each other in this concentration of destructive force, it is questionable whether even among the people of New Zealand to-day there is as clear an understanding as there should be of the full measure of her services and her sacrifices as a nation in arms, mobilised to the near limit of her fighting manhood, enrolling and equipping, and then transporting to the other end of the world, the largest number of men in proportion to population of the overseas Dominions. And, also, as short memories are the rule in the crowded and fevered life of the world, and the obliterating hand of time has an unchanging habit of dealing not too tenderly with much that should be regarded as sacred to the nation, it is the duty of New Zealand to-day, not only to those of her soldiers who still live, but even more so to those who have fallen, and not less as an inspiring message to future generations of New Zealand, to see that the valour of her soldiers, and the loyalty of her people to a great cause, are given a permanent and honoured place in her national literature.

This is conceived to be history in its highest form. It stands as an implied, if not direct, repudiation in language and spirit of those ideals that may imperceptibly lead young nations, fresh from the discovery of their prowess in war, in directions not conducive to their ultimate happiness and security. But while history discountenances what is known to-day, in an aggressive and lawless sense, as militarism, it should stand for everything that makes for national patriotism, for the strengthening of the traditional love of freedom, the development of vigour of national character, and proficiency in the use of arms for the protection of our shores and the security of our liberties. Towards the attainment of such objects the lessons of the Great War may be wisely and profitably employed.

The rapidity with which a succession of dramatic events of the profoundest import to the world followed the assassination of the Austrian Archduke Francis, at Serajevo, on June 28th, 1914, threw the nations concerned into a delirium of feverish anticipation, without the power to visualise even in the remotest degree the vastness of the calamity that was about to desolate the world. One month after the Serajevo tragedy, which, viewed from any human standpoint, concerned only a very small number of people, Austria had declared war on Serbia. Then followed that succession of terrible events which plunged almost the whole world into the abyss. Five days after Austria's declaration of war, Germany sent her troops into Luxembourg, violated French territory without even a formal declaration of war, made war on Russia, and opened her campaign of savagery on the practically defenceless people of Belgium. England, up to this point, had been tirelessly engaged in efforts of peaceful negotiation, remonstrance, and protest, and despairing of stemming the tide of war by such means, declared war on Germany on August 4th, 1914, and immediately entered the lists on the side of France and her Allies.

Three days after England's declaration of war with Germany, the New Zealand Government cabled to the Imperial Government offering to provide an Expeditionary Force, and on August 12th the offer was accepted. Already, on July 30th, preliminary arrangements had been made by the Defence Authorities of the Dominion for raising a voluntary Expeditionary Force for service in Europe or elsewhere, and the moment the cable of acceptance reached New Zealand this prepared machinery was set in motion. Concentration camps were established in the Military Districts, in which the Mounted Rifles

Regiments and Infantry Battalions were formed, and received their preliminary training. Volunteers for the Artillery, in common with those for other Divisional Units, were concentrated at the Awapuni Racecourse, near Palmerston North. At the outset it was decided to send away with the Force one six-gun 18pr. Battery, a Section of Brigade Ammunition Column, one Section of Divisional Ammunition Column, and one Small Arms Sub-section of a Horse Artillery Brigade Ammunition Column. But by the time these units had been formed it was decided that something more ambitious should be attempted with the large number of young men volunteering for the Artillery. Ultimately it was decided to equip and despatch with the Expeditionary Force a whole Field Artillery Brigade of three 18pr. Batteries, each of four guns, and one Field Artillery Brigade Ammunition Column; also to form a Howitzer Battery of four guns to be sent away with the Second Reinforcements.

Command of the Brigade was given to Lieut.-Colonel G. N. Johnston, R.A., one of the Imperial officers whose services had been loaned to New Zealand to assist in the training of her Territorial Forces. Lieut.-Colonel Johnston remained in command of the New Zealand Artillery during the training in Egypt and throughout the Gallipoli campaign, and going to France as C.R.A. of the Division, held his command until the close of the war. The Adjutant of the Brigade was Lieutenant J. M. Richmond, R.N.Z.A., 2nd Lieutenant W. L. Moore being Orderly Officer.

The officers of the three batteries were:—1st Battery— Major F. Symon, Captain C. McGilp, Lieutenant C. N. Newman, and 2nd Lieutenants J. C. Dunnet and F. M. Turner. 2nd Battery—Major F. B. Sykes, R.A., Captain G. E. Daniell, Lieutenant V. Rogers, Lieutenant R. C. Wickens, and 2nd Lieutenant A. E. Horwood. 3rd Battery—Major I. T. Standish, Captain C. V. Leeming, Lieutenant R. Richards, Lieutenant C. Carrington, and 2nd Lieutenant T. Farr. Brigade Ammunition Column—Captain F. G. Hume, R.N.Z.A., Lieutenant N. Purdie, and Lieutenant S. W. Morton.

The gunners who had been posted to the original six-gun battery were distributed amongst the three new batteries, and on this nucleus the establishment of gunners was built up by selection from the many who clamoured for inclusion. Practically all the non-commissioned officers had had considerable experience either in the volunteers or Territorials, or in the Permanent Artillery. But the equipping of batteries on an active service footing was a harder problem than the selection of personnel, and actually was only made possible by the experience and foresight of those who had been instrumental in equipping the Territorial batteries with modern guns and howitzers. The field artillery of New Zealand's citizen army comprised at the outbreak of war four Brigades, each of two batteries and an ammunition column, and with the exception of D (Mountain) Battery (Wellington), all the batteries possessed modern 18prs. or 4.5in. howitzers. D. Battery was awaiting the arrival of new guns from England. The 18pr. batteries were A. Battery (Auckland), and G. Battery (Hamilton) of the Auckland Brigade; F. Battery (Napier) of the Wellington Brigade; E. Battery (Christchurch), and H. Battery (Nelson), of the Canterbury Brigade; and C. Battery (Invercargill) of the Otago Brigade. The two 4.5in. howitzer batteries were B. Battery (Dunedin) and J. Battery (Palmerston North) of the Otago and Wellington Brigades. The original volunteer batteries had always been able to attract a good class of recruit, and had maintained at once their popularity and strength even in the days when volunteering had grown so unattractive that it had to give way to a system of compulsory training. Nor did they lose their keenness under the new system; and undoubtedly they gained a great deal in efficiency. It was these batteries, then, which may be said to have furnished the foundation on which the artillery of the Expeditionary Force was built up.

The horses were a fairly mixed lot. The best of the gun horses came from the stables of the Royal New Zealand Artillery. These were few in number, however, and so the drivers, good horsemen most of them, had a busy time for a while schooling the raw material in the way that a gun horse should go. During the few weeks that elapsed before the Brigade moved down to Wellington in readiness for embarkation, details of organisation and equipment occupied most of the energies of commanding officers and their subordinates, and the amount of training carried out was inconsiderable. The closest secrecy was being maintained as to the probable destination of the Force, and the date of its departure, but towards the end of September the fitting out of the vessels which had been chartered as transports was complete, and preparations were made for embarkation. The Brigade was to embark at Wellington, the 1st and 2nd Batteries on the *Limerick*, and the 3rd Battery and the B.A.C. on the *Arawa*. On September 23rd the Brigade entrained at Palmerston North for Wellington, and on arrival there shortly after mid-day marched through the streets of the city to the barracks at Mt. Cook. Embarkation was carried out the following day.

The Main Body, as the first Expeditionary Force has always been called, comprised one Mounted Rifle Brigade, one Infantry Brigade, an independent Mounted Rifles Regiment, a Brigade of Field Artillery with a Brigade Ammunition Column, Field Troop N.Z.E., Signal Troop, Signal Company, Mounted Field Ambulance, No. 1 Field Ambulance, and Divisional Train. The force which actually sailed totalled 8,417 of all ranks. Of this total 6,900 had had some previous military training, 3,600 having served in the Territorial Force at the time of enlistment.

The 4th (Howitzer) Battery was not formed at the same time as the 18pr. batteries, as the offer of a howitzer battery was not accepted by the Imperial authorities until shortly before the embarkation of the Main Body. When its formation was decided on, one officer and a few N.C.O.'s who had acquired experience in howitzer batteries in the Territorials were withdrawn from the 18pr. batteries to assist in the training of the new unit, which it was then decided should leave New Zealand with the 2nd Reinforcements. The Battery was organised and trained at Trentham Camp, and when it left New Zealand was commanded by Captain N. S. Falla, who had with him Lieutenant H. J. Daltry, Lieutenant R. Miles, Lieutenant E. Gardner, and 2nd Lieutenant J. G. Jeffery.

An official farewell was tendered to the units which embarked in Wellington, at a big parade held in Newtown Park on September 24th. The Wellington Mounted Rifles Regiment, the Wellington Infantry Battalion, and the Artillery

Brigade, and other Divisional Units paraded in full strength, and were inspected by His Excellency the Governor, the Prime Minister, and the Minister of Defence. Great crowds assembled in the Park to witness the parade, and afterwards lined the streets and cheered the soldiers as they marched down to the wharves. The transports backed out from the wharves before dark, and anchored in the stream, where they were were joined during the evening by the *Ruapehu* and *Hawke's Bay* from Port Chalmers, and the *Tahiti* and *Athenic* from Lyttelton. The fleet stood ready to sail with the dawn, but before the morning it was known that its departure had been indefinitely postponed. The *Waimana* and *Star of India*, which had left Auckland the previous night, had been recalled to that port by a wireless message, and the transports at Wellington went alongside the wharves again and made ready to disembark all the mounted units with their horses. The fleet would not sail, it had been decided, without a sufficiently powerful escort. On disembarking, the Artillery with their horses and vehicles marched out to the Lower Hutt Racecourse, and went into camp. During the three weeks that elapsed before the Force finally sailed away the batteries were able to devote their whole energies to training, and the time was very profitably spent.

The escort for which the Force had been waiting arrived at last on the afternoon of October 14th, to the surprise and delight of the soldiers, who were growing tired of the long delay. Two big cruisers, H.M.S. *Minotaur* and the *Ibouki*, the latter flying the Japanese flag, steamed quietly and unannounced into the harbour at Wellington, and were at anchor almost before the city was aware of their arrival. By the following afternoon the mounted units, which had been encamped around Wellington, had embarked again with their horses and vehicles, and the transports one by one moved out into the stream. The *Maunganui*, which was the flagship of the convoy, and on which was Major-General A. J. Godley, commanding the Expeditionary Force, was the last transport to leave the wharves; and as she went past the cruisers in the gathering dusk, the men-of-warsmen gathered aft and woke the echoes with their cheers.

The Main Body Sails.

Whoever looked to the heavens for an omen in the early morning of October 16th, when the cruisers and convoy one by one put out to sea, must have been well content with what they read; for the sky was cloudless, and only the soft early morning mists obscured the first rays of the sun. Everyone was on deck by *reveille*, to watch the two big cruisers plough their way out through the Heads, followed by the convoy, led in two divisions by the *Psyche* and the *Philomel*. There was no demonstration and little noise; but the soldiers turned their eyes again and again to take another glimpse of the city before it disappeared from view, or to look at the little knots of people who had gathered on the heights to bid them a silent farewell. Very soon the last boat had cleared the Heads, and the convoy, gathering speed, proceeded through the Straits and out into the open sea. Led by the *Minotaur*, far in advance, the transports sailed in two parallel "divisions," with the *Ibouki* half a dozen miles off on the starboard side and the *Psyche* a similar distance away on the port side. The *Philomel* brought up the rear some three or four miles astern. This first day came in companionship with perfect weather, and the troops revelled in the warmth of the sunshine and the novelty, for most of them, of life at sea; but on the following day the weather freshened. The glamour of blue skies and placid seas was gone, and the majority of the voyagers found that getting their sea-legs was a rather painful ordeal. The great majority of the men were sea-sick, and some of the seasoned travellers were obliged to admit the force of example. The horses were well looked after during this period, as the men who still kept their legs were always willing to do more than their share. Within a couple of days' sail of Hobart the breeze fell away, and, cheered again by the bright sun, the afflicted made a rapid recovery. The prospect of getting ashore and stretching their legs was hailed by all ranks with the utmost enthusiasm. The coast of Tasmania was sighted on the morning of October 21st, and before noon the transports were safely in the harbour.

The troops from five of the ships were taken for a route march after lunch, and the remainder went ashore the following morning. The weather was fairly warm, and marching was hot work after a week in cramped quarters at sea; but the discomfort was forgotten in the delight of getting ashore again. The unexpected arrival of the convoy had taken the townspeople by surprise, yet they mustered in great numbers and lined the streets to watch the marching columns go by, cheering the men on their way with gifts of fruit and flowers. Twenty-four hours after its arrival, the convoy left Hobart for Albany, where the New Zealand ships were to join those of the Australian Expeditionary Force. The wharves were crowded as the transports slowly backed out to the accompaniment of the music of the regimental bands and the mingled cheers of soldiers and civilians. During the night a heavy fog enveloped the fleet, which for some hours was obliged to feel its way slowly forward at reduced speed, amidst a tumult of sound from screeching syrens. A heavy swell made matters seem more uncomfortable, but by 7 a.m. the fog had lifted, and normal speed was resumed. There had been gloomy forebodings of rough weather in the Australian Bight, but the swell soon subsided, and pleasant conditions again prevailed.

Early on Monday morning, October 25th, a signal went round the fleet that a private of the New Zealand Medical Corps had died the previous night on board the *Ruapehu*; and the intelligence of this first death came almost as a shock to men who had thought only for that side of war that promised excitement and adventure, that stirs the blood and fires the imagination, and little for that other side on which lay its tragedy and suffering and death. In the afternoon an impressive burial service was held. At 3 p.m. the *Ruapehu* moved up to the centre of the two divisions, and the troops on every transport were paraded facing inwards. Five minutes later all engines were stopped, and the convoy rode motionless on the water while a brief funeral service was held on every ship, and the body was committed to the deep. The customary volleys were fired on the *Ruapehu*, and the Last Post sounded; the *Ruapehu* hauled her ensign close up, and the convoy proceded on its way. The service was very brief, but the circumstances invested it with an impressiveness that was not lost on the thousands who paid their tribute of respect to the dead.

Albany was reached on Wednesday, October 27th. The head of the long line of transports entered the outer harbour about 7 a.m., and saw disposed about the broad waters of King George's Sound the transports of the Australian Expeditionary Force, ranging in size from the fourteen thousand ton *Euripides* down to ocean tramps of a third her tonnage. Australians and New Zealanders having come within hail greeted each other with cheers and coo-ees on the one hand and fantastic Maori war-cries on the other. During the four days the fleet remained in the Sound the majority of the New Zealand transports stayed at anchor, but some went alongside and advantage was taken of the opportunity to give the troops a march ashore. The day before the voyage was resumed Major-General Godley paid a visit to all the New Zealand transports.

At daylight on Sunday, November 1st, the *Minotaur* led the way out to the open sea, followed in slow procession by the transports, their decks thronged with troops, who watched in silence the stately setting out of the great Armada. By the time the last of the New Zealand transports had cleared the heads the long line extended almost as far as the eye could reach. The escort now consisted of the *Minotaur* in the lead, the *Ibouki*, and the two Australian cruisers, *Sydney* and *Melbourne*. Once clear of the land, the Australian transports formed into three parallel divisions spaced a mile apart, each transport keeping an interval of 800 yards from that in front. The New Zealand ships, still in two divisions, steamed in rear. The strictest orders were issued regarding the danger of showing lights at night; beyond necessary navigation lights ships were to be absolutely darkened; and as a further precaution no rubbish was to be thrown overboard that would float and leave behind a tell-tale trail, but was to be consigned to the stokehold or galley fires. The faulty station-keeping of some transports was a matter of much concern to the *Minotaur*, which frequently sent out messages pointing out the danger to which the whole convoy was exposed by the straggling and consequently broken formation which took place at night. These criticisms, however, did not apply to the New Zealand transports, which were complimented on their orderliness. The voyagers had by now become thoroughly accustomed to the sea, and had settled down to the daily routine, in which, for the artillerymen, stable duties formed a very important part. A certain amount of war news was received by wireless occasionally, and a few days out from Albany news was received of England's declaration of war on Turkey, an event which was destined to have incalculable consequences for every member of the Force.

A week after leaving Albany the *Minotaur* said good-bye to the convoy, and her place as leader was taken by the *Melbourne*. Before leaving, the *Minotaur* sent the following farewell message to the New Zealand transports:—"I am ordered on another service; wish you the very best success when you land in France. Give the Germans a good shake up. It has been a great pleasure to escort such a well disciplined force and convoy. Good-bye." Later in the day all transports were enjoined to take the strictest precautions with regard to lights during the night as the Cocos Islands would be passed before dawn. The night passed uneventfully, but in the morning, shortly after six o'clock, everyone was thrown into a fever of excitement, first by the significant manœuvring of some of the escorting cruisers, and then by the news that S.O.S. signals had been received from the wireless station at the Cocos Islands. The operators on most of the transports picked up these messages, which stated that a strange warship was entering the harbour. Other messages were received mixed up with a string of meaningless words, which evidently were being sent out in an attempt to "jam" the station on the island.

Meanwhile the *Sydney* had made off at top speed in the direction of the Islands, her place on the flank of the convoy being taken by the *Melbourne*, which was joined a little later by the *Ibouki*. The *Sydney* was soon hull down, and very shortly was lost to view. The convoy proceeded on its way at normal speed, with the *Melbourne* and the *Ibouki* cruising well out on the quarter from which any threat to the fleet would be most likely to come.

For the next few hours the soldiers were obliged to content themselves with conjecture as to what was happening away beyond the horizon, but at 9.30 a.m. it was announced that the enemy ship had been brought to action, and shortly after 11 a.m. the wireless was busy again with the electrifying intelligence that "the enemy had beached herself to prevent sinking." Even yet it was not known that it was the notorious *Emden* which had been brought to book at last; but the restraint was over, and the men expressed their relief after the period of anxious waiting by cheering long and vigorously. It required only the news that it actually was the *Emden* which had been defeated by the *Sydney* to complete their satisfaction and start them cheering anew. However great the pride with which the Australians viewed the honours which had fallen to their young Navy, it was fully shared by every New Zealander, and the official congratulations of the Force were duly offered to the *Sydney* on the results of the Australian Navy's first engagement. The *Sydney* had two men killed and thirteen wounded, but the list of killed and wounded on the battered *Emden* ran into big figures. Three days after the engagement was fought the big liner *Empress of Asia* passed the convoy on her way to pick up the *Emden's* prisoners and bring them on to Colombo.

On November 13th the New Zealand transports quickened their speed in order that they might arrive at Colombo in advance of the Australian boats, and so lessen the congestion which would be caused by the simultaneous arrival of the whole fleet. During the previous night the Line had been crossed, and so on all the transports the afternoon was devoted to the traditional ceremonies. King Neptune and his Consort came aboard, were received with fitting ceremony, and impartially exacted tribute from all of high or low degree. A few days later, on Sunday, November 15th, the transports arrived at Colombo, getting close in to land in the early morning, while the air was yet fresh and cool. As the boats crept slowly in towards the harbour and edged their way in the narrow entrance they passed through swarms of small craft of every known and unknown design, all of them very insecure looking, but skilfully managed by their brown, scantily-clad occupants. The harbour itself, by no means commodious, was crowded with ocean-going steamers of every class, transports, and men-of-war.

Soon after the New Zealand transports had come to anchor in the harbour the Australian transports commenced to arrive; then came the *Empress of Asia* and the *Sydney*, fresh from her victory at the Cocos Islands. The *Sydney* bore little trace of her engagement, but all about her decks were rows of stretchers on which lay her own and many of the enemy wounded; and so there was no cheering or noisy welcome. As she entered the harbour and passed the transports the troops crowding the decks stood to attention in a silence that was more eloquent than cheers. The prisoners from the *Emden*, totalling about one hundred and forty, were divided into parties of half a dozen, and distributed over the various transports.

While the boats were being coaled and watered the troops were given shore leave, parties two hundred strong being sent ashore from each transport at a time. The men revelled in the freedom and in the opportunity of seeing something of a place and people so unlike anything to be seen in their own temperate clime. Borne along by the lean, sweating rickshawmen, many of them explored the outskirts of the town, or drove about under the cool shade of the fine avenues that decorate the thoroughfares. The majority considered the chance of a change of diet too rare to be neglected, and in the hotels and restaurants they regaled themselves with the best that money could buy. The persistent and persuasive vendors of "precious" stones and antiquities reaped a harvest, and few there were who did not take back to the ship some small memento of their first visit to Colombo. Coaling and watering were completed by the morning of November 17th, and before noon the New Zealand transports and some of the Australian ships had moved out of the harbour, and, escorted by the *Hampshire*, had set out on the way to Aden.

From Colombo to Suez was the least interesting portion of the voyage, and certainly the most trying for the horses, many of which were on the lower decks or in the holds, where the air was close and stifling. For days there was not the slightest breeze to ripple the mirror-like surface of the sea, or to temper the scorching heat of the sun. The men shed most of their clothing, and in leisure times lounged about the decks under the canvas awnings; at night they brought their blankets up on deck and slept under the stars. The days became very monotonous; interest flagged in the performances of the flying-fish; and even the sunset with its riot of glorious colour palled after a while, so that it was something of a relief when the convoy steamed into Aden in the early morning of October 25th. There was no shore leave, nor was anyone very disappointed in consequence. An arid, rocky spot shimmering in the blaze of the tropical sun, and its harbour infested with hungry sharks, it was sufficiently unattractive to make the crowded transports seem pleasant by comparison. After bringing on those Australian boats which had been last to leave Colombo, the *Ibouki* said farewell to the convoy, and steamed away for her home waters. From this point onwards the *Hampshire* was the only escort, and she led the way when the convoy, united again, left for Suez. As the convoy proceeded up the Red Sea a wireless message was received warning the whole Force to be prepared to disembark in Egypt. Most of the men had firmly believed that they were on their way to England, and would ultimately go from there to France, and they parted with their illusions regretfully, but once it had been definitely stated that the voyage would end at Egypt they were quick to realise the cogency of the reasons which probably lay behind this decision. At Suez, where the leading transports anchored for an hour or two, detailed disembarkation orders were brought out to the flagship, the Canal pilots were taken aboard, and the *Maunganui* led the way into the Canal. A powerful electric light was installed in the bows of each boat so that they might feel their way along the narrow channel in the darkness.

Of the town of Suez little could be seen—a glimpse of the palm-shaded water-front, a glimmer of lights, and then the boats were in the Canal with the low banks on either hand so close at times that it seemed almost possible to leap ashore from the decks. Armed guards had been posted on the deck of each transport to keep a look-out to eastward, but there was no sign or sound of an enemy. The soldiers clustered up forward and silently watched the canal-banks slip by like the unfolding of a cinematograph film; but, late at night a heavy fog enveloped everything, and the leading boats anchored till the morning in the Bitter Lake. Proceeding by day, the entrenchments and fortified posts skirting the canal, with their garrisons of English and Indian troops, provided a first impression of the seriousness attached to the Turkish threat to the precious waterway, and of the elaborate preparations being made for its defence.

The first transports to pass through the Canal reached Port Said by the evening of December 1st; others continued to arrive during the following morning, and late in the afternoon the New Zealand convoy set out on the final stage of its long journey. Definite orders as to the disembarkation at Alexandria had been issued, and there was no delay when once the boats were alongside the quays. The city was in sight at dawn, and very soon after breakfast the transports had berthed, and men and horses and stores were pouring out on to the wharves. The Force was to be encamped on the outskirts of Cairo, so there was still a train journey of almost 150 miles before its travels would for the time being be over. Once the batteries had marched their horses down the big ramps, and slung their guns and stores up from the holds, they had to set to and pack them into the long troop trains which were in waiting to carry them off to their new home on the edge of the great desert.

Strenuous Days in Egypt.

The site chosen for the New Zealanders' camp was on the edge of the desert, about eight miles out from Cairo, on the outskirts, almost, of Heliopolis, a suburb built on modern ideas, with clean, broad, paved streets and substantial buildings. The camp was skirted by the main road that ran out from Cairo, and within a mile was the railway. Pipes had been laid for the water supply, which was always plentiful, but nothing else had been done, and the first train loads of troops to arrive made shift as best they could. Although the express trains from Alexandria to Cairo did the journey in about three hours, the troop trains seldom took less than eight hours, and the first train load of troops, leaving Alexandria in the late afternoon, did not reach Zeitoun until somewhere about midnight. Arrived at the camping area the men threw themselves down to snatch a few hours of sleep before dawn, when the task of establishing the camp began in earnest. The colonial's adaptability and faculty for making himself at home under any circumstances stood him in good stead, and units settled down very quickly after their arrival. Day and night trains continued to arrive at the stations, and within a week horses, vehicles, and men had all been transported from the fast-emptying transports at Alexandria to the rapidly growing camp on the desert. A road was constructed through the centre of the camp, dividing the areas of the Infantry Brigade, whose tents stood in serried rows on its left, and the lines of the Artillery and Mounted Brigades on the right. At the cross-roads in the centre of the camp stood the Supply Depôt, where each day units drew their stores and forage for the animals.

Despite their seven weeks at sea in cramped and often ill-ventilated quarters, the horses came off the transports in very good condition. They were weak, of course, and uncertain on their legs, but they improved rapidly. For the first few days they were led out for a very modest spell of exercise, which was increased by progressive stages until within a fortnight they were pronounced fit for normal work. During this period manœuvres were out of the question, but the Brigade, in common with all other arms, had embarked without delay on a thorough course of training, which began at the most elementary stage. The drivers devoted the greater part of their time and energy to grooming and exercising their horses, and the gunners grew fit at standing gun-drill, and studied afresh the complexities of their pieces. This individual training, which was thorough and complete, was followed by section and battery training, after which the batteries were exercised as a brigade. The country was not eminently suitable for artillery training, and the heavy sand made hard going for the horses, and heavy work for the gunners; but every disadvantage and every deficiency were overcome by the seriousness and determination with which all ranks faced their work. This spirit, which permeated the whole Force, was more than a transitory enthusiasm; it kept alive the keenness of the men through the long months of unremitting hard training, and the more trying period of waiting; and it was the foundation of the magnificent spirit which afterwards animated the New Zealand Division through all the long years of war.

In the evening, after their day's training on the desert, the Colonial soldiers poured into Cairo like a human tide—the New Zealanders from Zeitoun, and the Australians from their big camp at Mena, by the foot of the Pyramids, and the Light Horse Camp at Ma'adi. There was a sprinkling of English Territorials, but it was essentially a slouch-hatted invasion. Leave was general until a fairly late hour; and from six o'clock in the evening onwards the streets were filled with this moving, restless throng, to whom the life of the age-old city came as a revelation in many ways. They filled the eating houses and saloons; and in the variety houses where, in "Continental" style, they could sit at little tables and be served with refreshments during the performance, they formed such a large part of the audience that it was matter for wonder how those establishments had existed before the advent of the colonial. There was no by-way and no corner in the city itself which they did not explore, full of life and the buoyancy and insatiable curiosity of youth. It was scarcely a matter for surprise, and perhaps even less for stricture, if some lost their heads for a little, transported as they had been with the swiftness of modern magic from the decencies and orderliness of their remote homes and set down amidst the distractions of a city the life of which was as novel as it was unbounded in its license. The shops and the quaint native bazaars were a never-ceasing attraction; the soldiers disbursed freely, and the shop-keepers and itinerant vendors of "antiquities" and all manner

B

of trifles reaped a golden harvest. In the eating-houses business never languished; and when it was discovered what a source of revenue lay in the appetite of the soldier new establishments sprang up, mushroom like, on every hand. From the city wonderful excursions could be made cheaply and easily to the Pyramids at Ghizeh, to the Gardens or the Zoo at Ghezireh, or to the great Barrage, where were stored up the precious waters of the Nile; in the city itself were the Citadel, with its famous Mosque of Mahommed Ali, and the Museum. Everyone went first to the Pyramids as a matter of course; the more energetic climbed perspiring up their giant steps, or were led inside along the smooth-worn, narrow passageways to see "the tomb of the Pharoahs"; but the majority were content to gaze at their mighty dimensions in silent wonder.

On December 18th Egypt was proclaimed a British Protectorate; the Khedive, who had made open avowal of his sympathies with Turkey on the declaration of war with that country, was deposed, and a new Sultan of Egypt in the person of Prince Hussein Kamel Pasha, was proclaimed at the Abdin Palace, Cairo, on December 20th. Three days later the New Zealand Expeditionary Force marched in strength through the streets of the city, such a display of force being rightly regarded as at once the most prompt and efficacious argument that could be addressed at the moment to the disturbed native mind. It was the first occasion on which the whole force had been publicly paraded since its arrival; and men and horses made a display worthy of the force. The field batteries turned out with their guns and wagons, and gave an impression of smartness and efficiency. The horses had completely recovered from the effects of the long voyage, and their smooth, well-groomed coats literally shone in the sun. In the Opera Square, in the centre of the city, the General Officer Commanding the British Forces in Egypt took the salute as the long column went by, and everywhere along the route the populace applauded the spectacle; but the average Egyptian is no mean dissembler. Christmas Day, two days later, passed quietly, but with due observance in the matter of Christmas fare.

By the New Year the camp was beginning to wear a more habitable air. Messing huts were erected in all the lines; wet canteens were properly established, and a big hall had been erected, where picture entertainments, lectures, and boxing competitions were held almost every night. These healthy distractions were of very great benefit in helping to keep the men in camp in the evenings, and served considerably to brighten the routine of the soldier's life. There was little or no sickness in camp; beyond the troublesome bouts of sand colic which afflicted all the newcomers, the process of acclimatisation was easy and rapid. The mid-day heat was trying, but the early mornings and the evenings were delightfully cool. The chief annoyance was the occasional khamseen, when for a space the wind lifted the face off the desert, blotting out the sky with great clouds of fine sand that penetrated everything and everywhere.

As the first Expeditionary Force fell considerably short of the establishment of a complete division it was decided to incorporate with the New Zealanders two brigades of Australian troops—the 1st Light Horse Brigade, and the 4th Infantry Brigade; at the time this policy was decided on the 4th Brigade was on its way from Australia, and was due to arrive in Egypt about the end of January, 1915. The composite division thus formed was styled "The New Zealand and Australian Division." There was a shortage of Divisional troops; but one company of Field Engineers and two companies of the Divisional Train were formed as reinforcements became available. Two Small Arm Ammunition Columns were also formed, and a section of Divisional Ammunition Column, which was sent out from England, was temporarily attached to the Division.

At the end of January the Artillery was strengthened by the arrival, with the 2nd Reinforcements, of the 4th (Howitzer) Battery. The transports carrying the 2nd Reinforcements arrived at Suez a couple of days after the New Zealand Infantry Brigade had been ordered to the Canal to assist in its defence against the Turkish attack, and at the time when the attack was being almost momentarily expected. The

Battery, on the *Knight of the Garter*, passed through the Canal, on January 28th; the vessel had anchored overnight in the Bitter Lakes, and before proceeding the guns were brought up on deck and lashed ready for action; but the precaution proved unnecessary. The gunners saw only the Indian and Colonial troops, who lined the banks as they steamed past, and with whom they exchanged enthusiastic greetings. The Battery disembarked at Alexandria, and on arrival at Zeitoun occupied lines adjoining those of the 18pr. Batteries. The gunners at once devoted their energies to training and the drivers to getting their horses into condition. The majority of the men had had no previous experience of practical artillery work, but they had received some sound elementary training in New Zealand, and once the horses were available for work the Battery grew daily more efficient. The flat country was not very suitable for howitzer work, and no live shell practice could be permitted owing to the great scarcity of ammunition. Beyond the 800 odd rounds brought from New Zealand there was no other 4.5in. howitzer ammunition in Egypt until shortly before the opening of the Gallipoli campaign. The Battery had reason to be proud of its weapons, which were of the very latest pattern, and the only guns of their kind in Egypt at that time. It is beyond question that had the howitzer batteries of the New Zealand Terriorial Force not been in possession of these very modern guns before the outbreak of war they would not have been available in Egypt, and the colonial troops would not have had the benefit of their protection on Gallipoli. Before the Brigade left Zeitoun a Howitzer Battery Ammunition Column was formed from personnel available in Egypt.

Right through February and on into March the Brigade persevered untiringly with its training out on the desert. The work was sufficiently strenuous to try to the utmost the stamina and endurance of the men; no constitutional or physical weakness could withstand such a searching test, and the few unfit were rapidly discovered. Training became much more interesting as it progressed, and the keenest interest was taken in the tactical evolutions in which the Brigade was exercised. On night operations with the Division, batteries marched out and bivouacked under the stars, the gunners digging their gun-pits and preparing their positions during the hours of darkness, and then carefully filling them in again at dawn, before the weary trek back to camp.

By the middle of March it was apparent that the long days —and nights—of training had brought the ample reward in the success which had attended the training of the Division, which from being merely a collection of units, had become a coherent, disciplined, and perfectly efficient force. Individually, the men were in perfect physical condition, and were full of eager anticipation when it became whispered about that the Division might not remain much longer training on the desert. The end of the month drew near, and it became definitely known that both the 1st Australian Division and the New Zealand and Australian Division, which constituted the Australian and New Zealand Army Corps, were shortly to be given an opportunity of proving their mettle in an actual theatre of war. The men were not told what their destination was to be, but the Mediterranean Expeditionary Force was then in process of formation; for what purpose it was not difficult to conjecture. The spectacular but costly naval attacks on the forts guarding the Dardanelles had failed, and the Mediterranean Expeditionary Force hoped to accomplish what had been found impossible for the Navy.

On 29th March the whole Division paraded on the desert to the north of the camp for inspection by Sir Ian Hamilton, Commanding the M.E.F. There had been other inspections and parades which had savoured more of the ceremonial; now they were to march past under the critical eye of the soldier who was to lead them on the Great Adventure. There was a wind blowing, and the movement of such large bodies of troops raised great clouds of dust which almost obscured the sky; but that was of no moment to men who for months had made the desert their element. The guns of the Artillery Brigade had already been prepared for war by coats of "camouflage" paint, which somehow gave them a strikingly business-like appearance; and, as the batteries went by the saluting base in succession they gave an undeniable assurance of strength and fitness.

By Easter definite orders were issued for the movement of the Division, less the Mounted Rifles and Light Horse Brigades, to Alexandria for embarkation. Preparatory embarkation parades were held by ships, and during the last few days all batteries devoted much time and energy to completing their equipment. With such a tremendous influx of troops into the country, the ordinary sources of supply had been strained beyond their limits, and the complete equipping of batteries became a matter of much concern. The appointment of a commissioned officer as Brigade Quartermaster proved a considerable help, and gradually every difficulty was overcome. On the night of April 9th the first train load of guns, horses, and men moved out from the main Cairo station on its way to Alexandria. The harbour and the wharves were crowded with transports and men-of-war, and the tremendous accumulation of stores and material of every description on the waterfront gave the New Zealanders some idea of the magnitude of the preparations involved in the great venture on which they were about to embark.

The Artillery sailed on four transports, Headquarters and 1st Battery being on the *Katuna*, the 2nd Battery on the *Surada*, the 3rd Battery on the *Californian*, and the 4th (How.) Battery on the *Australind*. These practised hands made light work of loading the horses and slinging the guns and vehicles, and once their loading was complete transports sailed away independently and without escort. The waters of the Mediterranean had not at that time the evil reputation which the activities of German submarines earned for them in later days. There was a risk of attack from Turkish torpedo boats, however, and there was some alarm on the *Surada* when S.O.S. signals were received from an English transport which was being attacked by a Turkish destroyer only some fifty or sixty miles away. With some effort one of the 18prs. was got up on deck ready to open fire; but in the meantime the Navy had gone to the scene of the attack and the Turkish destroyer was driven ashore on a neighbouring island.

On all the transports the soldiers were busy during the trip to Lemnos perfecting the arrangements for a speedy disembarkation. In every battery there were men who at sea or elsewhere had learnt the trick of handling ropes and slinging a load with safety and despatch, and in most cases batteries were able to improve materially the existing facilities for unloading. This was particularly the case on the *Katuna*, where the gunners were so dubious as to the ability of the Lascar crew to do the job decently that they did everything themselves. One by one the transports made their way through the island-studied Ægean, and were escorted through the narrow entrance to Lemnos harbour by the destroyers cruising about in the outside waters. The big land-locked harbour presented an unforgettable spectacle. Close at hand were the fighting ships, the battle cruisers of France, England, and Russia, and stretching away in the background were the long lanes of crowded transports. Of greatest interest to the colonials was the big *Queen Elizabeth*, of whose formidable strength romantic minds had woven many a fanciful story. There was much to interest the eye and stir the imagination in the big harbour, where there was never a quiet moment, but always the coming and going of patrolling destroyers, the buzzing of an occasional 'plane bent on a reconnaissance, and the incessant flitting to and fro of naval cutters and despatch boats.

During the week or more that they lay waiting the fateful day of the attack, gunners and drivers assiduously practised unloading the guns and wagons on to pontoons, and slinging the horses fully harnessed. The final plans for the landing were being concerted; maps were issued, and the great scheme was unfolded to the soldiers. The Australian and New Zealand Army Corps was to force a landing on the coast of the Peninsula to the north of the headland known as Gaba Tepe, and endeavour to force a way across to the Narrows. The remaining three divisions of the M.E.F. were to operate at the southern end of the Peninsula. The 29th Division, the last of the British regular divisions to take the field, was to land with the Royal Naval Division at Cape Helles; the French Division was to land at Kum Kale, and after destroying the forts at that spot on the Asiatic shore was to join the two British Divisions at Helles.

CHAPTER II.

THE LANDING AT ANZAC.

At last on the afternoon of April 24th the great fleet of men-of-war and crowded transports began to clear Mudros harbour, and set out for the shores of Gallipoli. The New Zealand transports lifted anchor early, and steaming down the long lane of ships, dropped anchor again near the netted and closely guarded entranceway. From this vantage point the New Zealanders watched with swelling emotions the vessels of the fleet, and the host of transports move in stately procession out into the open sea. Elated at the thought that at last after their weary months of training and waiting they were to be tried on the testing ground of battle, and thrilled by the moving spectacle, the men cheered vociferously as each ship went slowly past. Night fell at last, calm and very dark, and at midnight, while the soldiers slumbered in their quarters below, the New Zealand transports steamed out to sea with darkened lights. They needed no *reveille* that morning. The boom of heavy gun-fire heralded the dawn, and clustering up on deck the troops caught their first glimpse of war. Looking shorewards they could see the hills of the Gallipoli Peninsula faintly outlined in the half-light of the coming day; and lined along the coast the dim shapes of great ships of war, which broke again and again into vivid bursts of flame.

By the time it was full day the transports had arrived opposite the little bay on which the covering force of Australians had landed, and which was to become famous for all time as Anzac Cove. The whole line of warships could now be plainly seen stretching away south towards Cape Helles until they became lost in the clouds of smoke. Close at hand were the transports, some of them moving out after having unloaded their troops; but the majority awaiting their turn to transfer their human freight on to the destroyers or big barges.

THE FIRST BATTERY IN ACTION

A section of the 4th (Howitzer) Battery landing on the beach at Anzac on the morning of April 26, 1915

[*Photo by the Author*

The New Zealand and Australian Division commenced to disembark at 9 a.m. The troops of the 1st Australian Division had driven the Turks beyond the tangled mass of spurs and steep ridges which overlook the beach at the landing place, and were then endeavouring in face of superior numbers to hold the ground which they had won. The task of the New Zealanders on landing was to extend the line on the left of the Australians, and particularly to support the left of the 3rd Australian Brigade, which had landed as the covering force at 5 a.m. The enemy had rushed some batteries of field artillery into action, and as the New Zealanders climbed from the transports into the barges and boats in which they were to be towed ashore, they could see the shrapnel bursting along the water's edge. The densely packed barges offered a very tempting target to the Turkish gunners as they drew slowly in to the shore; but though casualties in the boats were frequent they were not heavy. As they landed the men were flung into the fight without regard to particular units. The need was desperate, and there was no delay. Discarding their weighty packs they went straight up the slopes and gullies and engaged in the desperate struggle against great odds. But the Division was being landed very slowly; night had fallen before the whole Brigade of New Zealand Infantry had been got ashore. For some hours in the middle of the day there was a complete stoppage in the disembarkation; and this at a time when the enemy had been strongly reinforced and was fiercely counter-attacking.

Artillery Headquarters landed with the boats of the first tow, which reached the shore a few minutes before 10 a.m., and the C.R.A. and staff immediately commenced to reconnoitre positions for the Brigade. It needed no reconnaisance to show that in such country it would be a matter of the greatest difficulty to select positions for the 18pr. batteries; it was, however, quite suited for howitzers. Efforts were made to get some of the guns ashore, but without avail; and Headquarters had to content itself with the selection of positions, and the partial preparation of some of them during the night.

The only guns that had been landed by evening were two Indian mountain batteries, and one solitary Australian 18pr.

The infantry's need was a desperate one, and they suffered severely owing to the absence of artillery support. The guns of the Navy, owing to their flat trajectory, could not search the gullies or engage the concealed enemy batteries, nor could they lend close support to the infantry. Two shore observation parties were provided by the New Zealand Artillery Brigade to direct and control the fire of the naval guns; but the difficulties of observation and communication were enormous. The Indian gunners did wonderfully good work with their light mountain guns, but they were few in number, and in any case could not hope to silence the Turkish guns. Advancing and fighting in the open, the infantry were exposed to the full effects of the bursts of shrapnel which swept the beaches, and sprayed the scrub-covered ridges where they stubbornly stood their ground, stemming each rush with a desperate courage that took no count of odds. Stretcher bearers of the Field Ambulance and volunteers were working tirelessly to get the wounded down on to the beaches, where the congestion of suffering men became so great that the doctors were overwhelmed, and almost every outgoing barge and boat was crammed full. Out in the Bay the artillerymen on their transports were consumed with impatience; from early morning they had been eagerly expecting the arrival of the barges which were to take them ashore with their guns.

The Artillery in Action.

Casualties during the day had been extremely heavy, and the troops were almost exhausted with their terrible and continuous struggles. The enemy, too, had suffered severe losses, but he had been constantly reinforced, and threatened at any moment to sweep the troops of the Army Corps from their precarious hold on the precipitous and hard-won ridges. The night brought no relief, and the anxiety was so great that a conference was held at which the possibility of a withdrawal was discussed; on the Artillery transports orders were received to stand by the boats in case a re-embarkation should be ordered. But the idea of withdrawal was peremptorily dismissed by the Commander-in-chief; it was decided that the force must hold on; and orders were issued for the hastening of the disembarkation of more troops, including the 4th (How.) Battery and more 18prs. During the night the guns of the 4th Battery were unloaded from the *Australind* on to barges. The Left Section of the Battery landed at 6.30 a.m. on the 26th April, and immediately went into action at the foot of Howitzer Gully, the guns being pulled along the beach by two teams of Australian horses which had been brought ashore the previous afternoon. The first round, fired at ten minutes to seven, was sent into the "blue" at a range of three thousand yards, so that the infantry might know without delay that their artillery had commenced to arrive, and an involuntary cheer went up from the hillside at the welcome sound. It was music to the ears of the battle-weary men in the line. Within a few minutes of firing its first round the section had been linked up with an observing station on Plugge's Plateau, and was busy engaging targets with an unvarying accuracy that certainly did not suggest that the gunners were having their first practice with live shell. Soon after coming into action this section was engaged by hostile guns firing from Gaba Tepe, but they were silenced by the fire of the warships. The remaining two guns of the Battery were landed about noon, and occupied positions which had been prepared overnight to the north of Ari Burnu Point. The first target was the Fisherman's Hut, from which enemy snipers had done a good deal of execution, and a direct hit was registered with the third round. These two guns remained in action on Ari Burnu during the whole period of the campaign, being moved only when the orders came for evacuation.

By the close of the second day a line had been established with some continuity; trenches were gradually being dug and strengthened, and ammunition, stores and water were being got up to the line by the carrying parties, who laboured up the gullies and precipitous slopes oblivious of the enemy shrapnel, or the snipers who took toll of their numbers from the scrub-covered tops. On the beach a pier had been improvised from some barges which had been stranded on the shingle, which on subsequent days was strengthened with planking and stout beams, and did service until the more substantial Watson's Pier was erected. On this narrow shelving strip of shingle everything was landed—mules, men, and guns, and stores of every description, and here grew up great square stacks of bully beef and biscuits, the staple diet of the soldier at Anzac. The transport mules were picketed in lines on the beach until the guns from either flank commenced to make the area so unhealthy that they took refuge up the deep, narrow gullies which ran up between the ridges.

Late in the afternoon of April 26th arrangements were made to disembark the 2nd Battery, but it was the early morning of the 27th before the guns were finally got ashore. Two big barges went alongside the *Surada* about dusk, and into each was loaded a section of guns and limbers, and a full complement of ammunition. About 9 p.m. a trawler took charge of the two barges and towed them close in shore, where the Battery was informed that it could not land that night. The gunners spent a cheerless night lying off-shore in the barges, listening to the patter of the stray bullets in the water all round them. At dawn the trawler took them to within a hundred yards of the shore, near Hell Spit, the gunners laboriously manœuvring the unwieldy barges over the remaining distance. As they were landed the guns and vehicles were drawn up on the beach and concealed as far as possible; but the disembarkation had hardly been completed when the enemy commenced to shell the beach with shrapnel. The Battery did not go into action at once, but the officers spent the day endeavouring to find a position for the guns which would be accessible besides being suitable in other respects. Everywhere they were faced with sheer cliffs or apparently impossible slopes; but it was recognised that the guns would have to be dragged up a track which must be prepared without delay. There was no alternative; as the flat trajectory guns could not shoot over the cliffs they must be got up on top of them. In the meantime the two guns of the Right Section were manhandled up to a temporary position on the shoulder of the ridge above Ari Burnu. The position afforded only a limited field of fire to the north-east; but the guns did some very effective shooting on this zone.

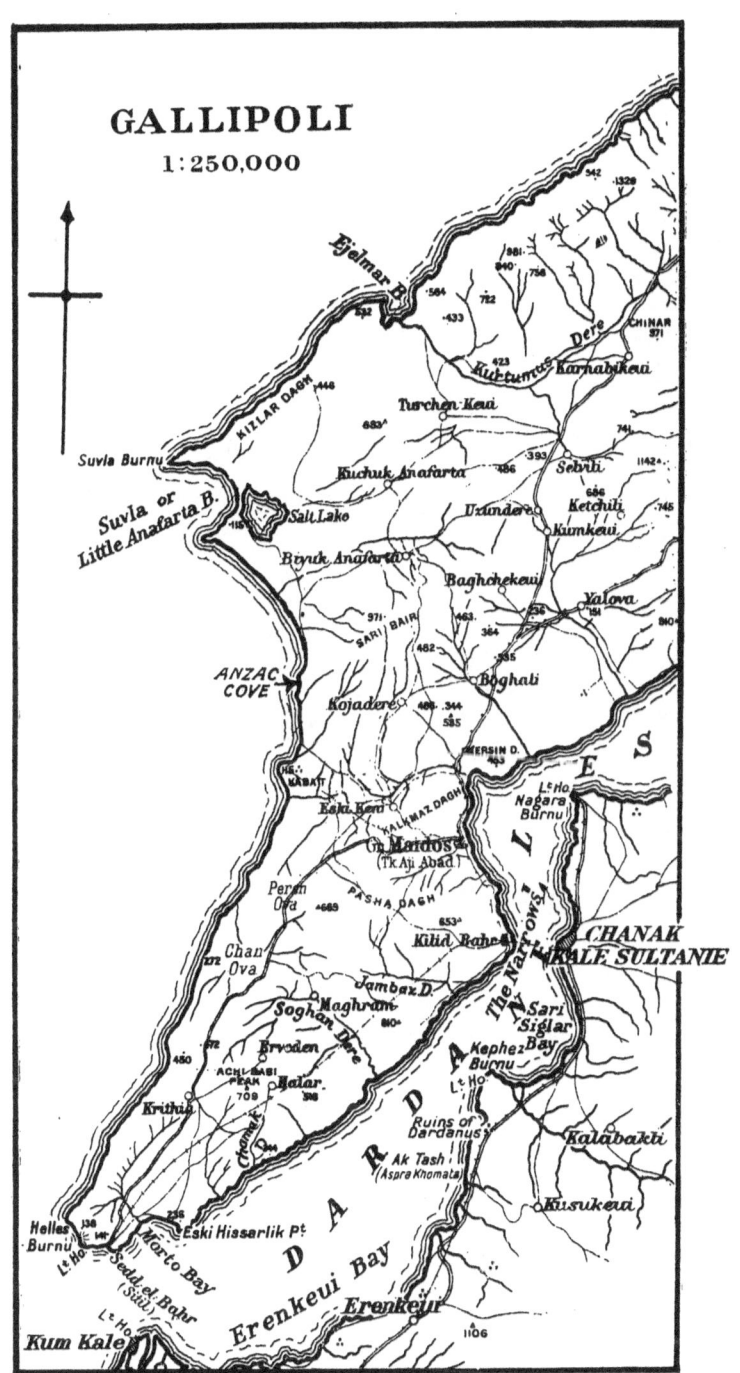

ANZAC POSITION

There was an exciting moment on the crowded beach during the afternoon of the 28th, when observers, watching through a telescope the busy movements of the Turks on the distant point of Nibrunesi, reported that a heavy gun was being dragged into position. A gun firing from Nibrunesi Point could enfilade the beach, and play terrible havoc on the crowded slopes sheltered by Plugge's Plateau and the shoulders running down to the sea. The left section of the Howitzer Battery opened fire, but failed to reach the Point, and beach parties working with feverish energy to get the ammunition from the beach to the shelter of Howitzer Gully, were filled with anxious apprehension. Messages had been sent out to the Navy, however, and a cruiser away on the left opened fire on the Point, and relieved the situation. A party of New Zealand Infantry, which made a successful landing on Nibrunesi Point at dawn on May 2nd, destroyed an observation post as well as capturing a number of prisoners, and reported the existence of a prepared gun position, but no gun.

The Left Section of the 2nd Battery, which had been in reserve on the beach, got a sudden call into action some time after midnight on the 28th. Infantry patrols had reported that the enemy was moving along the flat to the north of the Cove, evidently with the idea of attacking the somewhat exposed left flank. All spare men and beach parties stood to arms, a defensive line was occupied, and the gunners dragged their two guns through the heavy sand to a position near the left section of the 4th Battery. Supplies of ammunition were brought up, and the guns stood ready for action, but the threatened attack was abandoned. Once again the Navy had come to the rescue, destroyers standing in and throwing a concentrated beam across the flat from their searchlights. On this brightly illumined path the Turk very wisely refused to show himself. As the two guns were in full view of the enemy by day, they were removed with the first flush of dawn.

A position had now been found for the 2nd Battery on the top of Plugge's Plateau, but the question of how the guns were to be got up had yet to be settled. However, a working party of infantry, some hundreds strong, was set to work to make a road up Maclagan's Ridge, and with such energy did they apply themselves to their task that the track was sufficiently prepared by evening to permit of the passage of the guns. Horses could not be employed on those sheer slopes, and accordingly, with long ropes and one hundred lusty men heaving in unison the guns were literally lifted up on to the plateau. Ten days later the Right Section was brought up from Ari Burnu, and there the Battery remained until shortly after the opening of the big August attack. The position was eminently one which in ordinary times would have been considered "impossible"; but so would most positions at Anzac. But to the bold imagination and indomitable spirit of the Australasians who took and held for so long that narrow sweep of barren, broken country, nothing appeared impossible. This position looked straight across to the Turkish trenches at Quinn's Post, and the Turks, on their part, were able to look almost down the muzzles of the guns.

Plugge's Plateau was an almost level piece of ground a few acres in extent which crowned the slopes of Anzac Cove. Standing on the Plateau and looking east across Monash Gully the forward trenches at Quinn's Post were in full view; while lower down were the communication trenches with which the beaver-like industry of sapper and infantryman had honeycombed the face of the cliff. Above these forward trenches, almost in the same line of sight with them, and a bare twenty yards further on, was the Turkish front line. The 2nd Battery watched this point, the most vulnerable in the whole system, and the most vital. It could see and shoot at scarcely any other; but though its arc of fire was so limited, the shooting the guns could do within this arc was so effective and of such value as to make the position one of great importance. Careful ranging and most accurate fuze-setting alone rendered it possible for the guns to engage the enemy twenty yards beyond their own line at a range of between nine hundred and a thousand yards. The deadly effect of this direct fire can be imagined; and after one or two experiences the enemy was little disposed to leave his trenches in the face of it.

Three guns of the 1st Battery arrived on the beach on the afternoon of April 30th, and were followed by the remaining gun at 6 a.m. on May 1st. A somewhat exposed position on the left flank had been selected and partly prepared for one section, and despite the risks, an attempt was made to occupy it during daylight. The two guns, drawn by six-horse teams, had not proceeded far north of Ari Burnu Point when the leading team came under heavy rifle fire. As the team could not turn in the heavy sand, the horses were unhooked, and the attempt to get the guns into position was postponed till nightfall. This position, which had been occupied with a view rather to moral than material effect, afforded only a restricted field of fire, and four or five days later the two guns were withdrawn to the beach at the Cove, where the Battery remained in reserve until May 17th. From that date until the evacuation the Battery occupied what was without doubt one of the best gun-positions, from a shooting point of view, in the whole of the Anzac area, commanding as it did a field of fire which practically extended from the sea on the right to the sea on the left. This position was on Russell's Top, the apparently insurmountable summit of Walker's Ridge, the guns being got there only by dint of the same initial labour and great exertions that had been necessary to place the 2nd Battery on the summit of Plugge's Plateau. Engineers and infantry working parties made a track up Walker's Ridge, and a big team of infantrymen, whose enthusiasm made them willing volunteers, pulled the guns up the long, dragging way from the beach to the top. As the 2nd Battery looked directly into Quinn's, so from the 1st Battery gun-pits the enemy works at Lone Pine and Johnston's Jolly lay in full view, at a range of from eight hundred to one thousand yards. These were the only field guns which could bear on these two places in the line, this fact alone making the position one of tremendous value.

It will readily be seen that in addition to possessing a preponderance in guns, and more plentiful supplies of ammunition, the enemy enjoyed every advantage of position and observation. In the Anzac area, circumscribed and altogether unsuitable for the use of field guns, batteries were obliged for the most part to occupy positions that might almost be described as inaccessible, and were plainly exposed to the enemy's view, or altogether nullify the value of their support to the infantry. There were no alternative positions, and even if there had been, the labour involved in moving the guns in such country would have rendered them of little use. Being thus plainly exposed to the enemy's view, there was no recourse for the batteries but to endeavour to protect their positions, and particularly their personnel, by digging trenches and constructing protective earthworks. The 1st Battery position in front of the Sphinx was fairly well protected on the left by the lie of the ground, which sloped up to the cliff-edge. The Turkish guns firing from Anafarta seldom did any damage, most of the shells striking the face of the cliff, or going right over. The 2nd Battery on Plugge's Plateau, was even more exposed to view, but the position was made very strong despite the almost total lack of materials. Sandbags were to be had in small quantities, but timber was unprocurable—through ordinary channels of supply, at any rate. This lack of material made it impossible to construct strong overhead cover on the gun-pits; but communication trenches were dug between the guns, approaches were prepared, and the accommodation for the detachments was much improved. This work was done as opportunity offered; much of it during the quiet days at the end of May, and in June. The gunners lived beside their pieces in small burrow-like dug-outs or excavations, which were often very comfortable and always clean, and models of neatness in the arrangement of their few personal belongings. Observing officers, with their telephonists, lived at the observing stations in or near the front line while on duty. They were usually relieved at intervals of a week, or thereabouts; but during those periods when there was a shortage of officers, chiefly due to dysentery and similar complaints, these hours of duty extended over very lengthy periods. An observation station for the direction of naval fire was also constantly maintained, and the data and information as to targets which were supplied to the vessels of the fleet, considerably increased the value of their fire. All messages were sent to a naval wireless station established in the Cove, and thence they were transmitted to the fleet.

One of the 3rd Battery Guns at Cape Helles

At the commencement of the campaign ammunition had all to be taken up to the guns by hand, but when the Corps settled down, and such things became better organised, the employment of transport mules relieved the gunners of a heavy burden. It was not a long carry to the howitzers; but few of the gunners will forget the dragging climb up to Plugge's Plateau, or to the 1st Battery's position on Walker's Ridge. Most of the ammunition for the 1st Battery was taken up by pack mules on the road constructed for the guns, and a fair measure of success attended a scheme for hauling it up the cliffside by a rope let down on the right of the Sphinx.

The Turk long cherished the illusion that it was possible by sheer weight of numbers to fling back into the sea the adventurous soldiery who had wrested this narrow footing on his coast, but the absolute failure of all his desperate attempts in the closing days of April must have gone some way towards dispelling it. During most of this time the 4th Battery was the only field battery supporting the Division, and the value of its support to the wearied infantry is almost beyond estimation. The only limit to its activities was the ammunition supply, which had to be husbanded with the most jealous care. For two hours, at one of the most critical periods, the guns were entirely without ammunition. This was on April 27th, and difficulty was at first experienced in getting fresh supplies sent ashore, but at last some arrived from the *Australind*, and the guns were able to resume shooting.

By the end of April the line had been reorganized by extricating troops which had become mixed with other units in the confusion of the early fighting, preparations following for an attack on May 2nd, with the object of improving the line by capturing a commanding knoll between Quinn's Post and Walker's Ridge. The attack, which was made at night over unfamiliar, broken country, was not successful. It was preceded by a bombardment by the field guns that were in action, and the guns of the Navy; but owing to the conditions it could not be directly supported by artillery fire. The attacking troops suffered heavy losses from machine-gun and rifle fire during the night, and when the dawn came found their positions so exposed as to be absolutely untenable.

C

The Turkish Attacks in May.

Three days later the New Zealand Infantry Brigade, with the 2nd Australian Infantry Brigade, left Anzac for Helles. The temporary withdrawal of these two brigades so weakened the line that the gravest anxiety prevailed, until the tension was relieved by the arrival on May 12th of the New Zealand Mounted Rifles and the men of the Australian Light Horse. On the arrival of these fresh troops the battalions of the Royal Naval Division, who had been assisting to hold the line, were embarked for Helles. While the line had been so thinly held the New Zealand batteries in action played a very responsible part in the defence of the position. The 2nd Battery, tirelessly vigilant in following every movement of the enemy in front of Quinn's and the neighbouring posts, lent invaluable aid to the infantry on the morning of May 10th, during a strong enemy counter-attack. On the previous night troops of the Royal Marine Brigade had made a sortie and captured some trenches, the possession of which would materially have improved the position at that point. The assaulting troops had succeeded in establishing themselves in the captured trenches, and reinforcements had been sent up, but at dawn the Turks heavily counter-attacked, and recaptured the trenches. The direct fire of the 2nd Battery's 18prs. on Plugge's Plateau, and the high explosive of the 4.5in. howitzers inflicted very heavy casualties on the enemy, who paid dearly for their success. Later in the morning the 2nd Battery so effectually shelled the trenches in front of Quinn's Post that the shooting drew warm praise and a message of thanks from Brigadier-General Trotman, R.M.L.I., commanding No. 3 Section of the line. Further evidence of the deadly effectiveness of the fire of these two batteries on this occasion was had some time later, when an entry was found in the diary of a Turkish officer to the effect that two Turkish regiments on May 10th lost 600 killed and 2,000 wounded.

Despite the fact that they were few in number and so ill supplied with ammunition, the three New Zealand batteries shot so well and so consistently on every emergency, and at every critical period, that invariably they received the warm thanks of the Infantry Commanders in the line. The gunner's regret was that his activities should be so drastically limited by the unkind circumstance that every round he expended had almost to be begged for. But by accurate service on the guns, and careful skill at the observation post, as much was done with the meagre supply as was humanly possible. The 4th Howitzer Battery suffered more by the shortage than did any of the 18pr. batteries. The only howitzer battery at Anzac for many months, there fell to it the multitude of tasks which the flat-trajectoried 18prs. were not able to undertake in a country so unsuited for anything else but howitzers. Not a day passed but requests were sent in to the howitzers for fire to be brought to bear on some particular target which the other guns could not reach, and very often the Battery Commander found himself without ammunition, and unable to accede to the request. A reserve had always to be kept on hand lest some critical emergency should suddenly arise; and to make inroads on it for the purposes of normal daily fire was out of the question.

On May 16th, the day before the 1st Battery guns were got up to Walker's Ridge, Major-General Sir A. J. Godley sent to the C.R.A. a message referring in appreciative terms to the shooting of the batteries then in action. "Please convey," the message ran, "to all your batteries now here my high appreciation of the excellent shooting they have made while in action here. All commanders of posts are loud in their praises of the support they have had from the howitzers and No. 2 Battery, and on behalf of the whole Division I wish to express to them our thanks for the good work which has led to such substantial results."

When the Turks made their big attack on May 19th, the shore artillery supporting the Division consisted of the 4th Howitzer Battery, the 1st and 2nd Batteries, and one 6in. howitzer manned by men of the Royal Garrison Artillery. This gun had been landed on the night of May 16th, and on the following day hauled up Walker's Ridge to an excellent position which gave a good field of fire, but its value was rather discounted by the fact that only one hundred and fifty rounds of ammunition had been sent with it. At the time of this attack the troops holding the line were disposed as follows:—

> No. 1 Section—3rd Australian Infantry Brigade, 6 guns A.F.A., 6 guns Indian Mountain Battery.
>
> No. 2 Section—1st Australian Infantry Brigade, 5 guns Australian F.A., one 6in. howitzer.
>
> No. 3 Section—1st Light Horse Brigade and 4th Australian Infantry Brigade, 3 guns Indian Mountain Artillery, 2 howitzers 4th Battery, N.Z.F.A., 2nd Battery, N.Z.F.A.
>
> No. 4 Section—N.Z. Mounted Rifles Brigade, 4 guns 1st Battery, N.Z.F.A., 3 guns Indian Mountain Artillery, 2 howitzers 4th Battery, N.Z.F.A., one 6in. howitzer.

The attack was expected and prepared for. Word had been received of considerable movement of enemy troops along the roads on the Peninsula, and reinforcements had been seen marching to Anzac from the southern zone at Helles. The Navy vigorously shelled these roads and communication ways; the Turkish response at Anzac making it clear at once that his artillery had received an accession of strength, including some guns of very heavy calibre, which had not previously opened fire. The attack opened suddenly at midnight on May 18th, when rifle and machine-gun fire more violent than anything that had previously been experienced, broke out along the whole Anzac front. All ranks had been warned of the imminence of the attack, both the riflemen in the trenches, and the gunners by their pieces, calmly awaiting the moment of assault. The crash of the Turkish shells punctuated this prolonged roar from rifle and machine gun. Towards 3 a.m. the fire slackened somewhat, but increased in intensity again when the Turkish infantry at last advanced to the attack. The first effort, which was directed against the left of No. 2 Section, was repulsed with rifle, machine-gun, and artillery fire; but it was only a foretaste of what was to follow. The Turks came on four times, always to be repulsed with loss. At the same time a heavy attack was delivered on the north-east salient of No. 4

Section; and between 4.30 and 5 a.m. fighting became general along almost the whole line. At Quinn's and Courtney's, and in front of the trenches held by the New Zealand Mounted Rifles, the Turks came on in masses, dimly seen in the smoke of battle, and the half light of the coming dawn. There was little doubt about their courage, and there was less doubt about their numbers. Concentrated rifle fire, and the terrible stream of lead from machine-guns, swept great gaps in their ranks, but there was no wavering; they faced death bravely.

The growing light gave the artillery observers a better chance, and while the 2nd Battery was pouring its short range murderous fire into the trenches opposite Quinn's and Courtney's, the 1st Battery and the Howitzers were making good practice on large bodies of the enemy assembling in Johnston's Jolly. Employing an increased number of guns, the enemy shelled the trenches, interior positions and the beach. The 2nd Battery in particular was subjected to a fairly steady fire from light calibre guns, but little damage was sustained. This Battery, whose left section was getting most of the targets, got some splendid shooting about ten o'clock; a large force of the enemy which had been unable to make any headway in an attack directed against the left of Courtney's Post and the right of Quinn's, swung round to the left of Quinn's, where they were so severely handled by the guns that their attack was completely broken up. By that time the impetus of the attack was spent, but the enemy was further harassed by gun-fire in the valley east of Plateau 400, where they were endeavouring to reorganise their shattered ranks.

For the not inconsiderable part which it had played in thus definitely checking this great attack, which it was later discovered was ambitiously designed by the Turks to drive the invaders back into the sea, the 2nd Battery received the thanks of Colonel Chauvel, commanding the 1st Australian Light Horse Brigade, and Brigadier-General Monash, commanding the 4th Australian Infantry Brigade, both of whom stated that the Battery saved Quinn's Post, as they could not have held the position without its support. When the enemy was attacking with such determination in front of the Post, the shells of the Battery were bursting a few feet beyond the front line trenches and covering the enemy with a hail of shrapnel. The expenditure of ammunition was of course considerable, but amply justified by the results. The 18prs. fired 1,360 rounds, the Howitzer battery 143 rounds, and the Mountain Guns 1,400 rounds, while the expenditure of small arms ammunition was estimated at little short of a million rounds.

Desultory firing continued until the afternoon of May 20th, when there came a marked lull, and about six o'clock Red Crescent and white flags appeared at various points in the enemy's line. The Turks appeared at first desirous of an armistice to get in wounded and bury their dead; but it soon became apparent that the flags were part of a ruse to gain time and cover the massing of troops for another attack after dark. Those of the enemy who had left their trenches were warned to go back, the 1st and 2nd Batteries were ordered to open fire, and troops in the line were warned against a possible attack. The enemy did actually attack during the night in the direction of Courtney's Post, but the attack lacked vigour, and was broken up. An hour and a half after midnight, however, the whole line was shelled, and a determined attack was made on Quinn's Post; but the attackers again fared badly at the hands of the 2nd Battery, whose fire drove them to the shelter of their trenches, and beat back all other attempts to assault. Slow fire was kept up on the enemy's trenches in this locality until 4 a.m., when all guns opened up in a general bombardment which extended over half an hour.

The following day negotiations of a formal character were opened by the enemy with a view to arranging a suspension of arms. A Turkish officer made his way along the shore from Gaba Tepe, under cover of a white flag, and was met and escorted, blindfolded, through the lines and along the beach to Army Corps Headquarters. The negotiations extended over some two or three days, but a suspension of arms was finally arranged for May 24th, to commence at 7.30 a.m., and to terminate at 4.30 p.m. At the appointed hour the armistice parties from each force met on the right flank of the Anzac position, and proceeded to mark out with small white flags a dividing line down the centre of No Man's Land. By ten o'clock this preliminary disposition had been completed, and the burial parties, Turkish and Colonial, set to work each on their own side of the dividing line. It had been agreed that in addition to burying its own dead, each side should carry to the centre line and hand over all the enemy dead for identification and burial. This was not found practicable when the task came to be faced, and it was therefore agreed that each side should bury where they lay all the dead within its zone. The burying was completed about 3 p.m., by which time it was estimated some 3,000 Turkish dead, killed on or since the 18th May, had been buried in the area between the opposing lines.

The day following the Armistice was marked by a tragic and dramatic happening, which for the time, at any rate, left an even more marked impression on the minds of everyone than had the grim business of the previous day. This was the sinking by a submarine of H.M.S. *Triumph*, in the light of broad day, and almost at the very feet of the watchers on the slopes of Anzac. A hostile submarine had been reported off Gaba Tepe on May 22nd, and in consequence all transports lying off shore had been ordered to Mudros, although this meant the dislocation of the supply arrangements for the force on shore. Extra precautions had also been taken by ships of the navy, which were kept under way as much as possible. The *Triumph* was standing about a mile off shore, a little south of Anzac Cove, when a great column of smoke and water rose up from her side, and she quickly commenced to heel over. The big ship must have flashed the news abroad that she was hit and in her death agony, for from every quarter came racing destroyers and naval small craft. From away down south in the direction of Cape Helles black shapes on the skyline, each of them a torpedo-boat destroyer, began to increase in size, and presently into plain view they came, spreading out fan-shape, with the foam rising to their decks almost, and the smoke spreading out in a black mottled wake overhead. One or two destroyers cruising nearer at hand had raced at once to the *Triumph*, and were busy taking off the crew, while picquet boats and pinnaces had put off from the shore with a like despatch. Slowly the *Triumph* heeled over until her decks were almost perpendicular and her port guns were tilted skywards, and within twelve minutes of being struck she had turned completely over, the great length of her red keel glistening in the sun. While the questing destroyers circled round, hungry for a sight of the submarine, the vessel gradually sank deeper in the waters, until with a little swirl she disappeared completely from view. The old ship had become familiar to everyone at Anzac, and the spectacle made a profound impression on the thousands who stood on the hills and watched her tragic end. At midday she rode trim and strong, the sun beating on her clean bare decks, and the smooth, shining length of her big guns; but within the hour she had been stricken to the vitals, and found her last resting place in the blue waters of the Ægean.

CHAPTER III.

THE ISOLATION OF ANZAC.

For nearly a fortnight after the landing the C.R.A., Lieut.-Colonel Johnston, had his headquarters at the foot of Howitzer Gully, close by the headquarters of the Division, on the northern end of the Cove. But these quarters were cramped and inconvenient, and it was soon discovered that the congested and exposed beach front was unsuitable for the location of the headquarters of the Division. Shelters were accordingly prepared on a terrace at the head of a small gully which ran almost to the foot of the precipitous slopes of Plugge's Plateau, where Headquarters remained from May 7th until the eve of the August offensive. Army Corps Headquarters was in a central and accessible position at the very foot of a gully running off the centre of the Cove, where General Birdwood, living as unpretentiously as the most junior member of his staff, directed the ceaseless activities of his soldiers. From the very day of the landing the Cove became the hub or centre from which radiated everything that was vital to the life of the Corps. There were located the Supply Depôts of the Army Service Corps, the Army Ordnance Stores, and the Field Ambulance stations. The Cove was protected from direct fire by the steep sides of Plugge's Plateau, from which two long shoulders ran down to the sea, terminating in the two points that marked the northern and southern extremities of the little strip of beach—Ari Burnu on the north, and Hell Spit on the south. Never was a force so precariously placed, clinging by virtue only of its tenacious courage to a strip of broken and barren coast-line three thousand yards in length, and a bare thousand yards in depth at the centre, with the sea at its back, and hemmed in on three sides by a foe superior in numbers and guns, and lacking little in courage and leadership. But no one ever doubted its ability to hold what had been seized. Who could have doubted in face of such bold confidence and intrepidity?

The difficulties of supplying the troops with ammunition and the bare necessaries of existence were enormous and never-ceasing. Consider for a moment that the country they held yielded nothing, not even a sufficient water-supply, and that all supplies had to be brought by sea from the base at Alexandria, 800 miles distant, and landed on the open beaches at Anzac. The ordinary methods of supplying an army's needs could not be employed; there was no precedent which might be referred to for guidance, the position being unexampled in military history. Only the intelligent and skilful co-operation of the Navy made the task practicable. Between the base at Alexandria and Anzac there were but two harbours, Mudros Bay, distant 60 miles, and Kephalos, over at Imbros; and neither of these harbours possessed any piers or facilities for the transhipment of stores. The position became further complicated when enemy submarines began to make the Ægean Sea dangerous to shipping, and it became necessary to prohibit the big transports and store ships from proceeding north of Mudros. Up to that time the transports had stood off the coast at Anzac, and discharged their supplies or disembarked their reinforcements into lighters, which were towed into the beach; but the advent of the submarines made another transhipment necessary. At Mudros supplies were loaded into steam trawlers and mine sweepers, which discharged them into lighters and barges off Anzac or across at Kephalos. At Anzac the Turkish guns commanded all the landing places, so that everything had to be landed under cover of darkness.

The working of the whole system was dependent on the vagaries of the weather. Even during the summer months the broad surface of the bay at Mudros was sometimes swept by a northerly or southerly wind, which seriously impeded or delayed transhipment, but in the autumn and winter Anzac was often isolated for days at a time by gales which swept the open bay at Kephalos, and made the exposed beaches at Anzac quite unapproachable. The establishment of a reserve supply of stores at Anzac was the only measure which could be taken to minimise the dangers of isolation incurred by these breaks in the lines of communication. Within the first week after the landing of the force, the little mounds of stores on the beach began to grow and expand, until the shelving beach flanking the landing piers was piled high with great pyramids of supplies of all descriptions, but chiefly bully-beef and biscuits.

The bulk of the water supply also came from overseas. A certain quantity of water was to be had at Anzac, and by seeking for water in likely places, and improving existing wells, the local supply was considerable increased. At the end of June it was estimated that there was a natural supply at Anzac of eighteen thousand gallons per day, a further thirty per day coming from Alexandria by transports and store ships. These vessels pumped their supplies into a water ship, from which it was taken to Anzac in water-barges which were moored to the shore, the water being finally pumped into tanks on the beach, where it was jealously guarded and doled out to the thirsty troops.

Though the maintenance of the army from a distant base over sea routes frequented by enemy submarines was certainly an arduous, and often a hazardous, undertaking, it was in the landing and distribution on shore that danger showed itself grim and in deadly earnest. From his vantage point to the south, on the bold headland of Gaba Tepe, the enemy could see almost everything that went on in the Cove, while his guns covered not only the beach but the sea for some distance offshore. The beach was occasionally shelled by light guns firing from the direction of Anafarta; but the guns so cleverly concealed near the Olive Groves beyond Gaba Tepe commanded a perfect enfilade of the water-front, the accuracy and frequency of their fire making them a constant and deadly menace. So effective was their fire that an attempt to land anything during the hours of daylight was a flouting of death that received a quick and final answer. So during the long day the beach was quiet enough except for the frolicking of the bathers, who, making the most of their opportunity, disported themselves in the sparkling waters of the bay between the bursts of shelling.

With the coming of night the narrow water-front began to swarm with the activities of beach fatigues, carrying parties, and the chattering muleteers of the Indian Supply Column.

The pinnaces brought the unwieldy and heavily-freighted barges in to the piers, and the sweating fatigues filed in ghostly procession from the piers with their burdens of food supplies, ammunition and stores. From this advanced depôt on the beach the supply columns loaded up their pack mules and handy little transport carts, and filed off in the darkness on their various routes to the forward dumps.

Reinforcements for the Division were usually landed an hour or two before daylight. Full of curious questions, and marvelling at the seeming animated confusion on shore, the newcomers were promptly led into the comparative safety of one of the gullies running off the beach, and thence taken by guides away to their respective units. By the time the stars had begun to pale before the first roseate flush of dawn, the tumult had subsided; the last lighters had been emptied, the Supply Depôt had sent out its last load of stores, the Ordnance Depôt its final consignment of ammunition, and the transport drivers were commencing to filter back and arrange their little carts in orderly rows on the beach. With the rising of the sun the water's edge and the piers were given over to the morning bathers, who came trooping down, lightly or not at all clad, from their burrows and shelters on the slopes overlooking the bay.

For an army so disadvantageously situated the daily ration was a liberal one, and the occasions on which there was anything approaching a shortage were very rare. But there was an appalling lack of variety about the ration, and this circumstance was a contributory cause of much of the sickness which so grievously weakened the force during the summer months. Tinned beef—"Bully-beef"—and the square white granite army biscuit formed the foundation of the ration, and a very firm foundation too. These two articles of diet were never in short supply; great quantities of them were always kept stacked on the beach, and they were perfectly secure from the attentions of acquisitive souls who visited the Supply Depôt under cover of night in hopes of agreeably supplementing their ration. The biscuits were impervious to climatic influences or change of temperature, but the beef was often found to be par-boiled when brought straight from the stacks standing in the blazing sun. But that was a minor affliction. Supplementary items were jam, always of a constant brand and variety, "Machonachies"—a meat and vegetable ration much appreciated as a variant from the tinned beef, and, as a matter of course, tea. Fresh vegetables would have been worth their weight in gold, but unfortunately they were almost unknown.

When the summer was advanced, and almost every soldier was weakened by the ravages of dysentery and kindred troubles, some efforts were made to alleviate the distress by introducing some variety into the ration, but they did not go far, and achieved little. There was no one who would not willingly have given a portion of his pay each week if thereby he could have secured an occasional change from a diet so monotonous that it became nauseating to a sick stomach. But the Gallipoli campaign was nearing its conclusion before any active steps were taken to provide canteens over at Imbros, and by the time the canteens had become well established, and the system of purchase by unit representatives was in running order, preliminary steps were being taken for the evacuation.

Obviously it is impossible for an army in the field to carry into practice all the laws of sanitation that ordinarily govern a civilised community. The soldiers are too busy fighting for one thing; too busy at times even to bury their dead; and for a host of other reasons the sanitation of a fighting army must always be a matter of difficulty, and, especially in a warm climate, a source of anxiety. At Anzac these difficulties were intensified a hundred-fold by the circumstance that for many months the force was confined to the narrow strip of country on which it first established itself. From the outset nothing was left undone to keep the area as clean as possible, and so minimise the risks of an outbreak of disease; but inevitably much of the ground became foul, and formed breeding places for myriads of flies, which swarmed everywhere, and seriously aggravated the already prevalent dysentery. The colonials had experienced the fly plague in Egypt, which was a natural breeding-ground for anything that had its origin in filth; but the flies in Egypt were a pleasant and soothing companionship compared to the voracious hosts that from dawn to dusk tormented the very souls of these unfortunate campaigners at Anzac. No efforts could keep them out of the food. They came from the unburied dead in No Man's Land, and from the gaping latrines, and buzzed about the supply depôts, and swarmed even on the very food as the soldier conveyed it to his mouth. Small wonder that the great majority of the force suffered from dysentery and diarrhœa as the season advanced.

The Fighting in Midsummer.

The varied activities of the artillery, both offensive and defensive, during the three weeks that had elapsed since the landing, culminating in the big Turkish attack in the middle of May, made such serious inroads on the slender ammunition supplies that a drastic curtailment of the normal daily expenditure became an imperative necessity. After the fighting of May 19th and the two following days had simmered down, an order was issued cutting down the allowance for 18prs., 4.5in., and 6in. howitzers to two rounds per gun per day. Two rounds per gun did not even suffice for the checking of registrations. Observing officers in their posts had to content themselves with gazing at targets which they could not engage, however tempting they might be. This was galling enough, but it was even harder for battery commanders to refuse, as they must, the frequent requests from the front line for support from the guns. Their cruel necessities forced them to deny to the infantry the support they expected and so sorely needed. The gunners employed much of this enforced leisure in further improving the gun positions, and their own accommodation. Here again they were faced with the almost absolute lack of materials. A few sandbags could be had, but nearly all the timber and sandbags that were landed went to meet the prior claims of the front line. So for the artillery there ensued a long period of irksome and enforced inactivity, which was broken in real earnest only when the guns were called on to help in countering a Turkish attack, as on May 29th, or in supporting some local operation by their own troops.

It had become apparent that the Army Corps could not hope to make any decisive move forward without first receiving strong reinforcements and a more liberal supply of ammunition. Although the enemy had been unable to accomplish his avowed purpose of sweeping the invaders into the sea, he had succeeded in confining them to the circumscribed area on which they had established themselves on the day of landing. Week by week the fighting began more closely to approximate to siege warfare. The failure of the series of attacks in which the New Zealand Infantry Brigade had been engaged at the southern end of the Peninsula early in May had similarly made it equally plain that no decisive step towards victory was likely to be achieved with the forces which Sir Ian Hamilton then had at his command in that theatre of operations. The situation was summed up in a Force Order issued by the General Officer Commanding the M.E.F. on May 11th, in which it was stated that "Owing to the numerous and well-planned entrenchments now held by the enemy in the vicinity of Achi Baba, and also at Gaba Tepe, the operations in the immediate future will approximate more to semi-siege warfare than to open operations in the field. Further progress must now be made by continuous and systematic attack on certain portions of the hostile line rather than by a general action involving the advance of the whole line at once. . . ."

The fact that trench warfare had set in and that no operations on a large scale appeared to be contemplated, did not diminish the aggressive alertness of the colonial troops at Anzac, nor did it mean any lessening of the constant struggle between the two opposing forces; a struggle which became more bitter and intense in those places where the front line trenches ran close together, and grave issues hung on the loss or gain of a few yards, or even of a few feet. At Quinn's Post, that vulnerable point in the defences where the defenders dare not yield one inch, so close to their backs was the edge of the cliff, the fighting assumed a character which invested it with new and fearful dangers. Despairing, doubtless, of ever advancing over the open against the devastating fire which his assaults always encountered from the trenches and the guns of the 2nd Battery, the Turk commenced mining operations in an endeavour to blow the Post and its defenders into the gully behind them. There was only one way to meet such a threat, and that was by prompt counter-mining. Experienced miners in plenty were to be had from the ranks of both Australians and New Zealanders, and to these men was entrusted the task of outwitting the Turkish miners who were secretly sapping into the vitals of the defences at the head of Monash Gully. Work went on unceasingly; cramped in the narrow confines of sap or tunnel the miners toiled and sweated, advancing their underground ways as cautiously as they might. Listening at intervals to the dim and muffled noises of the Turkish miners, they endeavoured to calculate, by sense and instinct, how far off they might be, and the direction of their drive. It was an uncanny game, in which skill and chance were mingled; and there was the ever-present possibility, despite the miners' untiring watchfulness and untrained judgment, that the Turk might advance his gallery undetected, and at any moment strike a surprise blow. And from surprises of that nature escape was difficult, if not impossible. Several Turkish galleries were discovered and destroyed by counter-mining in front of Quinn's; but about 3.30 a.m. on May 29th, the enemy succeeded in springing a mine which almost wrecked No. 3 Sub-section of the Post. The explosion was followed by a heavy bomb attack by a storming party of Turks, who succeeded in penetrating the front trenches, and isolating the sub-section of the left from the other two on the right. Some inevitable confusion resulted and for a few moments the situation was dangerous and obscure; but the garrison on each flank of No. 3 Sub-section desperately resisted all enemy attempts to extend their gains. Meanwhile reinforcements were clambering up the slopes, and the 2nd Battery and the 4th Battery's section of howitzers on the beach at once opened fire on the enemy's trenches and his reserves in front of Quinn's Post and at the head of Bloody Angle. About dawn a counter-attack succeeded in re-taking the lost trenches, and the attack was thus finally and decisively defeated. The batteries of the New Zealand Artillery engaged did good work in assisting to beat off the attack, and in addi-

The "Water-Queue" on the Beach at Anzac

[Photo by the Author

tion to keeping the enemy's trenches under constant fire and shelling his reserves in the open, several enemy batteries were engaged and silenced.

Close fighting continued in front of Quinn's Post for the next couple of days. The Turks had an apparently unlimited supply of bombs with which they constantly harassed the defenders of the Post, who replied as best they might with the "jam tin" bombs made at Anzac. Two enemy saps were actually pushed forward to within five yards of the front line, and these it became necessary at all hazards to destroy. At 1 p.m. on May 30th two parties of thirty-five men each went forward under covering fire from the 2nd Battery and the guns of two batteries of Indian Mounted Artillery, the operation being preceded by a heavy fire from the 2nd Battery on the enemy trenches, 100 yards in rear of their front line. The storming parties cleared the sap-heads and penetrated into the trenches beyond; but in spite of the supporting fire they were gradually driven back by a series of counter-attacks in which the enemy's lavish supplies of bombs placed the attackers at a grievous disadvantage. Colonel Chauvel, commanding the 3rd Section of Defence, was again warmly appreciative of the 2nd Battery's shooting, and in a message to the Divisional Commander expressed the opinion that the guns had caused great execution amongst the enemy, and fulfilled their task of keeping down hostile fire.

Practically ever since the day of the landing the weather had been consistently fine except for an occasional shower of rain. The days had been bright and warm and the nights fine, but somewhat cool to men who had been tempted by the brilliance of the sun to discard most of their warm clothing. But the hot summer season was advancing, and by June the heat had become oppressive, and combined with the ills and afflictions that it brought in its train, was a grievous burden to men who had already been sorely tried in body and spirit. As the heat increased, the amount of clothing worn by the average individual became less and less, until the absolute minimum was reached by the many, who contented themselves with a very short pair of "shorts," boots, and headgear of the variety that most appealed to their own particular tastes. Clad thus in abbreviated uniforms that were anything but uniform, the rank and file of the army grew bronzed, and some even heightened the suggestion of the primitive by becoming bearded, for the morning shave had become but a memory of another existence. Thoroughly verminous as they were, and often lacking sufficient fresh water even for drinking purposes, the soldiers might almost have been pardoned for ceasing to worry about personal cleanliness; but good habits persist as well as bad, and the desire to wash and be clean never waned. The gunner provided himself with a small pannikin-full of water, when it was to be had, and went about his toilet with the gravity of a man engaged in an absorbing morning ritual. Under such conditions it can be easily conceived what a joy to the soldier were those invigorating swims in the clear, cool, sparkling waters of the Cove.

Every day the guns from the Olive Groves swept the beach with their deadly enfilade, and hardly a day passed when they did not exact a toll in killed and wounded, but none ever thought of foregoing his swim in consequence of these risks. It was certainly a characteristic of Anzac that immunity from constant danger was to be sought nowhere; but there was something infinitely more tragic and terrible in being stricken down while enjoying an hour off duty on the beach, than while in the trenches, or serving the guns in the heat of battle. The guns usually fired in short bursts at uncertain intervals; and as they were firing at a considerable range the shells gave some warning of their approach and enabled the most active to dive for the shelter of the big stacks of boxed provisions or the lee side of the iron barges that usually lay alongside the pier. There they crouched while the shrapnel swept over their heads with that familiar but frightful swishing sound; and the stretcher-bearers rushed the wounded to cover. In a few moments the shelling would cease, men would straighten themselves up with an air of mingled relief and caution; then one, more intrepid than the rest, would lead the way again into the tempting waters, and in a few minutes it would seem as if there had never been anything to disturb their splashing and frolicking.

The summer dragged on slowly enough. The strength of the force was slowly dwindling through the wastage from sickness and the daily casualties in killed and wounded, and the prospect of making some decisive move without the addition of strong reinforcements became more and more remote. At every point the Army Corps was faced with wire entanglements and deep entrenchments which the enemy, strongly reinforced and enjoying every possible advantage that the position could offer, was daily making more formidable. For the garrison at Anzac there was never any rest. The inactivity of the force was only comparative. Because it was not called upon to make any prodigious effort there was none the less no lessening of the incessant and arduous fatigues, no respite from the constant dangers and alarms, the sniping, night patrols, and the fierce bombing encounters at those places where the opposing lines ran closely together. Before the commencement of the lengthy preparations for the August offensive gave them a heartening indication of big events at hand, the soldiers were inclined sometimes to wonder how much longer the depressing routine of "holding on" was to continue. The monotonous waiting during the hot summer weeks was calculated to do more to lower the morale of the soldier than all the exhausting struggles that had preceded it. In men of another temper it would have produced a fatal lethargy, and a decay in their fighting spirit, but in the Australians and New Zealanders it bred only a restlessness and a growing desire for some decisive action to end the seeming *impasse*.

In this frame of mind everyone turned with anxious interest to the theatre of operations at the southern end of the Peninsula, where the British and French forces were laying siege to the great natural fortress of Achi Baba. Those battles and the possibilities they suggested were a constant topic of discussion in June; and there were always at least one or two rumours in circulation that Achi Baba had fallen or was about to fall. Every time the noise of the guns at Helles rolled up to Anzac in swelling volume, and the shoulders of the big hill were cloaked in the sullen gloom of war, it was freely prophesied that its fall was imminent. So strongly does hope spring up in the heart of the soldier! But the story of those heroic but fruitless struggles is now well known. Achi Baba did not fall, and at last, hope shattered and prediction falsified, those who had long and valiantly persisted in the belief of its ultimate capture, came to regard Achi Baba as some great indestructible barrier which barred the path to victory. And so in a measure it was.

The fighting at Helles, however, had a more immediate material effect on the affairs of the Army Corps, inasmuch as any big attack by the Allied forces in the south always found an echo at Anzac in the shape of a local operation undertaken in the hope of diverting some of the Turkish reserves from the real attack. In rear of his positions on the Peninsula the enemy possessed ample sheltered country in which to dispose his reserves, and with lateral communications was able to move men to either Anzac or Helles at short notice. A diversion at Anzac was liable to be of a costly nature; but at any rate it never failed to attain the dual object of retaining the Turkish forces opposite the colonials and attracting some portion of his reserves.

On the occasion of the big attack at Helles on June 4th, the efforts made at Anzac to distract the attention of the enemy took the form of three distinct enterprises—a demonstration in the direction of Gaba Tepe, and raids on a section of trench opposite Quinn's, and on German Officers' Trench, opposite Courtney's Post. New Zealand infantrymen carried out the raid from Quinn's Post, the assaulting party numbering sixty men. They were to leave their own trenches at 11 p.m., under cover of artillery fire, make a dash across No Man's Land, and capture the selected portion of trench, which was then to be put in a state of defence, and linked up with their own front line. The first phase was accomplished swiftly enough, the trench being successfully seized, and some Turks bayoneted, in addition to twenty-eight who were taken prisoners. The raiders were supported by the 2nd Battery, N.Z.F.A, the 4th Australian Battery, and the 21st Indian Mountain Battery, firing on the front and left front of their objective, while a section of the 4th Howitzer Battery accurately shelled the enemy's main communication trench leading to the captured trenches. The 1st Battery engaged the northern face of Johnston's Jolly. When they endeavoured to consolidate their gain the raiders found themselves enfiladed by machine-gun fire as a consequence of the non-success of the attack by the Australians on German Officers', Trench, and all night long the Turk assailed them with bombs. By dawn the two flanks had been driven in to such an extent that the raiders occupied only a narrow strip of trench, which the enemy was doing his best to render untenable. Heavy casualties had been suffered; further endeavours to hold on could be productive of no good, and ultimately the raiders were obliged to relinquish what they had gained, and withdraw to their own front line.

The closing days of June were marked by further heavy fighting, but this time it was the Turk who attacked, and the Turk who suffered heavy losses. Activity commenced with another containing movement to assist the forces at Helles, local attacks being made on the right of the Anzac position by the Australians. Whether or not this diversion simply succeeded beyond expectations, or whether the enemy had been planning an attack upon Anzac is not quite clear, but at any rate the Turk assembled in great force in his trenches during the hours following the attack, and himself advanced to the assault shortly after midnight on June 29th, after a preliminary bombardment of great intensity, and a torrent of rifle and machine-gun fire. On the right of the Anzac sector the enemy's reserves had already been severely handled by guns of the Australian and New Zealand Artillery during the afternoon, the 1st Battery having effectively engaged large parties behind Lone Pine. Again when the enemy determinedly launched several heavy columns against the left and left-centre of the line, shortly after 1 a.m., the guns played havoc with his reserves, and cut gaps in his ranks as they moved forward to the attack. Showing more than usual determination, the attackers still pressed on in face of a murderous machine-gun and rifle fire, and some few even penetrated into the trenches held by the 3rd Australian Light Horse Brigade, where they were promptly bayoneted. A large force then endeavoured to work round the left flank, but advancing with fixed bayonets they blundered against a concealed sap, and, being met with a devastating fire, lost over 250 of their number. Completely beaten everywhere, the enemy retired in some disorder, harassed by the fire of the 18prs. and howitzers. This, the last attack on the Anzac position, was to have been a decisive effort, and it was stated by prisoners that Enver Pasha himself was on the battlefield to share the expected triumph of his soldiery. How little their sanguinary repulse agreed with his great expectations!

Chapter IV.

HOW THE GUNS WERE STARVED.

From the earliest hours of the Gallipoli campaign it needed no master of strategy to divine that one of the most fatal weaknesses of the Mediterranean Expeditionary Force lay in its shortage in guns, especially howitzers, and in shells. This weakness in a potent and indispensable arm detrimentally affected the fortunes of the army at every stage and in every phase; and the appalling casualty lists were undoubtedly swelled by reason of the necessarily inadequate artillery preparations for infantry assaults against strongly fortified and naturally formidable positions, and across broken and difficult country, the like of which was unknown in France or Flanders. The New Zealand batteries which landed on the Peninsula successfully overcame obstacles which might well have been considered insurmountable. They dragged their guns up the precipitous hillsides, and fought them for months under the direct gaze of an enemy more liberally supplied with both guns and shells. But despite their skill and devotion they were handicapped and at times almost crippled by a factor beyond their control—the shortage of shells.

In chronicling the part played by the New Zealand Field Artillery in the Gallipoli campaign it is unnecessary and inadvisable to attempt to deal with the events leading up to the inception of this "immortal gamble," to analyse the causes of its failure, or to speculate on the far-reaching consequences that success would have had on the general course of the war. But the artillery were so directly affected by certain of the shortcomings under which the Expedition suffered, that no history would be complete without some reference to them.

From the outset the War Office seemed to display a tragic lack of understanding of the magnitude of the undertaking to which the country was about to commit itself in the Gallipoli Expedition. The Army was but ill-equipped with guns, many of them out-of-date, and the ammunition supply "was not calculated on the basis of a prolonged occupation of Gallipoli." So the War Office informed Sir Ian Hamilton early in May. Maps were scarce, and those that were available were old and inaccurate. None of them was reliable. The idea of despatching an army to Gallipoli was conceived in an atmosphere of irresolution and doubt, was regarded with "hesitating reluctance" in many official circles at Home, and was bitterly opposed by generals on the Western Front. Launched under these discouraging auspices the Expedition from first to last was regarded as a "side show" for which almost anything was good enough. Even as late as June Sir Ian Hamilton, in endeavouring to persuade the War Office to increase his supplies of ammunition, pointed out that he had only the artillery of two divisions for the infantry of five, which fact vitiated all comparisons based on expenditure per gun, as the guns at Gallipoli had to do twice the work of those in Flanders. Both the colonial divisions at Anzac were armed with 18prs., but at Cape Helles the 29th Division was the only division in possession of these modern weapons. The Royal Naval Division had no guns at all! The 15prs. with which the 42nd Division was armed, were obsolete and worn. On one occasion when the force at Helles was in the greatest straits for 15pr. ammunition, a good many hundred rounds arrived, but on being landed were found to be suitable only for the Royal Horse Artillery guns in Egypt, of which, however, there was none on the Peninsula.

In contrast to this pitiful weakness the French troops which landed at the southern end of the Peninsula were well equipped with guns and howitzers, and were always well supplied with ammunition, so that they became the envy, as well as the admiration, of the British gunners. On occasions the French generously lent some of their batteries to the British in order to help them in their preparations for an assault. In the attack at Helles on the 12th and 13th July the French placed some thirty or forty guns and howitzers under British command; and on account of the shortage of British ammunition the French guns undertook the whole of the preliminary artillery preparation for the assault.

Situated far distant from the source to which he must look for the supplies of men and munitions, which were vital for the successful prosecution of the campaign, and almost for the very existence of his army, Sir Ian Hamilton could present his pleas or press his demands only in the comparative brevity of a cable, or by the slow process of a despatch. In neither way was he likely to carry conviction to the War Office against the arguments and influence of those who were opposed to any diversion of strength from the main issue on the Western Front, insisting that not a man nor a gun could be spared from France. Yet what incalculable consequences might have followed from the diversion to Gallipoli of some very small proportion of the forces that were expended in the indecisive battles fought by the British and French on the Western Front in 1915! Had the original British forces on Gallipoli not been literally starved in guns and shells there are reasonable grounds for the belief that their efforts might have been crowned with success, and the Dardanelles opened and made secure for the passage of the Fleet. At any rate it is certain that the losses in killed and wounded would have been very considerably less, and those of the enemy incomparably greater. The British armies in France and Flanders suffered severely from the shortage of guns and shells throughout the whole of 1915, but surely no other troops had ever to advance against such strong positions with less artillery support than was afforded the infantry of Anzac and Helles.

The messages which passed between the Commander-in-Chief of the Dardanelles Army and Lord Kitchener, then Secretary of State for War, afford illuminating evidence of Sir Ian Hamilton's urgent and almost incessant, but for the most part fruitless, appeals for more guns for his army, and of his endeavours to quicken the sluggish and uncertain flow of ammunition supplies. After having very early in the campaign described the ammunition question as acute, Sir Ian Hamilton placed the position with much fullness before the Secretary of State, and pointed out that a liberal supply of ammunition, especially H.E., would enormously reduce the loss of life. Only three aeroplanes were available, and trouble was being experienced from the enemy's heavy guns, which could not be located, and were doing a lot of damage. Significantly enough, a few days later the ammunition allowance at Anzac was reduced to two rounds per gun per day. About the middle of June the War Office reported that it was impossible to send out more ammunition than was being sent. Four days later the Commander-in-Chief cabled pointing out to the Secretary of State that the Turkish trenches were deep and narrow, and the howitzer was the only effective weapon for dealing with them, and succinctly summed up the position regarding the need for munitions in the following terms:—"We realise for our part the necessity in matter of ammunition and guns it is no good crying for the moon, and for your part you must recognise that until howitzers and ammunition arrive it is no good crying for the Crescent."

But the War Office, apparently convinced that the needs of the far-distant campaign must not be permitted to interfere with the paramount claims of the cause near at hand, remained unmoved by all appeals and every demand. For the great battle of August, inexperienced troops were sent to reinforce the Gallipoli army—to meet an enemy whom Sir Ian Hamilton had already described to the War Office "as a very formidable foe, and individually better fighting men than the Germans" —and any increase in the rate of ammunition supplies was insignificant. During the tremendous fighting in August the 18pr. ammunition sent out averaged only eleven rounds per gun per day.

The total artillery strength at Anzac by May 17th. was just under forty guns and howitzers, included in which were the twelve guns of the Indian Mountain Artillery, and the two 6in. howitzers which had just been landed. Both these howitzers were old, and badly equipped with stores; and as only 150 rounds of ammunition were sent with each piece their usefulness was rather limited. In June Anzac asked G.H.Q. for more of these howitzers, but there was only one available, and there was no ammunition. In their attack on May 29th, the Turks had a numerical superiority in guns of about two to one, and as they were mostly well-concealed and liberally supplied with ammunition, they were able to make the most of their advantage. Throughout June and July the garrison was subjected day by day to galling and destructive fire from the Turkish guns, the most active of which it was impossible to locate without aeroplanes, or to silence without howitzers and shells. Throughout this trying period the shore guns of the Army Corps fired with any freedom only on those few crucial occasions of attack or counter-attack which were regarded as epochal in the monotonous succession of summer days.

Every effort was being made at this juncture to build up a store of ammunition for the big operations which were being planned for the month of August, but notwithstanding that this meant submitting to hostile fire without retaliation, the situation was accepted in the cheerful, self-sacrificing spirit that was characteristic of Anzac. Battery commanders managed to achieve surprising results with the small number of rounds that were made available from time to time. The guns of the 4th Howitzer Battery were constantly in request for breaking up enemy works and strong points, and engaging targets that lay in "dead" ground for the flat-trajectory 18prs. On June 12th one of the 4th Battery guns at the foot of Howitzer Gully was taken up to Plugge's Plateau, near the 2nd Battery position, thus giving it a more effective range for engaging distant targets. More particularly on the right flank there were always plenty of tempting targets out of range of the shore artillery, and for a considerable time the Commander of the Australian Field Artillery had made urgent representations for two 4.7in. naval guns with which to engage them. It was not, however, until July 11th that one very old and much-worn gun arrived, and was placed in position on the right flank, firing its first round on July 26th. As it was frequently out of action its usefulness was very limited.

The Turks no doubt experienced difficulties and anxieties about their own ammunition supplies, but never at any period was there anything to indicate that they were in the same sore straits as the Army Corps at Anzac, or the British Forces at Helles. On July 10th, indeed, a memorandum was issued by G.H.Q., stating that news had been received to the effect that a secret order had been issued four days previously by the Turkish Commander-in-Chief, enjoining economy in regard to ammunition. A General Staff memorandum issued at the same time stated that it had been learned from a source believed to be "absolutely reliable," that for the next three weeks the situation of the Turks on Gallipoli Peninsula would be most critical unless munitions of war were allowed to pass freely through Roumania. At the end of that period it was believed Turkey would be in a position to manufacture her own munitions. But however critical the position may have been for the Turk, his guns were persistently active throughout July; and in addition to periodical bombardments of the trench systems, he freely shelled the "inner circle" and the Headquarters' area, making work on the beach and piers dangerous and costly.

The expected arrival of two more batteries from New Zealand, the 5th Battery of 18prs. and the 6th Howitzer Battery, made necessary some reorganisation in the composition of the New Zealand Divisional Artillery at the end of this month. In an order published on July 26th, the details of this reorganisation were set forth. In place of the existing Brigade of four batteries, two Brigades were created, each consisting of three Batteries. Major F. Symon, 1st Battery, and Major F. B. Sykes, 2nd Battery, were promoted Lieut.-Colonels, and given command respectively of the 1st and 2nd Brigades. Lieut.-Colonel G. N. Johnston, commanding N.Z. Divisional Artillery, was promoted Colonel. The composition of the Brigades was as follows:—

1st Brigade:—1st Battery—Major C. McGilp; 3rd Battery —Major I. T. Standish; 6th (How.) Battery—Captain G. E. Daniell; 1st Brigade Amm. Column—Captain A. E. Horwood.

2nd Brigade:—2nd Battery—Major F. G. Hume; 4th (How.) Battery—Major N. S. Falla; 5th Battery—Major G. J. Beattie; 2nd Brigade Amm. Column—Captain T. Farr.

The Divisional Ammunition Column, an attached British unit, was commanded by Lieut.-Colonel J. E. Cochrane, D.S.O. The 3rd Battery was of course at Cape Helles, and the Brigade Ammunition Column in Egypt.

CHAPTER V.

THE 3rd BATTERY AT HELLES.

When Sir Ian Hamilton decided at the beginning of May to make a supreme effort to capture Achi Baba, the big hill that dominated the southern extremity of the Peninsula, he drew upon the Australian and New Zealand Army Corps for two brigades of infantry and five batteries of artillery. Included in the latter was the 3rd Battery, N.Z.F.A., which still lay off-shore from Anzac in the transport *Californian*. The Battery received orders to disembark at Helles on May 4th; Major Standish, who had been ashore at Anzac with an observing party, rejoined his command, and the transport sailed for Helles at midnight on May 3rd. The battery, complete with guns, horses, and wagons, went ashore in two big pontoons, and disembarkation was complete at midnight on the 4th. A position for the guns having been reconnoitred on the left flank of the line, was occupied by the evening of the 5th, and wagon lines were established near the landing beach. The Battery was attached to the 147th Brigade, R.F.A., commanded by Lieut.-Colonel F. A. Wynter, D.S.O., and covered portion of the line held by the 29th Division.

The British and French troops, which had made good a landing at Helles, were in somewhat better case than the Colonials at Anzac. With each flank resting on the sea, they held a line running across the base of the Peninsula, and the nature of the country, together with the extent of ground occupied, afforded more freedom of movement in rear of the line. The Turks had fallen back some distance on a prepared, though not continuous, line of entrenchments and redoubts, protected by wire and skilfully disposed machine-guns. Behind them rose the shoulders of Achi Baba, which their industry and valour was to convert into a stronghold so formidable as to be described some months later by the Commander-in-Chief as "the strongest fortress in Europe."

The 3rd Battery opened fire for the first time at 11 a.m. on May 6th, on the commencement of the big attack which, at the close of three days' fighting, left the Allied forces relatively no better off than it had been at the commencement. The close of a day's desperate fighting on May 6th found the attacking brigades virtually in the positions which they had occupied in the morning. At most an advance of a few hundred yards had been made at certain points, but at great cost. A long day's fighting on the 7th was equally without results, but it was decided to make one further effort on the following day. Accordingly, orders were issued for the renewal of the attack on the 8th, at 10.30 a.m. The New Zealand Infantry Brigade, which, as part of a composite Division had hitherto remained in reserve, was now attached to the 29th Division, in place of the Lancashire Fusilier Brigade, withdrawn into reserve. The attack was preceded by a heavy bombardment from the Navy and shore batteries, which plastered the Turkish trenches and the slopes of Achi Baba with shrapnel and high explosive; but the moment the attacking infantry moved forward from their trenches they were greeted with a roar of rifles, machine-guns, and field-guns, which the altogether insufficient bombardment had failed utterly to silence. The New Zealand Infantry Brigade, advancing towards Krithia, over "The Daisy Patch," a perfectly smooth stretch of ground swept by rifle and machine-gun fire, suffered terrible casualties, but still pressed doggedly on until very flesh and blood could go no further. An advance of a few hundred yards had been made, and to this dearly-won strip of ground the New Zealanders clung with desperate tenacity. It was impossible to go further, but they refused to go back. At no other point in the advance were the gains more appreciable, and by nightfall the attack had definitely failed.

It had become evident that victory by open movement on the surface could hardly be hoped for. Barbed wire entanglements and scientifically disposed machine guns had so strengthened the enemy's power of defence that open assault must be terribly costly in lives, and barren in results, unless it was accompanied by an intense artillery preparation and support, such as the Dardanelles Force was incapable of affording. Orders were issued that the line held was to be consolidated; and it was decided that further progress must be by continuous and systematic attacks on selected portions of the enemy's line.

During the three days' battle the 3rd Battery assisted in the preparatory bombardments, and lent valuable supporting fire to the infantry on its front. The battery fired a total of 420 rounds during these three days—more than half of them on the first day of the attack. A few Turkish shells fell round the position on the 7th; but the pits gave some shelter, and a trench dug in rear of the Battery afforded cover for personnel when not engaged on the guns. On the day following the conclusion of the attack, a new position was chosen for the Battery on the cliff-edge overlooking the western shore of the Peninsula, the guns covering the extreme left of the line. This position was occupied by the evening of May 10th, and there the guns remained until their departure for Anzac in the middle of August. The wagon lines remained in the position they had first occupied near the landing beach. All ranks worked very hard to improve the gun and ammunition pits and to create as much shelter as possible from the flying shrapnel. The guns were connected by trenches, deep and narrow, and dug-outs were cut on the face of the cliff overlooking the blue and sparkling waters of the Ægean Sea. A sheltered track ran along the cliff-side from the Battery to the Observing Station, situated some five hundred yards forward of the guns. The position was overlooked by the enemy, but the gun emplacements were concealed by scrub, which was always kept freshly cut, and in the hot weather the dust was kept down by sprinkling sea water in front of the pits. All the trenches and communication ways on the front covered by the Battery were carefully registered, as well as enemy redoubts and salient points along the front. These targets afforded good shooting within the limits imposed by the ammunition supply, but it was a matter of more difficulty to locate and successfully engage the Turkish machine-guns, which were invariably cleverly concealed, and the field batteries, which, as at Anzac, certainly had all the advantages of position.

Except on the occasions when the guns were called on to provide covering fire for some local operation, or assist the infantry against a counter-attack, the daily expenditure of ammunition was small; often it was insignificant, and there were days when the guns did not fire at all. A supply of ammunition had always to be carefully accumulated for a pending operation, and if stocks were depleted by any sudden call or emergency a lean period must follow until a reserve had been once more established. Over two hundred rounds were fired on the evening of May 12th in supporting a successful surprise attack by a party of Ghurkas, who scaled the cliffs on the extreme left and carried the formidable work known as "Ghurka Bluff," situated to the north-east of Y. Beach. By this operation the left flank, which a succession of costly efforts had been unable to advance, was moved forward nearly 500 yards.

In the big battle of June 4th the Battery fired just under a thousand rounds, a record at that time for one day's shooting or for any single operation. A considerable reserve of ammunition had been built up, and the attack was preceded by a more thorough and careful bombardment than had yet been possible. As on previous occasions, the British 8th Corps, consisting of the remains of the 29th Division, with the Indian Infantry Brigade, the 42nd Division, and the Royal Naval Division, in that order from left to right, held the left and centre of the line, while the two Divisions of the French Corps Expeditionaire held the right. The French, who were relatively stronger in artillery than the British Divisions, and were better supplied with ammunition, lent the British two groups of their 75's for use in the attack. The guns of the fleet with such heavy guns as the Force had on shore, opened a deliberate bombardment at 8 a.m., and continued until 10.30 a.m. At 11 a.m. the bombardment recommenced, and continued until 11.20, when a feint attack drew heavy fire from the enemy's guns. At 11.30 a.m. the bombardment became general, guns of all calibres joining in, and firing with great intensity until 12 noon, when the guns lengthened their range, and protected by their "barrage," the infantry advanced in earnest.

Lieut.-Colonel F. B. Sykes, D.S.O., (d), R.A.

For the first half hour the advance was rapid, especially in the centre, and hope of decisive victory ran high. But the further advance of the 29th Division was checked through the Sikhs on their left being held up by barbed wire at the first trench remaining undamaged by the bombardment. Reinforcements were hurried up from the reserve, but even the new battalions were unable to advance, and the left of the British line thus found itself kept in check. The French at first made good progress. The formidable Haricot Redoubt, commanding the approach to the southern slope of Achi Baba, which had barred the way almost since the first advance, was rushed and captured. Within an hour, however, the Turks made an overwhelming counter-attack upon the redoubt, shelling it heavily, and pouring masses of troops down the deep communication trenches. A fatal gap was thus opened between the French and British lines, and the fortune of the battle turned. The Royal Naval Division and the 42nd Division were forced in turn by enfilade fire to fall back from the position they had won, and when night came on and the battle closed the gains at most did not exceed two or three hundred yards in depth. Again the hopes of victory had been dashed by a costly but gallant failure.

So far as the 3rd Battery was concerned a succession of quiet days followed the big effort of June 4th. During the ten days following June 7th, the Battery expended on an average less than ten rounds a day. Then on June 18th the guns were busy again assisting to repel Turkish counter-attacks on the left of the line, and on June 28th they supported a most successful attempt to dislodge the enemy from his hitherto unshakable hold on the western coast. Pivoting upon a point in the line a mile inland from the sea, the assaulting troops took all their objectives, the attack being carried out in two phases. The greatest gains, of course, were on the coast furthest away from the pivotal point. There five lines of Turkish trenches were captured, and the British line was advanced nearly one thousand yards. For several days following this success the Turk made strong counter-attacks, which led to bitter fighting, but he was able to press none of them home. For their close and accurate shooting in support of the infantry on these occasions, and particularly on June 5th, the Battery received the thanks of the Indian Infantry Brigade, and the congratulations of Brigadier-General H. Simpson Baikie, G.O.C., R.A., at Helles.

On the 12th and 13th July an attempt was made to seize the enemy's foremost trench system along the centre and right, and so conform with the advance that had been registered on the left flank. Two days' solid fighting, in which the French again lent the British the support of some of their batteries, achieved only a partial success. The 3rd Battery and two R.F.A. Batteries fired in support of a diversion by troops of the 29th Division on the left, the allotment of ammunition per battery, being 500 rounds. During the preliminary registration the enemy opened fire on the 3rd Battery position, and one or two casualties were incurred. The Battery was again freely shelled during the operation; more casualties were suffered, material damage was done to some of the wagons, and a fire was caused in the thick dry scrub in front of the guns, one of the wagons being burnt, and the position swept clear of cover.

The Battery remained at Helles until the middle of August, taking part in all the operations undertaken by the British troops in that zone, including the containing attacks in August. On August 17th the Battery received orders to proceed to Anzac to join the New Zealand Division, and embarked the same night on the *Queen Louise*.

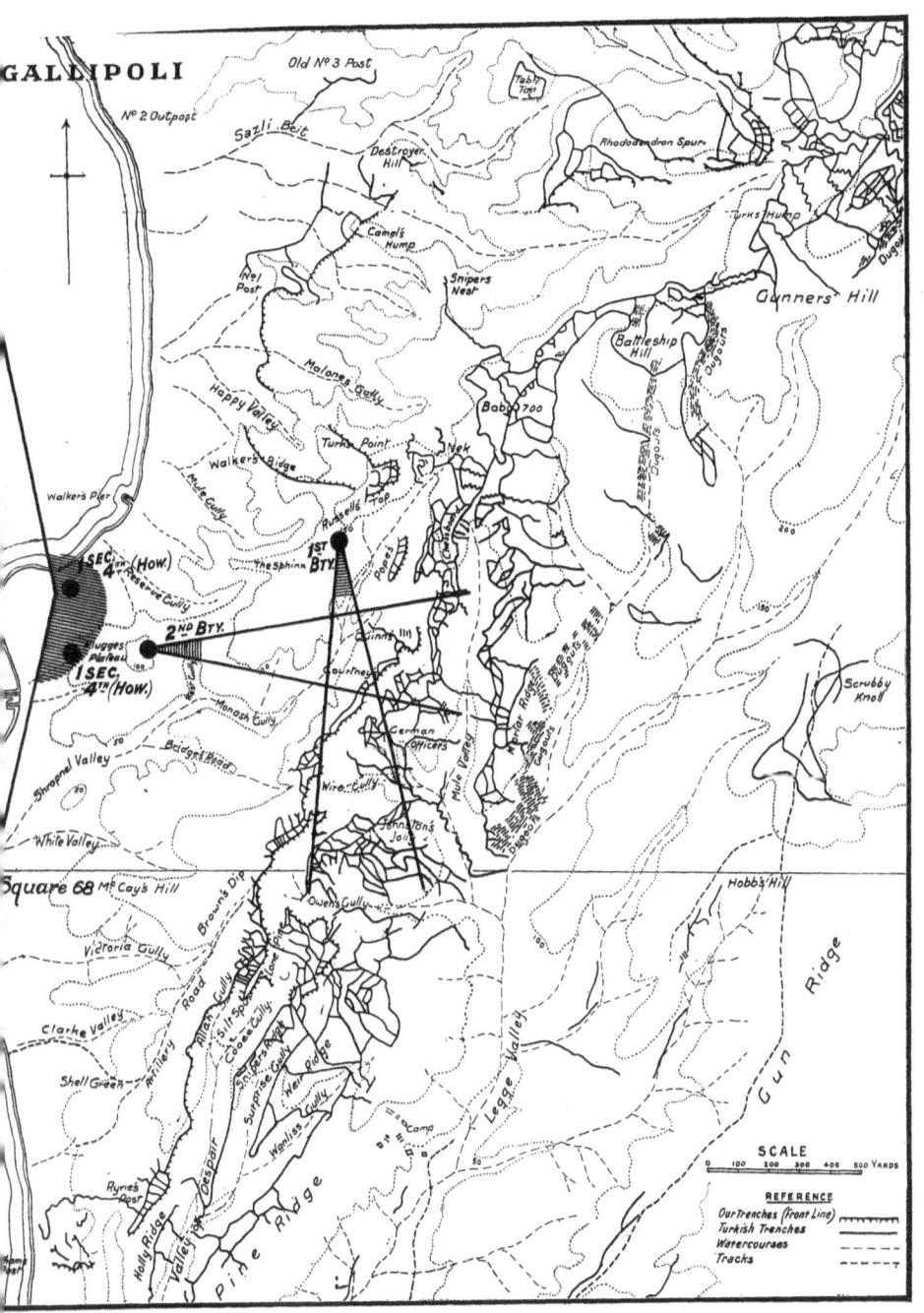

THE ANZAC AREA

Showing the positions held by the 1st and 2nd Batteries and the two sections of the 4th (Howitzer) Battery prior to the August offensive.

CHAPTER VI.

THE AUGUST OFFENSIVE.

At last, while the summer was yet at its height, events began to shape themselves for the great battle of Sari Bair, which was at once to set the seal on the heroism, the endurance, and the self-sacrifice of the soldiers at Anzac, and to mark the culmination of their hopes. Early in the campaign it had been made apparent to the Commander-in-Chief that neither at Anzac nor at Helles were his forces strong enough to fight their way through to the Narrows. On May 10th Sir Ian Hamilton had cabled to the War Office asking for two fresh divisions, and a week later another cable was sent, stating that if the Force was going to be left to face Turkey on its own resources two additional Army Corps would be required. The 52nd (Lowland) Division had been sent to Gallipoli, but whilst it was *en route* Russia, owing to the serious turn of events on the Eastern front, had given up the idea of co-operating from the coast of the Black Sea, and as a result several more Turkish divisions had become available for the defence of the Dardanelles. Finally, during June, Sir Ian Hamilton was promised three regular divisions plus the infantry of two Territorial divisions. The advance guard of these troops was due to reach Mudros by July 10th, and their concentration was to be complete by August 10th. A decision as to the method of employing these reinforcements was arrived at only after every practicable scheme had been exhaustively considered in all its aspects. These schemes were readily narrowed down to four in number, which may best be summarised in the terms of the Official Despatch:—

> (1) Every man to be thrown on to the southern sector of the Peninsula to force a way forward to the Narrows.
>
> (2) Disembarkation on the Asiatic side of the Straits, followed by a march on Chanak.

(3) A landing at Enos or Ibrije for the purpose of seizing the neck of the isthmus at Bulair.

(4) Reinforcement of the Australian and New Zealand Army Corps, combined with a landing in Suvla Bay. Then with one strong push to capture Hill 305, and working from that dominating point, to grip the waist of the Peninsula.

The considerations in favour of an assault from Anzac combined with a surprise landing at Suvla appeared conclusive; the plan seemed to afford a reasonable prospect of success, and was not subject in any measure to the unanswerable arguments which were responsible for the rejection of each of the other three schemes. Furthermore, the scheme was acceptable to the Navy, and it was considered that the bay at Suvla would afford a good submarine-proof base, and a good harbour excepting during south-west gales. As the season was advancing, and the enemy was making his position more secure each day, there were manifest dangers in unduly delaying the launching of the attack. The last drafts of the reinforcements were due to arrive on the 4th or 5th of August, and August 6th was therefore fixed as the date on which the battle would open.

The fresh troops available for the impending operations consisted of the 10th (Irish) Division, the 11th (Northern) Division, and the 13th (Western) Division, all comprising the 9th Army Corps, and the Infantry Brigades only of the 53rd (Welsh) Division, and the 54th (East Anglian) Division. The 9th Corps was composed of New Army troops, and the 53rd and 54th were Territorial Divisions. All were without experience in war. The 13th Division and one Brigade of the 10th Division were to reinforce the Australian and New Zealand Army Corps at Anzac, and to the remainder of the 9th Corps, under Lieut.-General Sir F. Stopford, was given the task of landing at Suvla Bay, and co-operating with the attack from Anzac, by first seizing and holding the Chocolate and Ismail Oglu Hills, together with the high ground on the north and east of Suvla Bay. If the landing went off smoothly it was hoped that these hills would be in the possession of the landing force before daybreak. In that case it was further hoped that the first division which landed would be strong enough to picket and hold all the important heights within artillery range of the Bay, when General Stopford would be able to direct the remainder of his force, as it became available, through the Anafartas to the east of the Sari Bair, where, in the words of the Commander-in-Chief himself, "it should soon smash the mainspring of the Turkish opposition to Anzac."

The elaborate dispositions which had to be made at Anzac for the reception and concealment in an already overcrowded area of large bodies of fresh troops, threw a heavy burden on the garrison. Sick of the monotony, and keenly alert for evidences of change, the soldiers were not slow to grasp the significance of the preparations, which they were called upon to undertake in July, and the momentous nature of the events impending was instinctively realised. The prospect of some great decisive movement, with its alluring possibilities of success, was a tonic to men worn by incessant endeavours and weakened by privation and disease, and the spirit in which the men faced their heavy task was as admirable as the heroism which they displayed in the subsequent battles.

The entire details of the operations allotted to the troops to be employed in the Anzac area were formulated by Lieut.-General Sir W. R. Birdwood, and all these local preparations, vast as they were, were carried out in their entirety by the garrison at Anzac, and faithfully completed by August 6th. Everything had to be done secretly and by stealth under the very eyes of a vigilant enemy. Two tasks of the first magnitude were the widening of the "Big Sap," the long communication trench which wound out to the outposts on the left flank, and the making of a road for wheeled traffic along the beach in the same direction. The sap was deep and narrow, and much of it ran through hard-baked clay, so that the task of bringing it to the uniform width of five feet involved a tremendous amount of sheer hard work for the sweating fatigues. Work on the road running along the exposed beach front had perforce to be done by night, a circumstance which enhanced the difficulties of the undertaking; but if the nights were short, the energy of the workers was unflagging, and gradually the road crept out towards the flank.

As the disembarkation of the fresh troops would extend over several nights some method had to be devised of securely concealing the newcomers during the few days which would elapse before the opening of the battle. Terraces and shelters were accordingly dug on the hillsides, and in these they lay hidden alike from the enemy aircraft and scouts on the heights. Great supplies of food were landed and ammunition in such quantities as the resources of the Force were capable of furnishing. The provision of an adequate supply of water was the most difficult of all problems, its solution calling for the most careful forethought and calculation so that no contingency might be unprovided for, and nothing left to chance. Little ever stood between Anzac and thirst, so dependent had it always been on the sea-borne supplies of tepid but welcome water; but in the battles that were to be fought on the sun-baked heights, water would be as indispensable almost as ammunition. Dependence on regular daily supplies involving too great a risk, a reservoir of great tanks was formed on the hillside above the beach. A system of pipelines and supply tanks was created, and the water from the barges after being pumped by hand into tanks standing on the beach, was lifted up to the reservoir by a stationary engine brought from Egypt. There were delays and mishaps of course, but anything that could not be supplied was improvised, and every obstacle was overcome by the fertile resource of minds which had been trained to cope with many desperate situations.

At last the long-expected reinforcements began to arrive. Throughout the nights of August 3rd, 4th, and 5th, they swarmed on to the beach from the crowded boats and barges that drew silently in out of the night, and as they landed were guided away to their concealed bivouacs to await the opening of the battle. The troops now at the disposal of General Birdwood amounted in round numbers to 37,000 rifles and 72 guns, with support from two cruisers, four monitors, and two destroyers. This force was divided into two main portions. To the Australian Division, strengthened by the attachment of the 1st and 3rd Light Horse Brigades and two battalions of the 40th Brigade, was entrusted the task of holding the existing Anzac position, and of making the frontal assaults which were to divert the enemy's attention and draw his reserves from the quarter in which the main blow was to be struck. The remainder of the force was to carry out the attack on the Sari Bair Ridge.

The artillery support in the operations was so planned as to make the most effective use of the very small number of guns available on shore. These numbered only 72 of all classes. In addition to the 18prs. of the Australian and New Zealand Field Artillery, and the one New Zealand 4.5in. howitzer battery, there were the 10pr. guns of the Indian Mountain Artillery, five batteries of 5in. howitzers, three 6in. howitzers, and the solitary 4.7in. naval gun on the right flank. There were in addition, of course, the guns of the fleet, but their effective value was limited, and they could not be used for the close support of attacking troops. In view of the great issues at stake, and the terribly difficult nature of the operations upon which the army was about to embark, it must be said that in material, whether in numbers of guns or in supplies of shells, the artillery at Anzac was pitifully inadequate.

The Attack at Lone Pine.

The New Zealand batteries played a very prominent part in paving the way for the frontal attacks which were made by the Australian Division on August 6th and 7th, and particularly valuable was their support to the 1st Brigade of Australians in their heroic and altogether successful attack at Lone Pine. During the 4th, 5th, and 6th of August, the works on the enemy's left and left centre were subjected to a slow bombardment; the 1st and 4th Batteries bombarding the Lone Pine trenches, which were provided with strong overhead cover, and well protected by barbed wire entanglements. The 1st Battery was given the task of destroying the wire; and wire-cutting, as experience showed in France, calls not only for accuracy of fire, but for a large expenditure of ammunition. Though this latter was impossible, the battery commander himself satisfactorily accomplished the task. Every round had to be conserved, so using one gun only, and observing from the forward trenches in the vicinity, he carefully and methodically prepared the way for the attack.

High explosive shell was used by the 18prs. for the first time on this occasion, and its effect on the wire was watched with interest. It was found, however, that low-bursting shrapnel was much more effective. The 4th Battery did a lot of shooting on the enemy's trenches at both Lone Pine and Johnston's Jolly; but the lack of ammunition made the work piecemeal, and the heavy overhead cover on the trenches at Lone Pine remained intact when the infantry attacked. Hostile batteries were very active, and one of the 1st Battery guns on Russell's Top was put out of action. One of the 4.5in. howitzers also went out of action owing to a broken buffer spring, but a new spring was rushed up from Cape Helles. The howitzer batteries (4.5 and 5in.) were limited to a mere 30 rounds per battery on the day before the attack, and 40 rounds only were allowed each battery on the day of attack for their fire action from 4 a.m. to 3 p.m., though this was supplemented by "a quick rate of fire" from 4.30 p.m. till 5.30 p.m. At the former hour an "intense bombardment" by all guns was commenced, and continued until the moment of assault.

The gunners did their utmost throughout with the hopelessly inadequate material at their disposal; more they could not do. The wire had been well cut up by the 1st Battery, which had expended over two hundred rounds on wirecutting since morning; about one half of the Turkish troops in the enemy fire trenches at the commencement of the bombardment were killed or wounded; but the result of the shooting in dealing with the massive overhead cover of the enemy's front line trenches was so inconsiderable as to be of little use to the infantry. After crossing No Man's Land in face of a storm of rifle and machine gun fire they found the overhead cover practically intact, and the weighty beams defied all individual efforts to remove them. Then came a pause while groups of the men bodily lifted the beams and then flung themselves in among the Turks. The hand-to-hand fighting in the obscurity of these covered ways was of a bitter and desperate character, but by 6 p.m. all the garrison had been killed or captured, and the whole of the trenches seized.

While the attack was proceeding the 1st Battery directed its fire on the trenches at Johnston's Jolly, the 2nd Battery engaging those opposite Quinn's and Courtney's Posts; while the 4th (howitzer) Battery assisted a strong effort to neutralise the fire of enemy guns that could bear on Lone Pine by shelling hostile guns on Mortar Ridge. Enemy guns on Scrubby Knoll, Battleship Hill, Gun Ridge, and at the Olive Groves and Wine Glass Ridge were similarly engaged by a force of guns made up of four 5in. batteries, two 6in. howitzers, the 4.7in. gun, and the guns of the Australian Artillery. There was little abatement in hostile fire, however; and it was considered that the expenditure of ammunition by the old and worn 5in. howitzers was not justified by results on this occasion.

From the very commencement the enemy made it quite plain that he was determined at all costs to regain the important work which had been wrested from him in such indomitable fashion. Within an hour the guns were called upon to assist in repelling a heavy counter-attack which swept in wave on wave, both from the north and from the south, and nearly a week elapsed before the Turks seemed willing to relinquish their efforts and accept defeat. For three days the Australians had to meet constant counter-attacks and continuous and heavy shelling and bombing, the enemy's supply of bombs being apparently inexhaustible. During this period the 1st Battery, in particular, and the 2nd Battery and the 4.5in. howitzers inflicted very heavy casualties on the enemy's reserves. Time after time the guns of the 1st Battery swept the enemy's ranks in a deadly enfilade as they pressed forward to the counter-attack, and more than once their fire was sufficiently destructive to break an enemy assault at its inception.

The battery was under heavy fire throughout August 6th and the following night, and the gun emplacements were so badly damaged that they had to be rebuilt. During the afternoon of the 6th Nos. 1 and 2 guns were temporarily out of action owing to the destruction of the emplacements, and several men were wounded. Notwithstanding this hostile shelling the battery was usefully employed during the night in shelling the enemy operating against Lone Pine, as well as his reinforcements arriving from the direction of Mule Valley, and at 6 a.m. it was largely instrumental in beating back with a heavy loss a local counter-attack from the direction of Mais Mais. The enemy came on a second time, but was again repulsed, the low-bursting shrapnel playing havoc in their broken ranks as they were driven back. The Australians lost heavily in the initial attack, and they continued to suffer severely in the desperate intermittent struggles of the succeeding days. They had the satisfaction, however, of knowing that the enemy's losses were much greater, and that in the end he was reluctantly compelled to accept defeat.

The Australian infantry were quick to acknowledge the valuable, and indeed vital, support they had received from the 18prs. of the 1st Battery, which had on occasions succeeded in crushing the Turkish assaults the moment the attackers moved from cover. This successful attack was eminently valuable as a diversion, and was considered by the Commander-in-Chief "more than any other cause to have been the reason that the Suvla Bay landing was so lightly opposed, and that comparatively few of the enemy were available at first to reinforce against our attack at Sari Bair." But the same measure of success did not attend other frontal assaults which were made from the existing Anzac position during the night and early morning of August 6th and 7th. There were two fruitless assaults on German Officers' Trench, and attacks by troopers of the Australian Light Horse from Quinn's Post, Pope's Hill, and Russell's Top. In the ill-fated ventures from Quinn's and Russell's Top, the Light Horse troopers, while conscious of the terrible odds against them, advanced over their parapet in ordered lines, and were swept away by an annihilating stream of machine-gun fire. Whatever advantages may have been gained by these heroic but hopeless assaults were dearly bought.

The Battle of Sari Bair.

As night began to fall, and while the Turkish reserves were gravitating towards the bitter struggle at Lone Pine, the attacking columns of General Godley's force were silently assembling for the master stroke—the night assault on the heights of Sari Bair. Now had arrived the most momentous phase of the whole campaign, for upon the issue of the struggle upon which the veterans of Gallipoli were about to embark side by side with the untried soldiers of the New Army, depended the success or failure of the whole great undertaking. The Sari Bair Ridge, the objective of the assaulting columns, ran roughly parallel to the coast line, and was flanked on the coastward side by a number of long broken spurs which ran down to within a few hundred yards of the beach. The gullies, or deres, in between were steep, broken, and scored with the rushing waters of many a winter's storm. In parts they were choked with a tangle of scrub and close undergrowth, which would add enormously to the difficulties and dangers of a night march up their unreconnoitred ways, yet through them lay the only road to the goal on which all hopes were set. It was manifestly impossible for an attacking force to break the Turkish line, seize the lower heights, and then fight a way up the gullies in the darkness and arrive at the top intact and in condition for an assault on the ridge. The attack must be made in two stages, the first of which must be devoted to the capture of the positions which commanded the entrances to the deres and the clearance of the lower portion of the deres themselves. Accordingly the force was divided into four columns, two of which, designated covering columns, were to open up a path for the two assaulting columns.

The total force available comprised the New Zealand and Australian Division (less the Australian Light Horse), the 13th Division (less five battalions), and the 29th Indian Infantry Brigade. The four columns into which they were divided were:—

Right Covering Force (Brig.-General A. H. Russell):—New Zealand Mounted Rifle Brigade, Otago Mounted Rifles Regiment, Maori Contingent, Field Troops, N.Z.E.

Left Covering Force (Brig.-General A. H. Travers):—4th Battalion South Wales Borderers, 5th Battalion Wiltshire Regiment, half 72nd Field Company.

Right Assaulting Column (Brig.-General F. E. Johnston): —New Zealand Infantry Brigade, Indian Mountain Battery (less one section), 1st Field Company, N.Z. Engineers.

Left Assaulting Column (Brig.-General H. V. Cox):—29th Indian Infantry Brigade, 4th Australian Infantry Brigade, Indian Mountain Battery (less one section), 2nd Field Company, N.Z. Engineers.

Divisional Reserve:—6th Battalion South Lancashire Regiment, 8th Battalion Welsh Regiment (Pioneers), 39th Infantry Brigade, half 72nd Field Company.

The Right Covering Force was to move out from No. 2 and No. 3 Posts at 9 p.m., and seize the enemy positions on Old No. 3 Post, Table Top, and Bauchop's Hill. The accomplishment of this task would open up the Chailak Dere and the Sazli Beit Dere for the passage of the Right Assaulting Column, which was to commence to move up these gullies at 10.30 p.m. The Chailak Dere and the Sazli Beit Dere both led up to Chunuk Bair, which the Column was to attack, after having cleared Rhododendron Spur on its way up to the Ridge. The Left Covering Force was to march northwards along the flat, and then turn inland and seize Damakjelik Bair, a hill which lay some 1,400 yards north of Table Top. The seizure of this position would protect the left flank of the Left Assaulting Column during its climb up the Aghyl Dere. The Left Assaulting Column, moving off at 10.30 p.m., was to cross the Chailak Dere and march northwards until it rounded Walden's Point, when it was to work up the Aghyl Dere and assault Koja Chemen Tepe or Hill 971, joining up with the left of the Right Assaulting Column at the head of Kur Dere, behind Hill Q.

Of the Divisional Reserve, portion was to be assembled in readiness at the foot of the Chailak Dere, and the remainder at the foot of the Aghyl Dere.

THE AUGUST OFFENSIVE

The total weight of artillery which was available to support the attack, was so small as to be almost insignificant, especially in view of the magnitude of the operations and the issues at stake. In addition to the three New Zealand Batteries there were available three 5in. batteries of the 69th Brigade, R.F.A., and the solitary 6-in howitzer on Walker's Ridge. To make matters worse, none of the New Zealand Batteries could lend their full strength to the support of General Godley's force, as they could not be spared from the areas which they covered on the centre and left of the Anzac line. Thus one section of the 1st Battery faced north from Russell's Top; the other section still watched Lone Pine, where its support was essential in face of the prodigious efforts being made by the Turks to redeem the loss. The 2nd Battery on Plugge's Plateau could not be spared from the defence of Quinn's Post, and so could direct only a very limited amount of fire on the Sari Bair Ridge, and that by map only. Only half of the 4th Howitzer Battery could be counted upon, as the section in Anzac Cove continued to cover the area from the Chessboard southwards to the sea. Thus of the artillery emplaced at Anzac before the opening of the battle there were actually available only two 18prs., two 4.5in. howitzers, three batteries of 5in. howitzers, and one 6in. howitzer. In addition, there were the ably-handled but obsolete 10pr. guns of the Indian Mountain Artillery, which went forward with the attacking infantry. A force, equal almost to an Army Corps, was to be supported in a major operation against a skilful, well-led, and more numerous enemy by two 18prs., little more than a dozen howitzers, and the fire of some ships of war. The value of the naval guns was greatly lessened by the fact that they could engage only the forward slopes of the hills, and that they could not be used for the close support of advancing infantry.

As the attack from the left flank was essentially a surprise attack in which much depended on the rapid exploiting of the strategical opportunities so created, there was no attempt at an artillery preparation of the initial objectives. A limited programme of artillery fire had been drawn up, however, under which fire was brought to bear at fixed times on the Nek, the

Chessboard, Big Table Top, and Rhododendron Spur. The trenches in front of Quinn's Post were also kept under fairly constant fire by the 2nd Battery from 9.30 p.m. onwards through the night. Commencing at 9 p.m., the guns of three Australian 18pr. batteries directed a slow rate of fire on to the Nek and the Chessboard, and maintained it until 4 a.m. on the 7th. At 9.30 p.m. C. Battery 69th Brigade R.F.A. joined in the shelling of the Nek, and continued in action until the Australian guns ceased fire. A group of guns consisting of one section of the 4th Battery, one 6in. howitzer, and a section of B. Battery 69th Brigade shelled Big Table Top from 9.30 till 10 p.m., and Rhododendron Spur from 10 till 10.30 p.m., at which hour they switched their fire on to the Nek, which they continued to shell until 4 o'clock next morning. Fire throughout was at a very slow rate, each battery or section firing only one round every two and a half minutes.

Stripped of all encumbering gear, in light fighting trim, the covering columns moved quietly out with bayonets fixed. Distinguishing patches of white calico were worn on the back of each man, so that there might be no fatal mistaking friend for foe in the confusion of close fighting in the darkness.

The Right Covering Force opened the fighting, advancing from Nos. 2 and 3 Posts shortly after 9 p.m. Its task of carving a path for the passage of the assaulting Brigades of infantry was all-important, as any failure to seize its objectives and fulfil its mission would imperil the whole undertaking. But imbued with the spirit of invincible resolution which animated the whole force this night, the mounted riflemen or the men of the Maori Contingent were not in the mood to be stayed by ordinary obstacles. No. 3 Post, which had been recaptured from the Mounted Rifle Brigade at the end of May, and which the enemy had since made very strong, was captured by stratagem, thus obviating the loss of life which would have resulted in an attempt to take the Post by open assault. For some considerable time prior to the attack the destroyer *Colne* had made it a nightly practice to shell the Post, illumined by the glare of her searchlight, from 9 o'clock till 10 minutes past, and again from 9.20 till 9.30 p.m. As each of these brief bombardments always began and ended at precisely the same time each night, the Turks in the Post had adopted the practice of temporarily seeking safer quarters in some dug-outs in their rear. Thus the garrison became practised in the part which unconsciously they were to play in the capture of their own stronghold. The stratagem succeeded admirably. The attackers crept out close to the Post under cover of the shelling, and the moment the guns were silent and the searchlight disappeared, they rushed straight for the enemy trenches. The surprise was complete; and although the garrison made an attempt to save the situation, the Post and the surrounding entrenchments were completely cleared in a very short time.

While the Auckland Mounted Rifles were carrying the fortress of Old Number Three Post by an admixture of boldness and strategy, the remaining sections of the Right Covering Force were advancing to their allotted tasks. The Wellington Mounted Rifles were stealing on Destroyer Hill and Table Top, and the Canterburys and Otagos were advancing on Bauchop Hill from the flat ground to the north of Number Three Post. In both attacks the enemy was met in force, and stood his ground, the attackers suffering severely from machine-gun and rifle fire as they closed in in the darkness on the entrenched positions. But the determination with which the attack on Bauchop Hill was pressed home, despite the loss of gallant officers and men, and the very audacity of the frontal assault against the forbidding face of Table Top, brought their deserved reward. By midnight the task of the column was virtually accomplished; the Sazli Beit Dere, the Chailak Dere, and part of the Aghyl Dere were open to the passage of the assaulting columns, and the New Zealand Infantry Brigade was making its way up to the assault on Chunuk Bair. The Otago, Auckland, and Wellington Battalions were to proceed by way of Chailak Dere, and the Canterbury Battalion by the Sazli Beit Dere.

It was half an hour after midnight before the Left Assaulting Column crossed the Chailak Dere and pushed on across the flats to the Aghyl Dere, which it entered hard on the heels of the Left Covering Force. This force, composed entirely of units of the New Army, had moved out from No. 3 Outpost when the attack on Bauchop's Hill had developed, and by 1.30 a.m. had completed the capture of Demajelik Bair and was in a position to protect the left flank of the army operating from Anzac. With the two assaulting columns fairly on their way up the deres, the attack was in full swing, but it had started late, and while the columns were slowly fighting their way forward, overcoming the resistance of the enemy, and struggling against the frightful difficulties of the broken, unreconnoitred country, the precious hours of darkness were fast slipping away. Though completely surprised, the enemy did not readily give ground, but in places offered a fierce resistance, his familiarity with the country giving him a great advantage over the attacking infantry. In the deep, scrub-covered ravines the darkness became intensified, and the troops were constantly in danger of being led astray from their path by blind alleys or offshoots from the dere. Mistakes of this nature always resulted in a certain amount of confusion, and a loss of valuable time.

The first light of the breaking day revealed the columns still laboriously struggling up the gullies and spurs, and yet beyond striking distance of the coveted crest of the Sari Bair Ridge. It revealed also the bay at Suvla crowded with the transports of the 9th Army Corps, an inspiriting spectacle to troops exhausted with the night's terrible exertions and conflicts with an unseen enemy. All hopes of a surprise attack on the Ridge had vanished, but the New Zealand Brigade pushed on in daylight until it reached a point afterwards known as the Apex, on the top of Rhododendron Spur, only a bare quarter of a mile from Chunuk Bair. Of the Left Assaulting Column, the Indian Brigade, which had advanced up the southern fork of the Aghyl Dere, had gained possession of the ridge west of the Farm below Chunuk Bair, and along the spurs to the north-east. It had succeeded in obtaining touch on the right with the New Zealand Infantry Brigade, and on the left with the 4th Australian Brigade. This brigade had fought its way up to the north of the northern fork of the Aghyl Dere, making for Koja Chemen Tepe, and had succeeded in gaining the ridge overlooking the head of the Asma Dere.

The enemy now showed signs of having thoroughly recovered from his surprise, and had received strong reinforce-

The 18 pr. Q. F. Gun

ments. Artillery support was called for and given in an attempt to push on up the ridge, but the Turks met the movement with a withering fire, and the idea of any further advance could not be entertained until the troops had somewhat recovered from their fatigue, and units could be reorganised for the assault. Both columns had made a magnificent advance, notwithstanding that it had stopped short of victory. The troops were exhausted, and their further advance was subject to enfilade machine-gun fire. It was decided to hang on during the day, and assault on a broad front at daylight on the 8th, after an artillery bombardment. The difficulty of preparing the way for the attack on the morning was enhanced by the fact that it had not yet been possible to move any of the guns from their positions at Anzac out to the left flank. It followed that either the fire had to be controlled from a great distance or the shooting had to be done by map. The section of the 1st Battery facing north was controlled from Walker's Ridge, but that station gave no view beyond the southern slopes of Chunuk Bair, and for the direction of fire on targets further north, and the better observation of most targets to the south, a station was established at Walden's Point. Even in a direct line this was a mile and a half from the battery, and breaks in the line were liable to occur at inopportune times.

With the three 5in. howitzer batteries of the 69th Brigade, and the guns of the 4th Battery, the Force was comparatively very strong in howitzers; but however ably handled, these unfortunately were not the best weapons with which to support an infantry advance across open country. During this period, however, there were a number of 18prs. lying idle on the beach at Anzac, waiting to be taken over by certain of the batteries which were to land at Suvla Bay. As the 9th Corps had as yet displayed little signs of life, the likelihood of these guns being claimed for a day or two seemed small, so it was decided to man them with such men as could be spared from other batteries and bring them into use. One battery of two of these guns, and two 18prs. borrowed from the Australians was placed under command of Captain G. E. Daniell. It was emplaced on the flat immediately to the north

F

of the old line, whence it shot at Chunuk Bair over open sights, and in return got freely shelled and shot at by enemy snipers to a very uncomfortable extent. A second battery, formed in a similar manner, was commanded by Lieutenant H. J. Daltry, but the guns were taken away very soon after the battery was formed.

For the attack at dawn on August 8th, the whole force was reorganised into three columns, of which the Right Column was to attack Chunuk Bair. This column was commanded by Brig.-General F. E. Johnston, and comprised the New Zealand Infantry Brigade, the Auckland Mounted Rifles, and the Maori Contingent, and two battalions from the reserve. The Centre and Left Columns, commanded by Major-General H. V. Cox, were to attack Hill Q. and Abdel Rahman Bair, and thus converge on Koja Chemen Tepe. The attack began promisingly on the right, where the Wellington Infantry Battalion and the 7th Gloucesters, supported by remaining units of the column, pressed forward with intrepid resolution to the very crest-line of Chunuk Bair. On the centre and left the attack fared badly, being unable to make any headway against the concentrated fire from the heights. But a footing had been gained on the coveted ridge; and it well might be that this would mark the turning point in the bitter and prolonged struggle. It had become obvious by this time that whatever successes were to be achieved must be gained unaided by the force at Anzac. The army at Suvla seemed to be stricken with some paralysing inertia, and the soldiers fighting on the slopes of Sari Bair, exhausted, tortured with thirst, but still of bold spirit, looked in vain for help from that quarter. If the hold on Chunuk Bair was for the valiant soldiers of Anzac a cheering presage of victory, for the Turk it was an ugly omen of defeat, and all day he made desperate efforts to throw the New Zealanders back from Chunuk Bair, and to break the line held by the left and centre columns. All day long and into the night the enemy assailed the shallow, hastily dug trenches on Chunuk Bair with artillery and rifle fire and showers of bombs, and attacked again and again with troops brought fresh from reserve; but the New Zealanders were determined at all costs to cling to their hardly-won footing on the heights.

A Glimpse of Victory.

At last night came, and if it brought no respite for the forward troops, it at least enabled them to be supplied with a little—a very little—water and food, and supplies of ammunition. To attack again and at once in an endeavour to exploit the success on Chunuk Bair was almost the only course left open; so the columns were again reorganised and preparations made for a further effort, on the issue of which would depend the success or failure of the whole operation. The attack was to be made by the following three columns:—

No. 1 Column (Brig.-General F. E. Johnston)—26th Indian Mountain Battery (less one section), Auckland and Wellington Mounted Rifles, N.Z. Infantry Brigade, and two battalions of the 13th Division.

No. 2 Column (Major-General H. V. Cox)—21st Indian Mountain Battery (less one section), 4th Australian Brigade, 39th Brigade (less the 7th Gloucesters), 6th Battalion South Lancashire Regiment, and the Indian Infantry Brigade.

No. 3 Column (Brig.-General A. H. Baldwin)—Two battalions each from the 38th and 29th Infantry Brigades, and one from the 40th Brigade.

No. 1 Column was to hold and consolidate its position, and in co-operation with the other columns to gain the whole of Chunuk Bair and extend to the south-east. No. 2 Column was to attack Hill Q. No. 3 Column, the units in which had been brought from reserve, was to make the main attack. It was to march by way of the Chailak Dere after dark on the night of August 8th, and after gaining touch with No. 1 Column, advance up the slopes towards Hill Q.

At 4.30 a.m., on August 9th, the most furious bombardment that it was possible to bring to bear was opened on the Chunuk Bair Ridge and Hill Q. by the guns on the left flank, and as many as possible from the Anzac area, assisted by the fire of the naval guns. The guns on the hills at Anzac, away on the right, with the 4.5in. howitzers on the beach, were able to enfilade the enemy's position on the ridge, their fire being quite as destructive as that of the guns firing at closer quarters out on the flank. This bombardment was timed to continue from 4.30 a.m. to 5.15 a.m., when it was to be switched off on to the flanks and reverse slopes of the heights. The bombardment was only comparatively effective; considering the number of guns engaged the results were surprisingly good; but the enemy still swept the slopes up which the attack must be pushed with a hail of lead.

While the troops of No. 1 Column fulfilled their task of holding on to their positions on Chunuk Bair, the 6th Gurkhas of the Indian Infantry Brigade, as well as some of the 6th South Lancashire Regiment actually fought their way up to the very crest of Hill Q. For a brief space the little band stood on the objective for which so many thousands had fought and bled and died, and gazed upon the Turkish communications— the roads winding far below them, and the Narrows, whose forts and mine-fields had blocked the way for the fleet, and across which the Turks brought troops and supplies from the Asiatic shore. But this prospect of victory was to be short-lived, and its termination sudden and tragic. Suddenly a salvo of heavy naval shells fell among the Ghurkas. The confusion which ensued on this shattering of their ranks by the shells of their own Navy was yet at its height, when the enemy, rallying, charged back on to the crest, and drove the Ghurkas and Lancastrians back down the slopes up which they had just fought their way at great cost. The loss was irretrievable. General Baldwin's Column, which was to have made the main attack, was hopelessly late, and was unable at this critical moment to exercise any influence on the fortunes of the battle. Instead of launching their attack from immediately in rear of the trenches held by the New Zealanders, as had been planned, the battalions of No. 3 Column had got no further than the neighbourhood of The Farm. The enemy's attempt at a decisive counter-stroke extended along the whole line, but the New Zealanders on Chunuk Bair, undismayed by the fury and frequency of the assaults, clung desperately to their grip on the heights.

That evening the line ran along Rhododendron Ridge, up to the crest of Chunuk Bair, where a lightly dug trench-line, some two hundred yards in length, was held by about 800 men.

Thence the line ran down to the Farm and almost due north to the Asma Dere southern watershed, whence it continued westward to the sea near Asmak Kuyn. The New Zealand troops occupying the trenches on the top of Chunuk Bair were relieved on the night of the 9th-10th August, after three days and nights of incessant fighting, and after having held this forward trench on Chunuk Bair for 36 hours. The position was handed over to two battalions of the 13th Division.

At dawn on August 10th, the Turks delivered a counter-attack against this precarious line with troops estimated at something over the strength of a division. Attacked from three directions at once, the New Army troops on Chunuk Bair were literally engulfed, the enemy pouring over their positions and down the crest like a human tide, but it was full daylight, and as the Turkish infantry topped the crest and came down the slopes, they were subjected to a perfectly annihilating fire from the shore and naval guns, as well as from the machine guns of the New Zealand Infantry Brigade. Never on the Peninsula had the New Zealand gunners been offered a better target, and never was an opportunity more eagerly seized. A section of the 1st Battery on Russell's Top did tremendous execution amongst the Turks streaming down Chunuk Bair towards the Farm; while from their positions on the flats on the left the scratch battery manning the 18prs. of the R.F.A. shot into the Turkish masses over open sights as fast as the guns could be reloaded. In the gullies, where they attempted to take refuge, the enemy were relentlessly pursued by the howitzers, the two guns of the 4th Battery north of Ari Burnu, and the 5in. howitzers shelling all the ground out of reach of the 18prs., and driving the enemy back into the open. The enemy suffered tremendous losses from this concentrated fire; but the line fell back, and the attacking army finally lost its footing on the Ridge.

The great attack had failed, and the Turks remained in possession of the dominating heights which had been the goal of three days' ceaseless endeavour and sacrifice. Instead of the strip of country a few hundred acres in extent, which had been the extent of the original position at Anzac, an area of several square miles was now held. The Colonials felt that they had room to breathe after having been huddled into the gullies at Anzac for so many months; but that was all. Success was still as far off as ever.

To meet the new situation a good deal of movement of guns was necessary. On August 10th the section of the 4th Battery which had been situated at Anzac Cove was moved out to Taylor's Hollow, the first re-entrant north of the Chailak Dere, the bed of which where it reached the beach had been itself the northern boundary of the old Anzac position. Four days later two guns of the 2nd Battery were moved from Plugge's Plateau to the left flank, where they joined one of the scratch batteries which had been formed during the offensive. On the 18th the arrival of the 3rd Battery from Cape Helles made a welcome addition to the artillery strength of the Division. The left section of the battery at once went into action on one of the spurs running up from the flat ground near Taylor's Hollow, with an arc of fire to the north-east in the direction of the "W" Hills. The day following the right section got into action in the same position, and the remaining guns of the 2nd Battery joined the section already in position near Taylor's Hollow. Such was the disposition of the batteries for the assaults on Hill 60 or Kaiajik Aghala, as it was otherwise known, which marked the last offensive action of the force at Anzac.

HILL 60.

After the failure of the attack on the Ridge Sir Ian Hamilton cabled to the War Office, pointing out the sadly weakened condition of his Divisions, and urging that large reinforcements must be sent at once if the campaign was to be brought to a rapid and successful conclusion. The answer to these requests effectually dispelled all hopes of a resumption of offensive operations on a scale that would be likely to produce any decisive results. Reinforcements could not be sent. Forced to make the best of a bad situation, Sir Ian Hamilton decided to strengthen his forces at Suvla Bay as far as lay in his power, and to make an attack on Ismail Oglu Tepe—known at Anzac as the "W" Hills. The possession of these hills would not only command the valleys running up to the two villages of Biyuk Anafarta and Kuchuk Anafarta, but would permit freer communication between Anzac and Suvla. To assist the 9th Corps in this operation troops from Anzac were to attack Hill 60.

The attack was fixed for the 21st of August, and the artillery support was to be rendered by the following guns:— 2nd, 3rd, and 4th (How.) N.Z.F.A., "Daniell's" Battery (two Australian guns), three 5in. howitzer batteries of the 69th Brigade, one 18pr. battery at Lala Baba (Suvla Bay), certain of the mountain guns, and naval guns. It had been intended that the guns at the disposal of Colonel Johnstone should give their support solely to General Cox's attack on Hill 60, and all the preparations were made to this end; but almost at the last moment these dispositions were upset by an order for a general bombardment of the Turkish trenches in front of the 9th Corps. Accordingly, at the eleventh hour the whole programme of artillery support had to be revised in order that for the first phase of the action support might be given to the 9th Corps alone. This seriously interfered with the preparation of the ground over which the Colonial and other units of General Cox's force were to advance, and instead of the bombardment commencing at 2.15 p.m., it did not begin until 2.45 p.m., when fire was switched from the 9th Corps' front.

From 3.30 p.m., when the infantry assault commenced, the 18pr. batteries were engaged on any target which presented itself. They made good shooting on enemy reinforcements advancing at Anafarta, and got particularly good results on various targets in the direction of Kabak Kuyu, Susak Kuyu, and the northern slopes of Kaiajik Aghala. Meanwhile the howitzers of the 4th Battery were bombarding enemy trenches on Kaiajik Aghala, where their shooting was accurate and effective, prisoners captured later reporting that this shelling caused heavy casualties. The attack fell short of success, the enemy rifle and machine-gun fire at some points being so intense that it was impossible for the attackers to make headway. On the left the Indian troops succeeded in gaining the well at Kabak Kuyu, but on Hill 60 the two hundred yards of trench line seized and held by the New Zealand Mounted Riflemen represented the sole gains. At the request of General Cox a steady rate of fire was kept up by the 4th Battery's howitzers during the night on the front occupied by General Russell's troops, in order to hinder any attempts at an assembly of enemy troops for the purposes of counter-attack. During the day of August 22nd the 4th Battery kept up this bombardment, and did excellent work in limiting the activities of the Turks, who were endeavouring further to entrench. On the lower northern slopes of the hill, where the enemy was in strength and strongly entrenched, they were subjected to a steady fire, which drove them into the gullies beyond observation. Hoping to clear this portion of the front, and acting on artillery advice, General Russell asked for the co-operation of the 9th Corps artillery, as it was thought that with the assistance of their enfilade fire this piece of ground could be denied to the enemy altogether. This assistance, however, was not forthcoming, the reason given for the refusal being that observation was difficult, and that the results to be expected were not thought to justify the expenditure of ammunition.

Late on the afternoon of the 21st one of the guns in "Daniell's" Battery was completely destroyed by a shell which burst in the bore, fortunately without wounding any of the crew. The gun, which had been borrowed from the Australians, was replaced by one from the 2nd Battery. On the evening of August 26th the right section of the 3rd Battery moved its guns to a new position on the north-western slopes of Damakjelik Bair. At the close of the month the whole battery was established in a position on the edge of the beach about a mile north of No. 3 Outpost.

In the interval which ensued before the second and final attack was made on Hill 60 on August 27th, the Hill was kept under fairly constant fire, especially during the hours of darkness. So frequently were requests for night-firing received from the infantry that the daily allowance of ammunition, which had again been reduced to five rounds per howitzer and ten rounds per gun, was almost entirely accounted for in this manner. The attack on the 27th, which was made at 5 p.m. by a force consisting of New Zealand Mounted Rifles, Australian Infantry, and Connaught Rangers, was preceded by an hour's heavy bombardment, over 500 high explosive shells being poured into the limited area on the front of assault. The batteries in action were the 4th (How.) Battery, and B., C., and D. Batteries, 69th (How.) Brigade. Field and naval guns assisted by shelling the flanks and rear areas. The bombardment inflicted heavy casualties on the enemy, whose trenches were found heaped with their own dead; but still the attackers were met with a heavy fire from machine-guns and field batteries. The attack achieved a very fair measure of success, only the troops on the right being held up by machine-gun fire from a trench, the existence of which had not been suspected. Initial gains were slightly enlarged on succeeding days; but substantially the line remained unaltered from this on to the close of the campaign.

CHAPTER VII.

NEARING THE END.

Although the second attack on Kaiajik Aghala had been in a large measure successful, the success was of purely local importance. It could not in any way affect the fortunes of the campaign, which had been already finally decided by the failure of the attack on the Sari Bair Ridge, and the tragic fiasco at Suvla Bay. But though all chances of success were thus irretrievably lost, the campaign dragged wearily on for another four months. During this lengthy period of stalemate the action of the artillery was of necessity largely routine, though the routine was never devoid of hazards and hardships, and its activities continued to be severely limited by the inadequate supplies of ammunition. The spirit of all ranks and arms in the Division was unaltered. The great battle had brought victory no nearer; there had been no amelioration in the conditions of living, and the rigours of a stormy winter were close at hand; but at Anzac confidence remained firm and faith unshaken. The condition of some of the units in the line was such, however, that a rest of some sort became imperative. During September the worn-out and sadly thinned infantry brigades and mounted rifle regiments of the Division were withdrawn for a brief period of rest at Lemnos. The Divisional troops, including of course the artillery, remained at their posts without relief until the evacuation.

The New Zealand batteries, together with the other attached batteries under the command of the C.R.A., covered during this period the fronts of the N.Z. and A. Division and the 54th Division. The strength of the artillery had grown considerably since the beginning of August, and the big area of country gained to the north of the original Anzac position gave scope for the employment of more heavy guns. The New Zealand Artillery itself had been strengthened by the arrival of the 3rd Battery from Helles, and the 5th Battery from Egypt. The 1st Battery was still on Walker's Ridge. The

2nd Battery had one section on Bauchop Hill, and the other on Damakjelik Bair, to which latter position the section from Bauchop's Hill moved on September 28th. The 3rd Battery was in emplacements built on the edge of the beach, some distance north of the Chailak Dere. The guns of the 5th Battery were near the road that ran behind Taylor's Hollow, and of the 4th Battery's howitzers two were in Taylor's Hollow, and two in their permanent positions in Ari Burnu Point. Of the three 5in. howitzer batteries of the 69th Brigade, which were attached to the Division, two were in the neighbourhood of Taylor's Hollow and the third was in the bed of the Aghyl Dere. The 24th Siege Brigade, R.G.A., had landed part of its strength, sending one 6in. howitzer battery (17th Siege Battery) out on to the flat north of the Chailak Dere, and mounting two 4in. naval guns on the beach half-way along to Suvla Bay. Finally, there were the 6in. howitzer which had been landed in the middle of May, two batteries of Indian Mounted Artillery, and a battery of 60pr. guns also situated on the flats out on the left. The 4in. guns, which did not open fire until the middle of October, were very old, and in very bad condition, and possessed only one dial sight between them. Very early they were out of action owing to buffer trouble, and when that was remedied they continued constantly to go out of action from various causes. Both these two guns and a 60pr. battery drew a great deal of hostile fire. On several occasions the 4in. were put out of action, and the 60prs. were so badly damaged that eventually they were sent away about a month before the evacuation.

At the end of August it became necessary to decide as to the disposal of some heavy artillery, including one 15in. howitzer, which had been held in readiness for use in the event of a successful issue to the battle of Sari Bair. Regarding the 15in. howitzer the C.R.A., G.H.Q., gave it as his opinion that as matters stood the army had no use for this weapon, and that it was inexpedient to land it on the Peninsula. The employment of heavy guns on the Peninsula had been depending for some weeks on the outcome of the recent operations, and if those operations had resulted in putting the army astride the Peninsula heavy guns landed at Suvla and suitably sited could have commanded all the country between the Anzac position and the Dardanelles. In confirming the opinion that there was no room for the 15in. howitzer, the Commander-in-Chief stated that there was a battery of Mark VII. 6in. guns, another of 9.2in. howitzers, and much field artillery then in Egypt because there were no positions for them on the Peninsula.

Thus when the campaign had almost reached its closing stages the artillery had grown so considerably in strength as to present an almost imposing array when compared with the few batteries which the Division possessed in the first months at Anzac. The increase in gun-power, however, was almost purely nominal, because guns are of no use without shells, and the supply of ammunition never showed any increase that was worth the name. The War Office informed Sir Ian Hamilton at the end of September that all available ammunition was needed for France, and so to the very end the artillery was always grievously hampered and handicapped by this never-ending dearth of shells. That the New Zealand batteries achieved so much and stood so high in the estimation of their own front line troops speaks volumes for the service at the guns and the careful skill of the observers, who had to see to it that the maximum results were obtained with each day's quota. There was never any lack of good targets; and requests were constantly being received from the infantry for fire to be directed on to some particularly troublesome enemy machine-gun, or perhaps a redoubt or strong point. Such requests were seldom declined, and generally the shooting was satisfactory in its results. But more difficulty was experienced in dealing with enemy batteries, which neglected none of the advantages of position. Almost all the battery positions at Anzac were overlooked by the enemy, and some of them, such as the 3rd Battery's position down near the beach, lay in full view of the enemy on the commanding height. On the other hand, most of the Turkish batteries were situated on their own side of the high ridges beyond observation. Possessing ample supplies of timber and abundance of labour, both scarce commodities at Anzac, they built innumerable covered emplacements which served as alternative positions to which they could move their guns whenever they were located and shelled. Aeroplane observers reported the existence of these emplacements, but could never indicate which of them were occupied. Several of the New Zealand batteries engaged hostile guns with aeroplane observation, but these shoots were seldom justified by results. Obviously incorrect "corrections" were sometimes sent down from the air, and on one occasion, after twenty odd precious rounds had been fruitlessly expended on an aeroplane shoot, the battery commander observed in his report;—"I conclude the aeroplane found a number of targets or the estimation of distance was poor."

Generally the activity of the enemy guns was most successfully countered by neutralising fire where the positions were known, or by prompt retaliation on to registered points in his lines. The enemy guns seemed to be liberally enough supplied with shells, and in addition to subjecting battery positions to periodic bouts of shelling, engaged in some destructive shoots round about the headquarters area near Nos. 2 and 3 Posts. The mules of the Indian Transport Columns suffered badly on one or two occasions, and some losses were also experienced amongst the New Zealand artillery horses which were picketed in Waterfall Gully. The 5th Battery had landed with all teams and waggons, but most of them had been sent back to Egypt, and there were kept on the Peninsula only a few horses per battery—sufficient merely for moving the guns when required.

The 1st Battery remained always up on the heights at Russell's Top, although application had been made to Army Corps Headquarters for its relief by an Australian Battery so that it might be employed on the left flank. About the end of September, however, one gun was taken out to the left to be used in an ingenious effort to obtain close range enfilade fire on some trenches on Hill 60. The plan adopted was to drive a tunnel through to the face of the cliff, which commanded these particular trenches, and bring the gun through the tunnel to a chamber from which an embrasure or port could be broken out in the cliff-side when it was desired to open fire. The gun, piece by piece, was taken through the tunnelway, and reassembled in the pit, but for some reason the position was never disclosed and the gun never used. There were few further moves of batteries or guns in the remaining month or two of the campaign. Practically the only one was the move of a section of the 5th Battery on October 2nd to a position on the lower north-western slopes of Damajelik Bair.

The 6th (How.) Battery, which had been despatched from New Zealand in June, arrived at Anzac from Egypt on the night of October 12th, and was parked for the night in Reserve Gully. On the night of the 15th-16th the Battery got into action on the left of Walden's Point. Though the artillery of the Division was relatively strong in howitzers, there was always plenty of work for modern weapons like those possessed by the 4th and 6th New Zealand Batteries, and the 6th Battery, which was commanded by Captain G. E. Daniell, established its usefulness from the very day of going into action. An unfortunate and tragic mishap occurred in this battery a few days before the evacuation, a premature, which burst immediately in front of the muzzle, destroying the piece and killing two and wounding three of the crew. About the same time one of the 2nd Battery guns also had a premature, the force of the explosion tearing the piece into strips, but the crew escaped without injury.

On the whole the batteries got off well in the matter of casualties, despite the fact that none of them escaped a share of the liberal attentions of the Turkish batteries. The low casualty rate was attributable in some measure to the industry which the gunners displayed in strengthening their positions and digging shelters. The skilful placing of batteries, so far as the limits of the terrain permitted, and their concealment where possible, also served to reduce casualties, although naturally the howitzers had more freedom of choice in selecting their positions than the 18pr. batteries. Dysentery, however, claimed an increasing toll, and at times the small drafts of reinforcements coming forward were barely sufficient to keep the gunners up to strength.

Seasoned campaigners as they were, the men did not wait for the onset of the winter weather before endeavouring to make their dug-outs as nearly weatherproof as possible. The impossibility of obtaining by ordinary means any timber or other material was a serious handicap, but the wreck and destruction in a sudden storm of a timber-laden barque provided a harvest for the needy. Some effort was being made by General Headquarters to alleviate the conditions of the soldiers on the Peninsula during the winter months, but in everything that counted the men had to rely on their own initiative and their own individual effort. General Headquarters experienced difficulty in procuring materials, and consequent difficulty in giving effect to their schemes. For instance, on August 21st, 15,000 tons of corrugated iron were ordered by cable from England, but the shipment of the first consignment did not commence until the last week in September.

The bad weather set in in good earnest on November 27th, when the Peninsula was swept by a violent gale, accompanied by heavy rain. The storm caused a tremendous amount of damage on the landing beaches, and for the time completely isolated the troops at Anzac. Snow fell heavily during the night to complete the discomfiture, and by the morning of the 28th the whole countryside was completely enveloped. The cold was intense, and the traffic on the roads and tracks up to the forward areas turned the snow to slush, and so churned up the clay that locomotion became almost an impossibility. The artillerymen were more fortunately circumstanced than the units in the line or in their scanty bivouacs in reserve, and by comparison they suffered little. Observing officers rapidly discovered the effect of the altered conditions on their shooting, and the necessity for making all calculations for the atmospheric conditions was fully demonstrated. Such tempting targets had not offered since the fighting in August. The first morning after the blizzard large numbers of the enemy freely exposed themselves outside their trenches, which seemingly were bad enough to make them think the risk worth while. The guns soon taught them to keep under cover, but before the lesson was fully learnt it had been dearly bought. Across the flat country towards Anafarta the labouring mule trains, silhouetted against the white expanse, also afforded some good shooting for several of the batteries.

The Evacuation.

On October 16th Sir Ian Hamilton was recalled to London, in order, as he was informed on his arrival, that the Government might have the opportunity of obtaining a "fresh, unbiassed opinion, from a responsible commander, upon the question of early evacuation." This was the first of the series of events which led to the evacuation of the Peninsula; but at the time its significance was not understood by the soldiers, to whom nothing was made known of the reason which lay behind the Commander-in-Chief's recall. His successor, General Sir Charles Munro, did not arrive at Gallipoli until the end of the month, and during the interval command of the Forces was temporarily held by General Birdwood. The visit to Anzac on November 13th of Lord Kitchener created a sensation in the trenches through which the famous soldier passed, and raised a perfect welter of picturesque conjecture, and set many rumours afloat, regarding his visit and its probable consequences. Lord Kitchener proceeded to the observing station of the 2nd Battery, from where he was afforded a comprehensive view of the Anzac country. Within a few hours he had left Anzac, and was proceeding up the coast to Suvla.

Before the decision to evacuate had been actually taken, preparations towards that end were quietly begun, and so successfully was the real aim hidden that for a long while it was completely unknown to the soldiers themselves. In order to accustom the enemy to such a thing, and so lessen the risk of raising his suspicions, a period of silence of forty-eight hours was ordered at the end of November. Not a shot was fired during this period, and all work that would be apparent to the enemy ceased. Whatever he may have thought the Turk made no move, but his trenches were seen to be strongly manned on the first morning that normal activity was resumed, and they were accordingly treated to a brisk bombardment from six batteries, shooting being good and effective in its results. That evening the 54th Division, whose front had been covered by the New Zealand Artillery since the close of the August fighting, was withdrawn. Before leaving the

THE TRAGEDY OF YPRES
The ruins of the Cloth Hall and the Cathedral

[*Official Photo*

Peninsula, the Divisional Commander, General Inglefield, sent the following message to Colonel Johnston:—"On leaving Anzac I wish to thank you very heartily for your cordial co-operation and assistance, and for the effective help your guns have always afforded us." On December 8th, General Birdwood, now commanding the Dardanelles army, was directed to proceed with the evacuation of Anzac and Suvla at once. Detailed plans for such a step had already been perfected, and immediately the whole prepared machinery was set in motion. The decision to evacuate could not long be withheld from the soldiers. The rapid embarkation, night after night, of surplus stores and animals, and the gradual reduction of the force to the bare limits of safety could suggest only one conclusion. Consequently the order issued on December 16th announcing the impending event did not create any sudden surprise in the minds of the majority, but came rather as a confirmation of strong suspicion. The decision was received with mingled feelings in which it would be difficult to say whether regret or relief was uppermost. Everyone felt bitterly the relinquishment of the hallowed ground on which so many of their comrades had sacrificed their lives, and lay, many of them, still unburied; but they viewed with relief the close of a struggle whose continuance under existing conditions could only result in useless sacrifice.

On the day on which the first detachments left the Peninsula, there arrived a large quantity of canteen stores, which had been purchased for the artillery by an officer who had been sent to Imbros some time previously. It was a bitter reflection that these stores of provisions, which the batteries had had no opportunity of buying for eight months, should arrive on the eve of their departure. The stores could not be taken away by units, so a certain amount of them were sold by auction, and the remainder were destroyed so that they might be of no use to the enemy.

The evacuation of the New Zealand Field Artillery, and the other batteries attached to the Division, extended over little more than a week. Orders to evacuate the guns were issued on December 10th, and the evacuation began the following night, when one section of guns from each New Zealand

Battery was sent away. In many cases the guns had to be manhandled for a considerable distance, across trenches and broken ground, before they could be got on to ground where they could be limbered up and taken to the beach by the teams, but these difficulties were made light of in the determination that the New Zealand Brigades should leave none of their guns behind when Anzac was evacuated. By the 12th seven 18prs. had been embarked, as well as six 5in. howitzers, three 6in. howitzers, and two 4in. guns. On the nights of December 13th and 14th three more 18prs. were evacuated, as well as all the guns of the 6th (howitzer) Battery. On the 15th three 4.5in. howitzers and two 18prs. were evacuated, three more howitzers on the 16th, and one 18pr. on the night of the 17th. By December 18th only two of the New Zealand guns remained—one gun of the 1st Battery and one of the 3rd Battery. These were finally evacuated shortly before midnight on the last night, December 19th. The 1st Battery had only two guns to embark, the others having been knocked out prior to the evacuation.

The number of guns withdrawn from the Peninsula during the evacuation totalled fifty-three, of which number twelve were evacuated during the last two nights. Two guns attached to the Division were destroyed. These were a 5in. howitzer in Australia Valley, and one 3pr. Hotchkiss gun in the Aghyl Dere. Both were blown up an hour or two before the evacuation was completed. Eight ammunition wagons were also left behind, and four horses, which had been ordered to be destroyed, but were turned loose at the last moment. Any ammunition that remained was buried or thrown into the sea.

The final stages of the evacuation were carried out with methodical quietness, and exactly according to the time-table which had been laid down. It was a trying and anxious time for the whole Army Corps, but for none so much as the small garrison which held Anzac during the last twenty-four hours, and whose lives may be literally said to have hung by a thread. Everything possible was done in order to create the appearance of normal activity, and even to encourage the enemy in the belief that fresh troops were being landed by night. The three thousand men who held the Division's sector during the 19th of December were divided into three parties—A., B., and C., which were to embark in that order. The embarkation of A. and B. parties proceeded without a hitch once night had fallen on the 19th, and by 11.25 p.m. had been completed. There was a considerable interval before the men of C. party began to withdraw, as it was necessary that their movement should synchronise with the withdrawal of the troops of No. 4 Section and of the 9th Corps at Suvla. In the meantime men moved rapidly but quietly up and down the trenches, and fired shots from the various points from which fire was usually delivered. Various devices were also employed by which fixed rifles were discharged after the last men had begun to make their way down to the beach. Exactly at the appointed time the remainder of the rearguard left the trenches and made their way in the darkness down the silent, deserted deres to the pier, where the lighters waited to take them out to the ships in the Bay. By 3.40 a.m. the evacaution had been completed, and the Turk was left in sole possession of Anzac and Suvla. At dawn the enemy commenced shelling the trenches at Anzac, but the men who had lately occupied them were at that time disembarking at Mudros, ninety miles away.

Thus ended the ill-starred Gallipoli campaign, in which the soldiers of New Zealand had tasted at once the thrill of victory and the bitterness of disappointment. They had faced all the changing fortunes of the campaign with determination and unflinching courage, and if final victory had not been theirs they at least had done all that was humanly possible to achieve it. The task of the Artillery had been one of peculiar difficulty; enough has already been said of the terrible nature of the country in which the guns were fought, and of the incessant anxieties caused by the meagre and uncertain ammunition supply. That the New Zealand batteries achieved so much in face of this combination of adverse circumstances, and that they indubitably earned the confidence and gratitude of the soldiers whom they supported must for all time stand to the credit of the men who fought the guns on Gallipoli, and to the honour of the Field Artillery of New Zealand.

PART II.—THE WESTERN FRONT.

CHAPTER I.

THE DIVISION SAILS FOR FRANCE.

The almost simultaneous evacuation of the troops from Anzac, Suvla Bay, and Cape Helles threw a tremendous burden on the transport services in the Mediterranean, and the return to Egypt of the troops of the New Zealand and Australian Division, although carried out as expeditiously as possible, was not completed until the New Year had dawned. The evacuation of Anzac having been a gradual process extending over more than a week, units arrived back in Egypt distributed on different transports, and in no particular order. On arrival at Alexandria some parties proceeded to Zeitoun, and others to Moascar. At this latter place, which was merely a railway siding a mile from Ismailia, on the banks of the Suez Canal, advance parties were proceeding with the establishment of a big camp where the Division was to be once more concentrated under canvas. With the arrival of the Infantry Brigades, the artillerymen with their horses and guns, other Divisional troops, and the Supply and Transport services, the camp took on an air of bustle and animation, and the men gradually settled down again to the routine of training.

By the time units had settled down in their new quarters and training had been thoroughly entered on, the Divisional Staff had completed a comprehensive scheme of reorganisation which had as its object the formation of a self-contained, complete New Zealand Division. This scheme, which was immediately put into operation, involved the withdrawal from the Division of the 4th Australian Infantry Brigade and the 3rd Australian Light Horse Brigade, a circumstance which was almost as sincerely regretted by the men of those Brigades as it was by the rest of the Division. With the exception of the Otago Mounted Rifles Regiment, which was retained as Divisional Troops, the New Zealand Mounted Rifle Brigade also ceased to be part of the Division. The Divisional Artillery was thrown into the melting pot, and the two three-battery Brigades which the Division had had on Gallipoli were expanded into four Brigades. Three Brigades consisted of four 18pr. batteries, each of four guns, and the remaining Brigade was to comprise three 4.5in. howitzer batteries. In addition, there were to be three sections of the Divisional Ammunition Column, and a Howitzer Brigade Ammunition Column.

The composition of Brigades with the names of Brigade and Battery Commanders was as follows:—

1st Brigade (Lieut.-Colonel F. Symon).
    1st Battery—Major C. McGilp.
    3rd Battery—Captain C. V. Leeming.
    7th Battery—Captain A. E. Horwood.
    8th Battery—Captain C. N. Newman.

2nd Brigade (Lieut.-Colonel F. B. Sykes).
    2nd Battery—Major F. Hume.
    5th Battery—Captain Beattie.
    13th Battery—Captain T. Farr.
    14th Battery—Major H. C. Glendining.

3rd Brigade (Lieut.-Colonel I. T. Standish).
    9th Battery—Captain R. S. McQuarrie.
    10th Battery—Captain R. Wickens.
    11th Battery—Captain V. Rogers.
    12th Battery—Captain H. A. Davies.

4th (Howitzer) Brigade (Lieut.-Colonel N. S. Falla).
    4th Battery—Captain J. L. H. Turner.
    6th Battery—Captain G. E. Daniell.
    15th Battery—Captain R. Miles.

The first essential was the provision of personnel, the equipment was to come later. The men for the new units were drawn largely from the ranks of the Mounted Infantrymen, and very good material they proved. Practised horsemen, and nearly all men of fine physique, they possessed individually and in the mass most of the qualifications which their new commanders might have desired in them. Above all else they were astonishingly keen. It was significant of their interest in this new branch of the Service that when the Third Brigade found itself considerably over-strength and proceeded to draft men back to the Mounted Rifles, many N.C.O.'s elected to revert to the ranks and remain in the Artillery. A good many commissions had to be granted to make up the establishment of officers; experienced noncommissioned officers had to be selected, and a leavening of experienced gunners and drivers had to be provided for each new formation. Out of the new material was gradually evolved the complete unit, and under the instruction of men who had served their guns on Gallipoli the initial and more wearisome stages of training were quickly passed. The fact that it was impossible to equip the new batteries with guns was a serious hindrance, and much of the work was perforce of a very general nature. It was a case of making the most of the guns which the Division did possess. Work on the heavy sand, under a hot African sun, was trying and strenuous, but it was never overdone, and interest was never allowed to flag. Surprising results attended the training. The whole alphabet of artillery training from standing gun-drill to battery manœuvres was traversed in an incredibly short space of time, and the success which attended the instructional fire practices on March 22nd and the three following days, provided ample assurance that the labours of the past three weeks had borne good fruit.

Although a great deal of hard work had to be done, life meanwhile was not without its pleasant interludes of sport and recreation; games of football were played in the evening and on Saturdays, and inter-unit matches created a great deal of interest and enthusiasm. Frequent swimming parades gave the men ample opportunity of disporting themselves in the pleasant and invigorating waters of Lake Timsah, and a system was introduced by which men in turn were granted twenty-four hours' leave to Cairo. Beyond these things there was little to vary the monotony of existence in a camp which was more or less isolated in the desert. Growing weary of inaction, and confident of their fitness to take the field again, men began presently to talk of France, and to look forward eagerly to the day when they would enter the lists against the most formidable of their enemies. They were not long to chafe at their inactivity. The syllabus of training which had been mapped out had hardly been completed when orders appeared announcing that the Division would shortly embark for France. Rumours on this absorbing topic had been in the air for some time, but once the move was announced events travelled swiftly.

On April 3rd the Division, which had already had a visit from H.R.H. the Prince of Wales, was inspected by General Sir Archibald Murray, Commander-in-Chief Egyptian Expeditionary Force, and two days later units began to entrain for the ports of embarkation. The preliminary movement orders showed that the Divisional Artillery was to entrain on the 5th, 6th, and 7th of April. Immediately the camp was thrown into that orderly disorder of preparation which always precedes an enterprise of any magnitude. Kit inspections and the checking of equipment, the return of surplus stores, and the making up of shortages were followed by the striking of camp as unit after unit moved off to the entraining point at the railway siding, where the presence of large native working parties added to the noise and confusion. Few said farewell to Egypt with any regret; on the contrary, the prospect of action and a change of environment was hailed with enthusiasm. Light work was made of the entraining, and as fast as trains were available they were loaded up and set off for Alexandria, where men and horses were to embark for Marseilles. Guns, wagons, and ammunition were not taken, as Batteries and Ammunition Columns were to be newly equipped on arrival in France. Transports proceeded to Marseilles individually, and without attached escort; and though the submarine menace in the Mediterranean was then a real and growing one, the transport of the Division was accomplished without serious incident.

Everyone was eager for his first glimpse of France, and the ship's rails were lined and every vantage point on deck was crowded as the transports made their way up the picturesque harbour and proceeded to their berth at the wharves. All civilians had been rigorously excluded from the vicinity of the wharves, so that most of the ships arrived without any welcoming fuss. The disembarkation was carried out with the same despatch that had characterised the embarkation, and as units came ashore they were packed into long troop trains, and set off on their journey northwards through the heart of Southern France. The countryside was clad in the fresh and tender verdure of spring, and looked fair indeed to eyes that for long had gazed upon nothing more attractive than the scarred slopes of Gallipoli, the bare hills of Lemnos, and the parched and boundless spaces of the Egyptian desert. Marseilles and the sea were quickly left behind, and soon the way lay through the Rhone Valley, with its blossoming orchards and orderly vineyards, its quaint little clustering villages, and its busy towns. It was a long, slow journey, and the not over comfortable accommodation gave little opportunity for easy rest or sleep; but the way was never wearisome. The beauties of the countryside, the sense of change, and the novelty of the surroundings left no room for dull thoughts or weariness of mind. Lyons, Dijon, Versailles (where a glimpse was obtained of the famous palace), and Rouen were all passed in turn, and finally Havre, the destination for the time being, was reached after a journey that in most cases had extended over fifty hours.

At Havre, where the Artillery were to be fully equipped before proceeding to join the Division in its billeting area, several days were spent in camp on an exposed hillside above the town. The weather was bitterly cold, and a chilling wind blew straight in off the sea, proving very trying to men so suddenly transported from a tropical climate. There was little time to worry about the cold, however, for the days were busily occupied with the drawing of every detail of equipment required by Batteries and Ammunition Columns. Units took their teams, in many cases freshly drawn from the Remount Depôt, to the great base stores on the quayside, and marching in at one gate were equipped with guns, wagons, and everything else that was essential before they left by the other. The extensive yards, literally crammed with guns of all calibres and stores of every description, furnished a convincing demonstration of the material resources which England was then beginning in earnest to place at the disposal of her armies in France. As soon as units were complete they moved off again to rejoin the Division, which by this time had settled down in billeting areas near Hazebrouck.

The billets which had been reserved for the Artillery were situated in and about small villages, such as Lynde, Le Ciseaux, and Blaringhem, small places with a poor estaminet or two, and little else of note beyond the church with its spire standing up above the clustering thatched roofs. The old barns and disused stables, which served as billets, were made comfortable enough with the aid of straw bedding, even if they were not overclean; but the season had been wet, and the gun-parks and horse-lines were for the most part quagmires. Nor were there any manœuvring grounds available, so that beyond a route march or two no departure from the ordinary routine was attempted. Before going into the line, however, batteries were called on to undergo a test of their shooting abilities. Each Brigade in turn was required to send a party of gunners from each of its batteries to Calais, where they carried out live shell practice on ranges on the sea-front. As a test of shooting ability, if it were so designed, the affair was very simple, but it served to demonstrate the discipline and smartness of the gun-crews. In congratulating the men of one battery on their shooting, which had been but typical of that of all the brigades, an English staff officer explained that all batteries were being so tested prior to going into the line in France since, on occasions, one or two batteries had inflicted as much damage on their own infantry as on the enemy!

Before the Division was ordered into the line at Armentieres some further substantial alteration was made in the composition of the artillery brigades. The howitzer batteries were distributed between the 1st, 2nd, and 3rd Brigades, and

the 4th Brigade was made to consist of three 18pr. batteries.
Brigades then stood as follows:—

1st Brigade (Lieut.-Colonel F. Symon, C.M.G.)—1st, 3rd, 7th and 15th (How.) Batteries.

2nd Brigade (Lieut.-Colonel Sykes, D.S.O.)—2nd, 5th, 9th, and 6th (How.) Batteries.

3rd Brigade (Lieut.-Colonel I. T. Standish, D.S.O.)—11th, 12th, 13th, and 4th (How.) Batteries.

4th Brigade (Lieut.-Colonel N. S. Falla, D.S.O.)—8th, 10th, and 14th Batteries.

Brigade Ammunition Columns were abolished, and a 4th Section was added to the Divisional Ammunition Column, commanded by Lieut.-Colonel M. M. Gard'ner. The four Brigades and the Divisional Ammunition Column were commanded by Brig-General G. N. Johnston, C.R.A. of the New Zealand Division. The Division was now commanded by Major-General A. H. Russell.

Armentieres.

Armentieres, where it had been decided the Division should serve its apprenticeship on the Western Front, had for long been a quiet sector, undisturbed by any of the fierce contests which had raged along other parts of the long battle front. It was a good breaking-in ground for a Division which had seen no previous fighting, and it was a suitable place in which to "spell" a Division which had been heavily engaged. The New Zealand Division, fully reinforced and rested and strengthened after its hard but splendid service on Gallipoli, came to France confident in its strength and vigour, and eager to prove its quality in the new arena; but there was yet much to be learned of the complexities of a system of warfare which, new in itself, was subject to changes almost every day. Without this necessarily accurate knowledge and the perfection and thoroughness of organisation insistently demanded as a primary condition of success, valour and endurance would avail but little.

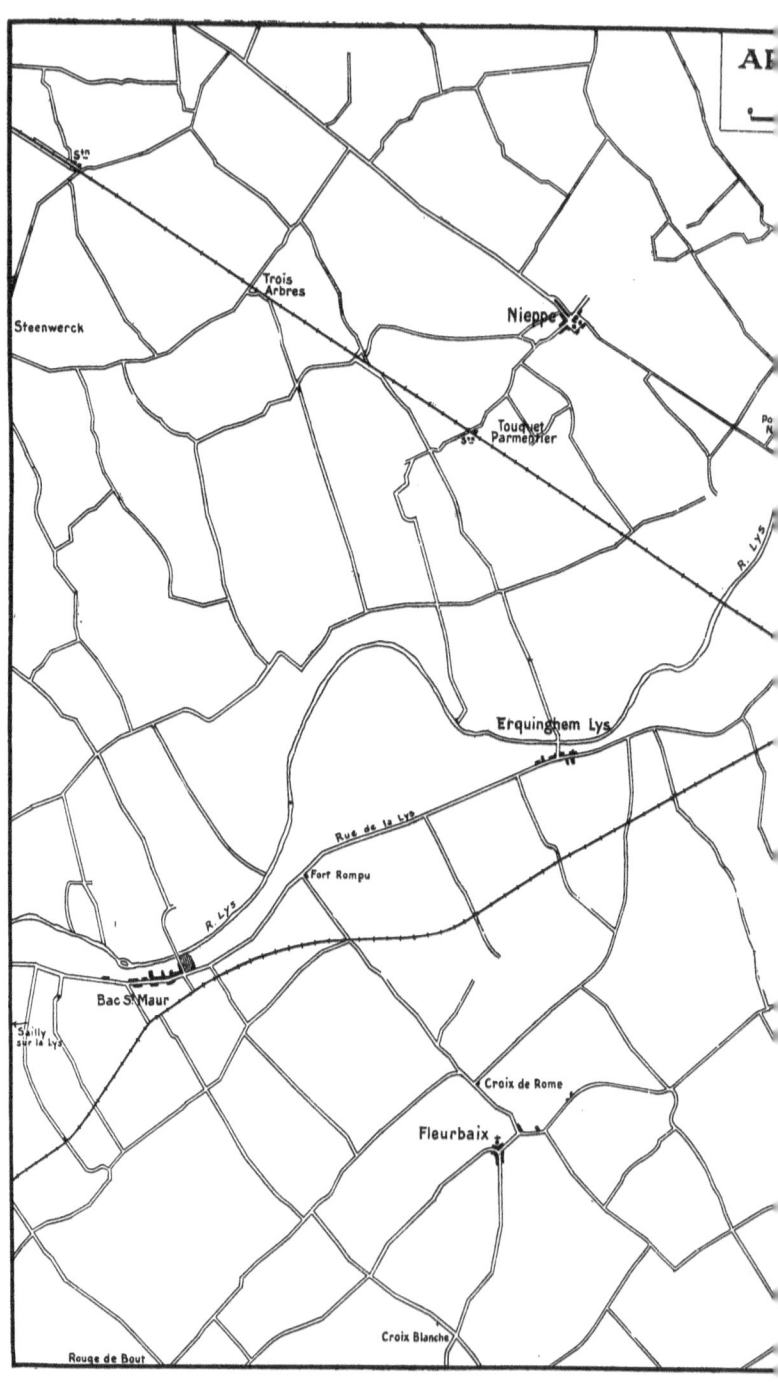

THE SECTOR ON WHICH THE NEW ZEALAND DI

FIRST WENT INTO ACTION ON THE WESTERN FRONT

The Division was now attached to the 1st Anzac Corps as part of the Second Army, commanded by General Sir Herbert Plumer, and about the middle of May orders were received to move up to Armentieres to relieve the 17th Division in the line. Artillery units made a two days' trek of the journey from the billeting area to Armentieres, and experienced fair enough weather, although it was still somewhat cold. Batteries had previously sent forward by motor 'bus small advance parties, who had quartered for a week with the outgoing batteries, and whose business it had been to familiarise themselves with the area covered by the guns of the battery they were to relieve, with the location of its observation posts, the system of communications, and all else that was essential. The relief was completed between the 16th and 19th of May, the greater part of it being carried out in daylight. Command of the artillery on the sector passed to New Zealand Divisional Artillery Headquarters at 10 a.m. on May 19th.

The new guns which had been drawn at Havre were not retained, but were handed over to the outgoing batteries, whose guns were taken over as they stood in the pits. This system of exchange, though often rendered necessary by circumstances, never came to be acceptable to the New Zealand gunners.

The 6,500 odd yards of front line trenches which constituted the sector was held by the New Zealand Infantry in two sections. At the outset the 1st Infantry Brigade held the right sector and the 2nd Infantry Brigade the left sector, the 3rd (Rifle) Brigade being in divisional reserve. For artillery support purposes the front was divided into three zones, right, centre, and left, each being covered by an Artillery Group. The 4th Brigade, as such, did not go into the line, its three batteries having been apportioned one to each group. Thus the Right Group, commanded by Lieut.-Colonel Sykes, consisted of the 2nd Brigade and the 10th Battery; the Centre Group, commanded by Lieut.-Colonel Symon, of the 1st Brigade and the 8th Battery; and the Left Group, under Lieut.-Colonel Standish, of the 3rd Brigade and the 14th Battery. Lieut.-Colonel Falla, being thus without a command, was entrusted with the charge of the Divisional

Artillery Intelligence branch. This work was carried out in conjunction with a Field Survey Company, and as it included the collection and recording of all data which could be of use to brigade and battery commanders, especially as regards the positions of hostile guns, it naturally had a strong influence upon the effectiveness of the Division's shooting.

In attempting to describe the conditions at Armentieres the first thing that might be said, so far at least as the artillery were concerned, is that they in no sense approximated to anything that had been expected or imagined. All preconceived notions relative to the place and the people under the existing conditions of war were dispelled on a first introduction to the new environment. After the active preliminaries of taking over the positions had been completed, attention was at once held by the calm, philosophic, but yet active and businesslike attitude of mind with which the people had accepted the conditions that suddenly confronted them. Nothing in the experiences of active warfare afforded a study so impressive and in many respects so interesting. The mind does not readily associate peaceful agrarian industry with the activities of war; but here in the open country, day by day, entirely regardless, or perhaps utterly oblivious, of danger, were the peasantry, men and boys too old or too young for war service, and even women, engaged in the labour of the fields in front of the British gun positions, and within close range of the guns of a merciless enemy.

Armentieres before the war was a fair-sized and busy manufacturing town, with a population of about thirty thousand, drab and uninteresting in many ways, and wearing an air of industry rather than of affluence. But what a contrast between this and that other theatre of war in which the Division had last figured—between Armentieres and Anzac. Gallipoli was bare, barren, and unpeopled, an inhospitable place in which the heat and cold and all the attendant hardships of the campaign were suffered without any of the alleviations which contact with a civilised community offers. In leisure times at Armentieres the soldier could go shopping, though the selection was limited and prices were high, and before returning to the guns or the billet enjoy afternoon tea, or sit in one of the numberless little estaminets and drink the pale beer or *vin ordinaire* which formed their stock-in-trade. At odd places in the Square and in the principal streets shopkeepers still plied their business, estaminets kept their doors open, subject to restrictions imposed by the military authorities, and did a brisk trade in the evening, when many of the troops in the town were freed from duty. Still more venturesome were others, women mostly, who kept their estaminets open at Houplines and across the Pont de la Targette, almost within sight of the German lines, and within easy range of their light field guns. These had escaped the occasional shellings which the town had undergone; but many of them were to pay dearly for their boldness in later days, when the town was subjected to savage bombardments by the enemy. In the meantime, however, they were led into an assumption of deceptive security by the periods of immunity which they had enjoyed in the past. For long the sector had been extremely quiet, little or no aggressiveness being displayed by the artillery on either side. The advent of the New Zealand Division, however, was marked by the institution of a policy of active shooting which had as its only limitations the exigencies of the ammunition supply. Even in the early days at Armentieres the expenditure of gun ammunition seemed prodigal after the jealous manner in which supplies had been husbanded at Anzac; but the question of ammunition supply was, no doubt, still a cause of concern and anxiety to the High Command.

The first duty of battery commanders on taking over their new positions was to register the enemy front line and all salient points within their group zone, and also an S.O.S. line on which a barrage could be laid down at any point on the Divisional front threatened by the enemy. Measures of defence having thus been decided on, a policy of active shooting was at once adopted. Exercises in concerted shooting were carried out with the dual purpose of obtaining proficiency in their execution and of harassing the enemy. One of the first of such shoots was the bombardment of a building reputed to be an enemy headquarters, by two Artillery Groups, each battery firing fifty rounds of high explosive. Whether headquarters or otherwise, the place had certainly been a centre of much activity, with many comings and goings; and after the welter of smoke and dust which shrouded it during the shooting had slowly drifted away it was seen to have suffered very severely, and was never again so much frequented. A programme of retaliatory fire was drawn up by Groups and distributed to batteries for use when required. This programme comprised a list of selected targets, each lettered for purposes of reference, and all carefully registered, upon one of which fire was promptly opened when the enemy's artillery became too active on any part of our forward areas. The method often worked quite well; but on occasions it provoked heavy bursts of shelling and counter-shelling. The enemy made no attempt to conceal his annoyance at this disturbance of his comparative quiet. He shelled the town, even battered the churches, and very assiduously he sought out the battery positions. Here it became a game of hide and seek with much at stake. Concealment was a battery's chief protection, for once a position was definitely located few of the gun-pits or shelters could withstand the impact of the heavy shells which were used in counter-battery work.

The study of the art of camouflage was at that time more or less in its infancy, but the majority of the battery positions in and around Armentieres were placed in positions which themselves afforded a good deal of concealment. As activity became more marked, both as regards normal shooting and the preparation and support for the frequent raids by the infantry, so the enemy developed his counter-battery work, and redoubled his efforts to reconnoitre positions by aeroplane, or to pick up the gun-flashes by balloon observation. The aeroplanes were the most to be feared. The balloon observer, riding high in the blue miles behind his own front line, could do little more than locate gun flashes; but the flying men, swooping through the frantic shelling of the anti-aircraft guns, could see a good deal, and, more dangerous still, carry away photographs, to be enlarged and microscopically examined by experts. To reduce the risks from this quarter a look-out was kept on duty at battery positions from break of day till dark. Equipped with binoculars and whistle he carefully scanned the sky for any signs of hostile aircraft, and gave shrill warning of their approach. On this warning signal of three blasts all movement would be suspended, and even shooting would cease if it were not of vital importance. The enemy scouts were apparently seldom challenged by our own 'planes, at least on that particular sector at any rate, and were consequently able to practice all manner of ruses, as for instance, making wide detours in order to approach from an unexpected quarter, or planing down from the distant clouds with their engines shut off.

The enemy was very thorough in his methods once he had marked his quarry, but the fact that these methods seldom varied was the saving of many lives. First came a deliberate and careful registration by aeroplane; so deliberate that there was generally ample time to withdraw the crews to a flank before the range was found and the "5.9's" which he favoured so much for this work began to stream in. The protecting fire, which might have been expected on these occasions from the heavy artillery in rear, was never available when it was most required—another consequence of the compulsory economy in ammunition. A bombardment of a battery position would last several hours, and if the range were effective would wreck pits and shelters and turn order and strength into chaos and ruin; but direct hits on the guns were extraordinarily few, and batteries were never put completely out of action. During the fiercest shelling communication was always maintained with Group Headquarters, from either the usual control post or an improvised one, and the personnel were always ready to man the guns on an emergency call. In the three months in which the Division held the sector battery after battery was shelled out by the enemy heavy guns; immunity was enjoyed by none, and often the shelling was so destructive that the pits and shelters had to be rebuilt or fresh positions sought. As instancing the persistence of these efforts to destroy the guns, the 3rd Battery positions was subjected to a three hours' bombardment from batteries of 77's, 4.2's, and 5.9 howitzers on the morning of July 9th. Over 2,000 rounds were dropped in and around the position. Three men were killed and seven wounded, but only one gun was put out of action, despite this terrible hail of shells. Attempts to locate the hostile batteries were unsuccessful. A British 'plane went up to reconnoitre and the firing ceased; but anti-aircraft fire forced the 'plane down with a broken wing, and the shelling recommenced with added fury.

Apart from the repairing of positions damaged by shell fire, or work on reserve positions which batteries had been ordered to construct, a great deal of energy was directed towards the strengthening of gun pits and the provision of better storage for ammunition, as well as in making the shelters for the crews safer and more habitable. Some diversity of opinion existed at that time as to the type of pit or shelter which would best stand the concussion of a heavy shell; the chief ambition seemed to be to devise something that would withstand the smashing impact of a 5.9in. howitzer shell. Handbooks on the subject were issued for the guidance of battery commanders; but the confidence which they expressed in various types of shelters was not always shared by the people who had to put these theories into practice.

The pits at Armentieres were of the two designs then most commonly followed. Two stout cupolas of heavy corrugated iron locked together in an arch and built over with sandbags to a good depth and width formed a fair shelter which could be further improved by a layer of "bursters" of concrete blocks. The bursters, of course, were designed to detonate the shell before it had penetrated, and so lessen its disruptive effect. More interior space was afforded by the square pit in which the roof of iron rails, sandbags, and bursters was supported by stout pit-props. In addition, the sandbag outer walls could be built high enough to support another superimposed roof, constructed in the same manner as the first roof, but raised sufficiently to leave an air space between the two, which, it was thought, would absorb much of the concussion of the bursting shell. In carrying out constructive work, whether on new or established positions, consideration had always to be given to the vital question of concealment, and obviously too many liberties could not be taken with positions that were more or less in the open. To alter their appearance substantially would be to court destruction.

One of the Massive German "Pill-Boxes" Wrecked by Heavy Artillery Fire [*Official Photo*]

The 4·5 in. Howitzer

Batteries were situated in all manner of places: in half-ruined dwelling houses, in factories in which they fired through the doors or camouflaged breaches in the walls, and in some back gardens of houses on the outskirts of the town. One 4.5in. howitzer battery for some time had its guns set just inside the big cemetery on the west side of the river, while an 18pr. battery had a gun dug right in under the railway embankment on the river's edge.

The country behind the line offered few natural advantages for observation, being flat and featureless. For shooting on the enemy front line or for wire-cutting, observation was naturally from the front line or support trenches, but observation posts there gave a restricted view, and were of little use for engaging targets at any considerable range. For this work recourse was had to the upper stories of buildings, or to one of the tall chimney stacks which stood in groups among the factory buildings in Houplines. This elevated post was gained by means of a perilous climb up the iron rungs set inside the chimney. To the uninitiated it was a trying experience. One seemed to be climbing for hours in a darkness as profound as night, and the slender rungs set at generous intervals rattled disconcertingly in the bricks. A small trapdoor gave on to the platform set just below the chimney top, and from there, seated on a stool, with his map on his knees and the telephonist at his elbow, the observer could command through peepholes set in the wall of the chimney a wonderful stretch of enemy country. Here at night, also, a sentry was posted to give instant warning over the telephone of the S.O.S. rocket from the Division's own lines. Doubtless the enemy suspected the existence of these eyries; sometimes he shelled them, and at least one observer suffered the experience of having the chimney beneath him "holed" by a shell which struck it as he sat aloft directing the fire of his guns.

The trenches taken over by the infantry on coming into the line had been in such a bad condition that a tremendous amount of labour had had to be expended in effecting an improvement; but this had not been allowed to interfere with a policy of unchanging aggression which found expression in many ways. Chief amongst them were the frequent raids made on the enemy's trenches, the almost invariable success which attended these ventures being in a certain measure due to the preliminary preparation by the trench mortars and artillery, and to their support during the operations. Of all the forms of minor aggression practised in trench warfare, raiding is one of the most hazardous, but yet the most profitable in its results if carried to a successful issue.

The issue of a raid depends on many factors, each vital to success, but none more vital than the human factor—the quality of the men who go over. The New Zealand infantryman possessed the qualities that make the ideal raider. He was disciplined and composed under shell-fire; he had initiative and intelligence to meet emergencies; and he had an adroitness and strength and desperate courage that made him feared at close quarters. The raiding party was always carefully selected, and the men were thoroughly schooled in their task. They were familiarised with every detail of the locality to be raided, and careful instruction and rehearsal made each individual perfectly familiar with his part in the scheme. From the outset the planning of the raid was marked by the closest co-operation between the infantry and artillery staffs, and detailed orders as to wire cutting and barrages were issued to Artillery Groups and the Divisional Trench Mortar officer. The registering of the guns was usually carried out as quietly as possible a day or two before the raid, every effort being made to avoid rousing the enemy's suspicions. Most of the wire-cutting was done by the trench mortars, assisted by the 18prs. The usual scheme of support provided for the barraging by both 18prs. and 4.5in. howitzers of the portion of trench to be raided, a vigorous bombardment under cover of which the infantry crept out from their own lines, their faces blackened, and some of them carrying knives, knobkerries, or such other weapons as seemed most suitable for close fighting in a trench. At the appointed time the barrage lifted, and the raiders rushed the trench, while the guns laid down a semi-circular curtain of fire about the scene of operations, closing all avenues of support for the raided enemy. Fire was maintained until groups had been notified of the raiding party's safe withdrawal. A howitzer battery from the group or groups supporting the raid was usually detailed for counter-battery work, and further to neutralize the enemy batteries known positions were engaged before and during a raid by the corps' heavy artillery.

The tactics employed on these occasions were naturally varied at times in order that the enemy might not be able to anticipate what was coming. On the occasion of a raid undertaken by the Pioneer Battalion, eager to emulate the achievements of the infantrymen, it was decided to have no artillery support during the raid, but to create a diversion at another point in the enemy's line. During this diversion, created by the Centre Group, the raiders proceeded to cross No Man's Land. The guns and howitzers of the Left Group were laid to cover them but the gunners awaited the ascent of a green rocket as the signal to fire. Apparently the raiders had some difficulty in clearing the enemy wire, which had been cut during the afternoon by 18prs. and trench mortars. On finally passing through the last belt the disposition of the enemy in some force on either flank led the raiders to suspect a trap, and they withdrew without casualties, calling on the Left Group to fire immediately they were inside their own wire. The soaring green rocket was answered by a simultaneous crash from the waiting batteries, and the enemy, who had been clearly visible from the trenches at one time, were believed to have suffered heavy casualties.

It could hardly be expected that a uniform degree of success could attend enterprises of this nature against an enemy who was himself brave and skilful, and strongly backed by artillery. Sometimes also the raiders found that the gaps in the broad belts of wire protecting the enemy's trenches had been imperfectly cut, or that repairs had been carried out under cover of darkness. There were risks and contingencies which it was not possible to provide against. A raid attempted by the 1st Battalion Otago Regiment on July 13th failed because of the totally unexpected and withering fire which the enemy brought to bear on the party, and which heavy guns were quite unable to neutralize. All three groups of artillery lent their support. The Centre Group directly supported the raiders; Right Group was engaged in counter-battery work; and the batteries of the Left Group were given counter-battery work, the engagement of any searchlights used by the enemy, and the shelling of his trenches north of the point to be raided. Hostile batteries responded very promptly to signals for assistance sent up by the German infantry, and their heavy shelling was supplemented by the fire of a number of machine guns, which batteries were unable to locate and silence. Over twenty active enemy batteries were "spotted," and no possible disposition of the means at the disposal of the C.R.A. could have succeeded in appreciably reducing their fire. It was during this raid that Captain J. L. H. Turner, M.C., Commanding 4th (Howitzer) Battery, was killed while fighting his Battery. The guns had been dragged from the pits into the open in order to obtain the necessary switch, and during the height of the firing the enemy sprayed the position with shrapnel. Captain Turner was the first battery commander in the New Zealand Division to lose his life. Command of the battery passed to Captain D. E. Gardner.

The observation balloons which the enemy kept up all day long behind his lines when the weather conditions were favourable were a source of anxiety and annoyance to everyone, and it is hardly necessary to say that an organised attempt to destroy them made by the R.F.C. on the afternoon of June 25th was watched with an eager and sympathetic interest. At 3.30 p.m. all guns stood by ready to engage hostile anti-aircraft batteries which might endeavour to impede the effort. The only batteries reported active, however, were in the areas to be covered by the heavy artillery and the guns of the 2nd Australian Divisional Artillery. On our own front the attack was very successful, three of the balloons being set on fire and destroyed.

At the beginning of July, orders were issued for the five batteries of the Centre Group to withdraw and relieve eight batteries on the left of the 2nd Australian Division, the Right and Left Groups to be responsible each for half of the Centre Group zone. On the night of the 2nd July the guns of four batteries of the Centre Group were withdrawn and handed over to the 2nd Australian Division, whose guns in position were taken over by the New Zealand gunners. The following night the procedure was completed in the case of the remaining battery, but the change-over was not allowed to pass uneventfully. A bombardment by the enemy of the Epinette trenches shortly after 10 p.m. heralded the advance of a small raiding party. Some confusion might possibly have been caused by the fact that the raid occurred on the zone which had just been taken over from the Centre Group; but, fortunately, on the commencement of the enemy's barrage battery commanders had made their dispositions in anticipation of the orders which were immediately issued, and within a couple of minutes from the enemy's first round a barrage had been put down. Simultaneously the enemy opened fire on Armentieres with guns and howitzers of all calibres, ranging up to 21 c.m. The heavy artillery were at once called on, and responded by counter-battery work and strengthened the barrage by shelling the enemy's supports. The town was subjected to heavy shelling, and the 11th Heavy Artillery Group retaliated by firing round for round into Lambersart; but it was early morning before the normal quiet of the night had settled down on the sector again. Such heavy bursts of shelling on the town itself were fortunately not of frequent occurrence, though about this time the enemy's artillery was being more than ordinarily active, and there was no indication that the desperate fighting on the Somme had caused the withdrawal of any of his guns from the front. The activity which had characterised the Division's holding of the sector doubtless formed a good argument against any such step.

A number of raids were carried out during July, and though they were generally successful, at least one was most disastrous in its results. This was the raid previously referred to, by the 1st Otago Battalion on the 13th of the month. On the occasion of a raid by the 3rd Battalion of the Rifle Brigade on the following night, supported by the Right Group, two mortars of "Z" Battery, and the 5th, 6th, 9th, and 10th Batteries, the raiders, 100 strong, successfully rushed the enemy trenches, but found them obliterated by artillery fire, the dug-outs destroyed, a good many dead Germans but none living. Two raids were undertaken on the night of July 19th, one by the Rifle Brigade and the other by the 1st Infantry Brigade, some guns and howitzers of the 2nd Corps Heavy Artillery being specially placed under the command of the Division in order to assist in the counter-battery work during the night. These operations were undertaken in order to give support to the Corps on the south in connection with an attack by the 5th Australian Division. Gas and smoke were to have been employed, but, as on previous occasions, the wind was not favourable. The raiders were successful in entering the trenches but found them unoccupied. Little more than an hour later a small party of the enemy entered the trenches at the Rue de Bois Salient, after exploding a mine, which buried about a dozen men. They were driven out by the 3rd Battalion Rifle Brigade, leaving two dead and one wounded behind. Through the night, and up to 3.20 a.m., the Left Group fired salvoes at the enemy's roads and billets; and on the following night the enemy's front line opposite the Rue de Bois Salient was subjected to a destructive bombardment as a form of retaliation for his action in blowing up trenches. Engaged in this shoot were the 106th Siege Battery, 2nd Corps Heavy Artillery, 15th (How.) Battery, and "Y." Trench Mortar Battery, and their combined fire was reported to have been at once accurate and effective.

Recognition of the work of the artillery of the Division on these occasions was contained in the following message sent by the G.O.C. of the Division, Major-General Russell, to Brig.-General Johnston:—

"Please convey to your officers and men the appreciation of the infantry and myself of their work in connection with the raids undertaken by the Division. They have by their good shooting earned the implicit confidence of those whom they support."

The concluding days of the month were quiet on both sides so far as artillery work was concerned. During the night of the 23rd-24th July the 11th Australian Field Artillery Brigade came in to strengthen the artillery on the front, and a week later an order was issued containing instructions for the reduction of the area held by the Division to the original front from Pear Tree Farm to the River Lys. The 11th Australian Brigade, less one battery, was withdrawn from the line on August 4th, and about the same time the 18th Divisional Artillery moved into unoccupied emplacements on our right. The 4th Brigade batteries returned to the command of Lieut.-Colonel N. S. Falla.

Little reference has so far been made to the Divisional Trench Mortars, the unit formed almost on the eve of going into the line at Armentieres; but it must now be said that of such value did the mortar batteries prove that they came to be regarded as an indispensable factor in almost every enterprise undertaken by the Division. Three batteries in all, X., Y., and Z., each equipped with four medium weight mortars firing a 60lb. bomb, their greatest usefulness lay in the very powerful support which they were able to lend to all the raiding and other trench activities of the infantry; a usefulness to which the courage and devotion of the personnel contributed very materially. The mortars were mounted on solid wooden platforms set in the front line, from where they could be used to greater advantage as regards range and accuracy. They were used principally for wire cutting and destroying enemy trenches, new works, and strong points. In preparing a gap in the wire for a raid, the spot selected would be ranged on in the daytime, and the same night, very shortly before the raid, the wire-cutting would commence. This method, if successful,—and it generally was—had obvious advantages over the cutting of the wire by 18prs. in broad daylight. In addition, the mortars nearly always directly supported the raid, either by firing on the enemy front line on either flank of the section of trench being raided, or by creating a diversion at another point. The work was arduous, involving a great deal of hard physical labour; fresh positions had frequently to be constructed, and all the ammunition had to be carried from the dump somewhere near the subsidiary line, although in this latter task the infantry helped with carrying parties. The gunners were usually relieved each week, spending a week in the line and a week in billets.

When the Division went to the Somme the trench mortars were not required in the line, and the officers were, therefore, in most cases temporarily attached to various batteries, the gunners being distributed between the batteries and the Divisional Ammunition Column, or employed on ammunition dumps. Both officers and men returned to their batteries when the Division left the Somme area, and in the sector to which it then proceeded the mortars carried out a great deal of active shooting.

CHAPTER II.

THE BATTLE OF THE SOMME.

After having held the line at Armentieres for three months, preparations were begun for the relief and departure of the Division, and almost immediately it was common report that its route would lie towards the Somme, where for over six weeks the British and French armies had been engaged in the most desperate series of battles which had yet been fought. The arrival of advance parties from the 51st (Highland) Division made departure a matter merely of days, and on the 17th of August the New Zealand battery positions were taken over by the batteries of the incoming Division, and detachments withdrew to the wagon lines. On this occasion the stir and incident attending a divisional relief were greater than usual. The New Zealanders displayed for the Scottish troops a regard greater than they had seemed to entertain for other Home troops with whom they had been associated; and this found expression in a great deal of fraternising in the streets and in billets as well as in the more congenial atmosphere of the numerous estaminets.

The 2nd and 3rd Brigades of Artillery and the Divisional Ammunition Column marched out from Armentieres on the 18th of the month, followed the next day by the 1st and 4th Brigades. All remained for a few days in the Blaringhem area, the time being devoted to "squaring-up" and ordinary routine duties. After this brief spell units marched to St. Omer and Arques, where they entrained and were taken to Pont Remy and Longpre, whence the 1st Brigade marched to billets at Erondelle, and the 2nd Brigade to Liercourt, the 3rd and 4th Brigades going to Fontaine-sur-Somme, and Bailleul, and Bellifontaine. The Divisional Ammunition Column was billeted at Longpre.

With the exception of one bad day of drenching rain while some of the batteries were out on an all-day training exercise, good weather was experienced during the week that was spent in this quiet and sheltered corner of the Somme Valley. Most of the time was devoted to hard training; but apart from the value of the training, the rest was beneficial to men who were soon to be engaged in a prolonged period of fighting of the most severe and trying description. Although no time was given to sport there was plenty of swimming to be had in the big pools that marked the course of the river, and everyone was in good heart when, on the 29th of the month, they set out on the next stage of the journey which was to bring them to the threshold of the battlefield.

For the artilleryman, who travels in greater ease than the heavily-burdened infantryman, a trek through new country in fine weather provides a pleasant interlude from the vicissitudes of life in the lines. Reveille sounds with the dawn, or earlier, and by the time breakfast is ready the horses have been watered and fed, and harnessed ready for an immediate start. Brigades move together, with a good interval between batteries, and every unit must be on the road at the appointed time. The early morning air is cool and invigorating; the horses are fresh, and swing steadily along with taut traces to the tune of jingling accoutrements and the rumble of the heavy vehicles of the long column half veiled in the morning mist. Every turn of the road brings something new to wonder at or to admire; and the driver sitting easily in his saddle exchanges sage observations with the gunner marching in rear of his gun. The ten-minute halts mark the passing of the hours; and then, if the journey be not a short one, comes the mid-day halt to water and feed the horses, and munch what the orders term "the unconsumed portion of the day's ration." A column on the march is always preceded by a billeting officer, who, riding hot-foot in advance, has the available billeting accommodation ready to apportion to units by the time they arrive at the night's resting-place. Trekking in heavy weather is disagreeable for the men and severe on the horses, which very frequently have to stand in the mud in some exposed horse lines after a hard journey on heavy roads.

Some such unfavourable conditions as these prevailed on the two days' march to Bonnay and Corbie. The first night was spent in Picquigny and neighbouring villages, whence on the next day the route lay through Amiens. It rained heavily both days, much to everyone's discomfort; and Amiens, which the Division was to know again under more tragic circumstances, looked sodden and grey as the columns swung down the slopes and wound through the outskirts of the town. Moderately fine weather was experienced during the week which was spent in the Bonnay-Corbie area before the artillery went into the line, and the men were able to dry their gear and clothing. Most of the guns were sent to the ordnance workshops at Heilly, and all equipment was thoroughly overhauled. The men were by this time wound up to a high pitch of uncertain but shoving expectancy; they had made the long journey down from Armentieres in easy stages, and for a week had waited on the very edge of the battlefield within close earshot of the guns, which filled the air with their incessant clamour and lit up the sky at night with their flashes.

On September 1st the C.R.A. with the Brigade-Major motored to Pommiers' Redoubt, about half a mile east of Mametz, and proceeded on foot to an O.P. near Longueval Windmill, whence they looked across the country on which the Division, at dreadful cost, was shortly to win the right to rank equal with the premier divisions that England had placed in the field. Brigade and battery commanders also rode forward to view the country and inspect the positions which they were to occupy. On the morning of September 5th a section from each battery and from the Divisional Ammunition Column moved up to the wagon lines of the units they were to relieve, and on the same day the guns were taken up to battery positions. The remaining sections followed next day. All the main roads for some distance behind the front were crowded with slow-moving columns of traffic, and as they approached their destination the drivers of the ingoing sections got a first experience of the congestion and pressure of traffic which was to be such a marked feature of all the roads on the Somme. The seemingly endless lines of motor-lorries, wagons, limbers, and vehicles of every description, with here and there bodies of marching troops, became at times so densely packed as to render movement slow and intermittent, much as a sluggish stream becomes at times completely dammed by some obstruction ahead of which no one can see the cause. The traffic control police did their best, but their task was a difficult one, and at times its magnitude seemed to have reduced them to a state of bewildered helplessness.

The guns of the remaining sections were taken up to battery positions on the afternoon and evening of the 6th September. The 1st and 2nd Brigades relieved two brigades of the 33rd Divisional Artillery, and were attached to the 14th Divisional Artillery, less the 15th Battery, which was placed under the orders of the 23rd Heavy Artillery Group, and during operations on the Somme was engaged on counter-battery work. The artillery of the 14th Division, with attached brigades, was commanded by Brig.-General Sandys, C.M.G., who was wounded by a shell on September 6th, close to the 9th Battery position, his command passing to Brig.-General G. N. Johnston, C.R.A. of the New Zealand Division. The 3rd and 4th Brigades formed a group under Lieut.-Colonel I. T. Standish, and relieved that portion of the 33rd Divisional Artillery which was attached to the 7th Division. The 7th Divisional Artillery was very shortly afterwards relieved by the 30th Divisional Artillery. The Divisional Ammunition Column relieved that of the 33rd Division.

Batteries of the 1st Brigade took over positions near Flat Iron Copse, and the 2nd Brigade batteries first went into positions due west of Montauban, in Caterpillar Valley. The 18pr. batteries of the 2nd Brigade assumed the formation of two six-gun batteries. The 6th (How.) Battery was in Caterpillar Valley about a thousand yards north of Montauban. The 3rd and 4th Brigades went into positions in the valley which lay a thousand odd yards south-west of Longueval. In misty or dull weather the road up to the guns was safe enough by day; and advantage was accordingly taken of the conditions prevailing to get most of the guns in during the afternoon of their arrival. For those that went up after dark, the obstructions on the roads or tracks that made locomotion difficult by day were enormously increased. Some guns got stuck for an hour or more, during which time a good many lachrymatory gas shells fell in the vicinity, and assistance had to be obtained before they were got under way again. The 2nd Brigade reported having completed the relief by 5.30 p.m. on September 6th, the 3rd and 4th Brigades by 6 p.m., and the 1st Brigade by 7 p.m.

All wagon lines were situated in the neighbourhood of Dernancourt and Becordel-Becourt. The dumps from which supplies of ammunition were drawn were near by, and horses were watered at the long line of canvas troughs which had been erected in the valley below the wagon lines.

No. 3 section of the Divisional Ammunition Column and fifteen G.S. wagons of No. 4 section were to assist in the supply of ammunition to the batteries of the 3rd and 4th Brigades, while the remainder of the column was employed in supplying ammunition to the 1st and 2nd Brigades. The supply of ammunition to the Divisions was carried out in two stages. The first stage from railhead to the dumps was by motor lorries, supplemented by the wagons of the Ammunition Column; from the dumps batteries drew their ammunition and carted it to the gun positions with the assistance of the Ammunition Column sections allocated to their particular brigade.

To give some idea of the part which the New Zealand Division was called upon to play in the battle of the Somme, it is necessary to refer briefly to the tactical position which existed at the beginning of September, about which time the Division was moving up into the line. The Allied offensive on the Somme, which had opened on July 1st, after a week's violent bombardment, had been undertaken with a threefold object: to relieve the strain on Verdun, where the Germans continued to exert a persistent and powerful pressure despite their frightful losses; to stop the further transfer of German troops from the Western Front, and so assist the Allies in other theatres of war; and, finally, to wear down the strength of the German armies, with always the possibility of breaking completely through on the front chosen for the launching of the offensive.

The positions held by the enemy along this front possessed great natural advantages for defence; and labouring for nearly two years, he had done almost all that human ingenuity and endeavour could do to render them impregnable. In spite of these formidable obstacles, in spite of the enemy's desperate resistance and the heavy losses sustained by the attacking divisions, rapid and almost substantial progress had been made on July 1st, the opening day of the offensive. By midday Montauban had been carried, and the whole of the ridge to the west of the village was cleared a little later. Mametz had also been entered, and Fricourt surrounded on three sides. It is true that these villages had been absolutely obliterated by a devastating series of bombardments and counter-bombardments; but their possession was coveted and fought for none the less bitterly despite that fact. At Thiepval, and north of the valley of the Ancre as far as Serre, on the left flank of the attack, the attack had made no headway, and terrible losses had been suffered. The nature and magnitude of the preparations which had had to be made for an offensive such as this had of course rendered concealment impossible; while the enemy, apparently, had considered himself secure in his heavily wired and labyrinthine system of trenches and dugouts. But the successes on the right and centre of the attack, and the vigour and resolution with which they had been followed up during succeeding weeks, quickly dispelled this feeling of security, and awakened him to a sense of his imminent danger; he had in consequence increased his gun power, and thrown picked divisions into the line in a desperate resolve to stem the tide, which ebbed and flowed a little, but always threatened to overwhelm his defences.

The position, as it stood at the end of the first week in September, was that practically the whole of the crest of the main ridge behind the enemy's original positions had been gained on a front of some five miles from Delville Wood to the road above Mouquet Farm, about a mile east of Thiepval. In those places where British troops did not completely hold the crest of the ridge they had most of the advantages of observation; while a firm footing had also been established on the ridge east of Delville Wood as far as Leuze Wood. It will thus be seen that the greatest measure of success had been won in the centre; on the flanks there was still difficult ground which had to be secured in order to avoid the creation of an awkward and dangerous salient. Events were now in train for a general resumption of the offensive on September 15th, to be preceded on September 9th by a preliminary attack mainly designed to straighten the line in certain places where it had been found impossible to conform to the general advance.

At the outset brigades expended anything from 800 to 1,000 rounds every twenty-four hours on normal shooting, and quite exclusive of any special tasks. Hostile batteries were very active round Longueval and Delville Wood, and in addition artillery areas were subjected to a fair amount of shelling with high explosive and gas shells, both lethal and lachrymatory. The 1st Brigade area was heavily shelled by 8in. howitzers from 7 a.m. till 1 p.m. on the 7th, while the 4th (How.) Battery lost a gun almost before the gunners had time to settle down into action. The enemy was slowly searching the valley with a few big shells when by an unlucky chance he got a direct hit on one of the gun-pits, destroying gun, ammunition, and pit, and killing one man and wounding five.

On September 8th orders were issued that the 4th Army would resume the attack on the following day at 4.45 p.m. The attack was preceded by a deliberate bombardment, which commenced at 7 a.m. on the 9th, with no intense fire previous to zero. The 1st and 2nd Brigades supported the infantry of the 3rd Corps, and the 3rd Brigade Group assisted in the support of the infantry of the 14th Corps. The bulk of the gains were on the right, where Ginchy was captured; otherwise the gains were inappreciable, and little or no progress was made at High Wood and east of Delville Wood. A counter-attack on Ginchy was repulsed.

Preparations were now being completed for the general resumption of the offensive on September 15th. Fresh troops were being brought in ready to take their place in the line, and the artillery were getting up stocks of ammunition for the prolonged bombardment which was to commence on the 12th. The general idea for the advance of the British armies was to pivot on the high ground south of the Ancre and north of the Albert-Baupaume road; while the Fourth Army devoted the whole of its effort to the rearmost of the enemy's original system of defence between Morval and Le Sars. Given success in this direction, the left of the attack was to embrace the villages of Martinpuich and Courcelette. The French were to co-operate by continuing the line of their advance from the Somme to the slopes above Combles, but their main effort was to be directed against Rancourt and Freigicourt so as to complete the isolation of Combles, already dominated by the British at Leuze Wood, and by the French to the south-east, and open the way for their attack upon Sailly-Saillisel. The whole of the Fourth Army, under General Sir Henry Rawlinson, was to take part in the attack, as well as the 1st Canadian Corps on the right of the Fifth Army. The New Zealand Division was now in the Fourth Army as part of the 15th Corps, which comprised also the 14th and 41st Divisions. In the attack on the 15th the New Zealanders were to be on the Corps' left and on the right of the 47th Division 3rd Corps. The objectives assigned to the 15th Corps were, first, the Switch Trench line; second, the line of Flers and Fat trenches extending along the front of Flers village, and practically parallel with Switch Trench; third, Flers village and a line extending from Flers support on the left up to Abbey road and then across the rear of the village and along Bull's road to the right; fourth, the final objective, which was to take in the village of Guedecourt and its outskirts and the intervening country and trench systems. In the New Zealand Division the 2nd Infantry Brigade and the 3rd (Rifle) Brigade were to take part in the attack, and the 1st Infantry Brigade was to be in Divisional Reserve. The artillery of the 14th Division with the attached 1st and 2nd Brigades of New Zealand Artillery was directly to support the New Zealand Infantry, which commenced to relieve in the line on September 11th. The 3rd and 4th Brigades N.Z.F.A. continued in support of English troops on the right.

On the 10th, battery commanders of the 2nd Brigade selected more forward positions for their guns. The two six-gun 18-pr. batteries were placed down the slope of the crest five

Lieut.-Colonel I. T. Standish, C.M.G., D.S.O., (d)

LIEUT.-COLONEL N. S. FALLA, C.M.G., D.S.O., (d)

hundred yards due north of Bazentin-le-Grand, and the 6th (How.) Battery near the Bazentin-le-Grand-Longueval crossroads. On the 11th the 15th Battery moved up to a new position near Longueval. New positions had also been reconnoitred for the other batteries of the 1st Brigade on the ridge between Bazentin-le-Grand and Longueval, and these were occupied on the afternoon of the 13th, batteries resuming their part in the bombardment in progress as soon as they were established in the new positions. Before the commencement of the bombardment battery commanders and their subordinate officers had made themselves familiar with the country over which the advance was to take place, by close study of the map and by visual observation from carefully chosen observation posts.

The bombardment opened on the morning of Tuesday, September 12th, all along the line from Thiepval to Ginchy, and continued steadily for three days. The 18-prs. were employed chiefly in cutting wire, searching communication trenches etc., while the 4.5in. howitzer batteries which were not engaged on counter-battery work directed their fire on enemy trenches, observation posts, and machine-gun emplacements. Each battery was given its programme of shooting; but its activities did not end there. Observing officers were constantly on the look-out for suitable targets, and any sign of life or movement in the trenches or on the roads behind the enemy line was instantly the target for several batteries. The whole enemy system of trenches for a great depth was battered with high explosive and sprayed with shrapnel, and any belts of wire entanglements that could be observed at all were methodically wiped out; roads and communications were shelled by day, and even more vigorously by night, when they carried most traffic, and groups of heavy guns concentrated their efforts on the destruction of enemy batteries; in short, the whole area behind the enemy lines was kept under a continuous and destructive fire, blocking the movement of troops and stopping the supply of water, rations, or ammunition. Gas shells, fired by the 4.5in howitzers, were here used for the first time by the New Zealand batteries. On the nights of September 13th-14th and 14th-15th the allotment of ammunition

I

to 18pr. batteries for the shelling of communications, road junctions, and similar targets was increased by 50 per cent.; but no limit at all was set to the expenditure of ammunition necessary for wire-cutting.

An order issued to the troops on the eve of the attack read:—"For the last two and a half months we have been gradually wearing down the enemy. His morale is shaken, he has few (if any) fresh reserves available, and there is every probability that a combined and determined effort will result in a decisive victory."

The morning of Friday, September 15th, dawned fine, but cool and misty—a typical autumn morning. For three days now the bombardment had gone on with unwavering persistence, neither diminishing nor increasing in volume, suggesting nothing so much as a giant machine controlled by a single mind; but at six o'clock, twenty minutes before zero hour, it seemed to increase in intensity and violence. One thought that nothing could exist under this annihilating storm of shells; but when at 6.20 a.m. the infantry left their trenches and moved forward behind the barrage, the enemy was manning his machine guns, and his artillery put down a heavy and accurate barrage. That day the new armoured cars or tanks, as they became universally known, were used for the first time, lanes being left in the barrage for their advance. Despite the fact that some of them broke down before they reached their front line, and that, of the twenty odd which managed to cross the German line, about a third were almost immediately crippled through some cause or other, they did very good work in fighting machine gun nests and strong points, and in flattening out belts of German wire. As yet, however, they were only in the experimental stage; and, undoubtedly, their greatest success that day lay in their moral effect, as they lumbered up to the German trenches, looming huge and uncertain in the half light.

All the objectives were reached on almost the whole front attacked, the chief exception being on the right flank, east of Ginchy. The New Zealand Infantry took Switch Trench, and finally fought their way into Flers, passing through it, and establishing their line a considerable distance beyond the village, where they refused to yield ground, and bloodily repulsed one counter-attack after another. The 1st and 2nd Brigades of Artillery, which were assisting to support their advance, kept in touch by sending forward observation officers accompanied by telephonists and linesmen. Switch Trench had been carried by 7 a.m., and by 9.30 a.m. observing officers from both brigades had succeeded in establishing communication with their batteries, and by observation were lending the best possible support to the advancing infantry Valuable work was done also during the day by these officers in spotting hostile batteries, reporting their location to Divisional Artillery Headquarters, and so securing for them the attention of the "heavies," and later by engaging, with every available gun, the enemy's troops as they mustered for the counter-attack.

On the front covered by the 3rd and 4th Brigade Group, English troops captured and consolidated their allotted portion of Switch Trench, closely supported by 18-prs. of the group. On pushing on to their third and final objective, however, the infantry had been unable to withstand the German counter-attacks, and had fallen back on to what was known as the Bull's Road line. In this case it had been deemed necessary to push the 3rd Brigade forward on the heels of the advancing infantry, and for this reason the brigade had moved its waggon lines forward from Becordel to the slopes of the high ground behind Montauban on the night preceding the advance. The 4th Brigade reverted to the command of the Brigade Commander, Lieut.-Colonel N. S. Falla, and remained in action behind Longueval awaiting orders to advance. Batteries of the 3rd Brigade commenced to move forward about 9 a.m. on September 15th, the advance of each one being covered in turn by the remaining batteries. The positions chosen were on the forward and reverse slopes of a long shallow valley, which extended eastwards of the road running from Longueval to Flers, and 1500 to 2000 yards in front of Longueval. The 11th Battery moved forward at 9 a.m., and was followed at hourly intervals by the 12th, 13th, and 4th (Howitzer) Batteries in succession. Each battery carried a light, portable platform in two sections, designed for use in crossing trenches, but they were not required that day. Early though the hour was, men of the Labour Corps and Pioneer Battalions had filled in the trenches that intersected the road, or what could be seen of it, and had removed the most formidable obstacles. Sandbags in such small quantities as it had been possible to procure, necessary tools, and, of course, ammunition, were taken up with the guns; while in some cases the gunners themselves, with wise prevision, had secured odd pit-props and baulks of timber, which they had lashed to the limbers. Thus burdened there could be no quick running of the gauntlet along the heavily shelled road, even had it not already been almost crowded with the parties of troops going up to the line and with the others who also had gone up so full of life but a little before, and were now being borne slowly back to the busy dressing-stations on the edge of Longueval. The drivers took their straining teams steadily along, while the gunners plodded in rear of the vehicles half curious, half apprehensive, and wholly alert.

Of those still living who went with the guns through Longueval that day, and down the tortured road that led on to Flers, assuredly none will forget it while memory lives. From the battery positions they were just leaving, a rough track led up the slopes and joined the main road that led into Longueval. There was but little shelling there, and only an occasional big shell fell into the village itself, but from High Wood, right along the crest to Delville Wood and beyond, the German gunners had laid down a deep, heavy barrage from seemingly every known calibre of gun. And through it ran the road to the forward positions. It might have been thought an impassable barrier; but the infantry had gone through it, and were fighting away in advance of it; and the guns went through. Battery after battery wound through the tumbled ruins of the village, and down past the ragged remnants of Delville Wood, a ghastly place where the big high explosive shells were sending up great gouts of black earth and pieces of wood, and Heaven only knew what else.

The postions were gained at last with surprisingly few casualties. The guns were unlimbered, the gear and ammunition dumped on the ground, and the teams with their lightened waggons set off to run the gauntlet again as fast as the broken ground permitted. The gunners set to work at once with feverish energy to get their guns into action, and to provide themselves with some cover from the flying splinters; but in this they were not always successful, and it was during the hours that followed, and before the fall of night intervened and brought a little quiet to the tormented valley that so many of the casualties were suffered by the gun crews. Battery commanders had preceded their commands by an hour or more, had marked out the positions, and laid out the lines of fire for the guns, so that once a platform was prepared from which the gun might shoot with some degree of stability, it was ready for action. A wooden platform for the gun was an essential, as the country everywhere had been riven and shaken with the concussion of the bursting shells, and nowhere could a solid foundation be found for a gun on the earth itself. Meantime the enemy unceasingly shelled the length and breadth of the valley; he was, of course, perfectly familiar with the country from which he had just been driven, and even had he not observed in the distance the ant-like activity which dotted the surface of the valley, he probably already had it set down as a likely location for the British field batteries.

Meanwhile the efforts of the 3rd Brigade observing officers to get their batteries into touch with the attacking battalions had not in all cases been successful. Infantry units had got mixed up in the advance, and could not be located in the confusion. Observation posts were established, however, and many targets effectively engaged, among them several hostile battery positions which were shelled by the 4th (howitzer) Battery. The difficulties of maintaining communication were common to all brigades. The wires laid forward from the batteries were continually being cut by bursting shells, and the maintenance of communications was terribly difficult. No sooner was one break in the line repaired than a bursting shell would gap the line somewhere else, and fling the loose ends perhaps half a hundred yards apart. The linesmen stuck to this apparently hopeless task with resolute courage, and the fact that communication was maintained at all is the highest testimony both to their contempt of danger, and to the value of their work. Similar difficulties were experienced in maintaining the vital link of communication between batteries and the headquarters of their brigade. In other battles, in later days, the system of communications in forward areas was made more secure by the provision of buried wires, which were laid down before the commencement of operations, but on the Somme the Division was entirely dependent on ground wires or visual signalling.

Towards the fall of evening the fury of the enemy's gun-fire seemed to have somewhat spent itself, work on the advanced battery positions, occupied, and in course of preparation, was pushed on during the night, and a great deal was accomplished before the shelling began to quicken up again with the first streaks of dawn. The tired teams were given no respite, being employed throughout the night bringing up supplies of ammunition to the guns. The 1st Brigade, which had kept its teams standing by on the afternoon of the 15th, in readiness for a move, had received orders to advance its guns on the morning of the 16th. By dawn the 7th Battery was in its new position to the east of High Wood, and close to the wood itself. As soon as this battery had registered, the 3rd Battery commenced to move up, and its guns were in position and registered by 1.50 p.m., upon which the 1st, and also the 15th (howitzer) Batteries advanced, the whole Brigade being in position by 6 p.m. The 2nd Brigade batteries did not move forward until the 18th and 19th, when they occupied positions to the south of High Wood.

On the 19th also, the 10th and 14th batteries of the 4th Brigade, with the 8th battery, which had hitherto been held in reserve, commenced to move into position in "Devil's Gully," near the 3rd Brigade batteries. The weather had broken on the 18th, a depressing, wetting rain having fallen almost incessantly from the Monday to the Wednesday. The roads were in an almost indescribable state. Wherever they had been constructed off the route of the one original paved road which ran through the area, it speedily became impossible to distinguish them from the surrounding sea of mud and shell holes. To bring up the guns was a task of some magnitude. The 10th

Battery, which started off with one section, reached the new position only after many hours struggling on the road, and with twenty horses hooked on to each gun. It was impossible to do more this day with exhausted men, and thoroughly exhausted horses; but on the 20th the guns of the 8th Battery, and the second section of the 10th, were got up and by dawn of the 22nd the 14th Battery guns were in position, and the move of the Brigade was complete. The rain had a ruinous effect on the gun-pits. The ground was so completely disintegrated by the bombardments that it would not hold, and when the rain came the sides of the pits slid in, and the platforms simply sank into the mud. The men suffered from constant exposure to the heavy rain, were up to their knees in mud, and slept in it when they got time to sleep. Under the weeping skies the battlefield, with its battered trenches and tangle of broken wire, its debris of smashed transport, dead horses, and unburied men, presented a scene of desolation, suffering, and death that must have awakened sombre and questioning thought in the mind of even the most war-hardened soldier as to the end and the purpose and the meaning of it all. But there was no time for melancholy reflections, and none were entertained. Quite cheerfully the men set to work and cleared out the pits and rebuilt the walls. Exercising a predatory instinct awakened by pressure of circumstances, they were soon in possession of timber and sandbags, and even sheet iron, and with these materials contrived to defy the elements, and restore their pits to a workable condition, and provide some cover for their ammunition. The weather commenced to clear on the 20th, but the ground was slow to dry.

The break in the weather so hindered operations that the offensive was not resumed by the British armies until Monday, 25th September, but this delay in no way interfered with the activity of the guns. Despite the unfavourable conditions for observation the field guns were ever busy, night and day, while the "heavies," screened by camouflage netting, and disposed round about the slopes near Longueval, or ranged in imposing lines behind the crest that ran west from Delville Wood, were continually sending over their big shells that went rushing through the air like giant birds in flight. The brigades covering the New Zealand Infantry assisted in supporting a small and highly successful advance by the 2nd Infantry Brigade on the evening of the 20th. All batteries also assisted in the breaking up of enemy counter-attacks which were reported by the infantry or by artillery observing officers.

Orders issued on the 17th regarding the expenditure of ammunition, laid it down that for night firing the nightly expenditure for brigades was to be five hundred rounds for the 18-pr. batteries, and one hundred and twenty rounds for the howitzers. Day firing consisted chiefly of careful registration to enable future barrages to be as accurate as possible, of wire-cutting, destruction of strong points, counter-battery work, and firing on hostile movement and dead ground.

On the morning of the 21st, the C.O. 1st Brigade and the Officer Commanding 1st Battery reconnoitred a wire-cutting position close to Flers, from which the battery had to cut wire in front of a portion of Gird Trench for the attack on the 25th. Digging was commenced and the guns moved up after dark. The battery registered soon after daylight, and at once commenced to cut the wire, a task on which it was still engaged on the 24th, while the bombardment for the attack on the following day was taking place.

Losses at the guns were continuous and heavy, brigade areas frequently being subjected to destructive shelling both of high explosive and gas; and, in addition, a number of casualties were also caused by prematures or faulty ammunition fired by other batteries in rear of the 1st and 2nd Brigades. One of these shells penetrated a gun emplacement in the 5th Battery scattering the ammunition, but fortunately no casualties resulted. In a gas shell bombardment on the 21st the 1st Brigade had four men killed and eleven wounded, and a little later the 3rd Battery was heavily shelled, and had one officer and three men killed and four men wounded, two guns put out of action, and a large quantity of ammunition blown up. Waggon lines were also shelled, and sometimes bombed at night, and as a consequence of the shelling some batteries which had established their waggon lines in more forward positions were compelled to withdraw them behind Montauban.

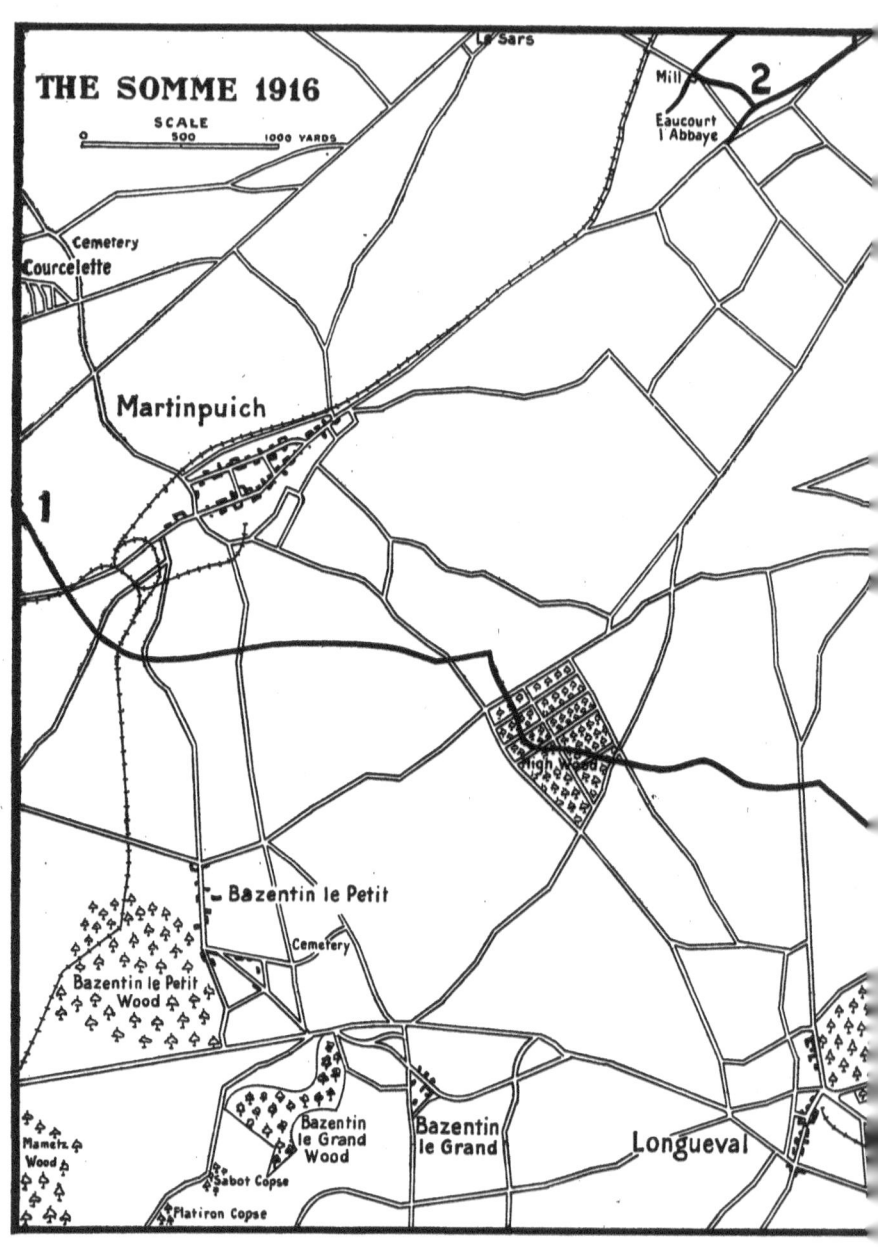

SHOWING THE PROGRESS MADE DURING THE

(The black line 1 represents approximate line when the New Zealand Di
the New Zealand A

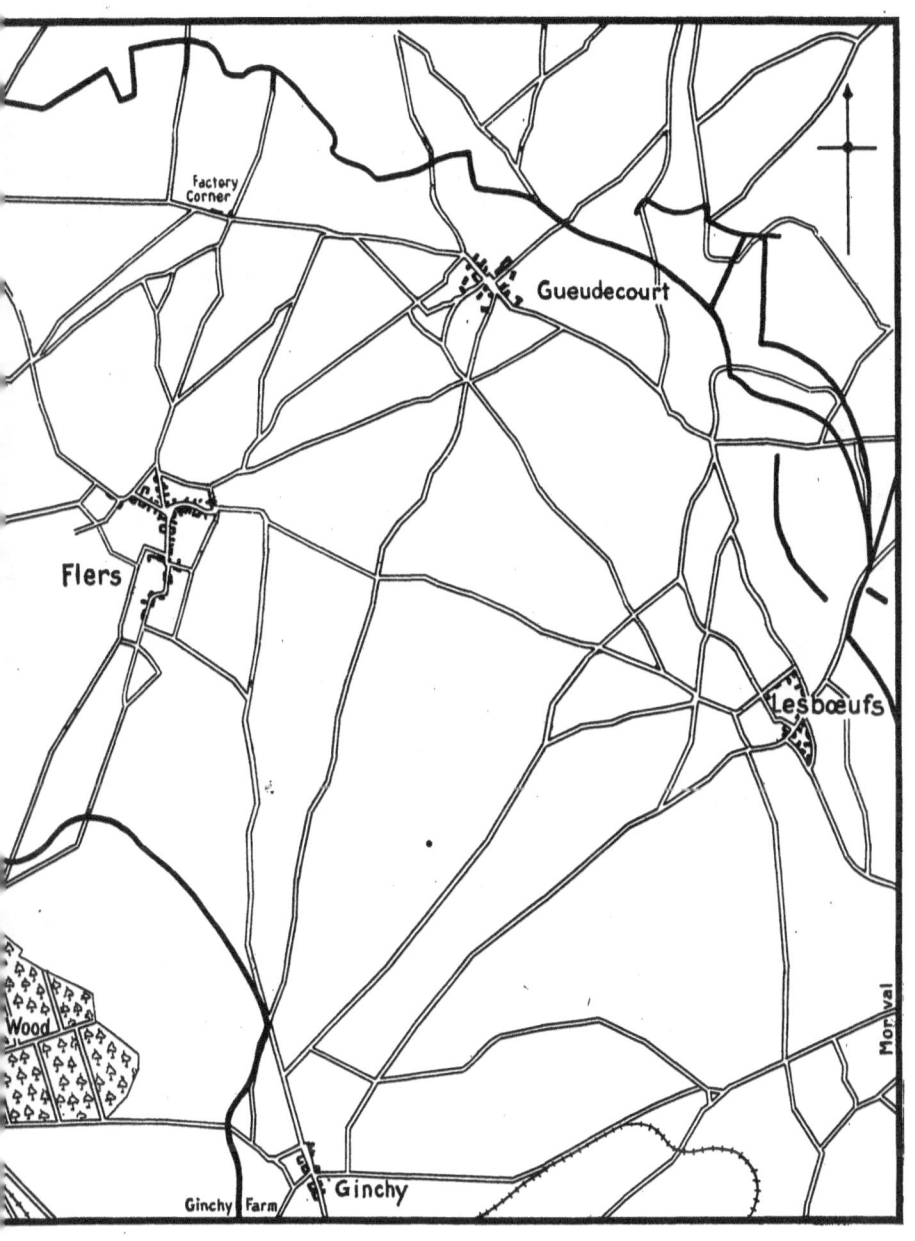

THE NEW ZEALAND ARTILLERY WAS IN ACTION

ent on to the Front in September, 1916, and black line 2 that covered when withdrew in October).

THE BATTLE OF THE SOMME

The attack on September 25th, which had been delayed by bad weather, was general along the Allied front, from the Somme to Martinpuich, and the objectives set for the attacking divisions included the villages of Morval, Les Bœufs, and Gueudecourt, and a belt of country about 1000 yards in depth, curving round the north of Flers, to a point midway between that village and Martinpuich. The New Zealand Divison was on the left of the 15th Corps with the 55th Divison on its right, and the 1st division of the 3rd Corps on its left, and was assigned as its objective, Factory Corner, and the establishment of a line thence to the division's junction with the 3rd Corps. The 1st Infantry Brigade made the attack, the 3rd (Rifle) Brigade and the 2nd Infantry Brigade being in reserve. The attack was preceded by a bombardment which began at 7 a.m. on September 24th, and continued until zero hour, 12.25 p.m. on the 25th, with no intense fire before zero.

The enemy made strenuous efforts to lessen the weight of this bombardment by heavily shelling battery areas, especially on the morning of the 25th, when he opened a searching fire with guns of all calibres on the 3rd and 4th Brigade positions in Devil's Gully. His fire was accurate and destructive, and a great number of casualties were caused. Captain F. S. Robinson and Second Lieutenant L. Jardine were both killed; both officers belonged to the 12th Battery, Captain Robinson having been given command on the death of Captain H. A. Davies, who was killed by a shell on September 15th. Fortunately the enemy's fire slackened before zero hour, and batteries were able to complete their programme of shooting.

A feature of the day's work was the employment against the enemy of two guns of a 77mm. battery which had been captured in the advance of September 15th, and which lay on the outskirts of Flers. There was a plentiful supply of ammunition, and an officer and a party of men from the 13th Battery went forward, manned the guns, and opened fire on a stranded tank which lay within the German lines, and which it was believed the enemy had converted into a strong point. Eighty rounds were fired at a range of 700 yards, direct laying, and a considerable number of direct hits were obtained. Hostile shelling wounded some of the detachment and caused a temporary withdrawal; but fire was opened again after half an hour's interval, and after about fifty rounds had been expended in enfilading an enemy trench, hostile fire put one of the guns out of action, and finally compelled the detachments to withdraw. Both these guns were subsequently repaired, and were used by the 13th Battery until the New Zealand Artillery was withdrawn from the Somme. Early in October they were placed in fresh positions west of Flers; there was a plentiful supply of ammunition, and, possessing a greater range than the 18-prs., these guns were able to engage targets beyond the reach of the Division's field batteries, including the town of Bapaume itself, which was shelled with German gas shell.

The barrage for the advance was effective, and the New Zealand infantry reported it as being even and regular. Advancing behind it they carried their objectives, and consolidated their position in characteristically workmanlike fashion. When night came on the advance along the front had reached its limits, except at Gueudecourt, where a stout and successful resistance had been offered by the enemy from a section of his fourth main system of defence. The fall of the village on the following day came as the sequel to an interesting little adventure, in which a tank was the principal actor. The tank started out from the line in the early morning, followed by bombers, and lumbered down the trench which had kept the English infantry from reaching their objective on the previous day. At the same time an aeroplane appeared on the scene, and promptly taking in the situation, sailed down the length of the trench, briskly machine-gunning the occupants as it went. Against these embarrassing attentions only one decision was possible, and presently the usual tokens of surrender were displayed. The tank rolled on and routed out a lot of machine gunners from their lairs in the village; the infantry followed up this advantage, and after some stiff fighting the village was cleared of the enemy. Batteries of the 3rd and 4th Brigades assisted in this operation by direct observation, and throughout the day observing officers were afforded some splendid shooting.

At one stage of the day enemy troops were observed massing for a counter-attack from behind Gueudecourt to Factory Corner; every available gun was immediately directed on the locality, and the attack broke down at its inception. On this day the enemy was being harassed at many points, and the right wing of the Fifth Army was attacking Thiepval and the Thiepval ridge. A great deal of movement could be observed in the enemy's back areas, and traffic was very dense along the main Bapaume-Peronne Road, out of range, of course, for the field guns. Officers from some of the 4th Brigade batteries, however, improvised communications to some heavy batteries, and directed their fire while they shelled the road. The fact that heavy artillery groups seldom maintained communications to the more forward observing stations must, on many occasions, have diminished the accuracy and effectiveness of their fire.

Throughout this day, the 26th, the 1st and 2nd Brigades were busily engaged cutting wire in front of Gird Trench, which the infantry were to assault on the following day. At the hour of assault, 2.15 p.m. on the 27th, both brigades co-operated in establishing a creeping barrage in front of the advancing infantry. The objective was gained by 3 p.m., and from that hour until 9 p.m. a protective barrage was put down, while the new positions were being consolidated. Throughout the night, also, the batteries searched and swept all the country in rear of the ground which the enemy had lost, in order to prevent any possibility of counter-attack.

Contending with the Elements.

At this stage of the offensive, when the enemy had been shaken by a series of shattering blows which seriously weakened his power of resistance, leaving him little time or opportunity to recover himself, a continuance of fine weather would have meant much to the Allied cause. But the weather broke at the end of September, and almost the whole of October saw a succession of drenching rains. It was a period of unremitting, hard, physical toil for all ranks. It had again become necessary to push the New Zealand batteries forward, and the task of dragging them over the almost non-existent roads, and across the trackless waste of mud to their assigned positions, became well-nigh hopeless. On September 29th batteries of the 1st and 2nd Brigades commenced preparing new positions which had been reconnoitred on the outskirts of Flers, to the west and north-west. On this occasion the 18-pr. batteries of the 2nd Brigade resumed their formation as four-gun batteries. The 6th (howitzer) Battery selected a position near High Wood. Work was very difficult owing to the rain and mud; but six guns and two howitzers were placed in new positions shortly after dark, and the remainder were got up about the same time on the night of the 30th. The 2nd Battery's position was shelled very heavily from dusk onwards.

Owing to the fall of the ground some of the batteries could be only partly concealed from the view of the enemy, and as a result they suffered heavily during the whole of the time they remained in these positions. For the same reason ammunition or stores could be brought up only under cover of darkness or in wet and misty weather. The only avenue of approach to Flers and the vicinity for wheeled traffic was by way of the road that ran down from Longueval, and this was under observation during the day. The 3rd and 4th Brigades had an alternative pack route past the east corner of Delville Wood, and similar routes were later reconnoitred and used west of the Flers road. This road had long since been rutted out of recognition, was badly pitted by shell holes, and at night when it was always thick with traffic the enemy shelled it more heavily than during the day. But picking a way across country through the maze of shell-holes and old trenches, following a track on which the horses floundered up to their bellies in the mud, was infinitely worse. It was a physical impossibility to take up stores or ammunition in the limbers; wheeled traffic being out of the question, everything had to be packed. There was no equipment on issue for packing, but the ammunition was carried on each side of the saddle in canvas bags, sandbags, or shell baskets which were salved on the battlefields. The horses suffered grievously from overwork, insufficient food and lack of shelter, some of them becoming so gaunt and weak that when they fell into a shell-hole they had not the requisite strength to drag themselves out, and died where they lay. Many of the horses had been in the hands of the same drivers since leaving New Zealand, and were treated with a consideration amounting to affection, being cared for, indeed, more than the men cared for themselves. Some that had seen service on Gallipoli, and had even been wounded, were rightly regarded as seasoned old veterans, sharers in the common misfortunes of war, and were, therefore, the objects of especial solicitude; while the loss of any of them on the battlefield was an occasion for mourning. One such well-known veteran was "Finnigan," an R.N.Z.A. horse, brought from New Zealand, that trod on a bomb on the road near Flers. Although very severely wounded, he gamely took his load three miles to its destination, on reaching which he dropped and died. This sentimental affection of a driver for his horses was worthy of encouragement on more than humane grounds, as the great wastage in horses which took place during such periods as the fighting on the Somme, was found to be considerably reduced in divisions where "horse-mastership" was something more than a name.

From the time in September when the wet weather set in, the conditions at the waggon lines grew steadily worse; overhead cover of any description was, of course, out of the question. Horse lines became quagmires, where the lean and jaded beasts stood up to their hocks in the mud; and batteries, with their reduced strength at the waggon lines, constantly employed packing ammunition, were unable to do anything to improve the position. Watering facilities were uniformly bad, also, and it was no uncommon experience for the horses of a unit to be led back to the lines without having watered, after a long and fruitless wait at the crowded troughs.

Following on local advances which had been made during the last days of September, between Gueudecourt and Courcelette, the enemy had fallen back on his defences running in front of Eaucourt l'Abbaye and Le Sars, and on the afternoon of October 1st an attack was launched against Eaucourt l'Abbaye and the defences to the east and west of it, the total front involved in the attack being about 3000 yards. From 7 a.m. on the 1st of October the trenches to be attacked by the

New Zealand infantry were bombarded by batteries of the 1st and 2nd Brigades, while at 2 p.m. certain other batteries shelled the ground over which the 47th Division of the 3rd Corps was to advance in its attack on Eaucourt l'Abbaye. At 3.15 p.m. an intense barrage was laid down, and behind its protection the New Zealand Infantry advanced to the attack. Heavy fighting was experienced, but by evening all the objectives had been reached. The attempt to take Eaucourt l'Abbaye was not successful; but a hold was obtained on the outskirts of the village, and by the early morning of October 4th its capture was complete. Oil projectors were used as part of the preparation for this advance, and when the infantry occupied the enemy trenches they found tragic evidence of their effectiveness.

Sections of the 3rd Brigade batteries went forward after dark on October 1st, to positions on the west of Flers, from where they were to support further advances which had been planned to embrace Ligny-Thilloy and le Barque. The positions were in most cases fairly exposed, and it was therefore deemed advisable to move under cover of darkness, and have the guns dug in and concealed as securely as possible before dawn. On the way up from the old positions in Devil's Gully some of the guns were delayed by heavy shelling on the Flers road, and when they left the road and struck across country the guide, unfamiliar with the route, and doubtless confused by the shelling, lost his way in the inky darkness. Precious time was lost in locating the positions, and by the time they had been reached by the joint efforts of the sorely tried horses and the gunners working with drag ropes and shovels the night was well advanced. The task of digging the pits in the heavy clay was attacked with feverish energy, and the guns were run into the pits as the first streaks of dawn appeared. Canvas camouflage screens were hurriedly thrown over the pits, and the effect was completed by a few shovelfuls of earth and weeds, after which the tired gunners had the satisfaction of seeing a German aeroplane fly all unsuspecting over their heads.

The New Zealand Division, less artillery, was withdrawn from the line on the night of the 3rd-4th October, on relief by the 41st Division. The Artillery remained in the line, all four brigades being attached to the 21st Divisional Artillery. On this occasion the following message was received by the Divison from General Sir H. S. Rawlinson, Commanding the Fourth Army:—

"I desire to express to all ranks of the New Zealand Division my hearty congratulations on the excellent work they have done during the battle of the Somme.

"On three successive occasions (15th and 25th September and 1st October), they attacked the hostile positions with the greatest gallantry and vigour, capturing in each attack every objective that had been allotted to them. More than this, they gained possession of, and held, several strong points in advance, and beyond the furthest objectives that had been allotted to them.

"The endurance and fine fighting spirit of the Division has been beyond praise, and their success in the Flers neighbourhood will rank high amongst the best achievements of the British Army.

"The control and direction of the Division during these operations have been conducted with skill and precision, whilst the Artillery support in establishing the barrage, and defeating counter-attacks has been in every way most effective.

"It is a matter of regret to me that this fine Division is leaving the Fourth Army, and I trust that on some future occasion it may again be my good fortune to find them under my command."

October was a bad month for the batteries. It rained almost incessantly; the batteries were heavily shelled in their advanced and exposed positions and lost a great many of their personnel; and for the drivers and the men of the Ammunition Column, the journey to the guns was a nightly struggle against the elements; while since the departure of the rest of the Division the rations had become so meagre and unvaried as to warrant the making of representations on the subject, after which there was an improvement. The enemy gunners harried the pack columns on the roads, and used their heavy guns unsparingly in the effort to destroy battery positions. With the absolute shortage of material and labour, nothing but splinter-proof shelters could be built at the most, and every battery suffered losses in guns and men, direct hits on the pits being suffered very frequently. In the 3rd Battery three direct hits were obtained on pits on October 3rd; and two days later, when the enemy shelled the area all day with 5.9in. and 8in. howitzers, a big shell landed on one pit, and destroyed the gun and ammunition, and killed the whole detachment. The 15th Battery had an ammunition dump exploded and lost one officer, Lieut. Watson, and four other ranks killed, as well as a number wounded. The explosion blew in the back of one of the gun pits, and set fire to the ammunition charges stored beside the gun, and a gunner, who had been caught by the falling beams, was in imminent danger of being burnt to death, until a rescue party extricated him after some minutes' work close to the burning ammunition. The leader of this party was, unfortunately, himself killed in action a few days later. On October 3rd there was an occurrence of equal gravity in the 6th Battery, when an explosion took place as the result of a premature at the mouth of the gun in No. 2 pit, and Captain G. E. Daniell, Second-Lieutenant E. M. Brookes, and four other ranks were killed and three severely wounded. On the death of Captain Daniell, command of the battery was assumed by Captain W. H. Johnston.

The 2nd Battery's new position was systematically shelled for three or four days at the opening of the month, and it was decided to move the battery in sections. One section was attached to the 5th Battery, and the other came under the command of the O.C. 9th Battery, and was dug in 500 yards north of that battery's position.

Although the conditions prevailing during October made the launching of an offensive on a big scale impossible, it was a month of hard fighting, in which the infantry were almost crippled from the outset by the difficulties under which they fought, and the results in consequence were of little value. On October 7th the Fourth Army attacked again from Les Bœufs to Destremont Farm, near Le Sars. Le Sars itself was captured and some progress was made east of Gueudecourt. On the front covered by the New Zealand batteries the attack was not successful. The 1st Brigade, to which "X" Battery, R.H.A.,

A PACK COLUMN GOING FORWARD TO THE GUNS AT PASSCHENDAELE

[*Official Photo*

Lieut.-Colonel R. S McQuarrie, D.S.O., M.C

had been attached, and the 4th Brigade assisted in the creeping barrage behind which the men of the 41st Division were to advance, the 2nd and 3rd Brigades firing in the stationary barrage. The bombardment commenced at 3.15 p.m. on October the 6th, and continued until 5.15 p.m., when the rate of fire was reduced. At 7.45 a.m. next morning the bombardment quickened up again, and kept steadily on until zero hour, 1.45 p.m. The enemy may not have been conscious of the impending assault, but he certainly made a strong effort to neutralise the fire of batteries by heavily shelling them with lethal and lachrymatory gas, in the hour before dawn. Fortunately a strong sou'westerly breeze minimised the effect of the gas, but later on the positions were "crumped" with 5.9's, and a lot of casualties were caused, particularly in the 15th Battery, where five other ranks were killed and several wounded with one shell. The 9th Battery, which had had a gun completely destroyed during the previous afternoon, had two guns buried at zero hour. They were, fortunately, not badly damaged, and in ten minutes' time the pits were cleared and the guns were in action again.

Altogether the advantages gained in this attack were somewhat disappointing, and it was in consequence decided to wait until weather conditions permitted of a further advance to be preceded by an ample artillery preparation. The enemy had brought up fresh troops on the front, and it was feared that he might use these in an attempt to win back some of the ground which had been wrested from him at such great effort. Certain arrangements of a defensive nature were accordingly made to render abortive such an attempt on his part. Enemy country was, if possible, kept under more constant observation from artillery observation posts, and forward communications were made more complete, and kept in good working order. At the batteries an effort was made to improve the overhead cover, and an order was issued by the 21st Divisional Artillery Headquarters to bring the reserve of ammunition at the guns up to 1000 rounds per gun.

On October 15th one section each of the 11th and 13th Batteries went forward from Devil's Valley, and occupied positions east of Flers which had been reconnoitred the previous

K

day, with the object of enfilading Gird Trench and Support Trench. A week later these sections were handed over, complete, to the 14th Battery, and the 11th and 13th Batteries each took over a section of the 14th Battery's guns in Devil's Valley. These guns the two batteries moved forward to their advanced positions west of Flers.

Further attacks were attempted on the 12th and 18th October, but the gains achieved were of no moment; the weather continued execrable, and as the Commander-in-Chief phrased it in his official despatch, "the moment for decisive action was rapidly passing away." In addition, the enemy was profiting by past experience; he made a better tactical use of his machine guns, his most potent weapon of defence; and the weather continued to aid him. In preparation for the attack on the 12th the guns commenced to bombard the enemy's defences at 7 a.m. on the previous day, and at quarter past three the same afternoon they opened a Chinese barrage, which, as the name might suggest, reverses the usual procedure by creeping back instead of forward. The enemy evidently read this as the preliminary to an attack, for he instantly replied with a furious barrage, even shelling his own line in his flurry; and at the same time his counter-battery guns commenced to shell the New Zealand batteries. When the attack really was launched at 2.5 p.m. on the following day, innumerable red rockets sent up all along the German line, brought the hostile barrage down five minutes after zero. His fire was, moreover, somewhat below normal, due to the shelling of his batteries by the heavy artillery, and gas-shelling by the 4.5in. howitzers.

The ensuing days were spent in thoroughly preparing the ground for the attack on October 18th, in which the objectives were very little different from those that had been set on the 12th, so far at any rate as the immediate front covered by the New Zealand batteries was concerned.

In addition to the shooting which usually paved the way for an attack, this preparation took the form of special bombardments, in conjunction with the heavy artillery, of enemy trenches and sunken roads, and other points which were likely to prove dangerous obstacles to the advance of the infantry. This went on uninterruptedly for several days, notwithstanding the persistent and heavy counter-shelling of battery areas. Despite this series of destructive bombardments, and the regular and well-timed barrage which preceded the infantry, the attack on this portion of the front yielded little better results than that which had preceded it six days earlier.

Throughout this period the work of the batteries had been carried on under an almost continual and destructive fire from the enemy heavy guns; but although casualties had been heavy and a great number of guns had been destroyed or put out of action, the various tasks assigned to the brigades in the preparation and support for infantry operations had been faithfully carried out, though necessarily with a reduced number of guns. When a battery was not engaged on any task of immediate importance the gunners were usually withdrawn from the pits if the positions were being very heavily shelled; but when firing in a barrage, on S.O.S., or any other task of vital importance, there was no question of "cease fire" or withdrawal, and it was on such occasions that most of the casualties were suffered at the guns. On October 10th, the 11th Battery had been forced to withdraw its advanced section, after having had one gun buried and the other completely destroyed. On the 13th, the 1st Battery had had a gun and several hundred rounds of ammunition destroyed; and on the following day several batteries had been deluged with gas shells. The detachments had to wear their gas helmets for several hours, and amongst other casualties suffered, Captain F. E. Cooke, 5th Battery, had been killed. The 1st Brigade, which was grouped with the 2nd Brigade, under the orders of the C.R.A. 12th Division as from the 16th of the month, had had its headquarters blown out the previous day by 8in. shells, and had to seek fresh quarters.

As instancing the desperate nature of these efforts to annihilate the batteries, of which each brigade had its experience almost every day, the 5th Battery was shelled for three days, the shelling on the 20th lasting over ten hours and two guns being put out of action. The shelling became so intense that the position had to be temporairly evacuated, and on the 21st Captain L. V. Hulbert, Captain N. F. S. Hitchcock, brigade medical officer, and Lieutenant S. W. Morton were killed outright by the same shell.

On the night of the 21st, the sections of the 3rd Brigade which still remained in Devil's Gully, where they also had been subject to frequent periods of shelling, joined the section which had been for some time near Flers, the guns going into pits which had been prepared for them. Most of the 18-prs. struggled through the mire, but the two howitzers of the 4th Battery got badly bogged after crossing the Flers Road, and fresh teams were required to complete the journey the following night.

A feeling of general satisfaction was experienced when word was at last sent out that a relief was impending by the batteries of the 1st Australian Divisional Artillery; but such is deferred hope that many of the men refused to believe the good news until they had actually seen the advance detachments of the relieving Australians, the reports of whose presence at the waggon lines they had at first regarded as a fable. To relieve the detachments was one thing, but to get the guns in and out was another in the unbelievable condition into which the roads had fallen. However, with treble teams, and by aid of much hard endeavour a section was got up to most battery positions on the night of the 25th. The following day, providentially enough, dawned dull and misty, so that it was possible to take teams up the Flers road, and carry on in daylight with the work of extricating some of the guns and limbers that had sunk deep in the mud the night before. After viewing the condition of the roads, brigade commanders agreed to exchange guns where it was impossible to get the New Zealand guns out. The 1st Battery, having no guns at their position, took four guns to Flers with ten-horse teams, under cover of the fog, and later on these were taken to the position in Abbey Road. In the case of the 14th Battery it was quite impossible to get the guns out, and the battery therefore exchanged guns with the 24th Australian Battery. The relief was finally completed about 9 o'clock on the night of the 26th, though the 4th Battery had to send a team back from Bonnay a couple of days later to take out one of their howitzers which had been left very badly bogged near the Flers road—but not so badly as to have prevented some enterprising person from removing a good many of the fittings in the meantime! Detachments spent the night at the waggon lines, and in the early morning of the 27th October batteries made their brief preparations for the road, and marched out for their billeting areas.

Thus ended one of the hardest periods of prolonged fighting in which the Divisional Artillery were ever engaged in the whole course of the war. For fifty-two days, from September 5th to October 27th, the guns had been continuously in the firing line without rest or respite of any description whatsoever; and such had been the nature of the fighting, and the length of the casualty lists, that most of the officers and many of the gunners had spent the whole period at the gun positions. It constituted at once a supreme test of efficiency, and a most severe trial of endurance, taxing the men's physical strength to the very fibre. In the positions which were first occupied there was not much to do in the nature of constructive work, as the batteries simply walked into established positions, but when they advanced after the attack on September 15th, and when they finally went forward to near Flers, the positions had to be completely made; had to be made in spite of the nature of the ground, riven by shell-fire, and then water-logged by the rains; and in spite of the fact, also, that sandbags and timber were practically unprocurable from the usual sources. In the second positions it was found that casualties were minimised by digging deep narrow trenches in rear of the gun-pits in which the personnel could take shelter from the flying splinters. In these positions, also, some form of protection from prematures from batteries in rear was imperative. The concentration of artillery along this portion of the British front was so great that it was a matter of difficulty to find positions for them all. Wherever the country offered any measure of concealment they were massed in row upon row, and at night when they all sprang into concerted action, or opened up in response to an S.O.S. from the infantry, the eye was bewildered by the myriad flickerings of the field guns and the vivid flashes from the heavy guns massed behind them.

After the last move forward a great deal of material was salvaged from the German trenches and dugouts in the neighbourhood, and used in providing overhead cover and weatherproof shelters for the ammunition. The heavy timber was also used for gun platforms, without which the guns became unsteady and the shooting less accurate. The almost incessant hostile shelling was responsible for a tremendous number of casualties in all ranks, and entailed also a great deal more work in digging out buried guns and rebuilding positions. The labour at the guns was increased by the fact that in wet weather almost every round fired had to be carefully cleaned by hand. Where it was possible the men at the guns were relieved occasionally by detachments from the waggon lines, but as the casualties became heavy this was found more difficult. The large batch of reinforcements which arrived from the Artillery Reserve Depôt in England, late in September, relieved the situation to a certain extent, but within a week or two the constant toll of casualties had again seriously reduced the strength of every battery.

The 3rd Battery suffered a higher percentage of casualties than any other unit in the Divisional Artillery; the total of killed and wounded being about eighty, including seven officers. As the number at the guns was normally about forty, this meant that the entire gun strength was casualtied twice over. Captain C. V. Leeming, who commanded the battery when it went into the Somme fighting, was wounded on September 30th, and Captain C. Carrington, who subsequently assumed command of the battery, was himself fatally wounded on October 8th. For the remainder of the fighting on the Somme the Battery was commanded by Lieutenant O. Opie.

The strain of the continuous firing was found to be very severe on the guns, and in addition to the number that were destroyed or put out of action by hostile shell fire, guns had constantly to be sent to the Ordnance Workshops for repairs, especially after any periods of particular activity. Buffer springs were a constant source of trouble, and as batteries did not carry spare springs, which they could have fitted themselves, a gun would have to be sent to Ordnance to have the springs renewed, and so be out of the firing line for three or four days.

Divisional Ammunition Column and battery drivers had an unenviable time; on the terrible roads nearly all night and every night with jaded horses that had reached the point of exhaustion, they had to squeeze through the traffic blocks, run the gauntlet of the shelling, and by some sixth sense find their way across the black waste of shell-holes and broken trenches to their own particular battery. Often they made two and sometimes three trips from more or less forward dumps to which they carted ammunition by waggon in the daytime. From the time the New Zealand Infantry left the Somme rumours were constantly circulated that the artillery were about to the relieved; but the dashing of these successive hopes in no way deterred the men, who retained their cheerful spirits until at last thy marched out muddy, verminous, and a good deal ragged, but quite satisfied.

CHAPTER III.

FLEURBAIX.

Two days after the Artillery withdrew from the Somme, Major J. M. Richmond, Brigade Major of the Divisional Artillery, proceeded by car to Sailly to make arrangements for the relief of the artillery of the 5th Australian Division, then supporting the New Zealand Infantry, which was by this time established in the line at Fleurbaix, on the right of the 2nd Anzac Corps, which was then in the Second Army. Units remained a day or two in their billeting areas at Bonnay and Corbie before setting out on the road, and spent most of the time endeavouring to get rid of the accumulated mud. A number of horses were evacuated on account of their extremely poor condition, and more had to be evacuated after the first stage of the journey to Sailly, the whole of which was done on the road by easy stages. The days were drawing in, and the weather was cold with a good deal of rain, and, as a consequence, the trek was attended with some discomfort. On the second day's march two brigades, which were to be billeted for the night at Amplier had to wait for several hours in the rain after reaching their destination, owing to the difficulty which was experienced in negotiating the only entrance to the lines, which were in such bad condition that the iron shelter huts in which the men were billeted stood out like islands in a sea of mud. On reaching their billeting areas behind Estaires, brigades and the D.A.C. rested for a day or two, after which on the nights of the 7th-8th and 8th-9th November, three brigades took over positions at Fleurbaix from the 5th Australian Divisional Artillery. The 2nd Brigade No. 3 Section D.A.C. and "X" Battery Trench Mortars went back to Armentieres where they relieved the 13th Australian Field Artillery Brigade in what was known as "Franks' Force," holding the left sector of the front occupied by the 2nd Anzac Corps.

The brigades which went into Fleurbaix were formed into two groups. The right group comprised the 1st Brigade and one battery of the 4th Brigade (the 8th) under Lieut.-Colonel Symon, and the left group comprised the 3rd Brigade, with the 10th and 14th Batteries of the 4th Brigade, under Lieut.-Colonel Standish. Most of the pits were in fairly good condition; but the season had been wet for some time, and the roads even were under water in places when the batteries marched in, so that a great deal of work required to be done to drain the pits of the water which seeped into them from the saturated ground, and generally to put them into a more workable condition. Where the pits could not be drained by ordinary methods, a sump hole dug in a corner collected the water which was then baled or pumped out. The sector was a fairly quiet one, however, and there was plenty of time to be devoted to the improvement of conditions in both the gun-pits and the men's shelters. Many of the latter were in half-ruined farm houses which stood near—by the positions, and it was possible in these cases to do a great deal to make them more comfortable. Some of the batteries had their waggon lines as much as seven or eight miles in rear, but this was not a matter of such consequence, in view of the good condition of the roads, and the small demands made on transport for the cartage of ammunition. The state of the different waggon lines naturally varied a good deal; but though some of them were in very exposed positions, and the approaches were axle deep in mud, a few week's work wrought wonders.

The cold weather, and the not over-generous horse ration, made it difficult to effect anything but the most gradual improvement in the condition of the horses, many of them indeed never fully recovering from their gruelling experiences on the Somme. Advantage was taken of every opportunity for grazing, and units themselves bought straw and cut it into chaff to supplement the ration; but it was an uphill fight. As at the guns the men at the waggon lines were able to make themselves comfortable enough, and everyone rapidly recovered from any ill-effects of the hard campaigning. New issues of clothes were made available, and the Divisional baths at Estaires provided facilities for the first thorough bath and change of underclothing that had been enjoyed since leaving Armentieres months before. Estaires, seven or eight miles behind the line, was a busy little market town to which the country people came weekly with their eggs and produce, but it was the only place within striking distance of the line that had any pretensions to cleanliness or comfort. Sailly, through which passed a great deal of the traffic to and from the line, was nearer at hand, but it boasted nothing better than a few frowsy-looking estaminets. Fleurbaix, yet nearer to the trenches, was almost in ruins, but even there one or two purveyors of "eggs and chips" still valiantly hung out their signs. A good many of the men walked across to Armentieres to renew acquaintances they had formed there, but the practice ceased when the town was put out of bounds for men not in possession of a pass.

On taking over the sector it was notified that the ammunition alowance for the period 7th to 17th November would total only 5,500 rounds for the 18-prs. and 2,300 rounds for the 4.5in. howitzers. The two medium trench mortar batteries and the one heavy mortar on the front were, for a while, the principal mediums of activity. In six days they fired over 800 rounds, including 280 rounds for a raid by the Rifle Brigade. This raid was supported by the Left Group Artillery and the trench mortars, which made a clean job of cutting the wire; but on the raiders entering the trenches they were found to be empty. During the whole month the trench mortars continued very active, and besides engaging strong points and other features in the enemy trench system, cut a lot of wire. In one day over 400 rounds were fired into the "Sugar Loaf" salient, doing considerable damage to the trenches and wire. In the early days of December hostile shelling showed something of an increase. At 5.15 p.m. on December 10th portion of the trenches came under heavy shelling, the bombardment being principally directed on Devon Avenue and Abbot's Lane, and a minute or two later the infantry sent up an S.O.S. rocket. Batteries promptly opened fire and frustrated an attempt to raid.

On December 20th, and for a few days following, the guns on both sides of the line were fairly busy; but on Christmas Day, which was cold and bleak, the enemy gunners remained silent, thought the New Zealand batteries carried out a special programme of shooting during the afternoon and evening. It was related that the enemy had sprung a surprise on the troops in line on the sector on the evening of Christmas, 1915, and possibly this activity was designed to provide against a similar occurrence. One day at the front is very much like another, and the only thing that outwardly marked this day as in any way different from the others was the provision of unlimited quantities of the traditional Christmas cheer. The material for these elaborate "spreads" was obtained almost entirely from farms in the back areas, where there was tremendous mortality among the cackling flocks, and from the Expeditionary Force canteens. It can hardly have been said to have been a "happy" Christmas; but at any rate everyone made the best of the untoward circumstances. The remainder of the month was uneventful enough, and batteries marked the passing of the year by a combined shoot on the enemy's roads and communications on the night of 31st December-1st January.

The most severe weather of the season was not experienced until after the New Year. Snow fell early in January, not a heavy fall, but sufficient to cover the ground lightly, and increase everyone's appreciation of the leather and sheepskin waistcoats which were being issued. A hard frost set in immediately after, and the weather continuing cold and dry it was many weeks before the snow had entirely disappeared. The long nights were bitterly cold, and even on the brightest days the cold and watery-looking sun had hardly vigour enough in its rays to pierce or scatter the mists that hung over the low-lying countryside. Pools and open ditches were frozen hard, and every clear piece of ice was the rendezvous for bands of skaters or "sliders" who considered themselves quite well repaid for an occasional bump on the head or for skinned elbows. Precautions were taken against the occurrence of trench feet, not unlike frost-bite in its effects, and despite its name, by no means peculiar to men in the trenches. Whale oil was issued, and it was made compulsory to rub the feet with it each day; on such a sector as Fleurbaix, however, Artillery personnel were generally able to keep themselves dry-shod, and to sleep warmly by night, and the occurrence of the complaint was, therefore, rare and regarded with disapproval. There was firewood of sorts to be gathered in the neighbourhood of most battery positions; and almost every shelter and "bivvie" boasted an improvised fireplace of some description. The cold was so intense from the middle of January to the end of February that braziers were set for an hour or so each day in the gun and ammunition pits, as the ammunition was injuriously affected by the extremely low temperature. The presence of the snow on the ground had one other serious effect, and that was to render it easier for the enemy aircraft, which crossed the line almost every day at this period, to detect signs of occupation around the positions. Movement was accordingly reduced to a minimum, but tracks made in the snow in the course of necessary work led to the shelling of at least one battery position. In order to conceal the tell-tale fan-shaped marks made in the snow by the gun-blast, big white sheets were issued, and these were spread in front of the guns after firing.

While at Fleurbaix the Divisional Artillery was subjected to a further and final process of reorganisation which effected big changes in its constitution by the breaking up of one Brigade and the establishment of six-gun batteries in the remaining three. The 4th Brigade was broken up, and its three batteries were apportioned by sections to batteries of the 1st and 3rd Brigades. The 16th (howitzer) Battery, which had been formed and trained in England under the command of Captain J. G. Jeffery, and had just arrived in France at the time, was similarly disposed of. By this means the batteries of the 1st and 3rd Brigades became six-gun units, and the strength of a brigade was increased from 16 to 24 guns and howitzers. The detail of the reorganisation was a follows:—

    8th Battery—Right Section to 3rd Battery, 1st Brigade.
                   Left Section to 1st Battery, 1st Brigade.

    10th Battery—Right Section to 13th Battery, 3rd Brigade.
                   Left Section to 7th Battery, 1st Brigade.

14th Battery—Right Section to 11th Battery, 3rd Brigade.
Left Section to 12th Battery, 3rd Brigade.
16th (howitzer) Battery—Right Section to 4th (howitzer), 3rd Brigade.
Left Section to 15th Battery, 1st Brigade.

It was not until the end of March that the batteries of the 2nd Brigade were brought up to six-gun strength by the absorption of three 18-pr. sections and one 4.5in. howitzer section, which were formed at the Reserve Depôt at Aldershot, and were composed of reinforcements, and men who had joined the depôt on discharge from hospital.

The Left Group, consisting of the 11th, 12th, 13th, and 4th (howitzer) Batteries of the 3rd Brigade, carried out this reorganisation on January 20th. With the exception of the 11th Battery, which moved to the 14th Battery position, no changes of position were involved. Two days later the change was effected in the Right Group, which comprised the 1st, 3rd, 7th, and 15th (howitzer) Batteries of the 1st Brigade. As a temporary measure and for tactical purposes only, the two sections of the 8th Battery, which were being incorporated in the 1st and 3rd Batteries, were formed into a four-gun battery.

About the same time the 2nd Brigade was made an Army Brigade, and as such came directly under corps for all tactical purposes. The principle of the Army Brigade was that they constituted a mobile Artillery Force, which could be moved conveniently by corps from place to place in the line to strengthen the local artillery or to support operations pending or in progress. Army Brigades were subject to frequent moves, often at very short notice, and the 2nd Brigade was often detached from the Division after becoming an Army Brigade; the most extended absence being in the late autumn when the Division was in the Ypres salient. During this period of nearly four months the brigade occupied a sector on the coast near Nieuport.

An extension of the front occupied by the Division took place on the night of January 26th, the 2nd Infantry Brigade relieving an infantry brigade of the 34th Division. That Division's right artillery brigade was also relieved by the 3rd Brigade, whose positions in turn were taken over by the batteries of the 2nd Brigade. The 2nd Brigade had been relieved in the line at Armentieres by the 8th Australian Field Artillery Brigade on the 18th of the month, and had since been in the reserve area at Doulieu. This was the first occasion on which one brigade had handed its position over to a relieving brigade, and then moved off to relieve another brigade the same night. Everything went smoothly, there was no hostile shelling, and by midnight the reliefs were complete.

About this time artillery activity on both sides of the line was somewhat on the increase, and the enemy commenced to pay a fair amount of attention to the New Zealand batteries; several of them were heavily shelled at various times, but the damage to either guns or personnel was small. Enemy trench mortars also were active, and had frequently to be silenced by the fire of one or other of the batteries. The policy adopted by battery commanders was to locate these mortars as accurately as possible with the assistance of the infantry and to register their position. On word then being received from the infantry or forward observer of the activity of any paticular mortars, neutralising fire was at once supplied. This system worked very well in practice, was prompt in its results, and undoubtedly did much to minimise the effectiveness of hostile trench mortar fire. Infantry activity displayed itself in occasional raiding, these excursions being supported by our guns and mortars with almost uniform success.

On February 14th advance parties of the 285th Brigade, R.F.A., 74th Division, arrived to prepare for the relief of the 1st Brigade. The relief was commenced the same night, one section of each battery being relieved, and was completed the following night, the outgoing sections proceeding to waggon lines at Steenwerck. However, a raid on a big scale had been planned to take place on the 21st of the month, and on the 17th, the 15th (howitzer) Battery, two guns of the 1st Battery, and four guns of the 7th Battery moved back into the line near Bois Grenier to assist in the artillery support for the operation. Commencing at 8 p.m. on February 16th, the Left Group carried out a dummy raid, which consists of all the settings in the way of artillery preparation and support without the raid itself. The enemy barrage came down three minutes after the guns opened; most of his fire, which was directed on to the support trenches, consisted of 15cm. shells. Three batteries of the 152nd Brigade R.F.A. came in for this raid, which was to have been undertaken by the 101st Infantry Brigade, but the infantry action was cancelled.

The raid in force, for which the 1st Brigade guns had returned to the line, took place at 5.35 a.m. on the 21st, and was supported by the whole of the Divisional Artillery in the line, the 285th Brigade, R.F.A., and the 2nd Anzac Corps Heavy Artillery. The raiding party consisted of 18 officers, 500 other ranks of the 2nd Battalion Auckland Regiment, and a party from the 2nd Field Company Engineers. The infantry moved forward in three waves at 30 seconds intervals; the plan being that the first wave should deal with the enemy front line, and the second and third with the supports; the Engineers were to make use of the time during which the trenches were held by demolishing dug-outs, etc. The Right Group 18-prs. and some howitzers of the 285th Brigade created a diversion on the right of the raiders, and the Left Group, specially composed of bateries from the 1st and 3rd Brigades and five trench mortars, created a diversion to their left. The raid was directly supported by thirty-nine 18-prs., ten 4.5in. howitzers, eight trench mortars, and certain guns and howitzers of the 2nd Anzac Heavy Artillery. The barrage came down like a dropped curtain, and was paticularly accurate and even. Severe casualties were inflicted on the enemy and forty-three prisoners were taken. Cease fire was ordered at 6.55 a.m., and the remainder of the day was very quiet. During the progress of the raid a shell landed close to one of the mortars of "Z" Battery, Trench Mortars, killing one and wounding three of the detachment.

Immediately following on this raid the headquarters of the 57th Divisional Artillery took over the sector from the headquarters of the New Zealand Artillery, which then moved to Steenwerck, in view of the pending relief of the 25th Divisional Artillery, in line near Ploegsteert. This relief was completed by the 28th of the month, when the 1st Brigade relieved the 110th Brigade, R.F.A., and the 3rd Brigade relieved the 112th Brigade. In the interval the 1st Brigade had gone to Armentieres to assist in supporting a successful raid by troops of the 3rd Australian Division on trenches in the Pont Ballot salient, east of the town. The batteries had now taken over a sector where they were to be called upon to do a great deal more fighting than had fallen to their lot since returning from the Somme. The winter months had passed uneventfully enough in the performance of the more or less routine tasks which fall to the lot of the guns when the Division is "holding the line." The men had wintered comfortably, as comfort went in such circumstances; there had been nothing to overtax their energies, and they were in remarkably good heart. But the winter had gone; spring was advancing, and bringing with it the promise of big events. Practically from the taking over of the sector at Ploegsteert the days of quiet were gone. At the outset there was a great deal of labour involved in improving, or sometimes rebuilding, the new positions; and then the coming of the dry weather and the long clear days brought a reciprocal activity that grew with the passing of the weeks, and found its climax in the battle of Messines.

A New Zealand Battery in Action near Kansas Farm

Wintry Conditions in the Ypres Salient. An 18 pr. in Action near Zonnebeke [*Official Photo*

Chapter IV.

THE BATTLE OF MESSINES.

For many months, indeed, since the late autumn of 1916, preparations for the attack on the Messines-Wytschaete Ridge had been proceeding steadily and unobtrusively, but in March they were fast reaching such dimensions that concealment was impossible; thenceforward they were pushed on with the utmost rapidity, and with all the resources at command. The railways which served the area had had to be extended, new roads constructed, and provision made for an adequate supply of water, which had to be brought forward by pipe lines from the Kemmel Hills or from sterilising barges on the River Lys. It was a huge constructive scheme, demanding much exhaustive and informed thought, and careful elaboration of multitudinous detail, and to its masterful handling throughout was due the complete success that attended it. The difficulties always attendant upon an enterprise of such magnitude were increased by the fact that the enemy's positions completely overlooked the British lines, and much of the area in rear. To deprive him of this direct observation over practically the whole of the Ypres salient was one of the objectives of this attack, and of the subsequent prolonged struggles, which began at the end of July, for the ridges further north. The launching of the attack on the Messines-Wytschaete Ridge had been fixed for a date early in June, and fully two months before that date all the country-side behind the forward positions was alive with the countless activities which must always precede such an offensive.

On March 15th the Division relieved the 36th Division on the left in the sector from St. Yves Avenue to the Wulverghem-Wytschaete Road, and handed over its sector to the 3rd Australian Division. The artillery relief was conducted on the 16th and 17th of the month. The 1st Brigade went in on the left to the positions vacated by the 153rd Brigade R.F.A., and the 3rd Brigade relieved the 173rd Brigade, R.F.A., and became right brigade. The 13th Battery remained in its old position with four guns, placing the remaining two guns in the position vacated by the 12th Battery. The 4th Battery, which went into the small square wood behind the group of buildings known as the "piggeries," left a section in its old position in the Bois de Boulogne, behind Hyde Park Corner. Batteries quickly settled down and registered their new zones; little offensive shooting being done meanwhile.

Since the beginning of March hostile artillery fire had been on the increase; several battery positions had been engaged, and some ammunition had been destroyed; while on the 8th, the enemy guns had been very active all day, and had destroyed Rutter's Lodge used by the 12th Battery as an observation post. After the Division had settled down in its new sector, this activity increased, and several raiding parties were launched by the enemy in an effort to secure identification. At 3.55 a.m. on March 23rd, the right group fired in response to an S.O.S. call; after heavily shelling the front line the enemy put down a box barrage and raided, but was driven back without obtaining identification. The following morning two enemy parties raided the line on the left goup sector, but both were driven off.

At the beginning of April work was commenced on the construction of battery positions to accommodate the mass of artillery which was to support the attack, and in the laying down of the network of tramways and light railways which were to serve the area for its supplies of ammunition and stores of all descriptions. Forward dumps were established for the provision of material required in construction work, and large working parties, generally a battalion or more in strength, were engaged on the burying of a cable running forward to a control station in rear of the trenches. This cable was buried to a good depth, and proved a tremendous improvement on the old system of ground wires, which could never be properly maintained in the heat of a bombardment. On April 1st the 3rd Brigade was entrusted with the building of ten battery positions. The infantry assisted by providing working parties, and a dump was formed and material issued to the batteries as it was required.

These *magnum opus* positions, as they were styled, had all to be carefully camouflaged, even before work was commenced, so that not the slightest indication of their presence might be observed by the enemy. Usually the site chosen was covered from end to end by great strips of green camouflage netting, and the men toiled under cover of this. Units of the Divisional Artillery constructed twenty-five battery positions on and near Hill 63 and in Ploegsteert Wood, the work being supervised by Major Glendining and Major C. McGilp.

In pursuance of the policy of resting the Division by units, the Artillery Brigades were withdrawn from the line in turn for a period of two weeks, which were spent in training and recreation in the Lumbres area, near St. Omer. By April 6th the 1st Brigade batteries had withdrawn to their waggon lines on relief by the 112th Brigade, R.F.A., and on the 9th the Brigade left on the march to the Lumbres-Tilques area for its period of rest. On the 6th, at midnight, the Division contracted its right, and the front was narrowed down to that on which it was to attack on the 7th of June, and following on the withdrawal of the 1st Brigade the right group, less the 12th Battery (which was temporarily under the tactical command of the C.R.A., 3rd Australian Division), extended its zone to embrace the whole divisional front. During this time one battery of the 112th Brigade was attached to the group. On the 19th and 20th the 3rd Brigade was relieved by the 110th Brigade, R.F.A., and marched out for the rest area on the 22nd. The 110th Brigade was relieved by the 1st Brigade on its return from Lumbres on the 24th. The 3rd Brigade returned from Lumbres on May 7th, but did not go into action until four days later; during this interval the Brigade supplied a daily working party one hundred strong for work on the *magnum opus* positions.

While out of the line batteries carried out a certain amount of training, but a good deal of time was devoted to sport in the way of football competitions, sports meetings, and cross-country races. The men benefited very much by the spell; but in the 1st Brigade the horses returned in rather poor condition, due to the cold weather which had been experienced and the work during training. No interruption in the works in progress had been suffered by the process of spelling the brigades, and once they had returned and settled down again, work went on with renewed energy. Such intense activity in forward areas, the construction of new roads and tramlines, and the growing volume of traffic had all been observed by the enemy from his coign of vantage on the ridge, and his artillery began to display an aggressiveness which was doubtless increased by the heavy shellings to which his own defences were being subjected in growing measure. Battery positions came in for a fair share of this hostile activity, and all through the night of May 5th, until four o'clock of the following morning, the rear areas along the whole front were heavily shelled. Several casualties were suffered at the waggon lines, and a number of horses were killed. At 3.30 a.m. a heavy bombardment was opened up on the front line, followed a little later by S.O.S. rockets along the whole front. All batteries immediately opened fire on the S.O.S. lines, and continued shooting until 4.7 a.m., when reports were received from the liaison officers, and fire was concentrated on the front of the left battalion. An enemy raiding party, which had been observed in No Man's Land, was driven off, and at 4.25 a.m. "All clear" was reported and batteries ceased fire.

On May 13th, the Divisional Artillery Horse Show was held near Westhof Farm; the condition of the teams and vehicles entered in the show was in all respects excellent, and reflected the greatest credit on the drivers, to whose zeal and labour such creditable results were due. The 7th Battery received the cup awarded for the best Battery Transport, and a number of prizes were secured by the sections of the Divisional Ammunition Column.

As the month progressed every day was marked by the most intense activity on the part of the British artillery, heavy and field, and by a corresponding increase in the enemy's retaliatory fire and counter-battery work. Wire cutting was carried out each day on the particular zones allotted to each Brigade, and targets at night included enemy tramways and roads, and places which had been shelled by the heavy artillery during the day; this latter practice was adopted in order to hamper repair work which might be attempted under cover of darkness. In order to secure the greatest degree of perfection in the elaborate and carefully schemed barrage which was to cover the advance there was frequent practice in the firing of creeping barrages, and the imperfections noticeable at the outset, especially in the timing of the lifts, gradually disappeared. The enemy gunners retaliated by shelling the roads and selected areas, and by a great deal of counter-battery work. In reply to a practice barrage carried out on May 25th, Gas Trench and the general neighbourhood of Hill 63 were heavily shelled with 10.5 and 15cm. howitzers. The same areas were shelled on the night of the 26th, and back areas were swept with fire for several hours. We suffered a good many casualties by these bombardments, the progress of work was often seriously hindered, and dumps of ammunition, some of them containing thousands of rounds for the field guns, were blown up; but these were checks not unforeseen that in no way stayed the momentum of events.

Brigadier-General Johnston had moved his headquarters from Steenwerck to Westhof Farm on April 30th, and on the 22nd and 23rd of May forward concentration areas which had been established for all units of the N.Z.F.A. were occupied. The object of these concentration areas was to have the headquarters of each brigade, the limbers, firing battery, and first-line waggons of each battery, and the sections of the D.A.C. grouped forward in a manner that would provide for better tactical and administrative control in the coming advance. Spare horses and men and transport were left at the rear waggon lines.

On the last day in May most of the batteries spent some time cleaning up uncut wire in their zones, and by the end of the day all the wire within wire-cutting range in group zones was reported cut. From 6 a.m. this day onwards fire was maintained continuously, day and night, on all roads, bridges, communication trenches, light railway junctions, and transport halting places on the front. Thus there was no road or approach by which the enemy could transport stores or ammunition, or bring up reliefs for his weary and harassed infantry without being subject to this incessant and destructive fire. What mental and physical agony this meant when prolonged for over a week may readily be conjectured. The enemy guns were very active during the night of June 1, Hyde Park Corner, where there was always much traffic, being persistently shelled. A practice barrage with 75 per cent. of the guns only, was fired on June 2nd, and the same night the German positions in front of Messines were liberally gas-shelled. The weather continued bright and warm, and practice barrages were fired again on the 3rd and 5th. On the 3rd enemy planes were active low down over battery positions and Ploegsteert Wood was heavily shelled; but on the 5th hostile fire was particularly severe and effective. The positions of three batteries of the 311th Brigade, R.F.A., which were attached to "G" Group, were shelled practically all day. About 1,300 rounds of ammunition were destroyed, and the position was almost burnt out. The personnel were withdrawn, but returned at 3 p.m. to take part in the corps practice barrage. Two minutes after this practice barrage started the men of one battery had to evacuate the position, owing to the danger from burning ammunition dumps in rear. All the rations and stores were destroyed, and the exploding ammunition put no fewer than five guns out of action. On the following day "G" Group did not fire as the positions, several of which were very exposed, were still being shelled at intervals, and it was not desired to give them completely away before the attack.

From June 1st the daily expenditure of ammunition had been 150 rounds per gun and howitzer, and this expenditure continued right up to the day of attack. Prior to the assault there was to be no intense bombardment and no departure from what had been for some time the normal and customary procedure in the daily and nightly attention given to the enemy. It was a critical moment in the consummation of the scheme—the hour preceding its tumultuous birth—and anything that might give the vigilant German mind any idea of the hour of the attack was to be rigorously avoided. "It is essential," said the order on the subject, "that there should be no increase or slackening in the rate of fire before zero hour, and that everything should appear normal." Such was the density of the smoke and dust resulting from the ceaseless shelling of the enemy front that the whole countryside was completely hidden from aerial observation. A cessation of fire was in consequence ordered for fifteen minutes each day, to allow aeroplane photographs to be taken.

The assault on the Messines-Wytschaete Ridge was entrusted to the 2nd Army, commanded by General Sir Herbert Plumer, and the front selected for the attack extended from opposite St. Yves to Mt. Sorrell inclusive, a distance of between nine and ten miles. The final objective was the Oostaverne line, running between these two points, and the greatest depth to which it was planned the advance should penetrate was about two miles and a half. The frontage allotted to the 2nd Anzac Corps, in which were the 3rd Australian, New Zealand, and 25th Divisions from right to left, extended from St. Yves to the Wulverghem-Wytschaete Road, and the objectives included the capture of the enemy's guns to the north-east of Messines and towards Oostaverne. For the Corps the attack was divided into two phases. In the first phase it was to attack and capture the Black line, which extended across the rear of Messines, involving of course the taking of Messines by the New Zealand Division in the centre. In the second phase the Corps was to capture the Green or Oostaverne line, which, on the front of the New Zealand Division, was about twelve hundred yards beyond the Black line. The three Divisions in line—3rd Australian, New Zealand, and 25th—were to carry out the first phase, and the second phase was entrusted to the 3rd and 4th Australian Divisions, the latter of which was to pass through the New Zealand and 25th Divisions, and capture the portion of the Green line opposite their front. In the New Zealand Division the 2nd Infantry Brigade, on the left, and the 3rd (Rifle) Brigade attacked side by side.

The projected operation had previously been thoroughly rehearsed by all the attacking troops on a large scale, exact model of the Messines area; and before June 7th arrived every man was perfectly familiar with the part his unit was to play in the battle. The signal for the attack was to be the explosion of a number of heavily-charged mines, which had been prepared during many months of unremitting and dangerous labour. Along the original Second Army front there was a total of twenty-four mines, which had involved the driving of eight thousand yards of galleries. Of this total four mines were outside the front of the attack, and one had been destroyed by the enemy. The remaining nineteen mines, charged with over one million pounds of powerful explosive were to be exploded under the enemy's positions at zero hour.

From first to last the operation in every detail, from the most important to the very minor, was thought out and planned with the most exacting care and, as far as was humanly possible every phase was carried out with clock-work precision. In the scheming of the barrage which preceded the infantry in their advance along the whole Army front no spot which might possibly prove an obstacle to the advance was left untouched. On the front of the New Zealand Division the barrage travelled a depth of less than two thousand yards in just over twenty lifts; so it may literally be said to have swept along in front of the advancing troops. A feature of the barrage in its earlier stages was the active presence of 144 machine guns along the Corps front, 56 of them being on the front of the Division. In addition to heavy guns and howitzers, one hundred and fourteen 18-prs. and thirty-six 4.5in. howitzers covered the Divisional front of 1,500 yards. The 18-prs. were divided into three groups; and there was one group of 4.5in. howitzers. "F" Group consisted of the 1st, 3rd, and 7th Batteries of the 1st Brigade, and A, B, and C Batteries of the 242nd Brigade R.F.A. The three 18-pr. batteries of the 3rd Brigade, the 11th, 12th, and 13th, were grouped with one battery of the 38th Brigade, and three batteries of the 311th Brigade R.F.A.

The system of grouping batteries did not generally affect administration to any extent, while it rendered the tactical handling of the artillery much simpler. Nearly all 18-pr. batteries were used on the creeping barrage, while the howitzer group was allotted special tasks. The standing barrage was generally a heavy gun barrage, although it also included 18-prs., and was laid well back, with the object of frustrating any attempt to bring up reinforcements as well as to keep down the fire of enemy riflemen and machine-gunners.

The last synchronisation of watches before zero hour took place at 9.30 p.m. on the June 6th. During the night the enemy threw over a great quantity of gas shell, chiefly lachrymatory on to Hill 63 and the vicinity. The shelling of battery positions which continued all day was also kept up during the

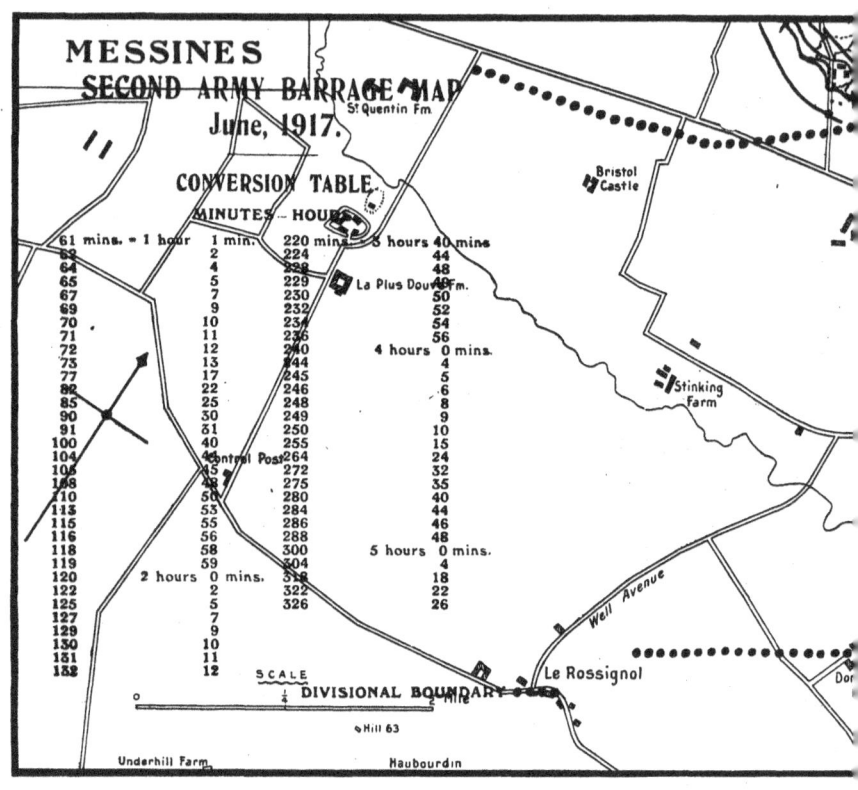

A Good Ex&

The lines between the Divisional Boundaries show the successive "lifts" of
"Black Line," etc

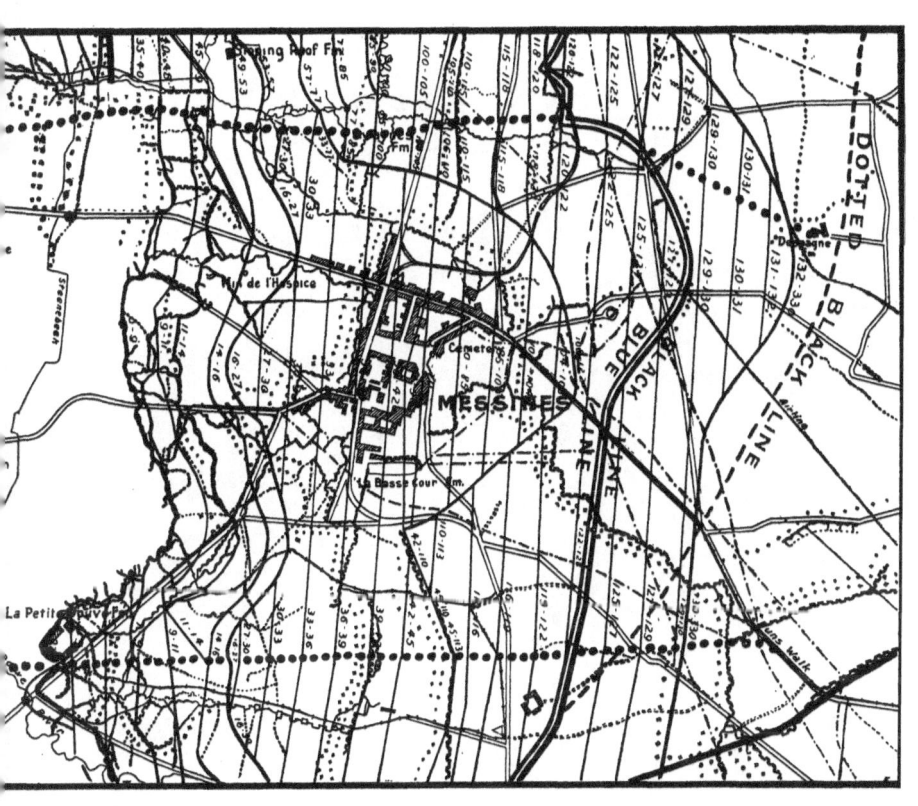

F A BARRAGE MAP

rrage as it moves forward in front of the advancing infantry. The "Blue Line,"
te the various objectives.

night and until 3 a.m.—ten minutes before zero hour. Those last ten minutes passed slowly for everyone, for the infantry awaiting the signal to advance, for the gunners standing ready by their guns, and for those who waited to press the buttons that would explode the mines under the German positions. Four minutes before zero hour a machine gun section opened its barrage prematurely, and then at exactly ten minutes past three the earth quivered and shook as the nineteen mines with their millions of pounds of explosives went up, and at once the barrage came down through the clouds of debris and dust. So dense were these clouds that until the attacking troops, preceded by the barrage, had passed beyond Messines Ridge, nothing could be seen from the observation posts. By 5 a.m., the New Zealand Infantry had captured Messines little opposition having been encountered in the enemy front line trenches.

The barrage was completely effective, and so successful in its purpose of opening a way for the attackers as to extort the highest praise from the infantry commanders. In order to make it as weighty and destructive as possible at the outset of the attack, all 18-prs. employed on the creeping and standing barrages kept one hundred per cent. of their guns firing for three-quarters of an hour after zero. At the expiration of that time every opportunity was taken of briefly resting the guns; but, meanwhile, those guns still in action substantially increased their rate of fire and swept in order that there should be no weakening of the barrage.

After capturing Messines the infantry pushed on, and finally reached the Black line, which was their obejctive for the time being. At this juncture troops of the 1st Infantry Brigade took up the task of establishing this line and the "Black Dotted Line" a little further down the eastern slopes of the ridge; these positions were to serve as the "jumping-off" place for the 4th Australian Division in its attack on the Oostaverne Line, the final objective. Following in the wake of the 2nd Infantry Brigade and the 3rd (Rifle) Brigade, the 1st Brigade troops had established themselves on the Black Line at 5.20 a.m. Stubborn resistance had been encountered at many points, and some light field guns, several machine guns, and many prisoners had been captured. At 8.40 a.m., after a pause of about three hours, the infantry moved forward again, and reached the limit of their advance. The artillery barrage was kept up in front of this line till a few minutes before ten o'clock, when it gradually slackened off and ceased. Shortly after 1 p.m. enemy troops were observed from several points to be massing for a counter-attack, and as they advanced from the vicinity of the Oostaverne Line they were preceded by a heavy barrage. The movement appeared to be general along the whole Divisional front, and the artillery barrage was promptly called for, and stopped the attack before it had time to develop.

The 4th Australian Division's attack on the Oostaverne Line was postponed for two hours, the "new zero" being 3.10 p.m. The final objective was reached about a quarter to four, after which a protective barrage was maintained for a further twenty minutes, and then all batteries reduced their fire to a very slow rate. As soon as word was received that the Oostaverne Line had been taken S.O.S. zones were allotted to each battery by group commanders, and all stood by ready to open fire upon the first sign of a counter-attack. Several S.O.S. calls were received during the early part of the evening, and all were promptly responded to, but it is doubtful if any real need existed for this vast expenditure of ammunition. At 9 p.m. "G" Group received a message from the group forward observing officer with one of the Australian Battalions that the line had been pushed back about three or four hundred yards; but Artillery Headquarters ordered the group to fire on the original S.O.S. line. A second message received by group at 9.20 p.m. stated that the Black Dotted Line was being held by the infantry, but Divisional Artillery Headquarters again ruled that fire should be kept outside the Green Line, as no definite information could be gained on the subject. Incidents of this description were of fairly frequent occurrence during the hours following a battle when communications were severely disorganised, and responsible officers were often obliged to make the most momentous decisions on the most meagre and uncertain information. Whatever doubt existed overnight had vanished by the morning, when the Australians were consolidated on their furthest assigned objectives.

On all other parts of the front the advance had been equally successful, and when time was gained to tally up the prisoners they were found to number over seven thousand; while in material the enemy had lost 67 guns, 94 trench mortars, and 294 machine guns.

During the first phase of the attack the field batteries were practically free from hostile fire. This was not an unusual experience, as it was frequently found that at the outset of an attack the enemy concentrated the heaviest weight of his artillery on barrage work, in his effort to stop the advancing infantry. In this instance, however, there were two other factors at work which undoubtedly had an effect on the situation. The first was that hostile batteries must have suffered heavily from the neutralising fire of our counter-battery guns; and the other was that a number of batteries on the front attacked were withdrawn to the rear. All the indications pointed to the fact that the enemy expected the attack to be pushed further than it actually was. The first hostile fire came from a flank, from the direction of Deulemont and Warneton, at about 9 a.m., principally directed against batteries on Hill 63, where one dump of about 3,000 rounds of ammunition was destroyed, and against Messines.

Groups experienced the usual difficulty in getting accurate and immediate information regarding the trend of events, but considering the difficulties of maintaining communication under such circumstances, much valuable information was received during the day from observing officers who had gone forward with the attacking infantry. Owing to the difficulty of maintaining communication by wire, these observers sent in many of their messages by runner or by carrier pigeon, by both of which methods, of course, messages were, unfortunately, subject to considerable delay.

Elaborate arrangements had, of course, to be made for supplying the enormous quantities of ammunition consumed by the massed batteries for days before and during the attack. It was a big undertaking, on the success of which great issues depended, and the fact that the system of supply never failed at any single point is the highest tribute that can be paid to the organising ability and range of vision displayed in its conception and control. The Divisional Ammunition Column, command of which had passed to Lieut-Colonel N. S. Falla about the end of March, had to supervise the delivery of ammunition to the twenty-five field batteries supporting the Division to the extent of 7,800 rounds per 18-pr. battery, and 6,600 rounds per howitzer battery prior to the attack. The most interesting feature of the system was the manner in which mechanical transport superseded the usual horse-drawn, limbered, and G.S. waggons. The ammunition came in by two broad gauge lines, one running to near Romarin, and the other to Kennabek. From these termini light railway lines ran up the Douve Valley and Ploegsteert Flat to forward dumps, and wooden spurs ran off to the different battery positions. It had originally been intended to use wooden rails in the construction of the light railway lines also, but later it was decided to use 9lb., and then 20lb., and even 40lb. rails.

All the construction work was done by Canadian and South African units, assisted by the New Zealand Pioneer Battalion, which maintained the system after its completion. It was late in the day when the lines were handed over for traffic, and it was imperative that the ammunition should commence to pour in without delay; there was little traction, however, and there were anxious moments when some mishap or breakdown threatened to dislocate the whole service. At one stage, the whole supply was dependent on the working of one petrol light line engine, and with the attack little more than twenty-four hours off another of these engines stopped, owing to a defect in a small but vital part and an officer of the D.A.C. had a midnight gallop to have it repaired. Nor did matters always run smoothly on the broad gauge; one night the second train to arrive failed to stop at the terminus, and ten trucks of ammunition went over the end of the line into a swamp. On occasions, also, enemy aircraft bombed the trains at Bailleul. But despite these mischances, and the destruction of a great quantity of ammunition by hostile shelling after it had been brought forward, supplies were always more than adequate. Between noon of May 31st and noon of June 7th the 18-pr. batteries expended 126,200 rounds, and the 4.5in. howitzers

33,700 rounds; up till noon on June 9th there was expended a further total of 76,000 rounds, of which over 63,000 were fired by the 18-prs.

This method of supply relieved battery transport of a big burden, and meant the saving of a great many horses and mules. A certain number of mules were used for haulage on the lines, and for hauling the ammunition up Hill 63. But the activities of the Divisional Ammunition Column did not end with the feeding of the field batteries; it handled a large proportion of the ammunition for the 6in. howitzers, took up small arm ammunition and bombs by mule-packs as far forward as it was possible to go, and then handed them over to the infantry, and night after night carted wire and stakes and material of all descriptions to within a few hundred yards of the front line.

The three medium trench mortar batteries and the one heavy battery did more than their share of shooting during the weeks preceding the attack; working under conditions of unusual difficulty they carried out a surprisingly big programme of shooting; and the thoroughness with which they dealt with dug-outs, strong points, and other features in the enemy's forward trench system, in addition to cutting great quantities of wire, marked a distinct development in their offensive use. The enemy retaliated strongly with artillery fire, and the mortar batteries were often forced to obtain covering fire from their own field batteries; on occasions, also, they fired under cover of a bombardment from the field guns. Enormous quantities of ammunition were fired away during the fortnight immediately preceding the attack, and the distinction of having achieved the "record" shoot was not lightly regarded by the mortar men themselves. On May 24th, three batteries of medium mortars fired a total of no less than 1,265 rounds; but this was eclipsed a few days later, when three batteries got through a total of 1,950 rounds. The trench mortars fired up to the opening of the attack, and then withdrew to Pont Nieppe.

There was little change in the situation on the 8th of June; throughout the day Messines and the ridge were bombarded by enemy guns from the direction of Warneton; but as Messines was not occupied by the infantry the effects of this shelling were not so serious.   Several S.O.S. calls were received during the afternoon and finally, at approximately 8.30 p.m., a barrage was called for and kept up till about 10 p.m. It was subsequently ascertained that no counter-attack had been delivered. At 9 a.m. on the 9th, the 4th Australian Division assumed command of the front held in advance of the New Zealand Division, which then went into Corps Reserve. At 5 p.m. command of the New Zealand Artillery passed to the C.R.A., 4th Australian Division; Brigadier-General Johnston went to Bailleul, where he remained until the 13th, when he moved to Steenwerck, and again assumed command of the Divisional Artillery. On this day there was an unfortunate and most unusual occurrence, Captain Primmer, New Zealand Veterinary Corps, having been killed by lightning at the Mobile Waggon Line, and seven other ranks injured.

Considerable changes were made in the composition of the groups immediately after the attack. After the capture of the Black Line the 38th Australian Brigade joined "G" Group, and at 4.15 p.m. A., B., and C. Batteries of the 311th Brigade left the group for another command. On the 9th, "F" Group lost the batteries of the 242nd Brigade but next day was joined by the 15th (howitzer) Battery from "H." Group. Batteries of both groups moved forward by the 12th June to positions below Messines, near the Wulverghem-Messines Road, and the mobile waggon lines were moved forward to fresh quarters east of Neuve Eglise.

The 2nd (Army) Brigade.

The 2nd (Army) Brigade was detached from the New Zealand Division for a period of practically three months—from early in March until the middle of June, when the Brigade came once more under the control of New Zealand Divisional Artillery Headquarters. During that period the brigade had been subject to a good many moves, and its batteries had figured in a number of minor operations on different parts of the front from Bois Grenier to Messines. At the beginning of March batteries were in action in rest positions at Fleurbaix, firing only on S.O.S. calls. On the 7th of March the Brigade, with the exception of the 2nd Battery, which remained under the 57th Divisional Artillery Headquarters at Bois Grenier, moved to waggon lines near Steenwerck, and the following day the 5th, 9th, and 6th, Batteries went into action under the 3rd Australian Divisional Artillery to assist in a rolling barrage in support of a raid by troops of that Division on the railway salient at Armentieres on March 13. On the 16th the three batteries returned to positions under the 57th Division for the purpose of assisting in certain minor operations. Little more than a week later, on the 25th of the month, the Brigade withdrew from the line, and went into waggon lines near Steenwerck for purposes of training and reorganisation. The arrival before the end of the month of the three 18-pr. sections and one section of 4.5in howitzers, which had been formed and trained in England, enabled batteries to be brought up to a six-gun standard, and thus completed the establishment of the Divisional Artillery on that principle.

At the beginning of April an operation was carried out on an extended sector running south from Armentieres, by which it was sought to impress the enemy with the belief that the artillery along the front was being strengthened, and possibly that active operations were projected. The method adopted was to move mobile batteries rapidly up and down the front, and to display the greatest possible degree of activity during the brief interval that each position was occupied. In accordance with this plan the 2nd Battery was attached to the 57th Division on the Laventie-Bois Grenier sector, and during the three days over which the operation extended, occupied no less than twelve positions. Each day four positions were occupied with one gun in each, and each gun fired 250 rounds per day. Observation posts were allotted to the battery before the guns were in action, the Divisional Signal Company assisting the battery staff in arranging communication between the "battery" and the observation post. Targets were chiefly roads, tracks, and salient points in trench systems, and the shooting was carried out in a manner that gave the impression that a great deal of registration was taking place. The operation certainly was successful to the extent that it brought down heavy fire on battery positions on the front.

The Brigade remained in waggon lines training and overhauling equipment until April 13th, when a move was made to Neuve Eglise, and parties 200 strong were supplied for work on the tramway system, trench mortar emplacements, and *magnum opus* positions in the neighbourhood of Hill 63. On the 22nd the Brigade returned to the vicinity of Steenwerck; and being again attached to the 57th Division, Brigade Headquarters moved into Armentieres, the 2nd Battery taking up a position at l'Armee, the 9th at Fleurbaix and the 5th and 6th (howitzer) at Houplines. On the nights of 3rd and 4th May the Brigade was relieved in the line by the 7th Australian Brigade, and on the 5th marched out *via* Wallon Cappel to the training area at Lumbres, being inspected *en route* by the G.O.C., 2nd Anzac Corps and the Corps G.O.C., R.A. The field training carried out at Lumbres included a field day with the 11th Australian Infantry Brigade, when operations were conducted somewhat on the lines of a rehearsal for the attack on the Messines Ridge. On the 20th the Brigade marched out for Wallon Cappel, under orders from the 25th Divisional Artillery, and proceeded thence to waggon lines at Bailleul. On May 22nd the Brigade went into positions east of Neuve Eglise. On the 23rd, Brigade Headquarters was installed near Neuve Eglise; the Brigade, less 6th (howitzer) Battery, now forming the nucleus of "C" Group, 25th Divisional Artillery. Mobile waggon lines were established by Dranoutre, the remaining men and horses being left at the lines at Bailleul. Batteries of the Brigade took part in the preparation for the Messines attack, and assisted in the barrage which covered the advance of the infantry of the 25th Division. On the afternoon of the 7th the Brigade moved forward to positions previously reconnoitred on Hill 63, all batteries being in action by 6 p.m. These positions were occupied until the 15th, when batteries moved forward again to emplacements already partly prepared near the old British front line at Seaforth Farm.

This Photograph, showing an artillery driver endeavouring to extricate his [*Official Photo*

St. Yves.

From June 12th onwards, enemy fire on artillery areas and roads began to display a marked increase; and the fact that a good deal of this fire came from opposite the Divisional front showed that the enemy had recovered his confidence, and brought his guns forward again. After the batteries of the Division had settled down in their advanced positions they commenced firing 900 rounds per battery per day on enemy roads and communications behind the Warneton lines in preparation for a further advance, which had been ordered for the evening of June 13th. The artillery were to support the infantry of the New Zealand Divison, which relieved the troops of the 3rd Australian Division in the line on June 12th, in the St. Yves sector. In this operation the line was to be advanced to a depth of 1,500 yards, and as it was not thought that the undertaking would prove particularly difficult, it was to be carried out without any artillery support in the way of a barrage. Late in the afternoon of the 13th, however, information was received that the 25th Division, which was to co-operate on the left, would not advance without artillery support. The New Zealand Division's original plans were adhered to, however, but the attack was only partially successful. The 3rd (Rifle) Brigade reached its objective, but the 2nd Infantry Brigade on the left came under heavy fire from the German artillery, and did not succeed in pushing home the attack.

A second attempt, supported by an artillery barrage, was more successful next evening. The attack was fixed for 7.30 p.m.; but it was after 6 p.m. when the instructions for the creeping barrage were received by Group Headquarters, and battery commanders got their orders from the runners barely in time. Fire died down to normal at 9.30 p.m., but the heavy shelling to which the Messines Ridge and the whole area between the ridge and Wulverghem had been subjected all day went on unabated.

From the 17th of June the amount of harassing fire carried out by the Division was gradually decreased, but hostile shelling of roads and villages and battery positions continued without diminution right to the end of the month; Ploegsteert Village and approaches, and Hyde Park Corner, being shelled at odd times of the day and night; and Neuve Eglise occasionally. On the nights of June 17th and June 18th, the 1st and 3rd Brigades N.Z.F.A., exchanged positions with the 3rd and 6th (Army) Brigades, Australian Field Artillery. The 1st Brigade batteries were in and about Ploegsteert Wood, and the 3rd Brigade batteries were further south, on the right of the Divisional front, the 11th Battery being near Le Bizet. Headquarters of the 3rd Brigade at Tilleul Farm were so heavily shelled on the 19th that a move was made to Grand Rabesque Farm. On account of infantry patrols being close to the River Lys no fire was to be placed west of that river. From June 19th the Divisional front was covered by six brigades of field artillery—the 1st, 2nd, and 3rd New Zealand Brigades, the 175th Brigade R.F.A., and two brigades Australian Field Artillery.

The activities of the artillery were now no more than normal, and the usual routine of events came as something of a relief after the strenuous happenings of the past month; no peace was had, however, from the enemy counter-battery guns, which continued persistently active. Heavy casualties were suffered on the 20th, and the 11th Battery, which was shelled all day, lost five men killed and three wounded. The position was made untenable and a fresh situation was reconnoitred and occupied the following night.

During the shelling on the 20th one section was located in a small cottage, the guns firing through the windows. This building was set on fire as a result of the enemy shelling, and the ammunition stored in the pits exploded and destroyed both guns. Three or four gunners managed to make their escape from the burning and shattered ruin, but the remainder were killed by the explosion. Including those guns which were casualtied during July, the battery had eleven guns put out of action during the fighting along this front, and of that total no less than seven were totally destroyed.

The Artillery covering the front was considerably weakened by the withdrawal on the 25th and 26th of June of the 2nd (Army) Brigade N.Z.F.A., which went out to waggon lines near Steenwerck, and of the 7th Brigade A.F.A. Orders were issued in consequence to decrease fire gradually in the hope that the enemy might do likewise. This policy, however, had not had the desired effect up to the end of the month, when the New Zealand batteries were withdrawn from the line for a brief period of rest. This was in the course of the relief of the New Zealand Division by the 4th Australian Division. The 1st Brigade batteries were relieved by the 10th Australian Brigade, and those of the 3rd Brigade by the 11th Australian Brigade, reliefs being completed by the night of the 1st July. Both brigades and the Divisional Ammunition Column were concentrated at waggon lines in the vicinity of Westhof Farm. Divisional Artillery Headquarters were at Vieux Berquin.

The 3rd Brigade was now commanded by Lieut.-Colonel N. S. Falla, *vice* Lieut.-Colonel Standish, who had proceeded to England on duty. Major Glendining, for the 11th Battery, assumed command of the Divisional Ammunition Column, and the 11th Battery was commanded by Captain J. G. Jeffery.

La Basse Ville.

Although the New Zealand Division did not go into the line again for nearly three weeks, the Artillery remained in rest for little more than a week only. Brief as it was, this period of rest proved beneficial to all ranks. A good deal of time was devoted to recreation, and a combined sports meeting proved a pronounced success. On July 8th the two Brigades, the Divisional Ammunition Column, and the Divisional Trench Mortars, commenced the relief in the line of the 4th Australian Divisional Artillery. Batteries took over the guns, which they had handed over a week earlier to the Australian batteries. On the night of the 16th-17th July the 311th Brigade, R.F.A., went into action on the front, which was then covered by three brigades of field artillery. By the 20th the New Zealand infantry had returned to the line in relief of the 4th Australian Division.

By the time the whole Divison had returned to the line preparations for the third battle of Ypres were so far advanced that the lengthy and careful artillery preparation which was to precede it had already been commenced. Although the enemy had been driven off the Messines-Wytschaete Ridge he could still overlook the Ypres salient from the high ground to the east and south-east, as well as from the Pilckem Ridge to the north. The attempt about to be made to dislodge him from those heights was to constitute the main summer offensive of the British armies, for which the Battle of Messines had been an important and, indeed, indispensable preliminary.

The front involved extended from the River Lys opposite Deulemont northwards to beyond Steenstraat, a distance of over fifteen miles; but the main blow was to be delivered by the Fifth Army on a front of about seven and a half miles, from Zillebeke-Zandvoorde Road to Boesinghe, inclusive. The Second Army, in which the New Zealand Division was still included, covered the right of the Fifth Army; it was required to advance a short distance only, the main idea being so to increase the area threatened by the attack that the enemy would be forced to distribute his strength and his gun-power. The First French Army was to co-operate on the left of the Fifth Army. The New Zealand Division, in the La Basse Ville sector, was on the extreme right of the front affected by the attack, and during the closing days of the month assisted the Second Army in its part in the scheme of operations by local operations, and an apparently significant increase in its artillery activity.

When the artillery first returned to the line the allotment of ammunition for all purposes was reduced to fifty rounds per gun per day for the 18-prs. and thirty-five rounds per day for the howitzers; but on the 21st of July it was raised to 75 rounds per gun and howitzer. Much of this fire was directed against enemy roads and approaches, and bombardments and practice barrages were also carried out. The enemy replied by severely shelling battery areas and bombing back areas by night. The batteries of the 3rd Brigade suffered heavily, and had a number of guns destroyed. The 11th Battery was shelled intermittently over a period of six or seven days; on the 13th it was shelled with 5.9in. and 8in. shells; on the 16th, some hundreds of 8in. shell were put round and about the position; more material damage was inflicted on the 17th, and an ammunition dump was exploded on the 20th; and finally, on the 22nd, the battery was shelled from 1 p.m. till dusk with 11in. shell, the battery in consequence being unable to take part in a practice barrage, which had been ordered for that day. On the 23rd another gun was destroyed and two others were badly damaged and the enemy shelling was so persistent and heavy that the position had to be temporarily evacuated. This battery was the target for a great deal of hostile fire, probably owing to the fact that it was at the time the only 18-pr. battery covering the infantry fronting Frelinghien, the remaining 18-pr. batteries on the divisional sector having moved further to the left, in order to support the attacks on La Basse Ville.

Some idea of the violence of the shelling to which the New Zealand batteries were subjected during the period that followed the Battle of Messines may be gained from the fact that the 15th (howitzer) Battery, which was fortunate to go through both the Battle of the Somme and the Battle of Messines without losing any guns by shell fire, lost a total of eight guns in this manner during the two months following the Battle of Messines.

At 2 a.m. on July 27th troops of the 1st Infantry Brigade attacked La Basse Ville, which had been heavily shelled by the artillery at intervals during the previous week. The infantry attacked under cover of a barrage which the infantry commanders described as entirely satisfactory. The village was captured, but at 5 a.m. the small garrison which had been left in possession was driven out by a strong enemy counterattack. The enemy's counter-battery guns were very active during the operation, and during the remainder of the day the front and support lines were heavily shelled at intervals.

A second attack was launched against La Basse Ville at 3.50 a.m. on the closing day of the month, and enemy posts in front of Warneton were also raided at the same time. Strong opposition was encountered in La Basse Ville, but the place was taken and held, an enemy counter-attack being repulsed. As from the 20th of the month artillery groups had ceased to exist, and tactical control was now by brigades, but for the operation against La Basse Ville a special group commanded by Lieut.- Colonel Symon, was formed of the 1st, 7th, 13th, and 15th (howitzer) Batteries and D Howitzer Battery of the 11th Brigade. Although the barrage was necessarily a thin one, it proved to be sufficient, and captured prisoners testified to its effect. Thirty-two 18-prs supplied the barrage for the minor operation, which was also successfully carried out.

The weather at the beginning of August was bad and the low visibility restricted the activity on both sides of the line, although the enemy gunners continued to devote a fair amount of attention to La Basse Ville. On the 10th the weather improved, and the sector became more lively. Our howitzer batteries commenced to carry out gas shell bombardments, chiefly with asphyxiating shell on selected points, such as suspected headquarters, etc. Retaliation was fairly prompt and in kind, 3rd Brigade Headquarters being twice shelled with poison gas shell on the night of the 13th. Although hostile fire showed a slight decrease during the month the enemy had continued to pay some attention to counter-battery work, and most of the New Zealand batteries had been shelled at one time or another. Though casualties had been light several guns had been destroyed, and the Division had the misfortune of losing one of its ablest battery commanders in the person of Major Horwood. As a sergeant-major in the R.N.Z.A., Major Horwood joined the Expeditionary Force shortly after the outbreak of war, and was commissioned in 1914, just before leaving New Zealand. He rose to the rank of Major, and commanded the 7th Battery, and was recognised as a capable officer and a skilful battery commander. On one occasion during the month also, the enemy shelled the ammunition dump at Romarin, killing one man and wounding five others.

On the night of September 4th the Artillery of the 8th Division, with its attached Army Brigades, commenced to relieve our artillery, following the usual method of relieving one section the first night and the remaining two the following night. Command passed to the C.R.A. of the 8th Division at 10 a.m. on the 6th. The same day units marched to the Morbecque area, *via* Steenwerck, Le Verrier, Vieux Berquin, and La Motte. After three days spent in this area Divisional Artillery Headquarters moved to the Thiembronne area, the 1st Brigade trekked to Flechin, the 3rd Brigade to Estree Blanche, and the D.A.C. to Laires. The trench mortar personnel proceeded in motor lorries to Thiembronne. On the 10th the two brigades and the D.A.C. completed the journey to the Thiembronne area. Little more than a week was spent there in training and recreation, the 19th of the month being devoted to a Divisional Artillery sports meeting near Merck St. Levien; the championship for the highest aggregate of points was secured by the 1st Battery.

On September 14th Lieut.-Colonel Symon proceeded to England for a course in artillery staff work, and on his departure command of the brigade was given to Lieut.-Colonel J. A. Ballard, R.F.A.

On September 20th the whole of the Divisional Artillery left Thiembronne at very short notice, and trekked to Wallon Cappel, the C.R.A. and staff moving to Hazebrouck. The following day the 1st Brigade moved to Boeschepe, and on the 26th the 3rd Brigade and the D.A.C. moved to Busseboom. After having been out of the line for little more than three weeks, orders were now received that the Division was to return to the line, to engage in the struggle which had been desperately raging for two months for the possession of the heights overlooking the salient.

CHAPTER V.

PASSCHENDAELE.

The Third Battle of Ypres had opened on the last day of July, two months before the New Zealand Division was moved into the fighting; but it had not continued without interruption during the whole of that time. On the afternoon of the day on which the first attack was launched rain commenced to fall, continued all night and for the four following days, and speedily transformed the battlefield into a vast morass, in which movement became so limited that a resumption of active operations was impossible until better weather permitted of more freedom and ease of movement underfoot. The slight improvement that took place in the weather towards the middle of August allowed of a second attack being launched on August 16th; but unsettled conditions again followed, and efforts for the remainder of the month were confined to a number of small operations east and north-east of Ypres. Desperate fighting was the rule during September, the enemy's positions having been attacked on a front of eight miles on the 20th of the month and again on the 26th, on a slightly reduced front. The enemy did not abandon the positions that were wrested from him in these attacks without a severe struggle, and his frequent counter-attacks led to fierce fighting; but except at one or two points the attacking troops succeeded in holding on to their gains. Very considerable but costly progress had been made by the end of September; but the enemy was still in possession of the main line of the ridge at many points. The advance was to be renewed on October 4th, when the main effort was to be directed against a front of about seven miles, extending from the Menin road to the Ypres-Staden railway, and preparations for this attack were being completed when the New Zealand Division relieved the 59th Division in the St. Jean sector east of Ypres.

The Division was still in the 2nd Anzac Corps which also included the 3rd Australian Division, and two attached Divisions, the 49th and 66th. In the attack on October 4th the New Zealand Division was to be on the extreme left of the 2nd Army. On its right was the 3rd Australian Division and on its left the 48th Division, XVIII Corps, Fifth Army.

A tragic experience befell the Artillery at the very outset. In accordance with orders received by the Division, both the 1st and 3rd Brigades went into certain positions near Frezenberg; but no sooner had they been occupied than further orders were received for their withdrawal and transfer to new positions south of St. Julien. During the brief interval, however, the locality had been subjected to a continuous and destructive fire, and both brigades suffered heavy losses in men and guns. The opinion that the orders were issued to the Division in error may not have been correct, but it was difficult to conceive of any circumstances by which they could be justified. Headquarters of the Divisional Artillery were established at Watou on the 28th of September, and the same night batteries commenced to go into the positions at Frezenberg in relief of batteries of the 42nd Divisional Artillery, the 1st Brigade relieving the 210th Brigade and the 3rd Brigade the 211th Brigade R.F.A. Batteries came under heavy fire from the moment of taking over, and the losses in men and guns were very severe. The 15th (Howitzer) Battery lost some of its guns, and the 11th Battery lost five guns before the artillery of the 3rd Australian Division relieved both Brigades, guns being exchanged. On withdrawal, a move was made to new positions which had been reconnoitred by Lieut.-Colonel Falla, south of St. Julien and east of the Steenbeek.

The new positions were situated in a locality which was at once innocent of cover or protection, and where the best was very little better than the worst. The whole area occupied by the Division was in a very bad state; it had been devastated by shell fire, and had become water-logged by the heavy rains, and during the early days of the month a tremendous amount of necessary work had to be done in repairing roads, tracks, and bridges, the existing conditions of which very seriously increased the already considerable difficulties of transport. Gas shells were thrown over by the enemy all through the night the batteries went in, and a few casualties were suffered; but there was subsequently not much hostile shelling on the positions and detachments were able to go ahead with the work of constructing gun-pits. As has been remarked, the countryside was completely stripped of natural cover, and in the confined space to which the selection of positions had been limited, there were few features that offered any degree of concealment for the guns. The positions were so close to the line, that in order to escape observation the guns were jammed together, wheel upon wheel, in order to get the shelter of a small hill. The disadvantages of concentrating all the batteries in such a circumscribed area were obvious enough, but it was the only alternative to placing the guns out in the open under the very eyes of the enemy only 800 yards off. The Steenbeek, swollen with the rains, ran in between the batteries, and had to be crossed on bridges of sandbags or any material that could be collected.

In view of the impending attack the trench mortars did not go into the line, and the personnel were attached to the D.A.C., which was concentrating all its energies on the task of co-ordinating arrangements for the supply of ammunition to the guns. It had taken over a dump near the railway at Ypres, and a more forward dump in Oxford Row, near Wieltje. Orders were issued on the 1st October stating the amount of ammunition to be at battery positions by the night of 3rd-4th October, at 960 rounds per gun for the 18-prs, and 760 rounds per howitzer. As the positions continued fairly free from shelling, the task of getting this ammunition up was made much easier, and Battery Commanders were able to register and calibrate their guns. The fact that the registration in some cases was carried out by direct observation from the battery positions will convey some idea of their proximity to the line and of their exposed nature.

Preparations for the attack on the 4th were speedily completed and detailed orders for the work of the artillery in the advance were issued to batteries. In addition to the heavy artillery on the front there was a strong concentration of field artillery. Brigadier-General Johnston had under his command ten brigades of artillery, five of which constituted the Right Main Group, and the remaining five the Left Main Group; in all there was a total of one hundred and eighty 18-prs. and sixty 4.5in. howitzers on a frontage of approximately 2,000 yards. The 1st and 3rd Brigades, N.Z.F.A., formed "E" sub-group in the Left Main Group, and were under the command of Lieut.-Colonel Falla. As the New Zealand Batteries were the most advanced in the group they were ordered not to fire, except for purposes of registration, so that the positions might not be given away prior to the attack. The scheme of artillery support provided for five barrages which were to take the infantry forward, break up counter-attacks, and afford protection after the objectives had been captured, and while they were being consolidated. The first of these barrages consisted of an 18-pr. creeping barrage, behind which the infantry were to advance, and which was to be laid down by 132 guns; a "B" barrage to precede the "A" barrage by a distance of 200 yards, and consisting of 48 18-prs. and 60 4.5in. howitzers; a "C" barrage of 65 machine guns to precede the "B" barrage by 200 yards; a "D" barrage of 6in. howitzers to precede the "C" barrage by 200 yards; and, finally, an "E" barrage made up of 60-prs., 8in., and 9.2in. howitzers to precede the "D" barrage by a similar distance. The "A" barrage was to advance in exact conformity with the infantry, moving as they moved and staying its progress as they reached their objectives, so constituting a constantly protecting wall of fire. It was also arranged that as each battery arrived on its protective barrage in front of each of the two objectives, its left hand gun would fire only smoke shell for five minutes to indicate to the infantry that the protective barrage was being formed.

The task of the Division was divided into two parts—the capture of the "Red Line" sited on the reverse slopes of the Abraham Heights Spur, and the "Blue Line," approximately 800 yards further on, and extending from Kronprinz Farm, through and including Berlin Wood, to near Hamburg. The attack was made by the 1st and 4th Infantry Brigades, with the 2nd Infantry Brigade in reserve. Zero hour was 6 a.m., and though the infantry met with strong opposition all objectives were captured and consolidated. The barrage was good, and counter-attacks were broken up by gun-fire. The Division secured over a thousand prisoners in the attack, and captured about sixty machine guns, besides gaining a deal of very valuable ground which gave excellent observation on to the north end of the Passchendaele Ridge. During the evening after the attack several S.O.S. signals were sent up on the Divisional front, but no serious counter-attack followed. When the sub-group replied to these signals the practice was for the "A" barrage guns to fire on the protective barrage in front of the final objective, and the "B" barrage guns and howitzers, 200 yards beyond it. This fire was continued until the infantry reported "all clear." Throughout the night prior to the attack the enemy shelled the forward areas vigorously, and at 5.15 a.m. he put down a heavy barrage which lasted until about 5.50 a.m. There was not much hostile fire directed on to battery positions, and casualties during the day were not heavy in either brigade. Most of the casualties were caused by a solitary high velocity gun, which fired from the direction of Houlthurst Forest, and directly enfiladed the long line of batteries. Every shot literally raked the position, and the shooting afforded a sufficiently convincing demonstration of true enfilading fire. A good many casualties were suffered, several guns were knocked out, and one or two batteries were temporarily put out of action. The gun fortunately ceased fire towards evening.

On this occasion, at least, the gunners had reason to be rather thankful that the ground on which they fought was so yielding, for the high velocity shells, hurtling in with frightful rapidity, plunged deep into the mud before exploding, and thus were robbed of much of their effectiveness. Had these shells been detonating on hard ground they would have annihilated the whole line of batteries.

The barrage in this attack gave general satisfaction, Brigadier-General C. W. Melville, Commanding 1st Infantry Brigade, reported on it in the following terms:—"The barrage was excellent, and all ranks were full of praise and admiration for it. It was easily followed, and very few shorts were experienced." The Divisional Commander, Major-General A. H. Russell, also congratulated Brigadier-General Johnston on the work of the artillery, which he described as splendid.

The success attained by the New Zealand Division was almost uniform on the whole front of the main attack in spite of strong opposition and the nature of the ground, sodden with the rains of the previous twenty-four hours. The enemy losses were very heavy for, in addition to the troops in the line, three fresh divisions which had been brought up for counter-attack purposes were also engaged in the fighting, and suffered badly at the outset from the barrage fire. These divisions were forming up in readiness for a counter-attack on the positions which had been won in the fighting on September 26th at Zonnebeke and Polygon Wood, but the British advance anticipated this stroke by ten minutes. The success of the day's operations marked a definite step in the development of the advance; it meant that the line had now been established along the main ridge for a distance of nine thousand yards from the starting point near Mount Sorrel.

The eastern approaches to Passchendaele were shelled with gas on the night after the attack, and harassing fire was continued the following day. On the evening of the 5th the New Zealand Division was relieved by the 49th Division, but the Artillery remained in the line under the command of the C.R.A., New Zealand Division. It had become necessary to move the batteries forward in preparation for the next stage of the advance, and positions had been reconnoitred a little east of Winnipeg by Brigadier-General Johnston and Lieut.-Colonel Falla, who had gone forward for that purpose on the 5th. The ground forward was found to be in a terrible condition, however, and it was at once seen that it would be impossible for the batteries to move forward till a road of some description had been made. This work was at once undertaken, and orders were issued for the positions to be prepared in the meantime, and supplies of ammunition sent forward in readiness for their occupation. Packing was, of course, the only possible method of supply, and the Divisional Ammunition Column was detailed to assist battery transport; each 18-pr. position was to be supplied with 600 rounds per gun, and each howitzer position with 450 rounds per howitzer. Rain had fallen again on the night of the 4th, and so bad had the weather become that it seemed as if the heavens and the earth had conspired to stay the forward flow of guns and ammunition. The terribly congested roads were rapidly churned into a condition that rendered them well-nigh impassable. The guns had to be fed, however, and the drivers struggled forward with their packs, at every step encountering obstacles that would have brought despair to all but the most resolute. There was one main road, which ran from Ypres through Wieltje, and on past Kansas Cross to Gravenstafel, and this had to feed the Division for practically all purposes; it had been almost destroyed by shell-fire before the rain, and the traffic had put the finishing touches on it.

On the night of the 4th-5th, two Brigades (the 295th and 296th Brigades, R.F.A.) were withdrawn from the line, leaving eight brigades supporting the divisional front. Following on this the Right Main Group was ordered to move three brigades up to forward positions, and the Left Main Group was ordered to move forward two brigades. An endeavour was to be made to adhere to the principle that at least two-thirds of these guns should always be in action covering the front whilst the moves were in progress. On October the 6th heavy rain fell again, and a visit to the forward areas revealed a most depressing scene; the roads were blocked by heavy howitzers, caterpillars, lorries, and field guns and under the rain and the shelling, men, so coated with mud that they moved with difficulty, were endeavouring to get them forward or off the road out of the way. Dead men and horses lay about; and a hostile long range gun was patiently searching for the battery positions.

The congestion finally became so bad that an absolute *impasse* resulted; and at 6 p.m. the routes forward were closed for a period so that they might be cleared. This expedient did not avail much however, and efforts to get the guns forward failed in almost every case as a result of the condition of the roads, and the blocks on the Wieltje-Gravenstafel and St. Julien-Winnipeg Roads. So many guns became stranded on the way to forward positions that on the evening of the 7th a reorganisation of zones became necessary; the Right Main Group being given one-third of the front to cover, while the Left Main Group (which included the New Zealand Brigades), having all its guns in action, covered the remaining two-thirds. Guns not in action were in every case either completely bogged or else blocked on the road; but wherever possible they were hauled off the road and got into action on the spot.

The heavy rain which fell on October 7th and 8th was not allowed to interfere with the resumption of the attack on October 9th on a front of over six miles, from a point east of Zonnebeke to the junction of the British line with the French north-east of Langemarck. On the left the French continued the attack to a point opposite Draaibank, minor operations being undertaken on the right to the east and south-east of Polygon Wood. The greatest measure of success was attained on the left, near the junction with the French. On the front which the New Zealand batteries assisted in covering, the 49th Division did not achieve substantial results; the assembly for the attack was carried out in cold, drenching rain, and inky darkness, whilst some of the attacking troops were on the march nearly all night, and arrived at the place of assembly only in time to take part in the engagement. As the infantry were held up at different points the advance did not proceed according to timetable; and finally the creeping barrage was stopped and brought back as a standing barrage on about the line of the first objective. Though the weather conditions continued to become steadily worse, orders were at once issued for a renewal of the attack on the 12th, and instructions concerning the artillery support were received by the New Zealand Brigades on the afternoon of the 10th.

Two days after the unsuccessful attack by the 49th Division it was relieved in the line by the New Zealand Division. The 3rd (Rifle) Brigade moved up to La Brique, north-east of Ypres, on the 9th and the following night commenced to go into the line, in company with the 2nd Infantry Brigade, which had been brought up to Ypres by motor 'buses. Meanwhile the weather continued unsettled and more rain fell. Command of the sector passed to the New Zealand Division at 10 a.m. on the 11th.

While this relief was in progress the New Zealand gunners were struggling to get their guns forward from the positions which they had occupied during the attack by the 49th Division. The night before this attack it was decided that an attempt should be made the next day to move the New Zealand batteries forward to a position near the Winnipeg Cross Roads, and instructions were issued by the C.O. Sub-Group that the 13th and 1st Batteries were to make the attempt with two guns, and the 3rd Battery with one gun early on the morning of the 10th. The Engineers and Pioneers had been working steadily on the roads, and had effected some improvement; but the material for their work had to be got up by carrying parties, and the consequent difficulty in getting supplies forward quickly proved a serious handicap. However, at 7 a.m. on the 10th, one gun of the 13th Battery was got out of its pit, and hauled to its new position; at 9 a.m. the 1st Battery succeeded in moving a gun on to the road, and the 13th another. Both, however, became bogged, but the men stuck resolutely to their task, and finally got them into position about 2 p.m. At 3 p.m. two howitzers from the 15th Battery were on the road, but just beyond St. Julien became so badly bogged that they finally had to be left till morning. So much, then, had been accomplished by dint of sheer hard endeavour and under a good deal of fire from enemy light calibre guns. Teams were brought up at 3 o'clock next morning by the 15th Battery, but the road was found to be badly blocked by smashed waggons and other transport, and littered with dead men and horses—the terrible aftermath of the night's shelling. The gunners and drivers redoubled their efforts, extricated the howitzers, and by 7.30 a.m. had dragged them to their new positions by the Winnipeg-Kansas Cross Roads. There was much scattered shelling during the day, and batteries suffered a good many casualties; but by 4 p.m. eight 18-prs. and four 4.5in. howitzers had been placed in their forward positions. Apart from the difficulties of haulage, the constant blocking of the roads by heavy guns caused a great deal of delay, and hung up the transport of ammunition as well as the moving of the guns. Only a small percentage of the guns had been brought forward, and they were without platforms to keep them from sinking in the mud. The situation was distinctly unpromising, but all had been done that was humanly possible in the time and under the conditions. The situation was such, however, that Brigadier-General Johnston, C.R.A. of the New Zealand Division, reported to both the Divisional and Corps Commanders that they could not depend on the artillery for the attack on the following day.

"On Trek" [*Official Photo*

A British Tank Going into Action [*Official Photo*

The Tragedy of October 12th.

The front of attack for the 12th was between the Ypres-Roulers Railway and Houthulst Forest, and the attack was to be made by troops of the Second and Fifth Armies, the latter being on the left. The objectives included Passchendaele Ridge and the village of Passchendaele itself. The New Zealand Division, with the 3rd Australian Division on the right, and the 9th Division of the Fifth Army on the left, was to attack with two Brigades disposed side by side. The two brigades chosen for the attack were the 2nd Infantry Brigade and the 3rd (Rifle) Brigade, the 4th Brigade being in Divisional Reserve. The Division's first objective was the Red Line which extended from the Ravebeek to the left across the Bellevue Spur, and the second objective was the Blue Line one thousand yards further on. When the New Zealand Infantry came into the line on the night of the 10th, there was only a very imperfect and confused understanding as to the general condition of affairs, but reconnaissances that night and early the following morning disclosed the fact that the enemy blockhouses were still intact and the wire uncut. A request was sent in for heavy artillery fire, but the amount of fire supplied entirely failed in its purpose, and another urgent request for heavy artillery fire was sent in on the afternoon of the 11th. Some time later the heavy artillery opened fire on Bellevue Spur, but the fire was of brief duration, and the damage to the enemy defences small.

The assembly of the infantry for the attack commenced at 6.30 p.m. on the 11th and, continuing through the night, was satisfactorily accomplished before daylight on the 12th, despite the darkness and the heavy condition of the ground. Rain held off during the night, but commenced to fall in the early hours of the morning. Zero hour was at 5.25 a.m., and about 5 o'clock the enemy commenced to shell the assembly areas, and a number of casualties was suffered. The attack was met with heavy machine gun fire, though the enemy's barrage was weak; with indomitable courage and tenacity the attackers pushed on until brought up by the pill-boxes and the uncut wire. The attack failed before it had reached the first objective. The artillery barrage proceeded according to programme, until messages were received that the infantry advance was held up, when fire was brought back to the protective barrage for the intermediate objective. At mid-day orders were received by the artillery that a fresh attack would be made at 3 p.m., when the barrage would recommence from a point slightly beyond the line Cemetery-Wolf Farm. But representations were made by responsible infantry commanders as to the inadvisability of attempting to continue the attack; they pointed out the exhausted condition of the men, the heavy casualties, the state of the ground, and the fact that the infantry were so close up under the enemy wire that they could not be extricated during daylight without incurring casualties, thus rendering re-organisation impossible. Fortunately any further effort to advance was abandoned, and at 2.35 p.m. the Artillery were informed that the afternoon operation was cancelled, and orders were received to make the Red Line the S.O.S. line. Fire on S.O.S. lines was called for at 3.50 p.m. and at 6.15 p.m.; no further calls were received during the night.

Very heavy casualties had been suffered by both Brigades of Infantry which took part in the attack; the losses in killed and wounded numbered 2730. Communications were utterly disorganised, the greatest difficulty was experienced in getting rations and water to the men in the forward areas, and the condition of the wounded was pitiable in the extreme. Many lay all night in the mud, exposed to the hail and rain and the bitter cold. On the night of the 12th-13th 1,200 men of the 4th Infantry Brigade, and every spare man from the Artillery and the Army Service Corps were engaged in getting out the wounded, a battalion of the 147th Brigade having been also loaned to the Division for the same purpose. Six or eight men were required to carry a wounded man on a stretcher over that veritable morass, and it took hours for each party to flounder down to the dressing stations.

From the moment the attack opened, the artillery barrage was weak and patchy as a direct result of the conditions under which the guns had to shoot; but this deficiency, though serious in itself, was not the chief factor in the tragic failure. The primary causes of the failure of the attack were the deep and continuous belts of uncut wire which faced the attacking infantry, and the massive concrete blockhouses, or pill-boxes, from which the enemy machine gunners shot down everything that moved. In short, it was lack of preparation. The Division was supported in the attack, in addition to heavy artillery, by eight brigades of field artillery, which totalled one hundred and forty-four 18-prs. and forty-eight 4.5in. howitzers. Some of these were still blocked on the road when the attack opened, and in the case of those that had reached the forward positions, the ground was so soft and water-logged that the guns simply sank up to the axles after the first few shots had been fired, and in some cases before a shot had been fired. The provision of stable platforms is an essential to good shooting at any time; but on the 12th it was only by desperate expedients that guns were kept in action at all. All the New Zealand batteries fired in the barrage; the gunners secured logs, odd bits of timber, anything, in fact, that would provide a foundation, and so contrived to keep their guns in action. The results of the day indicated nothing more clearly so far as the Artillery is concerned, than that if reliance is to be placed upon the adequacy of their support under such conditions provision must be made both for getting the guns forward and for the construction of platforms. The experience gained in the Messines operations in the use of light railways for the supply of ammunition might usefully have been applied in these operations even to a limited extent; besides being economical in point of time and in man-power such a system would have considerably relieved the congestion of traffic on the roads and been the means also of saving the lives of a great many horses.

Despite the fact that the artillery was almost reduced to total immobility and that even movement on foot was a matter of extreme difficulty, orders were actually issued to certain batteries about this time regarding the provision of mobile sections of 18-prs. in readiness to co-operate in case of a rapid advance on the front by cavalry. And this at a time when even unburdened animals became so hopelessly bogged that extrication became impossible and they had to be destroyed. Obviously Corps Headquarters must have possessed a better knowledge of the conditions prevailing in forward areas than such an order would seem to suggest; needless to say the opportunity of assisting the cavalry in a "rapid advance" never arose.

Notwithstanding the adverse conditions with which they had to contend, the shooting of the New Zealand batteries was not allowed to suffer, and careful checking of registration was frequently carried out in order to obviate any risk of inaccurate shooting. Several complaints were made regarding short shooting, however, and on the afternoon of the 14th October reports of "shorts" were received from one of the brigade observers; but it was ascertained that the New Zealand batteries had not been in action at any of the times stated, the officer commanding the sub-group having visited the infantry in the afternoon for the purpose of having the matter cleared up. On the 16th all 18-pr. guns on the Divisional front fired two rounds per gun on the S.O.S. line, and an hour later a report was received that some of the shells had fallen short. Lieut.-Colonel Falla expressed his conviction that none of the batteries of the New Zealand sub-group was responsible, and asked that they should be permitted to fire alone on the same lines. Permission was granted, and the shooting was reported to be quite satisfactory. This test exonerated the batteries from any suspicion of blame; but it also did more in strengthening the confidence of the infantry of the Division in their own Artillery.

At 11 a.m. on the 13th batteries were ordered to reduce fire to thirty rounds per gun every twenty-four hours; but this made matters little easier for the drivers, as supplies of ammunition had to be got up to the forward positions yet to be occupied; it was almost impossible for horses to get into the positions, and the ammunition had often to be dumped at the side of the road and carried to the guns by hand. The decision having been come to that all guns were to be moved forward to the positions near Winnipeg-Kansas Cross Roads with as little delay as possible, a company of New Zealand Pioneers was detailed to help repair the roads and assist in extricating the guns from their positions, and moving them forward. This was on the 15th of the month, but nothing was done towards moving the guns that day, owing to the condition of the roads. On the following day two 18-prs. and three 4.5in. howitzers were brought forward; but on the 17th, when the day was fine and the ground was drying fast, the roads were so heavily shelled that considerable delay was caused, and by the evening rain had set in again. The movement of the guns was continued, however, in the face of almost incredible difficulties. The whole countryside was one vast quagmire, and the roads were little better. The employment of horses was out of the question, as they sank up to their bellies at almost the first step, and some even were submerged and lost in the seemingly bottomless mire. At times even the guns threatened to sink out of sight; and tracks for the wheels had to be contrived from lengths of planking, which were taken up as the guns went on and laid down in front again, so that progress was by short and toilsome stages. The Pioneers, two hundred strong, and the gunners devoted their whole strength to each gun in turn, and it required the united effort of this powerful team to drag the gun along foot by foot. It was a task which only men of powerful physique and great endurance could have faced, and on which the Pioneers expended every ounce of their strength. Their hands became blistered and cut with the wet ropes, and often they were waist-deep in the mud; but they hung on, heaving in unison to the Maori cries of their leader, and very, very gradually the work progressed.

The position by the 20th was that about two-thirds of the New Zealand Artillery had been got up to the forward positions, where the simultaneous packing of ammunition had provided 800 rounds per 18-pr. and 450 rounds per howitzer. During this period the enemy had persistently shelled the whole area with guns of every calibre up to 11in., the shelling being particularly heavy round Spree Farm, Nos. 5 and 6 Tracks, Kansas Cross, and the whole of the Gravenstafel Spur. He had also systematically searched for battery positions, both forward and rear, and had made a favourite target of the Schuler Galleries, where the New Zealand batteries had their control posts. Night bombing of the waggon lines and rear areas had become systematic, whilst the enemy bombing planes had also begun to come boldly over by day, bombing battery positions and the traffic on the crowded roads. At 10 a.m. on the 20th command of the artillery on the Divisional front passed to the C.R.A., 3rd Canadian Division, which was relieving the New Zealand Infantry; command of the Left Main Group passed to Brigadier-General Forman, C.R.A., 49th Division, and Lieut.-Colonel Falla remained in command of the sub-group.

During the six days which elapsed before the Canadian Corps joined in the renewal of the attack, the New Zealand Brigades were occupied in vigorous harassing fire, most of which was carried out at night, and in taking part in preparatory barrages, which were designed to thoroughly sweep the enemy's territory to a considerable depth. Steps were taken to deal with all uncut wire, and vigorous counter-battery work was done along the whole front, the 4th (Howitzer) Battery being attached to a counter-battery group for this purpose. In short, a thorough effort was made to remove the obstacles which had chiefly been responsible for the arrest of the advance on October 12th. The activity of the enemy batteries chiefly found expression in the heavy shelling of battery positions and communications. The attack was launched at 5.45 a.m. on October 26th, on a front extending from the Ypres-Roulers Railway to beyond Poelcappelle, the Canadians attacking on the right on both sides of the Ravebeek, a small stream flowing south-westerly from Passchendaele. On the left bank of the stream they advanced astride the main ridge, and established themselves on the small hill south of Passchendaele; strong resistance was encountered on the Bellevue Spur, however, which was only captured on a second attempt in the afternoon.

The supporting barrage, advancing in lifts of 50 yards every four minutes, went through all its phases till 10.30 a.m. when cease fire was ordered, and at noon the S.O.S. line was given as the line of the protective barrage for the first objective. Hostile fire throughout the day was mostly directed on forward areas, but back areas and battery positions were heavily shelled throughout the night with howitzers of all calibres and high-velocity guns. Batteries were subjected to equally heavy fire practically every night until the next attack on the 30th. On this occasion the front of attack extended from the Ypres-Roulers Railway to the Poelcappelle-Westroosebeke Road. On the right the Canadians continued their advance along the high ground, and reached the outskirts of Passchendaele, but the village was not finally captured until November 6th, some days after the New Zealand batteries had been relieved. Zero hour on the 30th was 5.50 a.m., and the supporting barrage was entirely satisfactory. Fire ceased at

9.10 a.m., but the enemy counter-attacked several times during the day, and S.O.S. calls were answered at 9.45 a.m., 11.30 a.m., and 5 p.m.

On November 1st batteries of the 1st Canadian Divisional Artillery commenced the relief of the New Zealand batteries, taking over the guns as they stood in the pits. The relief was completed the following night, when the personnel of the New Zealand batteries, which had not received any guns in exchange, withdrew to the waggon lines. Both Brigades and the Divisional Ammunition Column moved out for the Watou area at 9.30 a.m. on the 3rd. While the relief was in progress waggon lines were heavily bombed, and casualties to men and horses were suffered, the 15th battery having twenty-six horses killed on the night of the 1st-2nd November.

After the New Zealand Artillery had withdrawn from the line the following letter was received by Major-General Russell, G.O.C. the Division, from Major-General L. J. Lipsett, Commanding 3rd Canadian Division:—"I must thank you very much for the great assistance given to us by your artillery during the Passchendaele battles. They have been very highly spoken of by all our people. They worked hard, and were keen on producing results."

The following letter was also received from Brigadier-General P. A. Mitchell, C.R.A., 3rd Canadian Division:—"Now that the New Zealand Artillery are leaving my command, I wish to place on record my appreciation of the high standard of efficiency maintained by them while they were assisting to cover the offensive operations of the 3rd Canadian Division. In spite of the difficulties of bad weather, and almost impassable roads, they kept their guns in action and their ammunition dumps filled with a regularity which would have been impossible without a high standard of discipline, energy, and efficiency. I should be glad if you would convey my thanks to all officers, N.C.O.'s, gunners, and drivers of the New Zealand Artillery for their gallant and faithful work in trying circumstances."

After spending three days in the Watou area, the artillery marched to the Wallon Cappel area on November 7th. For several days the weather was wet and disagreeable; but both men and horses were thoroughly exhausted after their prolonged and tremendous exertions at Passchendaele, and the rest, despite the unfavourable conditions, was much appreciated. On the 25th of the month both the 1st and 3rd Brigades and the Divisional Ammunition Column marched to waggon lines in the Boeschepe area, under orders of the C.O., 3rd Brigade, moving *via* St. Sylvestre-Cappel. In this area units remained until they received orders to return to the line in the Ypres salient.

The 2nd Brigade at Nieuport.

Three weeks after the battle of Messines the 2nd (Army) Brigade was withdrawn from the front then covered by the New Zealand Division, and concentrated at waggon lines at Le Veau, near Steenwerck. The brigade did not rejoin the Division until the first days of December, 1917, when in company with the 1st and 3rd Brigades it went into the Ypres sector in support of the New Zealand Infantry. During almost the whole of the intervening months the Brigade was in action on the Belgian coast, where, about the end of June, British troops had relieved the French on the sector from St. Georges to the sea. This relief was effected in accordance with an arrangement by which the French should take part in the Third Battle of Ypres, by extending the British flank northwards beyond Boesinghe, on the left of the 5th Army. Though the 2nd Brigade was not in consequence in the fighting at Passchendaele, its experiences on the coast were strenuous enough. The enemy had on the sector a strong concentration of artillery which pursued an extremely aggressive policy during the period from July to mid-November, when the Brigade marched south again. From an artilleryman's point of view the sector was remarkable for the amount of labour which the French had devoted to the construction of strongly-protected, almost shell-proof, battery positions. The New Zealand batteries, however, had to build their own pits, as well as those for half-a-dozen other batteries, and were not afforded the shelter of any of these reinforced positions until a few weeks before their departure.

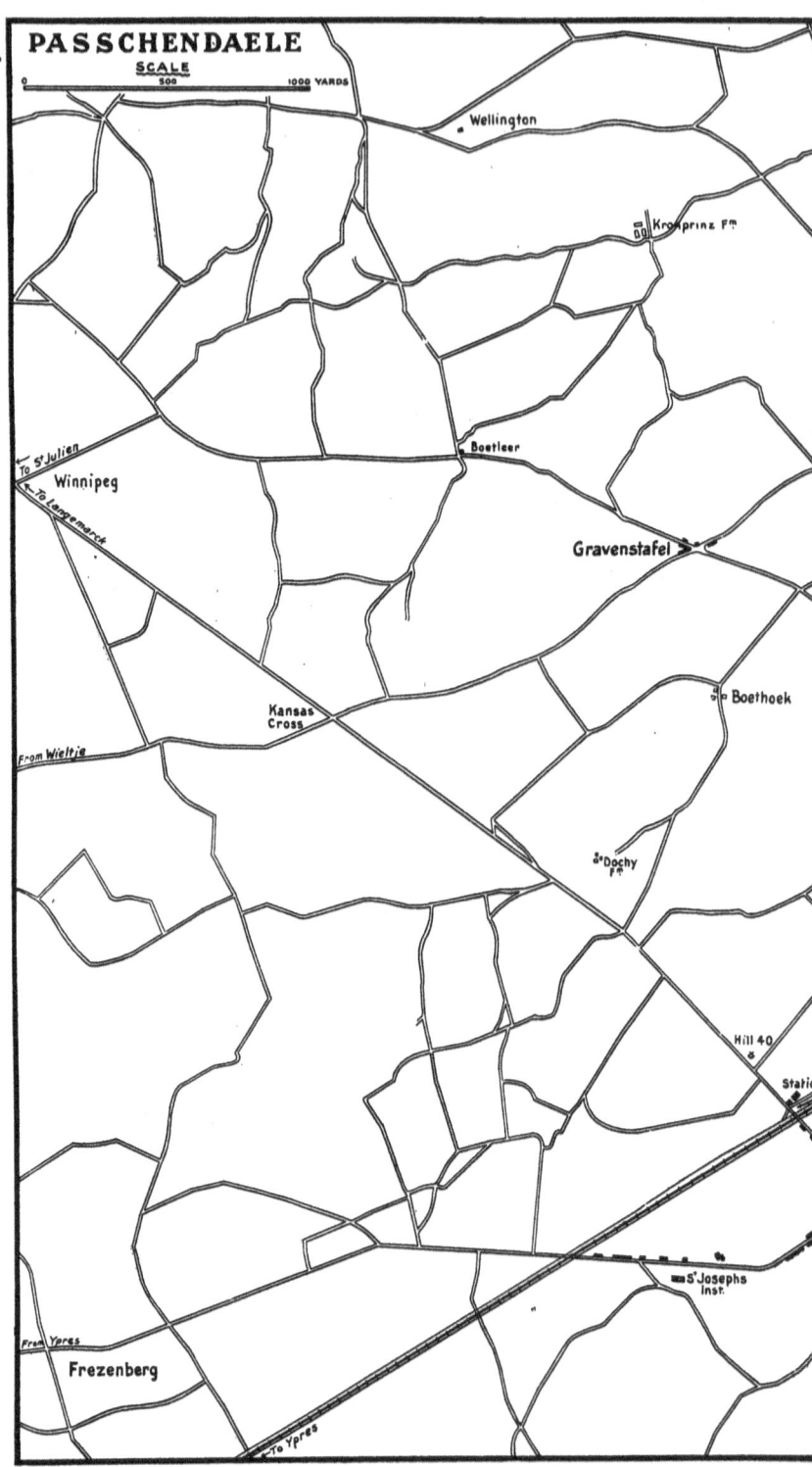

After withdrawing from the line near Messines, on June 26th, batteries spent until 10th July in refitting and general training, after which the Brigade and Brigade Ammunition Column marched off *en route* for the coast, where the brigade was to go into the line near Nieuport, under the 1st Divisional Artillery. The first night was spent in billets in the Staple area, whence the march was continued on successive days to Wormhoudt, Ghyvelde, and finally Coxyde, where waggon lines were established. The long warm days were, in a measure, pleasant enough for trekking; but the midday heat on a dusty road was likely to be trying to both horses and men, and a welcome departure from the ordinary routine was made by travelling in the cool of the early morning. The column was on the road by 4 a.m., and the day's journey was generally completed by 10 or 11 a.m.

On arrival at Coxyde the Brigade learned of the attack which the enemy had made on the British positions on the Yser Canal, near Lombartzyde, a few days previously, and the batteries were ordered to go into the line next day. The positions were situated on the sand dunes, and guns fired across the Yser Canal. Positions were partly prepared, the pits being camouflaged and provided with platforms. A good deal of work was, however, required to render them satisfactory; but the Brigade was unable to concentrate its efforts on the improvement of its own positions. Working parties had to be furnished for the construction of positions for three batteries for the 330th Brigade, R.F.A., which, with the New Zealand batteries, were to compose "C" group. Positions had also to be prepared for three batteries of "E" group, and one battery of "D" group, and the Brigade was occupied with these extra labours for two weeks. There were big concentrations of both British and German artillery along the front, and the liveliest activity was displayed on both sides; the enemy's shelling of battery areas became more and more a feature of his activity, until it gradually came to be regarded as a normal part of the day's events. The flat country afforded very little cover; and by the end of July the brigade had suffered a good many casualties, six other ranks having been killed and two officers and twenty-six other ranks wounded. Batteries had embarked on a policy of harassing and destructive fire, immediately they had completed their registration, and programmes of shooting on these lines were arranged almost every day, the daily allotment of ammunition for this purpose at one stage being 600 rounds per battery.

Ammunition and rations were brought up by the road from Oost Dunkerke, which ran straight towards the line for about two miles, until it reached the canal, providing a perfect enfilade for the enemy guns. It was almost continually under fire from guns of all calibres and, to avoid the shelling, supplies were packed up to the guns by devious routes. Occasionally trainloads of ammunition were taken forward a certain distance and dumps formed, but this was not always possible. Bad weather was experienced in the early part of August, and much discomfort was caused by the heavy rains; the flats became flooded, increasing the difficulties of transport, and the gun-pits in the low-lying dunes were under water for some time. In digging the pits, water was generally struck about two feet below the surface of the ground, and it was accordingly a case of building up rather than digging in. Conditions were not improved by more violent shelling of battery areas. A trial barrage on August 5th, on the opening line of a projected operation in conjunction with the 66th Divisional Artillery, was answered by heavy retaliation; but the only battery which the enemy succeeded in locating was B Battery of the 330th Brigade, where a gun was put out of action, and a number of casualties inflicted. The 6th (Howitzer) Battery experienced a bad day on the 12th, when three of its guns were put out of action, and on the following day Brigade Headquarters and the vicinity were shelled with what were afterwards discovered to be 17in. shells from one of the big coast guns along by Ostend. The brigade's counter-activity took the form of harassing fire programmes and practice barrages in company with other brigades and the destruction of an active hostile battery by the 6th Battery; support was also lent to two projector gas attacks.

At the close of the month the personnel at the guns was withdrawn for rest to the waggon lines, which were situated in particularly pleasant quarters in the sand dunes at Coxyde-les-Bains. During this brief spell all ranks were able to enjoy bathing and football on the beach nearby, which was also used for exercising the horses. The town of La Panne, with some civilian population and open shops, was within easy distance, and was provided with a bathing establishment well equipped, and with an abundance of hot water.

On September 2nd the Brigade went into action again under the 42nd Divisional Artillery at Nieuport Bains, but five days later came under the orders of the 32nd Divisional Artillery, and as the projected operations had been cancelled offensive shooting was reduced to normal limits. The enemy, however, was apparently still fearful of some offensive action on the part of the British forces, and kept his guns aggressively active. Brigade Headquarters and battery positions were shelled both day and night, and on fine nights the congested camps and waggon lines in the back areas were bombed. Emplacements were destroyed and guns damaged, and on one occasion an eleven inch shell demolished the headquarters mess—fortunately unoccupied at the moment. Even some time after the fire of the brigade had been reduced to moderate limits the enemy fiercely retaliated in response to anything that suggested a departure from the normal; and his observing aircraft were always active when conditions permitted. Casualties in the brigade during the month totalled thirty-three.

October, ushered in with broken weather, brought no diminution in the enemy's shelling; "shell storms" or violent bursts of fire on some selected area were of frequent occurrence, and on occasions were of such duration and intensity that the heavy artillery had to be called on for neutralising fire. On October 16th the brigade took part in a bombardment of the Palace Hotel, Westende Bains, the enemy retaliating with a series of shell storms round and about batteries and on the east dunes, causing several casualties in the brigade. During severe shelling on the 8th the 2nd Battery had seven casualties, one of the two who were killed being 2nd Lieutenant T. S. Grant, who had only that day joined the unit, after passing through an Officers' Training College in England.

French troops commenced to take over the sector again in November, and on the 17th of that month a brigade of French Field Artillery marched in to relieve the 2nd New Zealand

Brigade. The following day the French batteries conducted their registrations under covering fire from the New Zealand batteries, and on the 20th the relief was complete, and guns were removed to the waggon lines. Some time before this the brigade had received instructions to prepare winter quarters for men and horses; material had been issued and the erection of very fine stables, and the making of dug-outs had almost been completed when the brigade left the sector to rejoin the New Zealand Division. Before its departure from the coast, Lieut.-Colonel F. B. Sykes left the brigade, in order to take command temporarily of the Divisional Artillery, Major R. C. Wickens assuming command of the brigade in his absence.

The column marched out from the waggon lines at Coxyde at 3 a.m. on the 21st, and spent that night in the Ghyvelde area, proceeding the following day to Winnezelle and so to Morbecque. Bad weather was experienced on the march, and conditions were in unpleasant contrast to those experienced on the way to the coast. The movement northwards of so many British troops, and the marching to the coast of the French, threw an enormous amount of traffic on the roads, and also made billeting accommodation both scarce and inferior, while good waggon lines were not to be had. At Morbecque, where the Brigade received orders to rest and carry out training and refitting, the vehicles and horses had to be parked on the roads about the Nieppe Forest. The roads were narrow and edged with deep ditches, which were a danger to the horses, but after strong representations had been made on the subject, permission was obtained to use some open fields as waggon lines. All guns and howitzers were handed into the 2nd Anzac Corps "gun pool" at Reninghelst, necessitating the borrowing of a few 18-prs. and 4.5in. howitzers from a nearby English brigade for training purposes.

On December 5th parties were sent forward to take over the guns of the 3rd Australian Field Artillery Brigade in the line at Ypres, and the following day the Brigade, which was rejoining the New Zealand Division after having been detached for five months, marched by way of Boeschepe to its new waggon lines near Dickebusch.

CHAPTER VI.

WINTERING IN THE SALIENT.

On the night of the 14th-15th November the New Zealand Division relieved the 21st Division in the line at Ypres, on a sector extending from the Reutelbeek, northwards to Noordemdhoek. The Divisional Artillery did not go into the line, but the C.R.A., Brigadier-General Johnston, with his headquarters staff, moved into the Ypres area to take command of the artillery supporting the Division. This command comprised the 3rd Australian Field Artillery Brigade and two Army Brigades R.F.A. The C.R.A. established himself at Chateau Segard, between Ypres and Dickebusch, where the headquarters of the Division was to remain during the winter months. On November 26th the front held by the Division was extended southwards to the Scherriabeek, thus embracing Polderhoek.

The Divisional Trench Mortars, which had accompanied the Division when it first took over the sector, and had since been engaged in preparing positions, assisted in the support of the unsuccessful attack made on Polderhoek Chateau by the New Zealand Infantry on December 3rd,—two days before the New Zealand batteries came on to the front. In this attack the Divisional Trench Mortars used for the first time the 6in. Newton trench mortars with which they had just been equipped. Some 850 rounds were fired, and one mortar was destroyed by hostile shell-fire. On the night of December 5th, the Division was relieved by the 30th Division on that portion of its front south of the Reutelbeek. Four days later the Divisional sector was extended northwards to a point approximately one thousand yards north of Noordemdhoek.

The New Zealand Field Artillery moved into the line in support of their own troops in the first week in December. Batteries being still without guns, the gunners were taken up from Boeschepe in motor lorries, and took over the guns of the artillery then covering the Division. In this manner the 1st

Brigade (less the 15th Battery, which did not go into action until some few days later) relieved the 14th Brigade, R.F.A.; the 2nd (Army) Brigade, which had returned from the Belgian coast at the end of November, relieved the 3rd Australian Field Artillery Brigade; and the 3rd Brigade relieved the 18th Brigade, R.F.A. The relief was completed by December 6th. The Brigades covering the Division were grouped as follows:— "B" Group—2nd Brigade and 52nd Brigade R.F.A., under Lieut.-Colonel Sykes; "C" Group—3rd Brigade, under Lieut.-Colonel Falla; "D" Group—1st Brigade, under Lieut.-Colonel Symon. Headquarters of "B" Group were at the Tuilleries, of "C" Group at Halfway House, and of "D" Group at Hooge Crater.

The prospect of wintering in the salient was faced with the philosophic acceptance of events that becomes a characteristic of the soldier. The men were nearly all quite familiar with the nature of the country, but the scene that unfolded itself as they left the lorries at the Birr Cross Roads, and proceeded on foot to the battery positions, was forbidding in the extreme. The way lay through the country over which the attacking divisions had fought their way in the Third Battle of Ypres, and on every hand the fighting had left its indelible impress. Nothing had been left untouched by the shell storms that had swept up and down and over every inch of the land. The roads, so busy through the long hours of darkness, were deserted by day and were littered on either side with broken waggons and limbers and ambulance carts, and all the wreckage of transport and material that accumulates along a road line during heavy fighting. Batteries of the 1st Brigade were situated about the slopes forward from Hooge Crater; the 9th and 6th (Howitzer) Batteries of the 2nd Brigade were near Glencorse Wood, and the 2nd and 5th, with the 12th Battery of the 3rd Brigade, were on the left of Westhoek; the remaining batteries of the 3rd Brigade, the 11th, 13th, and 4th (howitzer) were very close together near the Westhoek Cross Roads.

Captured German blockhouses situated near the positions were used as battery headquarters and sleeping quarters, but like the gun positions themselves, they were in a very bad condition. Some of them were feet deep in dirt and debris of every description, and even German dead were unearthed in the cleaning-out process, but the blockhouses were tremendously strong and afforded complete protection against anything but a direct hit from a very heavy shell. Few there were indeed who did not feel grateful for their shelter at some time or other as they sat inside and counted the familiar "5.9's," as they poured in on a terrifying crescendo, making the stout walls and even the very earth quake. Their chief weakness lay in the position of the entrance, which faced the line, and on one or two occasions a shell found its way through the door and wiped the inmates out of existence.

Many of the gun positions were in an indescribable condition; the pits were water-logged and innocent of approaches or decent platforms, and were littered about with empty charge cases, and odd piles of ammunition which seemed on the point of sinking out of sight in the mud. Too much could not be expected in an area where a prolonged period of heavy fighting had been followed by persistently bad weather; but improvements were possible, and steps were at once taken to have them effected. Pits were drained, cleaned up, and provided with weather-proof ammunition racks and stable platforms, and splinter-proof sleeping shelters were built for the crews. Before the hard weather came and bound the surface of the earth in its iron grip, nearly all the ammunition lying about the positions had been cleaned up, and most of the charge cases salved; little of the ammunition was used, however, as it was found to have seriously deteriorated by exposure and damp. All this was achieved, not in a day or a week, but after long and patient toil during the short daylight hours, and subject to the interruptions of enemy shelling. An immense amount of salving was done by the Division during these months, and the value of the material and ammunition collected from all parts of the sector ran into very big figures. Every waggon or ration cart that visited the forward areas returned with a load of material of some description, and every man in formed parties marching down from the line carried some small thing back to the "dump," where, in striking letters, was displayed a notice which queried of the passer-by what he had salved that day.

The front offered excellent facilities for observation, but communications were hopelessly inadequate at the outset, and improvements were not effected until the Division had been some considerable time in the sector. Shooting a battery under decent conditions as regards observation and communication has a strong fascination for an observing officer, but it is more exasperating than fascinating when communication is constantly being broken, and orders take minutes to filter through to the battery. At Ypres a message had often to go through four or five stations to reach the guns, and a telephonist had constantly to be on the alert to ensure that another station did not "cut in," and take the wire. Shooting suffered under such conditions, and opportunities for effective fire were frequently lost. It was only after long endurance of these difficulties that buried wires were run to the headquarters of infantry battalions, whence batteries linked up their observation posts with ground wires which were laid on the bottom of the communication trenches or pegged to the sides.

When brigades first established their waggon lines there were no shelters of any description for the horses, and in a great many cases there were not even any standings. The 1st and 3rd Brigades and the D.A.C. were allotted lines in an exposed area, about a mile north-east of Dickebusch, and the 2nd (Army) Brigade and the Brigade Ammunition Column had their lines together somewhat nearer to Dickebusch. With the winter well advanced, and the horses still low in condition after the hardships suffered at Passchendaele, it was imperative that something should be done to provide them with dry standings and shelter from the bitter winds that swept across the open countryside. A number of G.S. waggons were employed carting broken bricks from Ypres, where the ruined and shattered buildings provided an inexhaustible source of supply. These were distributed to units, and standings were gradually provided for the horses, and the approaches to the lines generally improved. The erection of suitable shelters provided a much more difficult task, owing to the difficulty of securing material; timber and roofing iron were to be obtained only in small quantities, and the supply was by no means constant. Parties of men had been sent forward to erect these shelters,

A Depressing Prospect: the Ypres Salient under Snow

[Official Photo

THE WATERING POINT AT LOUVENCOURT [*Official Photo*

while the brigades and the D.A.C. were still at Boeschepe; but the work was always hampered through shortage of materials. By mid-winter most of the horses were under cover, and a good many shelter-huts of the semi-circular standard type had been built for the men; but the winter was practically over before some batteries succeeded in getting their horses under cover. In such cases the animals suffered severely from the exposure, and many of them lost condition; horse-mastership alone could not do what shelter and a more generous ration would have done.

Encouragement was given to every form of sport during the winter, and a variety of amusements and entertainments were promoted to brighten the tedium of existence. Rugby football took pride of place among the sports, and the most fervid enthusiasm was aroused by a series of matches between batteries and brigades in the final of which the 1st Brigade defeated the 3rd Brigade. A Divisional Fifteen was selected after a series of trial matches, and after defeating the Welsh Division's Fifteen at Merville by 14 points to 3 journeyed to Paris, and there defeated a team representative of the French Army. The most popular and successful entertainment ever presented by any party of entertainers from the Division, was the pantomime which was produced on a really elaborate scale in a big marquee near Dickebusch, and attracted crowded "houses" for a lengthy period. At the Artillery lines a commodious recreation hut was erected by the Y.M.C.A. for the use of the artillerymen; its construction was long delayed by the non-arrival of necessary material, and it was not till early in February that it was officially opened by Major-General A. H. Russell. In addition to reading and supper rooms, there was a big hall, in which entertainments ranging from Pierrot shows to debates were held almost every evening.

A Defensive Policy.

By the time the Divisional Artillery had settled down in the Ypres sector the general situation in the West had assumed a very different aspect from that which it had worn a few months earlier. The succession of tremendous events which had culminated in the disappearance of Russia as a factor in the

Allied cause, threatened the most momentous consequences. The bulk of the German Armies on the Russian front were set free, and as early as the beginning of November, 1917, the transfer of divisions to the Western Front had begun, and continued steadily until it became merely a matter of time when the enemy would have a big numerical superiority and a preponderance in guns. The British Army had suffered severely in the desperate fighting of 1917, and required reinforcing and rest and training to enable it to successfully withstand an offensive on the scale projected by the Germans. A defensive policy was adopted; measures were at once undertaken to prepare for a strong and sustained hostile offensive; and only such minor enterprises were undertaken during the winter months as were essential to secure information of the disposition of the German forces holding the line. The difficulty of resting divisions, and of training them in defensive warfare during a period when all available labour was required for the construction of rear line systems of defence, was not lessened by the extension of the British front at the end of January, 1918, when over twenty-eight miles of the French front were taken over by British troops. On the completion of this relief the British Armies held about 125 miles of active front.

In conformity with this altered tactical situation the New Zealand Division began to take thorough measures for the defence of the Divisional sector in the event of an enemy attack on a big scale. A comprehensive defence scheme, dealing with all the probable phases of such an attack, was prepared and issued to units, which immediately set about making such dispositions as were required of them under the scheme. A reserve infantry line was laid out, and the digging of trenches and communication trenches was at once undertaken. The captured "pill-boxes," which were dotted about the slopes, were utilised to the fullest extent in the construction of strong points, and the system was well wired. Reserve artillery positions were selected by each group, and each battery at once set to work on their preparation. Positions were built for six guns, but on completion only one section was to be withdrawn to the rear or reserve positions. The work was done by stages, each in its order of importance. Platforms for the guns were constructed first, then command posts, shelter for the crews, ammunition pits, and, finally, some sort of overhead cover for the guns. The work was, of course, camouflaged as it progressed, and everything possible was done to conceal the positions from observation. Approaches had to be made, and a brigade reserve ammunition dump constructed somewhere in the neighbourhood. Work proceeded slowly owing to the difficulties presented by the ground and the fact that almost all the material for construction had to be salved.

The positions were being constructed on country which had been the scene of desperate fighting, and which was then but a wilderness of shell holes, half filled with water. It was heavy, tedious work, and often as the men dug they found grim reminders of the fighting that had ebbed and flowed on these slopes, in the unburied dead who had gradually sunk into the soft ground or had been half buried by the bursting shells. Always the greatest caution had to be exercised to screen the work from the prying eyes of the German airmen who came over the line on clear days spotting for their batteries or taking photographs. Work on the new positions was frequently suspended owing to hostile shelling in the neighbourhood; their proximity in some cases to the road made them less secure; and the 3rd Brigade reserve dump, which was very close to the plank road that led up to Westhoek, had no sooner been completed than it was seriously damaged by shell fire. Reserve positions were placed in communication with Group or Brigade Headquarters, headquarters of the infantry in the line and forward observation stations, as well as with the main battery position, and after they were occupied by a section of guns an officer always remained in command at the position; though the orders were that the guns were to fire only on S.O.S. call or counter preparation. Counter preparation was one of the measures to be taken in the event of a threatened attack, and was fired only on orders from Divisional Artillery Headquarters. The defence scheme further provided that in the event of an attack penetrating the foremost defensive system the guns at main battery positions would be withdrawn to the reserve positions, whence the fire of the battery would be directed from specially selected and prepared observation posts.

Each brigade maintained four anti-tank guns, which were situated in suitable positions immediately in rear of the support trenches. These guns, which were got forward only with great difficulty, had of course, to be taken from the strength of the 18-pr. batteries in the brigade, as the 13-prs. which were normally used for this purpose were not available in sufficient numbers. It was considered as essential, however, that some provision of this nature should be made to guard against the possible use of tanks in an enemy attack.

Throughout the greater part of December, enemy artillery was continually active. Shooting on the forward areas was mostly from lighter calibre guns, but the battery areas and roads were shelled with heavy howitzers. On the afternoon of December 23rd, the 3rd Battery was heavily shelled with 5.9's, and there was a good deal of shelling on both forward and rear areas on the following day. Warning was issued from Divisional Headquarters that all ranks were to be specially prepared for attacks from the enemy on Christmas Day, but nothing of this nature followed, though the infantry sent up an S.O.S. at 2.45 a.m. Batteries at once opened fire, but after fifteen minutes the situation was reported clear, and firing ceased. During the remainder of the day the enemy's artillery activity was slightly above normal, while the New Zealand batteries contented themselves with firing two concentrations—one at 8 a.m. and another at 5 p.m. Snow fell during the day, just sufficient to lightly cover the ground and give the traditional setting for an Old World Christmas. All did their best to spend the day as suitably as circumstances permitted, and at the waggon lines at any rate the dinners which had been prepared were of a kind and quantity sufficient to tire the appetite of even such trenchermen as sat round the tables that day. The C.R.A. paid brief visits to the waggon lines about mid-day, and spoke a few words to the assembled men.

There was little change in conditions during the remaining days of the month; the enemy continued to shell the roads and battery positions at intervals, and also commenced to use an increased amount of gas. During the night of the 28th-29th the 12th Battery was heavily shelled, and two guns had to be taken out for repairs. The opening days of January saw an

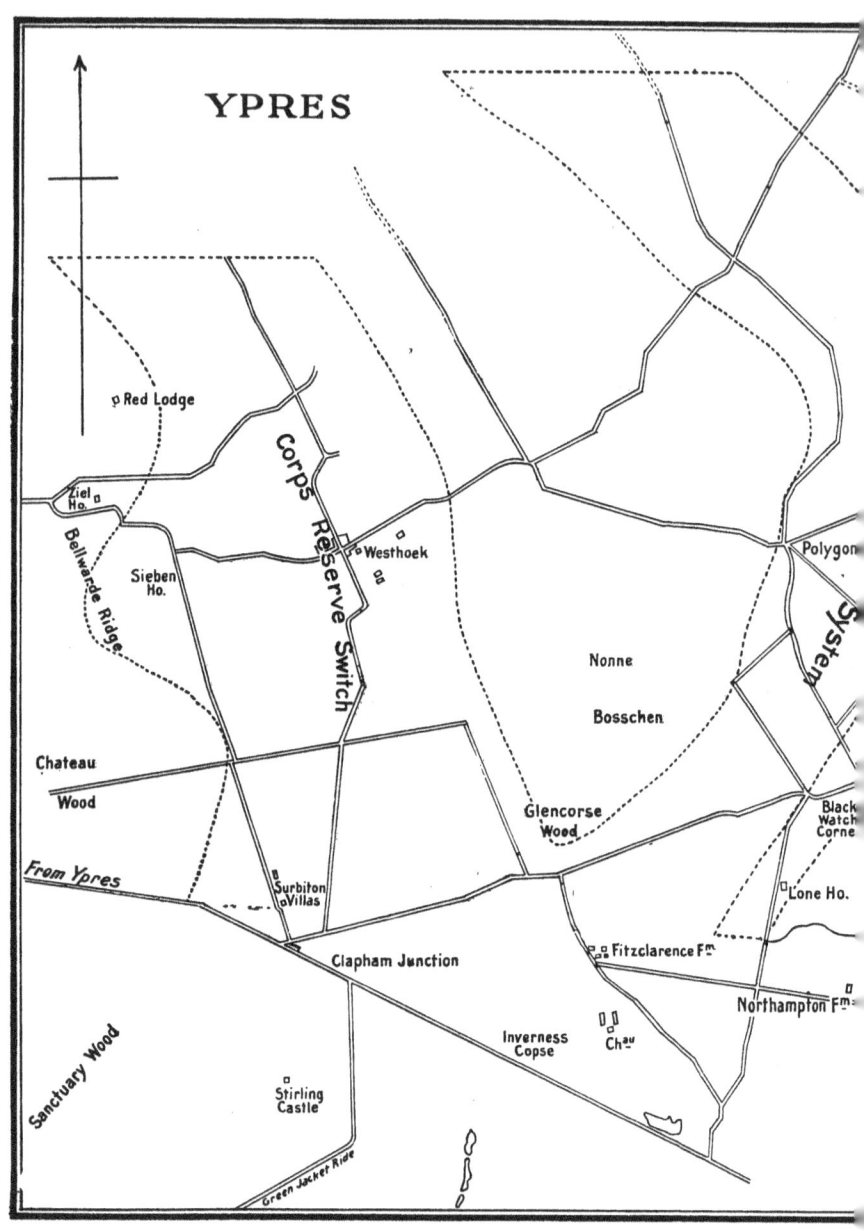

THE SECTOR ON WHICH THE ARTILLERY W

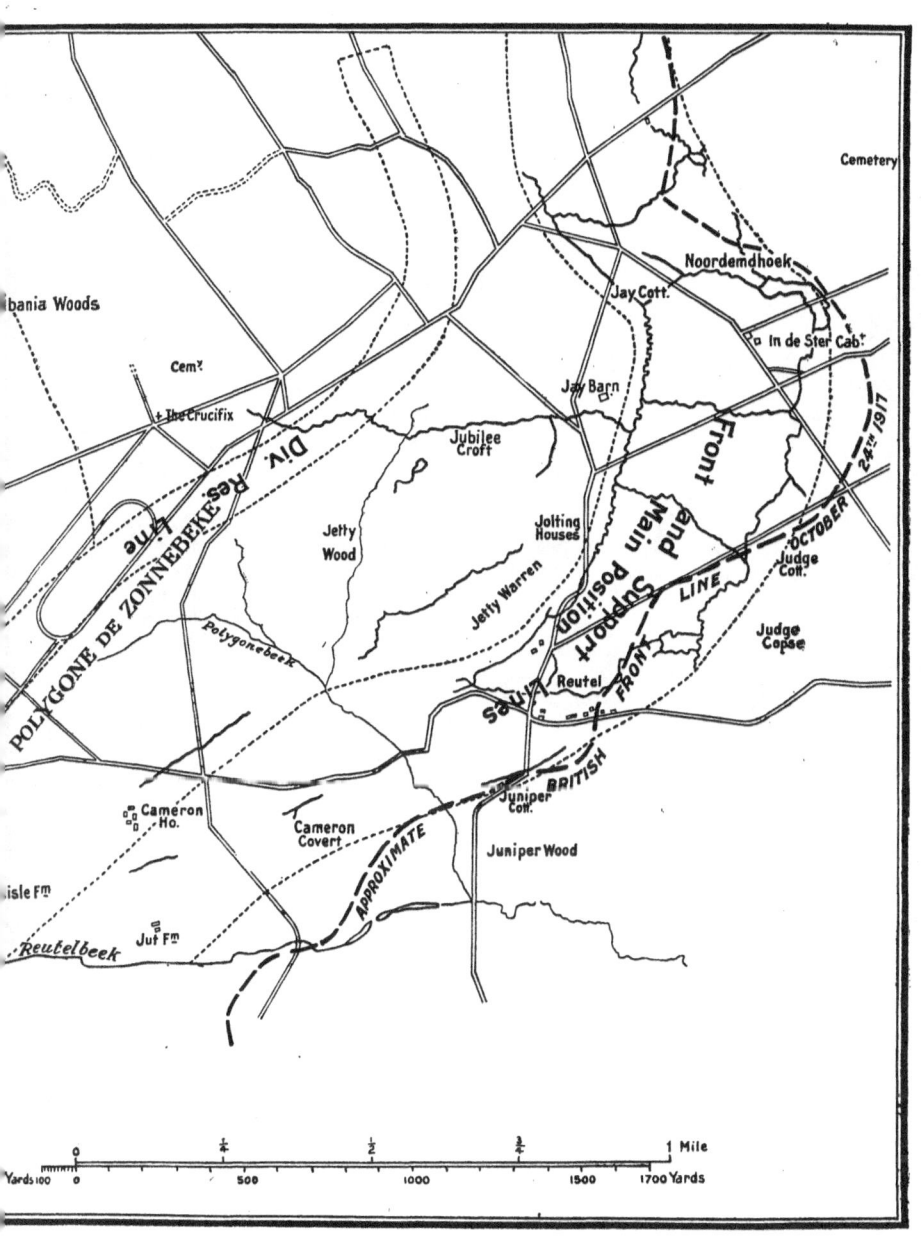

CTION DURING THE WINTER MONTHS OF 1917-18

increase in harassing fire on enemy communications, and shoots on occupied areas were carried out in conjunction with the heavy artillery and machine gunners. This harassing fire was kept up during the whole of the month, and the vigilance of forward observing officers effected a marked reduction in enemy movement during the hours of daylight. Batteries succeeded in stopping an attempted raid on the 22nd January, and the number of dead in front of the enemy's wire the following morning bore witness to the effect of their shooting. A few days earlier a derelict tank which lay in the enemy's lines and was used as a strong-point was successfully engaged by the 6th (howitzer) battery. Direct hits were obtained on the tank very shortly after fire was opened, and some of the enemy who fled across the open were brought down with machine gun fire, while an infantry patrol which went out later reported a number of dead in the tank. Hostile shelling was responsible for a number of casualties at gun positions, one unlucky shot on the night of the 9th January penetrating a dug-out in the 3rd Battery and killing all five occupants. Casualties and material damage were also inflicted at the waggon lines by periodic shelling from a long-range high velocity gun, which searched rear areas as far back as Poperinghe. The lines of the 1st and 3rd Brigades and the D.A.C. were concentrated in a confined area, and must have looked a tempting target to the German aerial observers, while the 2nd (Army) Brigade lines were unpleasantly close to the Engineer's big dump on the railway line at Busseboom. The shelling usually started in the morning and continued on throughout the greater part of the day; a high velocity shell has an unusually disconcerting effect, owing to the frightful suddenness with which it shrieks down out of the sky, and one of these shells could inflict tremendous damage in a crowded horse line. The horses were promptly removed to a flank after the first shell in or near the lines, and were kept out in the open until the shelling had ceased; but casualties to men and horses were frequently suffered before the lines could be cleared.

Events in February followed their course without notable change, except that the much-discussed German offensive was regarded as being increasingly imminent, and every precaution was taken to detect signs of unusual activity behind the enemy lines. When it was ascertained that the trenches opposite the Divisional sector were held by a German division newly transferred from the Eastern Front, it was decided to accord it a reception calculated to increase the disfavour with which these transferred divisions were said to regard service on the Western Front. This took the form of a creeping barrage, fired by the Divisional Artillery in co-operation with the heavy artillery and the guns of the 66th Division on the left. Fire was maintained for forty minutes, and so far as could be judged the results were considered to have been very satisfactory.

The enemy, who invariably made good use of his observation balloons when conditions were favourable, effectively engaged some of the battery positions during this shoot. At the 11th Battery's position he secured a direct hit on one gun just as the battery was firing its last round, completely destroying the gun and killing all five members of the gun crew.

Hostile artillery fire during this period frequently took the form of area shoots, in which a selected area was subjected to a brief, violent burst of fire from one or more batteries; the enemy also sent over a lot of gas shell, especially at night time. The practice in which he indulged of sometimes mixing a percentage of gas with high explosive shells, and so concealing the presence of the gas until it had made itself apparent, occasioned casualties, until the soldiers grew more alert. On one occasion a working party, twenty strong, who were going to Cameron Covert to assist in digging an approach to an observation post for the 2nd Brigade, were all more or less badly gassed in one of these "mixed" shell storms.

Some readjustment of the Divisional sector took place as a result of the withdrawal from the line of the 66th Division, on the left. The New Zealand Division was at the time in the XXII Corps, which held the corps front with three Divisions in line—the 20th, New Zealand, and 66th. On the withdrawal of this latter Division on February 8th, the command of the Cameron Covert sub-sector on the Divisional front passed to the 20th Division, on the right. On the north the Division extended its front for a distance of about one thousand yards, to a point immediately south of Broodseinde.

As reports of abnormal activity behind the enemy's lines had been received, Corps Headquarters ordered counter-preparation to be fired at 5.30 a.m. on the 20th of the month, but the situation remained normal.

Some slight alteration in the disposition of certain batteries was necessitated as a result of the change in the Divisional sector. This chiefly affected the batteries of the 3rd Brigade, which moved individual sections somewhat further north, the 4th (Howitzer) Battery putting a section near the Ypres-Roulers Railway, north of Zonnebeke.

On February 9th the 2nd Brigade had the misfortune to lose one of its battery commanders, in the person of Major V. Rogers, D.S.O., commanding 5th Battery, who was killed by a shell on the road between the Bellewarde Ridge and Westhoek while returning to the guns at night. Major Rogers was a very popular officer, with a lengthy record of service, and the news of his death came as a shock to every artilleryman in the Division. Command of the 5th Battery then passed to Captain P. J. Ellis, who was, however, severely wounded a fortnight later, after which the battery was commanded by Captain W. H. Jones.

Some important changes in commands occurred during the latter half of March. On the 14th Lieut.-Colonel F. B. Sykes, D.S.O., R.A., who had commanded the 2nd Brigade of Artillery since its formation in Gallipoli, left the Division to join the British Army. Lieut.-Colonel Sykes left New Zealand with the Main Body, in command of the 2nd Battery, and fought the battery on Gallipoli, until he was appointed to the command of the newly-formed 2nd Brigade. He possessed a vigorous personality and characteristics which made him a well-known and popular figure in the Artillery. Lieut.-Colonel N. S. Falla was appointed to command the 2nd Brigade, his departure from the 3rd Brigade, which he had up till then commanded, being viewed with regret by all ranks in the Brigade. Major R. S. McQuarrie, commanding 9th Battery, was promoted Lieut.-Colonel, and given command of the 3rd Brigade, command of the 9th Battery passing to Captain F. W. Reed.

Major McQuarrie did not actually assume command of the 3rd Brigade until the eve of its departure for the Somme at the close of the month. In the interval he was given charge of a Divisional Artillery Training School which was established in Scottish Camp, near Poperinghe. Training schools for the various arms had always been maintained in France by the several British Armies, and from time to time a small number of officers and non-commissioned officers from the Divisional Artillery had been despatched to the Artillery School of the Army to which the Division was at the time attached, and there received instruction in the most modern ideas concerning artillery warfare. The establishment of a Divisional School was a new departure. Its career, however, was very brief, as it was closed immediately warning orders came for the move south to the Somme.

On the 24th of February the New Zealand Division (less Artillery), was relieved in the line by the 49th Division, and went back into the Corps Rest Area. The 1st Brigade, N.Z.F.A., remained in the line under the orders of the C.R.A. 49th Division. The 2nd Brigade was relieved by the 245th Brigade R.F.A., but the personnel of the 2nd Battery remained in the line to man anti-tank guns on the Divisional front; the Battery, therefore, did not accompany the 2nd Brigade when it marched on the 27th of the month to Westoutre, under orders from the XXII. Corps.

The 3rd Brigade batteries were relieved by those of the 246th Brigade R.F.A. on February 25th, and withdrew to their waggon lines, only to be ordered into the line again the following day under the tactical control of the 37th Divisional Artillery Headquarters. The orders to move were received without warning shortly before 9 p.m. on the 26th, but despite the fact that the waggons had to be loaded with ammunition, the move was completed very shortly after midnight. All batteries were close to the road which intersected the Menin Road at Hell Fire Corner, and ran in rear of the Halfway House dug-outs. A few days later the 12th Battery withdrew from its position near Hell Fire Corner, and moved its guns to pits near Zillebeke Lake, in relief of a battery of the 213th Brigade, R.F.A., which had gone to the Artillery School at Tilques as demonstration battery. The 11th and 13th Batteries also moved forward a few hundred yards to positions immediately in front of Halfway House. On March 19th the 12th Battery, which had endured a great deal of heavy shelling at Zillebeke, was withdrawn from the 213th Brigade, and rejoined its own brigade, the guns going into action in front of the 11th Battery position.

The enemy displayed marked activity along the whole of the Ypres sector during March. In addition to a small local attack north and south of the Menin Road on the 8th of the month, hostile batteries were persistently active on forward areas, and there was a recrudescence of long range shelling in back areas. Anxiety was felt as to whether the heavy shelling of forward areas might not be the prelude to infantry action, and counter-preparation was ordered and fired in the early morning of the 10th, and on the three following mornings. There were constant alarms during the week that followed, but the tension remained unbroken until on the 21st March intelligence was received that the long-expected German offensive had been launched in the south. Details at first were meagre and, as always, rumours and vague reports of the most varied description sprang to life with a fecundity that is usual at such times. It was soon learnt, however, that the enemy had struck on a very wide front with tremendous weight, and that the situation was one of extreme gravity. On March 22nd Brigades and the D.A.C. were warned to be ready to move, and detailed instructions regarding reliefs were issued.

CHAPTER VII.

THE GERMAN BID FOR AMIENS.

The great German offensive, planned with all the skill of the nation's military leaders, and prepared for with all the vast resources at their disposal, had for months been so unceasingly written of in the English newspaper press, and so long discussed and anticipated in the Army itself, that the anxiety and strain of waiting for this formidable onslaught had become intense. When the offensive was at last launched on the morning of March 21st, it was startling enough in its magnitude and sustained violence, and in the rapidity with which it developed. In its first phase, which may be said to have ended on April 5th, the offensive was directed against the fronts held by the Third and Fifth Armies. The preliminary bombardment opened at 5 a.m. along practically the whole front held by those two Armies, while violent bombardments with gas and high explosive were opened along various other sectors on the British and French fronts. The weather favoured the enemy; a thick white fog obscured the countryside, being so dense in some localities that nothing could be seen, behind the line, of the S.O.S. signals sent up by the British infantry on the opening of the attack. The hour of assault was not everywhere the same, but by 9.45 a.m. the enemy had attacked on a front of fifty-four miles between the Oise and the Sensee Rivers. By noon his infantry had reached the first line of the battle positions in strength on practically the whole front of attack. Fighting continued with the greatest intensity throughout the afternoon and evening, the attack making particularly rapid and serious progress south of St. Quentin.

The enemy exploited his gains on succeeding days; sweeping down north and south of the Somme before reserve divisions could be hurried forward from other parts of the Allied front, he was soon threatening Amiens at comparatively close quarters. On March 26th, the day on which Marshal Foch assumed supreme command of the Allied Armies on the Western Front, the enemy's advance north of the Somme was practically checked. Between Hamel and Puisieux, however, the situation was obscure, and a gap existed between the V. and IV. Corps, through which enemy detachments worked forward and occupied Colincamps.

When the offensive opened on March 21st, the New Zealand Division (less Artillery), was still in XXII. Corps Reserve in the Staple area. Of the three Brigades of Artillery, the 1st and 3rd were in action at Ypres, being attached respectively to the 49th and 37th Divisions; the 2nd (Army) Brigade was in rest at Westoutre. A few hours after the offensive had opened warning orders were received by the Division to be prepared to move south at any hour after midnight on March 22nd, as G.H.Q. Reserve. On the 23rd orders were received directing that the entrainment of the Division (less Artillery) should commence at 2 p.m. on the following day. Owing to the rapidly changing situation orders issued regarding the detraining stations and the area in which the Division was to concentrate on its arrival at its destination, were subject to frequent alteration. Finally, at 1 a.m. on March 25th, orders were received that the detraining stations would be Hangest, Ailly, and St. Roch. Late on the night of the 25th, further and final orders were received from the Third Army for the Division to march by the Hedauville-Mailly-Maillet-Puisieux Road, and fill the gap between Hamel and Puisieux-au-Mont.

The Division was concentrating at Hedauville, where Divisional Headquarters had opened at 1.30 a.m. on March 26th, and as units arrived they were despatched straight into action. Contact was first gained with the enemy about 11 a.m. on March 26th, about five hundred yards east of Auchonvillers. The left flank of the advanced guard found the enemy in superior force, and fresh troops were reported advancing along the Serre Road, but the enemy was at once hotly engaged, and his advance was stayed. As further infantry units arrived a definite line was established, and touch was eventually gained with the troops on each flank, considerable assistance being given in one phase of these operations by a detachment of light tanks, or "whippets," which were being used in action for the first time. It was not until the evening of the 27th March, that the New

Zealand Artillery arrived on the front, and at once went into action in support of their infantry, who in the meantime had been almost without artillery support.

It is now necessary to turn again to Ypres in order to follow the movements of the Divisional Artillery, which, as has been shown, was still in action there when the first news was had of the launching of the smashing German attacks in the south. Warning orders were issued on the 22nd for the 1st and 3rd Brigades to be prepared to move at short notice. The relief of these two brigades was expeditiously carried out, but the stream of troops moving down to the threatened area threw a heavy strain on all transport arrangements, and precious time was lost standing by at the entraining stations waiting the arrival of trains. The 1st and 3rd Brigades were relieved by brigades of Australian Field Artillery on the night 22nd-23rd March, and on the 23rd were busily engaged getting everything in readiness for a move and cleaning up the waggon line areas. Guns requiring overhaul were hastily sent off to Ordnance, and the "sick lines" were cleared by evacuating all animals that were not fit to take their share of work on the march. Marching order parades were held, and kits were cut down to normal limits by calling in the surplus gear and equipment which always accumulated during a lengthy stay in one area.

The 3rd Brigade marched out from its waggon lines for the entraining stations at 9 a.m. on March 24th; Brigade Headquarters and the 4th, 11th, and 12th Batteries marched to Godewaersvelde, and the 13th Battery to Caestre. The 1st Brigade marched out the following day to Hopoutre, but as no trains were available preparations were made to bivouac near the station. At 10 p.m., however, 1st Brigade Headquarters commenced to entrain, and finally moved off at midnight, followed in succession by the 1st, 3rd, and 7th Batteries. The 15th Battery entrained at noon on the 25th. All day on the 25th the 3rd Brigade stood by waiting for trains without result. The night, which was wet, was spent in bivouac and it was finally late in the afternoon on the 26th before entraining was under way. The Divisional Ammunition Column travelled, in small sections, with units of the two brigades.

The train journey occupied about twelve hours, following a somewhat indirect route running north through St. Omer towards the coast, and thence through Calais, Boulogne, Etaples, and Abbeville, to the detraining stations south of Amiens. The 1st Brigade detrained at St. Roch, and the 3rd Brigade at Ailly and Hangest. After watering and feeding the horses the 1st Brigade marched right through to Hedauville, where batteries bivouacked, while the Brigade and Battery Commanders went forward to the vicinity of Mailly-Maillet to reconnoitre positions.

Headquarters of the 3rd Brigade also proceeded direct to Hedauville, but the batteries broke their journey during the night to feed and rest their horses; the 11th, 12th, and 13th stopping at Picquigny, and the 4th Battery at Warloy. After this spell the columns took the road again and marched straight through to Mailly-Maillet. The enemy vigorously bombed Amiens all night, the crash of his heavy bombs punctuating the incessant popping of the anti-aircraft guns. Some of the 1st Brigade batteries, which marched through Amiens during the night, had to run the gauntlet of this bombing, but fortunately escaped without casualties.

Already closely menaced by the German advance from the north and east, and thus violently assailed from the air by night, the inhabitants were fleeing from Amiens, and their numbers swelled the streams of refugees from the villages in the battle zone. The road traversed by the batteries as they went towards Amiens in the early morning presented a pathetic and extraordinary spectacle. Along the broad highway, bordered with lofty poplars, slowly moved an endless stream of women and children and old, old men, all on foot, except for the few, more fortunate, who rode on top of their heavily burdened waggons and country carts. All who were strong enough had contrived to take away some few small possessions which they wheeled in barrows and even perambulators, or carried on their backs. Mostly they trudged through the dust stout-heartedly enough, but others sat wearily by the roadside with hardly the courage to smile, sad fugitives of war, who knew not if ever again they would see their homes. Amiens itself appeared almost deserted, and many of the buildings showed evidences of the severity of the bombing to which the town had been subjected.

The 1st Brigade, less the 15th (Howitzer) Battery, moved up from Mailly-Maillet after 1 p.m. on the 27th, and by 5 p.m. was in action in positions which had been reconnoitred on the northern edge of the village. The 15th Battery went into action the following morning. Officers from the 3rd Brigade batteries arrived at Mailly-Maillet late in the evening of the 27th, and had just sufficient time before dusk to reconnoitre positions which were all to the east of the village, two of them being near the ruins of the railway station. Batteries arrived a little later, and were in action by 11 p.m. Beyond some hostile shelling the night passed uneventfully; but the movement of enemy troops opposite the Divisional front aroused fears of further attacks in the morning, and as an urgent provision batteries and the Divisional Ammunition Column were hard at work getting ammunition up to the guns, the batteries alone bringing up a total of ten thousand rounds during the first twenty-four hours. Harassing fire was maintained on the enemy's forward areas during the night and counter preparation was fired for two hours from 4 a.m. As battery staffs were still occupied during the day in establishing forward communications to infantry headquarters and front line observation posts, most of this shooting was done off the map; but observation showed it to be accurate and effective.

Very good observation was to be had over the enemy's country, and once communications had been laid no time was lost in engaging the splendid targets offered by the German infantry, who showed themselves very freely during the first few days, and could even be seen in bivouacs on the slopes of the ridges behind Beaumont-Hamel. Although the indications were that the enemy had not yet brought up a great weight of artillery, his batteries were very active on the villages and roads behind the Divisional front and on battery areas, and he made free use of captured guns, ranging from 4.5in howitzers and 60-prs. to heavy calibre howitzers. During hostile shelling on the 28th Lieut.-Colonel R. S. McQuarrie was slightly wounded, and command of the 3rd Brigade passed, temporarily, to Major C. Somerville. An unlucky shell the same night destroyed the headquarters of the 3rd (Rifle) Brigade in Colincamps, and killed Brigadier-General Fulton, the Brigade Commander, and his Brigade Major, besides wounding several other officers.

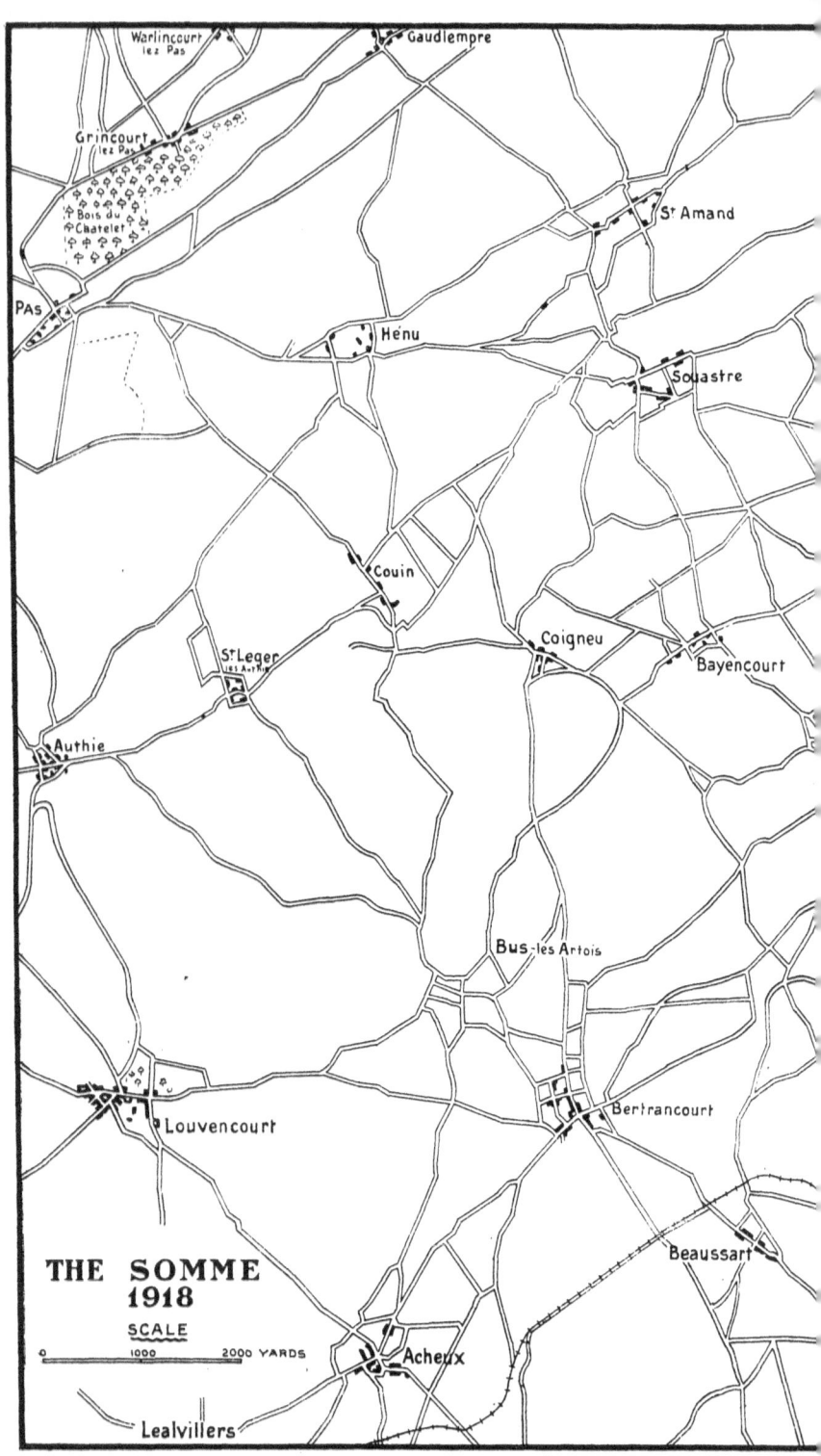

Showing the Sector held by the New Zealand Division aft[er]

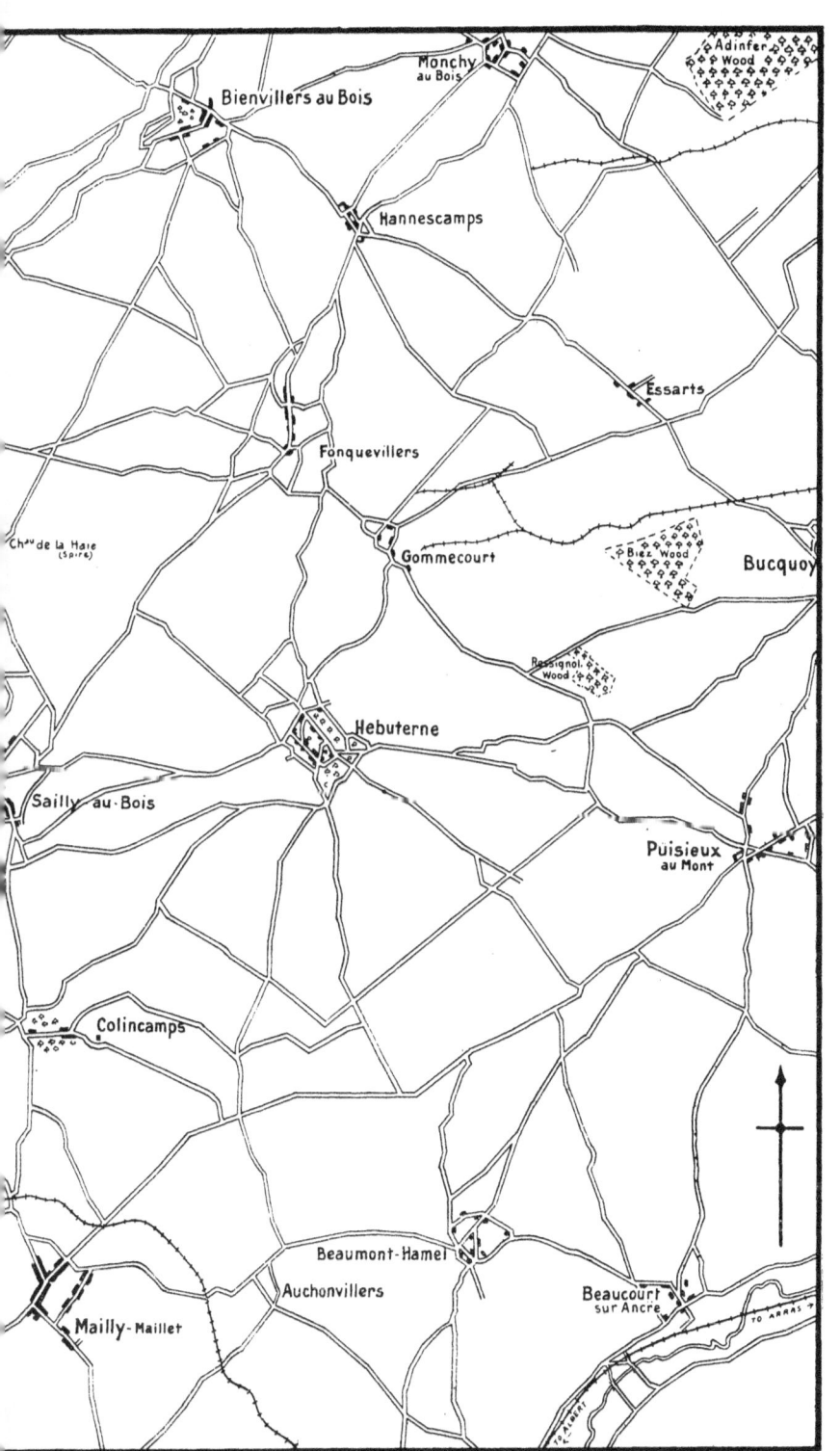

PING TO CHECK THE GERMAN ADVANCE AT THE END OF MARCH, 1918.

On 27th March Divisional Headquarters had moved from Hedauville to the Chateau at Busles-Artois, and the C.R.A. assumed command of the artillery covering the front, consisting of the two New Zealand Brigades, the 25th Divisional Artillery, the 104th (Army) Brigade, R.F.A., the 29th and 90th Brigades, R.G.A., and the 56th Siege Battery. At the beginning of April the 4th Australian Infantry Brigade took over a few hundred yards of line on the left, and a few minutes later the Divisional front was reorganised on a two brigade front, with one brigade in reserve. The 2nd Infantry Brigade remained on the right, and the 3rd (Rifle) Brigade took over on the left from the 1st Infantry Brigade which went into Divisional reserve. The construction of rear defence systems was by this time well forward, the Pioneers in particular, having done an immense amount of digging. These rear defences consisted primarily of a Divisional reserve line, known as the Purple Line, which skirted Forceville on the east and ran in a north-easterly direction past Beaussart and Courcelles-au-Bois to Hebuterne; a switch line known as the Colincamps Switch; and a third system, designated the Red Line, and situated several thousand yards in rear of the Reserve Line. The principle of defence in depth was also followed in the selection of reserve positions for the artillery, and the selection and partial preparation of these positions was actively proceeded with during April.

During the 28th March the guns supported minor attacks which were made by the infantry to regain a short length of line which had been seized by the enemy the previous night, and to improve the observation at one or two other points. In the early afternoon two brigades of enemy infantry were reported moving down the valley from Serre towards the Ancre; every available gun was turned on to them for an hour, and they were not seen again. Harassing fire was maintained day and night, and by day a tremendous amount of observed shooting was done by all batteries. Heavy rain fell during the night of the 29th, and as no duckboards were to be had the condition of the old trenches was very bad. An operation to further improve the line was carried out at 2 p.m. on the 30th March by the 1st Infantry Brigade and the 3rd (Rifle) Brigade. The advance was supported by a well-placed barrage and was quite successful, except in one spot where the enemy clung to a small "pocket," from which, however, he was eventually driven the following morning. So rapid was the success of the centre and right battalions in this attack that their objectives were reported occupied within seven minutes; the prisoners totalled nearly three hundred, and over one hundred machine guns, and five light minenwerfers were captured, while about two hundred and fifty enemy dead were counted on the front attacked.

The situation now became much more settled, and with the arrival of further heavy artillery on the front, it was possible to take advantage of some of the targets which presented themselves beyond the range of the Division's field guns. Several of the batteries had run forward single guns for sniping and engaging these "opportunity" targets, but had the Division possessed a battery of 6in howitzers or 60-prs. the additional advantage gained from their active presence on the front would have been very considerable. The enemy paid a good deal of attention to the battery positions of both brigades at the end of March and the first few days of April, and shelled Auchonvillers, Colincamps, and Mailly-Maillet at odd intervals during the day and night, doing a good deal of material damage, and inflicting many casualties. Headquarters of the 3rd Brigade, which had been located in a glass-fronted establishment in Mailly-Maillet, were obliged to move to more secure, if less convenient, quarters on the edge of the village, which itself was speedily becoming a less popular resort for the foraging parties who had levied toll on the wine cellars and the kitchen gardens. The inhabitants of the village had left everything when they fled on the approach of the enemy, and for the first few days troops in and about the place were able to supplement their rations with fare of a sort that seldom comes the way of a soldier. Though there was wine in abundance the men exercised a disciplined moderation in its use. Of the inhabitants of Colincamps but one was seen; an old fellow, who drove a white horse in a high-sided waggon out from Mailly-Maillet and up to his own village to bring down his store of grain. He made several trips, plodding along in leisurely unconcern, although the road was

A British Heavy Gun in Action on the Front of the New Zealand Division [*Official Photo*

Well Concealed : A 4·5 in. Howitzer in one of the cupola style pits [*Official Photo*

A German Tank captured by the New Zealand Division [*Official Photo*

subject to violent "crashes" from hostile batteries, but his judgment or his luck never failed him in choosing a quiet interval.

On the 3rd and 4th of April hostile fire was normal, and there was nothing to indicate that the enemy was strengthening his artillery along the front; although he had brought up a number of observation balloons, which stared down at the battery positions from the first peep of dawn till dark. It soon transpired, however, that this comparative calm was of the sort that precedes a storm. Apparently the enemy had not been able to accept the fact that his advance on this front had been completely blocked, and cherished the hope that he might yet re-open the road to Amiens; for on the 5th he launched a series of strong attacks accompanied by strong and sustained fire from a reinforced artillery against the front of the Division. It so happened that the Divisional Artillery was that morning assisting the 37th Division in an attack on Rossignol Wood, by putting down a smoke screen, and creating a diversion on enemy trenches elsewhere. The 37th Division was to attack at 5.30 a.m., but shortly after the guns opened up the enemy commenced a heavy bombardment with guns up to 21 c.m. calibre, and extending from the forward areas to well behind battery positions.

Particular attention was paid to all the valleys and dead ground in rear of the front line system. These places were almost deluged with high explosive, and swept with shrapnel—chiefly captured 18-pr. ammunition, with which the enemy gunners managed to get very effective bursts. Practically all the ground wires to observation posts and infantry headquarters were broken at the outset, and communication was made difficult and uncertain; but the enemy's trenches were kept under a slow rate of fire, and counter-preparation was fired for several hours. Strong attacks were launched against the Left Brigade in the morning, but beyond gaining a little ground at one particular point, they were repulsed with heavy losses.

At 2 p.m. the Right Brigade beat off a further attack and captured some prisoners, who stated that they were originally to have co-operated with the attack on the left in the morning, but that the weight of artillery fire to which they had been subjected had then made their advance impossible. This was the enemy's final effort, for the time being, and by 3.30 p.m. hostile fire had practically died down. The casualties at the gun positions during the day had been numerous, and considerable material damage had been done. The 3rd Battery position having been badly knocked about with eight-inch shells, was temporarily vacated during the night. The fact that the day had been dull, with low, overhanging clouds, was probably a fortunate circumstance for the batteries, as the enemy was unable to employ his observation balloons.

An enemy aeroplane, which had flown in and out of the low clouds above the batteries all day, was shot down by Lewis gun fire at 4 p.m., and both the pilot and observer were taken prisoners. At 5 a.m. the following morning counter-preparation consisting of a creeping barrage over the enemy's trenches to a depth of five hundred yards, was fired by all batteries in case the enemy should be assembling for another attack; but the night had been wet, and the situation remained normal.

On April 6th the 25th Divisional Artillery was withdrawn from the command of the New Zealand Division, and was replaced by the 93rd and 293rd (Army) Brigades, R.F.A. The artillery covering the Divisional front was then grouped into Right and Left Reserve Groups. The Right Group consisted of the 1st and 3rd Brigades, under Lieut.-Colonel F. Symon; the Left Group, of the two newly-arrived R.F.A. Brigades; and the Reserve Group, of the 104th (Army) Brigade, R.F.A. The situation remaining quiet, except for reciprocal artillery activity, the work of completing the defensive systems behind the Divisional front was vigorously proceeded with. The digging of the Divisional reserve line made steady progress, and a great deal of wiring was done in front of this line and the Colincamps Switch.

In view of the ever-present possibility of a renewal of the enemy's offensive on the front on a grand scale, the construction of a strong defensive system was regarded as of paramount importance, and the whole enemy country for a considerable depth behind his front line was kept under the fire of the guns with such excellent effect as to make preparation for an advance both difficult and costly. The greatest importance was attached to this harassing fire, and groups were ordered to keep it up during every hour of the twenty-four. The minimum daily expenditure of ammunition for this purpose alone was 600 rounds per 18-pr. battery and 300 rounds per 4.5in. howitzer battery. An elaborate and lengthy defence scheme was issued by Divisional Artillery Headquarters, together with instructions showing the normal course a hostile attack might be expected to take, and the manner in which it could be most effectively dealt with.

Owing to the shape of the salient held by the enemy in front of Hebuterne it was possible to bring enfilade fire to bear in support of the flanking Divisions, and accordingly arrangements were made for "mutual support" barrages. The action of the artillery in the event of an enemy attack was divided into three phases. The first was counter-preparation, during which the enemy assembly areas were thoroughly searched by all guns. The second phase was the neutralisation of enemy guns, principally with gas shell, during the hostile bombardment; this task was to be carried out by the heavy artillery and field howitzers, the remainder of the field artillery standing by on S.O.S. lines. Finally, the actual assault would be met by all guns firing on their carefully registered S.O.S. zones.

All the gun positions which had been selected in rear for the defence of the reserve line were accurately resected by the Corps Topographical Section and fighting maps prepared. No pits were dug, each position being simply marked with a numbered board and gaps being left in the wire through which the guns could be withdrawn. A supply of boxed ammunition was provided near each position. Trench mortars were to assist in the defence of the Colincamps Switch, and pits were dug on the eastern edge of the village for medium mortars. Some of 6in. mortars were placed in the line, and carried on an active programme of shooting. Forward waggon lines were established by each brigade, and gun limbers and teams were kept there in readiness to move the guns at a moment's notice. On 9th April the 1st Brigade batteries moved to positions behind Mailly-Maillet, from which the guns would be able to cover the right flank in the event of the enemy endeavouring to advance up the valley to the south of the village. A few days later the R.F.A. Brigade which had been in mobile divisional reserve, ready to move at an hour's notice, was ordered into positions selected for the defence of the Purple Line. In these positions the batteries were to fire only on S.O.S., remaining silent at all other times.

On April 21st and 22nd the 1st Brigade, exchanging positions with the 232nd Brigade, R.F.A., moved from the outskirts of Mailly-Maillet to north of Beaussart, and the 3rd Brigade went into the positions on the Divisional reserve line, with headquarters in Bus-les-Artois. Three days later the Division sideslipped a little to the north, handing over a short length of front to the 12th Division on the right, and relieving the 42nd Division in the line to a point just north of Hebuterne. In the readjustment of artillery caused by this change, the 93rd, 232nd, and 315th Brigades, R.F.A., were transferred, *in situ* to the 12th Division; the 235th and 236th Brigades, R.F.A., and four 6in. trench mortars being attached to the New Zealand Divisional Artillery.

By the end of April, Lieut.-Colonel McQuarrie had returned from hospital, and again assumed command of the 3rd Brigade, which continued to occupy the Purple Line positions. Further changes in the composition of groups took place during May. On the 7th the 235th and 236th Brigades were withdrawn from the Division, and as they were replaced by one brigade only—the 187th—it was found necessary to dispense with the Divisional Mobile Reserve, and accordingly the 104th Brigade, which had been in reserve since the beginning of the month, went into action again. On 21st May the batteries of this brigade were relieved in their positions near Sailly-au-Bois by the 3rd Brigade, and a day later the pits vacated by the 3rd Brigade were occupied by the 2nd (Army) Brigade, which had marched down from Hazebrouck. At the same time one of the 2nd Brigade batteries took over the two 18-pr. anti-tank guns which the 3rd Brigade had established near the Sugar Factory in front of Colincamps some two or three weeks earlier.

In addition to the normal tasks which were carried out during May, support was given to an infantry operation undertaken with a view to advancing the line on the left of the Divisional front some five hundred yards. The 42nd Division on the left, was to co-operate by conforming with this advance and also by creating a diversion. Zero hour was at 8.50 p.m. on the 4th May, and the attack was directly supported by the fire of eight 6-in. Newton trench mortars, two brigades of field artillery, and some heavy guns. For three days the ground to be covered in the attack had been thoroughly prepared by heavy howitzers, and a diversion was created at La Signy Farm immediately before zero hour, by a sudden bombardment being laid down on certain trenches which had been very deliberately registered during the day. The diversion was so far successful that the enemy placed a heavy barrage at La Signy Farm and only lightly shelled the actual front of attack. The objective was successfully reached and prisoners were taken; but as the 42nd Division was held up on the left the captured ground could not be held, and the troops were withdrawn.

Towards the end of the month there was a very marked increase in hostile artillery fire, although at the time the weather was dull and visibility was not good. The enemy carried out a great deal of counter-battery work, and heavy concentrations were put down on trench areas. This may, in some measure, have been due to nervousness consequent on the raiding activities of the Divisional infantry; but it was more probably a general activity accompanying the launching of his offensive on the Soissons-Rheims front. After the opening of this offensive hostile fire on the front died down a good deal, except for an increase in the shelling of rear areas with long range high velocity guns.

About the middle of May a silent area was laid down within the limits of which no active batteries could be placed. Guns in this area were situated well forward, so that they could engage at close range hostile troops breaking through on the front. It was considered that their inactivity in normal seasons would enable them to escape the enemy's counter-battery shooting in the event of an attack. Brigades which maintained a battery in this silent area thus had two 18-pr. batteries and on 4.5in. (howitzer) battery for normal fire purposes, while all guns and howitzers were available for fire on S.O.S.

On June 7th the New Zealand Division was relieved by the 42nd Division, and withdrew from the line for a period of rest and training. The relief did not extend to the New Zealand

Brigades of Artillery, which remained in action in support of the 42nd Division. Weather conditions were almost uniformly fine during June, and conditions for artillery work were correspondingly good. The period was not marked by any particular activity, but brigades expended on an average from eight hundred to a thousand rounds per day on normal tasks—observed shooting by day and harassing fire by night. Hostile fire was below normal; apart from the usual attention paid to the trench system, it consisted chiefly of bursts of fire on the small villages immediately in rear of the line, particularly Mailly-Maillet, Beaussart, Courcelles, and Colincamps. Some attention was also paid to Sailly-au-Bois, the positions of the 3rd Brigade batteries in and around the village being shelled at dawn for several days in succession with high explosive and blue cross gas shells, the latter containing a mixture of gas and high explosive. The damage to positions was inconsiderable. The enemy also frequently placed brief concentrations of small calibre shells with instantaneous fuzes on the open country forward of the artillery zone; but although their unexpected and sudden appearance made them very disconcerting to parties on the move, casualties were fortunately infrequent.

Batteries of the 2nd Brigade withdrew to their waggon lines on June 10th, and for the remainder of the month the Brigade remained in mobile reserve, still continuing, however, to man the two anti-tank guns near the Sugar Factory in front of Colincamps. As corps mobile reserve the brigade had to be prepared to go into action on an hour's notice by night, and two hours' notice by day. On the 14th of the month a test was given by Corps Headquarters, on which batteries turned out, and within thirty-five minutes of the order being received had reported themselves in occupation of their late positions. During this period in reserve a good deal of useful training was carried out, and batteries also proceeded in turn to the Third Army gun range near Frohen-le-Grand to calibrate their guns.

On June 16th Lieut.-Colonel I. T. Standish assumed command of the 1st Brigade, in place of Lieut.-Colonel F. Symon, who proceeded to England to command the New Zealand Field Artillery Reserve Depôt at Ewshott.

ROSSIGNOL WOOD.

The area in which the artillery waggon lines were situated afforded a striking and pleasant contrast to the quarters in which the battery transport had spent the winter at Ypres, and the artillerymen, in common with the Division generally, were not slow to appreciate the changed environment. The enemy's sweeping advance in March had been checked on or about the line held by the British forces before the launching of the first great offensive in July, 1916. For considerably more than a year all the country in rear of this line had been almost completely freed from the shadow of war, and the passage of the seasons had already restored to the fertile countryside much of that air of peaceful industry which it must have worn in happier days. Nothing had been done to repair the wreckage in the villages nearest the line; but the peasants had restored the fields to cultivation, and within a month or two of the Division's arrival on the front the crops were beginning to ripen, and the luxuriant fields of clover and rich meadow lands afforded splendid grazing for the horses. Traffic over growing crops was avoided as much as possible, and owners of fields on which batteries grazed their animals were always compensated, though not on the liberal scale on which they invariably based their claims. The country was undulating, at times hilly, and freely dotted over with typical French villages, whose small clustering woods and shelter plantations spoke in language both picturesque and eloquent of the comfort traditionally associated with those peasant homes. The Divisional Ammunition Column, and most of the batteries, had their transport lines in or nearby small villages like Bus-les-Artois or Louvencourt; but the 3rd Brigade lines were situated along the sheltered slopes of a small valley which ran up from the foot of Louvencourt Wood, which the soldiers themselves styled Happy Valley.

The natural tendency of the colonial soldier to beguile his leisure hour with sport or recreation of some active description was given a very full measure of encouragement during the summer months. There were weekly cricket matches, and occasional sports meetings, and in June, when the infantry were out of the line, there was a series of horse shows, at which jumping and other competitive mounted events bulked largely. The Divisional Artillery held its Horse Show, and the 3rd Brigade held an unofficial, though highly successful race meeting in Happy Valley. The Divisional Horse Show, held on June 16th, near St. Leger, eclipsed anything of the kind that had previously been attempted in France. Batteries and sections of the ammunition column competed very keenly in the events for which they were eligible.

When the New Zealand Division returned to the line at the beginning of July it took over the front immediately to the north of its old sector, involving a change of position for the New Zealand batteries which were still supporting the 42nd Division. The new sector extended from the southern edge of Hebuterne to a point immediately south of Bucquoy, and included the greater part of the small salient held by the enemy at this portion of the line. In changing over, the New Zealand batteries did not retain their guns, but exchanged pieces with the outgoing batteries, and dissatisfaction was again expressed regarding the condition of the guns and the pits in which they were handed over. Two of the batteries of the 3rd Brigade had their guns in the old trenches which had formed part of the British front line system before the Somme offensive of 1916. A few hundred yards away were the old German defences on the edge of Gommecourt and Gommecourt Wood, where the attacking British infantry suffered so severely in the first furious assaults at the beginning of July, 1916. The old enemy trenches, with their deep and safe timbered dug-outs, were still in a fair state of preservation, and when the guns moved forward on the eve of the great attack on August 21st, some of these old dug-outs provided temporary shelter for the gun crews. Most of the waggon lines moved to the vicinity of Souastre.

Of the five brigades of field artillery primarily available for the defence of the sector, four were in the line, one brigade, R.F.A., being in corps reserve. In addition, there were fourteen 6-in. Newton trench morars, and one brigade of heavy howitzers. There was also a call on two batteries of 60-prs. and counter-battery guns. The defensive scheme outlined in great detail the programme of normal fire, action in case of attack, counter-bombardment, barrage fire, response to calls from the air, gas attack, mutual support barrages, anti-tank defence and counter-attack. Observing officers were already familiar with the greater part of the front, and from the moment guns were "shot in," the full programme of harassing fire was carried out night and day. Facilities for observation were good, though no single station afforded anything like a comprehensive view of the whole sector. The entire front was kept under the closest observation from dawn to dusk, however, and this vigilance and close liaison with the infantry combined to render the fire of the guns so effective that as the month progressed signs were not wanting that this constant punishment was beginning to tell severely on the enemy infantry. Rossignol Wood was a favourite target for light and heavy guns, and entries in captured diaries supplied convincing testimony of the miseries endured by the unfortunate garrison in this gaunt and shattered wood.

During the afternoon of July 15th the infantry undertook a highly successful operation with the object of advancing the line a short distance in the vicinity of Hebuterne. The attack was preceded by a short bombardment from all active guns on the Divisional front; by guns of the right divisional artillery, and by two 6in. howitzer batteries. The Divisional Trench Mortars provided a diversion by bombarding Rossignol Wood. On the following day all the New Zealand batteries co-operated with corps heavy artillery in a bombardment of Puisieux-au-Mont with the threefold object of discovering any possible concentration of hostile artillery on the front, of searching out enemy ammunition dumps amongst the ruined buildings in the villages, and of drawing the fire of hostile batteries, and then engaging them by aeroplane observation. So far as could be be judged the shoot was fairly successful in its results, though it did not disclose any concentration of enemy guns. From this day onwards the ordinary forms of harassing fire were supplemented by a system of double "crashes," by which sudden brief bursts of fire were turned on to a particular area by every available field gun and howitzer on the front, at times notified by Divisional Artillery Headquarters. The first crash opened with a salvo from all guns, and the second, which was fired after an interval of three minutes covered all the ground within a radius of 200 yards of the target. It was seldom possible to estimate the results of this shooting by actual observation, but from the statements of prisoners captured from time to time, it was learnt that casualties from artillery fire were constant, and at times heavy.

About the middle of July a series of small operations were initiated in the neighbourhood of Rossignol Wood, and were carried out with such skill and determination that within a very few days the capture of the Wood became imminent. But so uncomfortable had his position apparently become that the enemy anticipated the event by withdrawing under cover of darkness. Explosions were heard in the Wood during the night—July 19th-20th—and at dawn patrols found that the enemy had destroyed his small concrete dug-outs, and withdrawn from the position. The infantry immediately followed up to keep in touch with the enemy, arrangements being made at Artillery Headquarters to meet the situation should the retirement become general. At the waggon lines everything was put in readiness for an instant advance, one battery in each brigade standing by for instant movement. The situation soon cleared itself, however, infantry patrols discovering that the enemy had merely withdrawn to the further side of the Wood. The enemy showed his irritation at these events by doing his best to make the Wood untenable, and fiercely and almost continuously shelling his lost trenches in front of it with light calibre guns. For several days this shelling was a feature of hostile artillery activity, but it did not deter the infantry from making a further forward move on the evening of July 24th, when they captured some high ground to the south of Rossignol Wood, taking thirty prisoners and a number of machine guns. The following evening the enemy counter-attacked after a heavy bombardment lasting half an hour, but the attack was crushed with the assistance of artillery fire. For the remainder of the month the enemy continued to shell the Wood and neighbouring area, the infantry on several occasions being compelled to ask for retaliatory fire. On the last night of the month counter-preparation was fired, the violence of the enemy's fire having given rise to the belief that he contemplated another counter-attack.

The work of the Division over this period was made the subject of appreciative reference by the Army Commander, in the following letter:—"G.O.C., IV. Army Corps. I would ask you to convey to the G.O.C. New Zealand Division my sincere appreciation of the operations of that Division which have led to the evacuation of Rossignol Wood and the adjoining trenches by the enemy. This operation, lasting over several days, has achieved a result which has reduced the extent of our front line and placed the enemy in an extremely difficult position. That this result has been obtained with few casualties and without check is due to the persistent enterprise on the part of all ranks, and to thoughtful preparation and skilful leading on the part of commanders. The Division is to be warmly congratulated on its spirit and initiative, and I desire that all ranks should be informed of these few words of commendation and gratitude. (Signed) J. BYNG, General, Third Army."

During this period batteries had been most successful in locating and engaging some of the enemy's light field batteries, and a great deal of valuable information as to the position of other enemy guns passed on to the counter-battery group of heavy guns. One or two sections, both of 18-prs. and howitzers, were placed well forward in order to engage gun positions and movement beyond the range of main battery positions, and a section of the 6th (Howitzer) Battery which was moved forward to Hebuterne for this purpose succeeded in destroying several enemy ammunition dumps. Shoots by 18-pr. and howitzer batteries, with aeroplane or balloon observation, were attended by a considerable degree of success, and afforded useful experience. Observations from the aeroplane observer were received at the wireless station attached to every brigade, and transmitted thence by telephone to the battery. Calibration shoots were also carried out in conjunction with the Field Survey Company, whose calculations were based on results recorded by extremely accurate and delicately adjusted instruments. These shoots were valuable as a check or confirmation of the results of calibrations carried out by batteries themselves; but calibration by direct observation from a forward station remained the general and most satisfactory practice.

CHAPTER VIII.

THE RETREAT FROM MESSINES.

When the 1st and 3rd Brigades of Artillery and the Divisional Ammunition Column moved out on short notice from the Ypres sector, to join the Division in its rapid march south to the fighting on the Somme, the expectations, so far as events could then be gauged, were that there was in store for them a good deal of hard fighting, and probably some open work such as could be expected in a "war of movement." The 2nd (Army) Brigade remained at Ypres outside the limits of the storm which had burst elsewhere with such dreadful violence, and seemingly was faced with no more exciting prospects than that of assisting to hold the line in a sector where the conditions of living were peculiarly bad. But none of these anticipations was justified by the turn of events. By the time the 1st and 3rd Brigades had settled into action near Mailly-Maillet the line there had practically become stable, and conditions were rapidly becoming normal again; and within a fortnight the 2nd Brigade, far from enduring routine duties at Ypres, was fighting a rearguard action in the Lys Battle—an experience which befel no other brigade in the New Zealand Division. A few days before the Division marched off for the Somme, the 2nd Brigade, which had been in rest at Westoutre, returned to the line at Ypres under the orders of the 37th Divisional Artillery. The brigade had spent about two weeks in the rest area, the time being devoted partly to training and partly to recreation, and during that period had been inspected by the G.O.C. and the G.O.C., R.A., XXII. Corps.

The old waggon lines near Dickebusch were occupied on the 16th of March, Brigade Headquarters going to Halfway House, and on the following two days the 5th, 9th, and 6th Batteries went into action in the neighbourhood of Birr Cross Roads, and the 2nd Battery near Kit and Kat. On the 19th the waggon lines were heavily shelled by high velocity guns, the resultant casualties to men and horses being so severe as to necessitate the establishment of temporary lines near Hallebast Corner. The brigade remained in action when the 1st and 3rd Brigade batteries were withdrawn; but on the 6th April orders were received for the relief of the 6th (Army) Brigade, A.F.A., in the Neuve Eglise-Ploegsteert sector. The relief was to be completed the following day, and as guns were to be exchanged the necessary personnel was sent forward in motor lorries. In this new sector the four New Zealand batteries, together with the 84th and 85th Batteries of the 11th Brigade, R.F.A., formed the Left Group Artillery on the front of the 19th Division. The group was commanded by Lieut.-Colonel Falla, and covered a front which extended approximately from the River Douve south to Pont Rouge, a little over 2,500 yards in extent. The 2nd Battery position was at Anton's Farm, in front of Hill 63, and the 5th and 9th were on the left in the valley below Messines. The 6th (Howitzer) Battery had its guns in Ploegsteert Wood, in the vicinity of Hyde Park Corner. Of the two R.F.A. Batteries attached to the brigade, the 84th was in front of Ploegsteert village, and the 85th was on Hill 63. Batteries were able to settle down in their new positions before their front became involved in the battle, which did not extend so far north until the second day. The settling-down process was made easier by the fact that everyone was perfectly familiar with the whole of the area.

Comparative quiet reigned on the 8th April, but at 3 a.m. the following day the enemy opened a most violent bombardment on the front running southwards from Armentieres. Although this did not extend north of Armentieres, and the front covered by the group remained normal, a heavy fire was maintained on the enemy's trenches, and back areas were subjected to harassing fire throughout the day. Towards evening the enemy bombardment to the south had moderated, and by 7.30 p.m. everything appeared quiet; but much had happened in the meantime.

After several hours' bombardment with gas and high explosive the enemy had attacked the front from Bois Grenier to the La Bassee Canal, and at the outset had overwhelmed the defences of the 2nd Portuguese Division, on whose front the attack first developed. So rapidly did the enemy overrun the positions held by the Portuguese troops, who were to have been relieved that day by a British Division, that the arrangements for manning the rear defences of the sector could scarcely be carried out in time. By nightfall the enemy had reached the River Lys, on the outskirts of Estaires, had crossed the river at Bac St. Maur, east of Sailly-sur-la-Lys, and after strengthening his forces north of the river, had pushed on northwards to Croix du Bac. Upon word being received of this advance at Fleurbaix, it was deemed advisable to withdraw the 2nd Battery about 500 yards to a position on Hill 63. With a view to emergencies an endeavour was also made to provide a track over which the guns of the 6th Battery could be withdrawn if found necessary. The ground about the position was badly pitted with shell holes, and in places marshy, and the operation of getting the guns out of the pits, and back on to the road would be both lengthy and difficult. The likelihood of the attack extending north to the group's front on the following day was recognised, and everyone remained on the alert. Anticipation in this instance, was unpleasantly verified, for at 2.30 a.m. on April 9th, heavy shelling broke out along the front from Frelinghien to Hill 60, and quickly developed into an intense bombardment with gas and high explosive, which extended from the front and support lines to the rear of battery areas.

A counter-bombardment was put down, but at 4 a.m. the enemy were reported to have penetrated the foremost defences. Ranges were shortened accordingly, and forward observing officers were instructed to engage the enemy at any point where he could be seen, irrespective of zones. The morning was misty, however, and communications in some cases broke down early in the attack. Communication with the 84th Battery was soon lost, but group was still in touch with the remaining batteries, and as the enemy had appeared on the Messines Ridge overlooking the positions, batteries were ordered at 6 a.m. to withdraw to the neighbourhood of Wulverghem. The 5th Battery withdraw first to Le Plus Douve Farm, in order to cover the withdrawal of the 2nd and 9th to the vicinity of Petawawa Farm, about 500 yards south of Wulverghem. Ammunition was brought to the positions by the Brigade Ammunition Column and battery transport, and by 11.30 a.m. the withdrawal was complete, and all three batteries were in action engaging the enemy with observation from various points. During the withdrawal the batteries were subject to a certain amount of machine gun fire from Messines Ridge; and in some cases part of the equipment had to be removed from the old positions under cover of darkness the following night.

Owing to the rapidity of the enemy's advance, other batteries of the group were unable to effect their withdrawal. British infantry retired through the 84th Battery, and very soon after 7 a.m. the battery was overwhelmed by the enemy. Similarly, the 6th (Howitzer) Battery found itself in danger of being encompassed at an early hour, and from about 6 a.m. had to deal with enemy infantry, who were working through Ploegsteert Wood, and round the Wood and the village of Ploegsteert. The guns of the battery were distributed over a considerable area; three were at the main position, one was in a forward position some six hundred yards in advance of the battery, and the remaining section was in the wood on the right flank. While the battery was firing on S.O.S. after the opening attack, the position was heavily shelled, and several casualties were incurred. When it was reported that the enemy was in Ploegsteert Wood, one of the battery Lewis guns was sent out to cover the right section; there were not enough men to enable the second Lewis gun to be used, as the battery had lost a complete gun crew in a direct hit from a heavy German shell on one of the guns at the main position. The enemy were by this time in Ploegsteert and in the neighbourhood of Hyde Park Corner, and the position of the battery was rapidly becoming critical. It was therefore decided to make an endeavour to drag the two right section guns on to the tramline, some little distance off, and bring the gun teams in from the road by way of the tramline. One gun was got out of the pit, but became hopelessly bogged half way to the tramline. Meanwhile the enemy had worked through to Butler's House, a building situated halfway between Ploegsteert and Hyde Park Corner, and in rear of the battery; the remaining gun of the right section was, therefore, turned round, and, firing out the back of the pit, shelled this building, the enemy being driven back

A 6 IN. TRENCH MORTAR IN ACTION [Official Photo

towards Ploegsteert. An Australian, one of three members of a trench mortar battery who had attached themselves to the 6th Battery, after their own mortar was destroyed by shell-fire, went forward to Butler's House, and found it occupied by only a few wounded Germans, the remainder having retired towards Ploegsteeert. The enemy's command of the road from Ploegsteert to Hyde Park Corner was so complete, however, that it was recognised that it would be impossible to bring a team in for the gun of the right section which had been got on to the tramline.

Attention was therefore turned to the guns at the main position, and one of these was got on to the road, with the assistance of a party of thirty British infantrymen; this party was obtained through the initiative of one of the Australian trench mortar men, who had gone over to the Catacombs, under Hill 63, where a considerable number of men were sheltering, collected this number and guided them to the battery's position. Of the other two guns at the main position, one had been destroyed by a direct hit, and the other was surrounded by a hopeless bog; it was, therefore, decided to get the remaining gun at the right section into action again, but on the way over to the pit the enemy was met in some force, and the battery commander (Major R. Miles) was wounded. The enemy was now near Hyde Park Corner, in rear of the battery, and it was therefore decided to abandon the position, taking sights and breech-blocks from the guns. A subaltern of the battery, however, volunteered to remain at the position with a party of two or three men, but no opportunity was had during the afternoon of getting the teams near the battery, and this small rearguard finally withdrew at 5 p.m.

Although teams which had attempted to approach Hyde Park Corner had been forced to retire under machine gun fire, the hope of saving the guns was very reluctantly abandoned. On the evening of the 11th an officer volunteered to go to Hyde Park Corner to see if a further attempt would be possible, but by that time the enemy had captured Hill 63, and it was recognised that any further effort would be foredoomed to failure.

The 85th Battery, R.F.A., fought from its position on Hill 63 until dusk on the 10th, training its guns on to the enemy in Messines and Ploegsteert Village. At nightfall the battery successfully withdrew to Neuve Eglise and rejoined its own brigade.

On the withdrawal in the morning of the 10th of the New Zealand 18-pr. batteries to the positions south of Wulverghem, in the Douve Valley, Brigade Headquarters found itself out of communication, and removed at 11 a.m. to new quarters near Neuve Eglise, in order to link up with the new battery positions. All the battery waggon lines were moved on to the Neuve Eglise-Dranoutre Road.

Some anti-tank guns which the brigade had manned on the Messines Ridge and in front of St. Yves were not called upon to stop any tanks as none were used; nor were their crews able to take advantage of targets offered by enemy infantry. Of two 15-prs. in front of St. Yves, which were manned by details from the 2nd Battery, one was put out of action on the opening of the attack by a 5.9 shell, which also casualtied the detachment. The other detachment got their gun into action against enemy infantry in the open, but the first round blew out the breech and casualtied two of the crew, leaving one man out of six. The two 15-prs., manned by gunners from the 9th Battery, on Messines Ridge, were put out of action and abandoned. The crews could see nothing of the advance, owing to the ground mist, and withdrew when the enemy were entering Messines on their immediate left.

At 8 p.m. enemy shelling, which had been severe all day, quietened down. Beyond the information sent in by the brigade's own observing officers, it was difficult to learn anything on which reliance might be placed as to the position of the enemy and the extent of his advance. Where doubt existed as to the precise position of the enemy's most advanced elements it was usually found necessary and profitable to detach an officer from one of the batteries to reconnoitre, and reports obtained in this manner were frequently found to anticipate information gained from Infantry Brigade Headquarters. On the evening of the 10th the line was reported to run from Hyde Park Corner, through St. Yves, to just west of Messines, the town itself having been recaptured during the course of the afternoon by the South African Brigade. On the right from Hyde Park Corner the enemy held the south-eastern portion of Ploegsteert Wood, Ploegsteert Village, and a line running through Nieppe to Steenwerck. During the night fire was maintained on Ploegsteert Village and the country immediately east of Messines; but enemy batteries remained quiet until 2.30 a.m., when they put down a heavy barrage on Hill 63, Messines, and the Douve Valley. Shelling became less intense after 6 a.m., but the enemy continued to advance from the positions he had gained on the previous day, and at 11 a.m. it was found necessary to move the 5th Battery back to Wulverghem.

Events developed quickly as the day proceeded. At 12 noon the enemy was advancing towards the slopes of Hill 63 from the east, and had occupied La Petite Munque Farm and Courte Dreve Farm, a thousand to fifteen hundred yards west of the road from Hyde Park Corner to Ploegsteert. Fighting took place in the afternoon round about Messines, which the enemy had regained. Throughout the afternoon batteries effectively engaged enemy infantry with observation from the brigade's observation posts on the ridge opposite Messines, and on the ridge at L'Allouette, west of Hill 63. Valuable information as to the trend of events was passed down from these stations, but the greatest difficulty was experienced in transmitting this intelligence to higher formations, owing to the defection of the personnel at the corps' test points, on the manning of which often depended the maintenance of a whole system of communications.

Towards evening the straggling which had gone on all day was intensified, the situation becoming critical at 7 p.m., when the enemy attacked and captured Hill 63. Brigade F.O.O's had already reported infantry retiring from Hill 63, and orders were issued to batteries to withdraw to previously reconnoitred positions off the main road running towards Dranoutre, about four thousand yards in rear of the positions they then occupied. Batteries expended all their ammunition, and commenced to withdraw about 8 p.m., the 5th Battery going first, being followed at intervals by the 2nd and 9th. Brigade Headquarters was also withdrawn to the same neighbourhood. Ammunition having been delivered to the positions during the afternoon by battery transport and the Battery Ammunition Column, the guns were in action again very soon after 11 p.m., and continued firing all night. The difficulties of communication became more pronounced after each withdrawal, owing to the shortage of wire, considerable quantities of which were, however, salved by brigade and battery signal staffs, and except during moves the brigade commander always maintained touch with the batteries and the Infantry Headquarters. F.O.O.'s were, in most cases, dependent on Lucas lamps for communication with batteries.

On the morning of the 12th, the line ran south from Wytschaete, a thousand yards east of Wulverghem and Neuve Eglise, and thence to Pont d'Achelles, whither the 34th Division had withdrawn from Nieppe during the night of the 11th. The enemy continued his pressure during the 12th, and severe fighting took place in the neighbourhood of Neuve Eglise, where effective observed shooting was done by the batteries on parties of German infantry. During the night this pressure increased, and by early morning of the 13th parties of the enemy had forced their way into the village. Batteries had been in action practically all the night, and S.O.S. had been fired several times, fire being regulated according to the volume of machine gun and rifle fire that could be heard. Shortly after 6 a.m., when the enemy were reported to have entered the village, orders for a further withdrawal were issued to batteries. The tired teams were brought up and by 11 a.m. the guns were in action again in positions which had been reconnoitred between Dranoutre and Locre. Headquarters was established near Dranoutre, and later, in Locre. By a successful counter-attack delivered during the morning by troops of the 33rd and 49th Divisions, possession of the village was regained, and the guns continued to shell the roads and approaches along which the enemy was endeavouring to force his way.

Although a small garrison still held out in Neuve Eglise on the morning of the 14th, the enemy had gained possession of Hill 75, due west of the town, and the direct observation which this spot gave him on to the battery positions between Dranoutre and Locre made another change of position imperative. The three 18-pr. batteries accordingly moved back nearer to Locre, the 9th being furthest in rear, a few hundred yards north of the village. The 6th (Howitzer) Battery, which had been equipped with new howitzers, went into action during the day in the same neighbourhood, and placed a forward section to the north-east of Dranoutre. By nightfall Neuve Eglise was definitely in the enemy's possession, but attacks delivered on the front running south-west from Neuve Eglise towards Bailleul were repulsed, and the attempt to seize the Ravelsberg Heights, almost midway between these two points, was for the time frustrated. After hostilities, directed against Wytschaete, on the following morning—15th April—the enemy launched strong attacks against the high ground west of Neuve Eglise, and gaining a footing on the eastern end of the heights, worked west along the ridge towards Bailleul, which he also attacked from the south at the same time. By 9 p.m. the troops holding this town had fallen back to positions between Meteren and Dranoutre, leaving the enemy in possession.

This new ground having given the enemy improved observation over the country beyond and around Dranoutre, the batteries of the brigade in the neighbourhood of Locre were heavily shelled at intervals during the 16th. Headquarters was also twice shelled out, and the gun positions were made more insecure by the activities of low-flying aeroplanes. Some uncertainty also existed as to the intention of the infantry, and in view of the possibility of a further retirement, the forward section of the 6th Battery was withdrawn, and the brigade took up positions further in rear. The 2nd Battery went into action five hundred yards south of Westoutre, the 5th midway between Locre and Westoutre, and the 9th and 6th near the junction of the main roads between Locre, La Clytte, and Westoutre.

Several S.O.S. calls were answered during the day and evening of the 16th, and again next morning, when the enemy placed a heavy barrage along the front. Waggon lines at Westoutre were also shelled by hostile guns during the morning, resulting in a loss of men and horses, and the evacuation of the positions.

Forward observing officers kept closely in touch with the situation during the day, and batteries placed protective fire on threatened points, and engaged a great deal of enemy movement. The enemy brought up more guns, and hostile fire increased in volume, battery areas being severely shelled. The 5th Battery suffered heavy casualties during the morning of April 18th, losing two officers and five other ranks killed and twelve other ranks wounded; the battery was forced to evacuate the position, and as the other batteries were also coming under fire, the brigade withdrew to fresh positions.

By April 19th the front covered by the Brigade had been taken over by French troops, but the artillery in support was not withdrawn, and the brigade remained in the line supporting the French infantry until the 23rd, when all batteries were withdrawn to their waggon lines. The brigade proceeded the following day to the Staple area, where it remained in billets for three days. During this period sixty-three reinforcements and seventy remounts reached the brigade, and the guns were sent to the Ordnance Workshops for much-needed overhaul.

The brigade suffered heavy casualties during this brief period of active fighting, which besides being a severe trial on the endurance of the personnel at the guns and at the waggon lines, must be regarded as a most severe and searching, and in all respects successful, test of the initiative of commanding officers and their subordinates and of the efficiency of the whole brigade. On the day of the attack at Messines the front covered by the brigade was under the 19th Division, but during the morning the C.R.A. of the 25th Division assumed control of the artillery. By evening the group had lost the two attached R.F.A. batteries, one having been overwhelmed by the enemy and the other having rejoined its own brigade; thereafter the Brigade Commander had an absolutely free hand in fighting his brigade. The orders received from the C.R.A. of the 25th Division were that he was to keep in touch with the situation on the spot, fight his own brigade, and if he found it necessary to retire to move generally in a north-westerly direction. No further orders were received from the rear until some days after, when the situation promised more stability. The brigade during this period was forced to act more absolutely on its own initiative, owing to the breakdown of rear communications at the very outset. The area possessed an elaborate system of bury and air lines, some of the former dating from the Battle of Messines; but it was a common experience to find the "exchanges" on the systems evacuated. After the first move rearwards brigade and battery signal staffs were sufficiently occupied in maintaining communication with each other, and with the headquarters of the infantry unit which they were supporting. A lot of old·wire was reeled up, in the absence of fresh supplies, and where the position of the batteries made that possible, a common wire was run through to headquarters. Forward observing officers in most cases were dependent on visual signalling for communication with their batteries, and orders to the waggon lines were always sent by mounted orderlies.

No other battery in the brigade suffered the unfortunate experience which befell the 6th Battery on the opening day of the attack. On all other occasions withdrawals were carried out without interference, and before the necessity had become too pressing, a policy which was dictated by the experiences of the 10th, and made still more imperative by the frequency of the straggling in some of the first-line units during the first three or four days of the fighting. This straggling was most marked on the evenings of the 10th, 11th, 12th, and 13th, and battery personnel were constantly engaged endeavouring to turn back parties of infantry who were making their way down from the line. One battery commander, whose guns were in action near Dranoutre intercepted a party of fifty strong in this manner, and sent them on to a battalion headquarters a few hundred yards in advance of the battery position. Most of the divisions which participated in the fighting on this front had already borne a share of the fighting in the enemy's first offensive in the south, and before going in to the line at Ploegsteert and Messines had received large numbers of reinforcements fresh from Home, and with no previous experience in the line.

In order to carry out the orders for withdrawal with the minimum of delay gun teams and limbers were kept fairly close to gun positions and fortunately suffered few casualties. The supply of ammunition was always constant; none was left at positions that were being evacuated, and small dumps were always formed at fresh positions before the guns had arrived. The normal supply at dumps was very soon exhausted, and it became necessary for waggon line officers to range the countryside in all directions in order to secure further supplies. Reinforced and somewhat rested after its strenuous experiences in the Ploegsteert sector, the 2nd Brigade went into action again on 26th April under the 1st Australian Division, which held the Hazebrouck front. Batteries were situated behind Strazeele.

After the guns had been registered and calibrated, batteries engaged on a very active programme of harassing fire and counter-battery work; a special hour in the harassing fire being devoted each day to Merris, during which every battery flung at least one hundred rounds into the village. Several enemy posts were engaged by the 6th (Howitzer) Battery, the fire driving the garrison into the open, where the Australians took toll of them with machine guns. A supply of incendiary shells was received early in the month, and these were very successfully employed against farm houses and other buildings occupied by the enemy. In fighting such as the brigade had recently experienced this class of ammunition would have proved invaluable in dislodging enemy machine gunners who often made a practice of establishing themselves in the farm houses dotted over the countryside. Shortly after coming in to the sector the Brigade Commander reconnoitred a very large dump of 18-pr. ammunition, at Strazeele railway station, which, however, was but a few hundred yards from the enemy's forward posts. By bringing the teams up under shelter of a hedge which ran close to the station and carrying boxes by hand from the dump some two thousand rounds were got away on successive nights; but it was feared that the ammunition might be too dearly bought, and operations were abandoned.

After having been in the line for little more than a fortnight, intimation was received from the XV. Corps that the brigade was to withdraw from action and be prepared to march away south to join the New Zealand Division. A day or two was spent at the waggon lines preparing for the road, and on 16th May the journey was commenced. The first night in billets was disturbed by the attentions of enemy aircraft who came over and heavily bombed Aire, a mile away, and the surrounding district. One member of the brigade signal staff was killed by a bomb, and a second received wounds from which he died. The second day's march on hot and dusty roads proved very trying, and to make matters worse difficulty was experienced in finding water for the horses. None was to be had at the mid-day halt, but later in the afternoon the column passed a stream at which the tired horses were able to slake their thirst. The night was spent at Magnicourt-en-Comte, and the following night at Etree Wamin (?), and finally on the 19th, the brigade marched into Couin. The C.R.A. inspected the brigade on its arrival, and the following day all officers accompanied him on a reconnaissance of the country behind the divisional front. On the 21st the brigade occupied the positions behind the Purple Line.

CHAPTER IX.

THE TURNING POINT.

The recovery of the British Armies from the smashing blows which they had sustained at the hands of the German legions in March and April had necessarily been slow; but it had been complete. The military situation on the Western Front at the beginning of August wore an outlook very different from the sombre uncertainty in which the future had been shrouded during those terrible days when the German divisions were sweeping forward with apparently irresistible impetus towards Amiens, and towards the Channel ports. Though the enemy achieved a great degree of success in those attacks, breaking completely through the organised defensive systems on the fronts on which the fighting centred, and making enormous captures of men, guns, and booty, his great strategic purpose still awaited fulfilment. The Franco-British Armies remained intact, and still barred the way to the coast. But the Germans still retained the initiative after the battles of the Somme and the Lys, despite their heavy commitments and heavy losses. The peril which menaced the Allied cause could not be said to have been effectually dispelled until after the definite collapse of the ambitious offensive launched by the enemy east and south-west of Rheims on July 15th, and the striking success of Marshal Foch's deliberately planned counter attack three days later on the front between Chateau Thierry and Soissons. That was the decisive turning point in the dramatic rush of events. The German army had made its great effort in the springtide of its strength, and the effort had failed. Thereafter the future of the Allied cause was no longer uncertain.

At a conference held on July 23rd, when the success of the counter-attack of July 18th was well assured, the Allied Commander-in-Chief asked that the British, French, and American Armies should each prepare plans for local offensives with certain definite objectives of a limited nature. These objectives on the British front were the disengagement of Amiens, and the freeing of the Paris-Amiens railway by an attack on the Albert-Montdidier front. The rôle of the French and American armies was to free other strategic railways by operations further south and east. It was subsequently arranged that attacks would be pressed in a converging direction towards Mezieres by the French and American Armies, while at the same time the British Armies, attacking towards the line St. Quentin-Cambrai, would strike directly at the vital lateral communications running through Maubeuge to Hirson and Mezieres by which alone the German forces on the Champagne front could be supplied and maintained.

The British attack in front of Amiens, which was entrusted to General Rawlinson's Fourth Army, was launched on August 8th, on a front of eleven miles, extending from just south of the Amiens-Roye road to the vicinity of Morlancourt. The attack was completely successful; within the space of five days the town of Amiens and the railway centring upon it had been disengaged, and the enemy had been driven back to the line of the old defences which he had held in the Somme in 1916. This sudden and striking success, following so closely after the Allied counter-stroke south of the Aisne, could not fail to exercise a strong influence on the morale of the German soldier. Without a doubt it must have implanted in his mind the first seeds of disbelief in the invincibility of Germany's arms, and created an uneasy feeling that after all his hopes of an immediate and decisive victory might yet be frustrated in the final issue. After the battle of Amiens, Sir Douglas Haig decided to extend the attack northwards to the area between the rivers Somme and Scarpe. In outlining the considerations which influenced him in arriving at such a decision, the Commander-in-Chief points out in his despatches that a successful attack between Albert and Arras in a south-easterly direction would turn the line of the Somme south of Peronne, with a promise of producing far-reaching results; it would also be a step forward towards the strategic objective St. Quentin-Cambrai.

In conformity with this plan the Third Army, commanded by Sir Julian Byng, was ordered to attack north of the Ancre on August 21st, on a front of about nine miles, and gain the line of the Arras-Albert railway.

This attack was to be delivered by the IV. and VI. Corps of the Third Army, with the object of pressing the enemy back rapidly, and preventing his destroying road and railway communications. The Divisions of the IV. Corps in line were the 37th, New Zealand, and 42nd. On the left the 37th Division was to attack and capture the high ground east of Bucquoy and Ablainzeville. This operation completed, the 5th and 63rd Divisions were to push forward through the 37th Division to the line Irles-Bihucourt. The New Zealand Division and the 42nd Division, on its right, were to co-operate in the first phase of the attack with machine gun and artillery fire, and by advancing their front to the general line extending along the eastern edge of Puisieux-au-Mont and the high ground to the immediate south; in the second phase, by advancing to conform with the 5th Division to a line extending along the western side of Miraumont. The attack was to be a preliminary to an assault on a grand scale on August 23rd by the Third Army, and the divisions of the Fourth Army north of the Somme.

During the week preceding "attack day," August 21st, the line held by the New Zealand Division was considerably advanced as the result of the enemy's withdrawal, hard pressed by the infantry, to a line running behind Serre, and through Puisieux. This movement involved the pushing forward of supporting artillery, and consequently there was considerable change in battery positions before the guns finally settled down, well forward, in position for the opening of the great offensive. Warning had been received on August 11th of a probable withdrawal of the enemy along the divisional front, and infantry patrols were constantly on the alert for indications of such a move. At dawn on August 14th suspicion was aroused by the abnormal quiet prevailing in the German trenches, and patrols went out and discovered that the enemy had evacuated his forward positions. Batteries were at once warned to confine themselves to observed shooting, and it was decided for tactical purposes to form the three New Zealand Artillery Brigades into two groups, each of which would cover the front held by an infantry brigade. Accordingly the 12th, 13th, and 4th

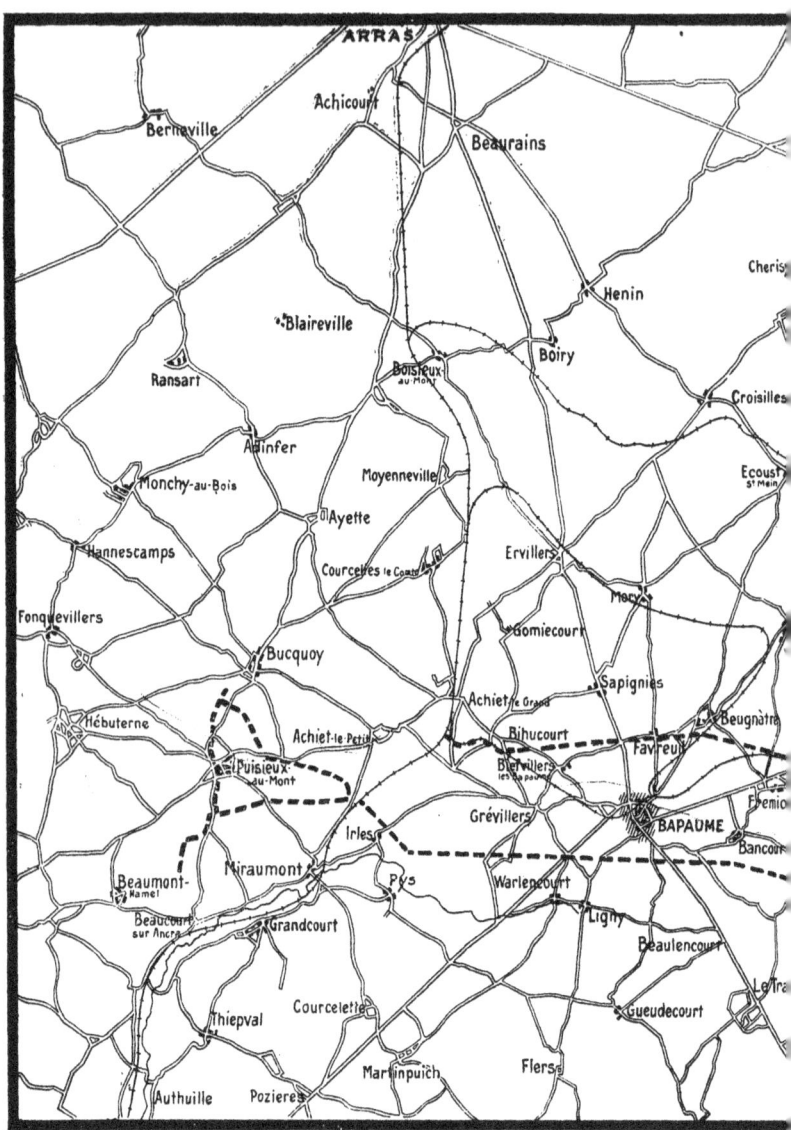

THE FINAL OFFENSIVE

Showing the line held by the New Zealand Division at Puisieux on the opening of the offensive on August 21, 1918, and the path followed by the Division in its advance until reaching the final line on the eastern edge of the Forest de Mormal.

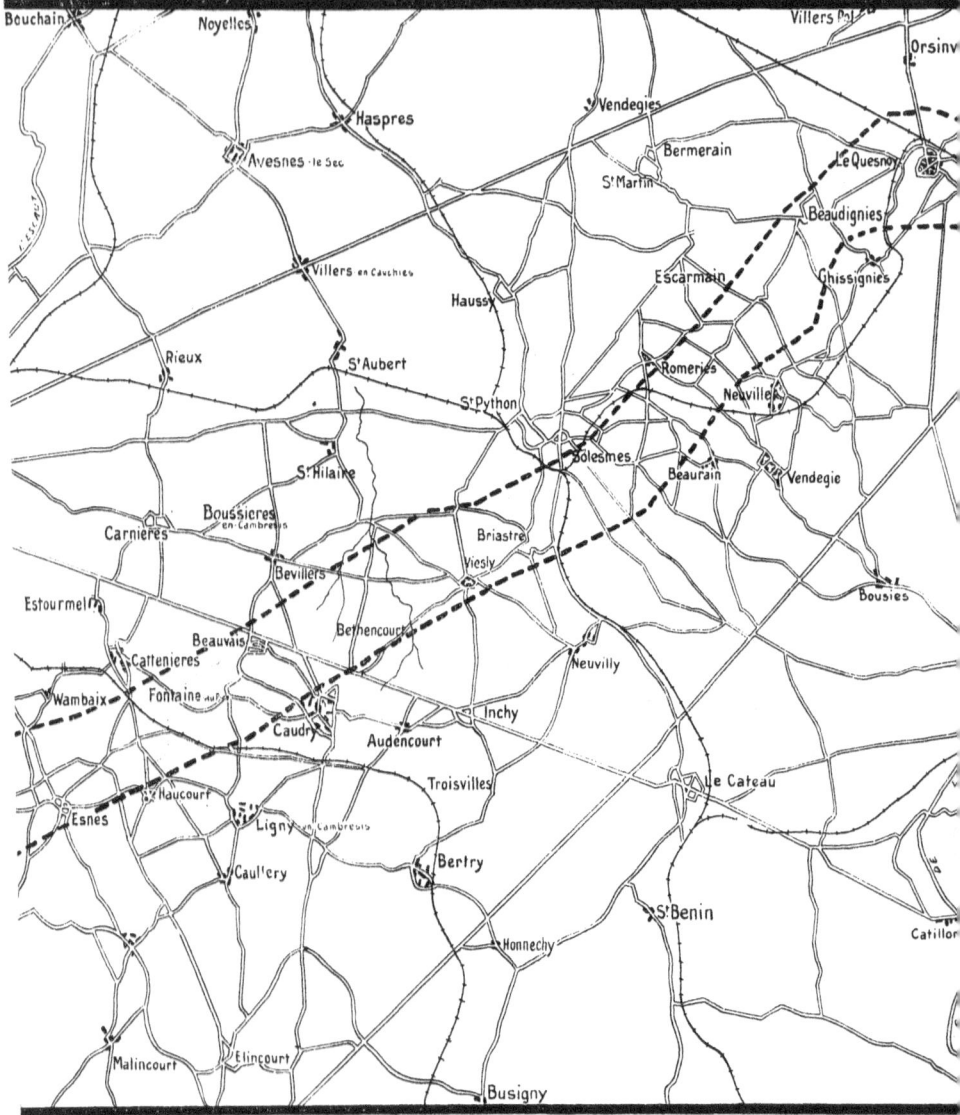

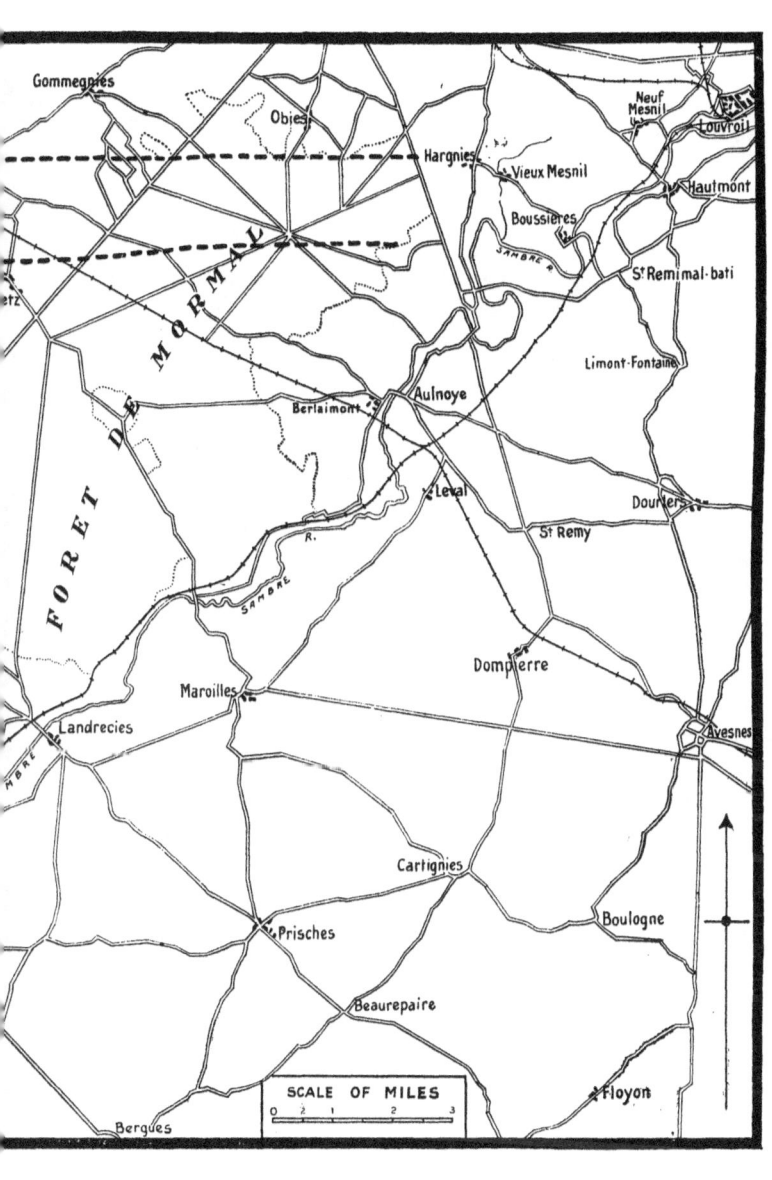

batteries of the 3rd Brigade were grouped with the 1st Brigade, and the 11th Battery was attached to the 2nd Brigade. During the day battery commanders reconnoitred positions and observation posts for forward sections from each group, these being occupied by 9 p.m. Valuable assistance was given to the infantry during the day by observed fire, and observing and liaison officers sent back to their headquarters a good deal of useful information. At dawn on the 17th the enemy counter-attacked at Puisieux, but without success. His artillery, which had been quieter than usual during the few days preceding his withdrawal, became very active again, and in addition to shelling the roads and forward areas, he engaged several of the new battery positions. A section of the 7th Battery in front of Hebuterne was heavily shelled on the morning of the 17th, and had both guns put out of action.

A remarkable feature of the opening assault on August 21st was the brevity of the preparations, and the suddenness with which, after their conception, the plans for attack were put into execution. The initial orders regarding the attack were not received by the Division until the night of August 18th, and everything had to be in readiness by the early morning of the 21st. For the first time in the experience of the Division on the Western front a great attack was to be launched without even the briefest preliminary bombardment. The necessary preparations for attack—the assembly of the infantry, and the pushing forward of the guns—were carried out so silently and unobtrusively as to leave the enemy quite unaware of the imminence of the storm which was about to burst. During the brief period available, batteries were very busy moving their guns forward under cover of darkness to their assigned positions for the opening of the battle, and the ammunition columns and battery transport were on the road from dusk till dawn bringing the ammunition supplies at the new battery positions up to the totals required for the attack. The New Zealand Division was to be supported by the 1st and 2nd Brigades only, the 3rd Brigade being attached to the 42nd Divisional Artillery, and forming the nucleus of "N" Group Artillery on that Division's front. Positions for all the batteries of the 3rd Brigade were found in front of Gommecourt. Of the 1st

Brigade batteries, the 7th and the 15th were on the right of Rossignol Wood, and the 1st and 3rd were fifteen hundred yards west of Puisieux. Three batteries of the 2nd Brigade, the 5th, 9th, and 6th, were all in the neighbourhood of Rossignol Wood, and the 2nd was in the valley south-east of Hebuterne. The C.R.A., Brigadier-General Johnston, and Staff, moved with advanced Divisional Headquarters to Foncequevillers on the eve of the attack.

The Division awaited with a feeling of settled confidence the commencement of the great series of struggles which was destined to culminate in the utter defeat of the powerful enemy whose wild ambitions, so nearly realised, had shattered the peace of the world, and carried ruin and desolation into the heart of Belgium and France. The courage of all ranks had remained unshaken in the darkest hours of March and April, their belief in a final triumph undiminished; and now they experienced a thrill of elation in the instinctive feeling that the final chapter in the bitter struggle of four years was about to open. The day of August 20th was dull, with occasional showers in the morning, and batteries displayed no more than the normal activity for such a day. A calm fell on the front with the coming of night, but in the forward areas the final preparations for the battle afforded little opportunity for rest. Tucked away in shell holes down by Rossignol Wood, or in the old German dug-outs near Gommecourt, battery commanders worked by candle-light, completing their orders for the barrage, and making their final dispositions for the advance.

The Attack Opened.

Zero hour on the 21st was at 4.55 a.m. The attack on the front of the New Zealand Division was carried out by the 3rd (Rifle) Brigade in support, and the 2nd Brigade in reserve. The barrage completely satisfied the infantry, who gained all their objectives early in the morning. By night the Division was on a line a thousand yards to the east of Puisieux, with patrols pushed out to a point midway between Achiet-le-Petit and Miraumont. The enemy artillery was very quiet during the day, although in the early morning the 1st and 3rd Batteries were shelled by light field guns, one gun of the 1st Battery being put out of action. When the barrage opened at zero hour the whole countryside was covered in a dense white fog, which effectually hid the enemy lines from the eyes of the artillery observers during the first few hours. In the evening, as soon as darkness set in, the guns commenced to move forward over the broken ground that led down into the Puisieux Valley. Batteries of the 1st and 3rd Brigades moved forward to the valley on the eastern side of Puisieux, the 2nd Brigade finding positions in the area to the immediate south of the village. The conditions encountered in the move were reminiscent of those which prevailed during the artillery's first advance on the Somme in 1916, before the advent of wet weather. The country was broken and intersected with trenches, and the roads, such as they were, torn and pitted with shell fire. Battery and ammunition column teams were on the road all night, bringing up ammunition, and by early morning on the 22nd 450 rounds per gun had been dumped at each position. The Puisieux Valley was heavily shelled during the early hours of the morning, severe casualties being incurred in running the gauntlet of the 5.9's. At 5 a.m. all guns were hotly in action answering S.O.S. calls from the 42nd Division, on the right; an enemy counter-attack was beaten off, although some batteries were under fairly heavy fire while answering the call. At one stage, when the line fell back to within close range of the 7th Battery, the battery commander had one gun run forward to the crest in front of the position, and engaged the enemy infantry over open sights.

As a result of the success of these preliminary attacks on August 21st and 22nd, the way was now clear for the launching on August 23rd of the main attack by the Third Army and the Divisions of the Fourth Army north of the Somme. A series of assaults were to take place on practically the whole front of thirty-three miles from the junction with the French, north of Lihons to Mercatel. In the IV. Corps, the New Zealand Division had the 42nd Division on its right, and the 5th Division on its left. The 42nd and New Zealand Divisions co-operated against Beauregard Dovecote and the high ground in the neighbourhood. In support of this operation the New Zealand Artillery fired a creeping barrage, which advanced due south from its starting point, in lifts of one hundred yards, until it reached the protective barrage line for the final objective. The 4.5in. howitzers were used to thicken up the barrage, keeping their fire fifty yards in advance of the 18-pr. barrage. The 5th Division assisted in the barrage with one brigade of field artillery, and the 90th Brigade, R.G.A., engaged selected points east of the Arras-Albert railway. Zero hour was at 2.30 a.m. on August 23rd, and though stubborn resistance was encountered in the neighbourhood of Beauregard Dovecote, this was successfully overcome. A second barrage was fired by all brigades in support of an attack made by the 5th Division on a line running east of Bihucourt and south-west of Irles, the New Zealand Division assisting in front of Irles and to the north of Miraumont. This attack was successful on the right, but was held up somewhat on the left. By evening the line held by the infantry was in advance of the Arras-Albert railway.

During the afternoon batteries of the 2nd Brigade moved forward to the valley fifteen hundred yards east of Puisieux, and teams of the 1st Brigade were assembled ready for a move. In the evening the 3rd Brigade, which up to this time had been attached to the 37th Division, rejoined the Divisional Artillery, and at 9.30 p.m. orders were sent out to the 1st and 3rd Brigades to move into positions in the valley south-west of Achiet-le-Petit. The march forward in inky darkness over totally unfamiliar country was not without its incident, apart altogether from the desultory shelling by hostile batteries, but the move was satisfactorily accomplished before dawn.

Two of the most serious difficulties that now beset the artillery were the shortage of water for the horses, and the incessant labour involved in keeping the guns fed with ammunition as they moved forward. At this stage of the campaign the occasional wells that were located were practically the only source of water supply; and, naturally, this method of watering a great number of animals proved tedious and consumed a great deal of valuable time. When batteries got

PEACEFUL SURROUNDINGS [*Official Photo*

immediate orders to move forward to fresh positions they generally left behind them a quantity of unexpended ammunition; but as waggon lines were generally established on the vacated gun positions, it was possible to bring this ammunition forward to the guns on succeeding nights. Where this was not possible the ammunition was picked up by the ammunition columns and re-issued to batteries. More serious difficulties arose as the result of the pooling, under Corps control, of the lorries which brought the ammunition forward to the divisional sub-park from railhead. The system of retaining these lorries under Divisional control had always worked smoothly and satisfactorily, but after corps headquarters assumed control in August there were constant delays and interruptions in the supply of ammunition to the Division.

While the guns were going forward on the night of August 23rd, arrangements were being made to continue the advance on the morning of the 24th. The New Zealand Division, attacking at 4.30 a.m., was to take Loupart Wood and Grevillers, the village to the north-east. The 37th Division of the IV. Corps operated against Biefvillers, on the left. The ultimate objective of the New Zealand Division was the town of Bapaume. For this attack the 1st Brigade, N.Z.F.A., and the 26th (Army) Brigade, R.F.A. were placed at the disposal of the G.O.C., 1st Infantry Brigade, which was to capture the first objective of Loupart Wood and Grevillers. The 1st Brigade batteries occupied positions east of Achiet-le-Petit. The 2nd Artillery Brigade was placed at the disposal of the 2nd Infantry Brigade, which was to follow up the 1st Infantry Brigade, and push through the first objective towards Bapaume and the high ground to the east of the town. Batteries of the 3rd Brigade were placed in divisional reserve, and occupied positions of readiness in rear of the 2nd Brigade. The orders for this attack were not issued until 2 a.m. on the 24th, and as the attack was timed for 4 a.m. it was found that the time available was too brief to enable detailed orders for a barrage to be issued to brigades, and thence to batteries. Brigades of artillery were, therefore, attached to the infantry brigades in the order mentioned, and artillery brigade commanders reported for instructions to the commander of the infantry brigade to which they were attached. The infantry attack was thus launched without any organised barrage fire, despite which fact it made good progress, and Loupart Wood and Grevillers were both captured. Both the 2nd and 3rd Brigades got their guns into position east of the Albert-Arras railway line to support the advance of the 2nd Infantry Brigade. Grevillers and Biefvillers which was taken by the 2nd Infantry Brigade, came under heavy enemy fire as soon as they had been captured. Any further advance towards Bapaume was found to be impracticable, for the time being, as the enemy was encountered in increasing strength west of the town, in the locality of the town and Avesnes-les-Bapaume.

Having crossed the battered stretch of country in rear of the enemy's old front line near Puisieux, batteries were now in action in open country. At last the prospect of open warfare, which the gunners had long contemplated, fair but elusive, had become a reality. The picture that presented itself to the eye as the guns went forward on the morning of August 24th, was remarkable and inspiriting. Infantry, guns, tanks, transport, and detachments of cavalry were all on the move, the roads and tracks leading forward being almost black with traffic. Overhead, in a brilliant sky, aeroplanes wheeled and circled, the insistent drone of their engines penetrating through the noise of battle. At one point where the roads converged, east of Achiet-le-Petit, the batteries streaming down the roads were obliged to defile through a narrow gap. The enemy was shelling the vicinity with a high velocity gun, but the great stream of traffic was capably controlled, and batteries passed safely through and on towards their positions. The Division, fighting in open country, no longer had at its disposal a complicated and secure system of communications, and artillery brigades and batteries were to a large extent obliged to improvise their own communications as they advanced. Visual signalling was used a great deal, especially by observing officers, in communicating with their batteries. The portable wireless set with which each brigade was equipped was sometimes used for communication between observers and groups or batteries, but the greatest use was made of ground wires and visual signalling.

The advance was resumed on the morning of August 25th after a night of heavy enemy shelling which culminated in a heavy barrage on the front line system about 4 a.m. At 5 a.m. under cover of a heavy fog and behind the barrage, the infantry swept forward to Avesnes-les-Bapaume, and gained the Bapaume-Sapignies Road. The enemy's heavy artillery was very active all day, but this did not prevent the guns from pushing forward. At 4 p.m., 1st Brigade batteries occupied positions immediately to the north of Loupart Wood, and in the evening the 3rd Brigade went into action west of Biefvillers. Hostile heavy artillery had been sweeping the roads and open country for some hours, and to get the guns forward was an anxious and difficult task. A section of the 12th Battery which was caught in the shelling, suffered several casualties and had some horses killed. All guns supported an attack on Favreuil at 6 p.m. The country was swept by a heavy thunderstorm at 9 p.m., and rain continued to fall all night. After a conference with the infantry brigade commander, it was decided to push the 2nd Brigade batteries forward towards Favreuil, on the western side of the Bapaume-Sapignies Road. Two of the batteries, the 2nd and 6th, were to be in action by 6 a.m. on the 26th to support an attack on the railway line running north-east from Bapaume.

The continuance of the unfavourable weather conditions on the 26th did not contribute to freedom of movement, but batteries limbered up again and advanced a little nearer to Bapaume. Before dawn the enemy commenced to shell forward and rear areas with all calibre guns and howitzers, and between 4 and 5 a.m. he put down a heavy concentration on battery positions and the valley between Biefvillers and Favreuil. During the morning New Zealand infantry reached the road running from Bapaume to Beugnatre, but as the division on the left was unable to get through or round this latter village, the advance was temporarily held up. It was then decided to bombard Beugnatre, and so from 1.15 p.m. to 1.30 p.m. the village was intensely shelled, after which the place was taken, and a line established on its eastern outskirts. The 3rd Brigade batteries moved forward to positions east of Biefvillers, and at 6 p.m. all guns fired in a creeping barrage to enable the New

Zealand infantry to go forward to the line of the railway running north of Fremicourt. This was successfully accomplished, except at one spot, which was very strongly held with machine guns.

While supporting this attack some batteries of the 3rd Brigade came under heavy and accurate fire from enemy 5.9in. batteries. The 4th Battery had four guns put out of action, several men killed, and eleven wounded, including the battery commander. The 13th Battery also suffered some casualties. Both batteries kept their guns in action, despite this sustained and destructive shelling, the gallantry displayed by officers and men of the 4th Battery under trying circumstances being of a high order.

The guns were now within close range of Bapaume, the position of which was hourly being made more precarious by the development of the encircling movement from the north. On the 28th, and the following day and night, the town was severely battered by the guns, which finally concentrated all their strength in a hurricane barrage which started on the western outskirts and rolled slowly over the town. This punishment, added to the threat of envelopment, compelled the enemy to withdraw; and at dawn on August 29th the infantry found that Bapaume had been evacuated. The Division passed through the town and advanced the same day some distance along the line of the Bapaume-Cambrai Road. At noon the 1st Brigade moved forward to positions south-west of the town, covering the high ground beyond Fremicourt and Bancourt. A section each of the 1st and 3rd Batteries was attached at the same time to the battalions in the line, their task being to deal quickly with enemy machine guns, and assist their own troops wherever they encountered any serious resistance. A section of the 12th Battery, and one from the 13th Battery, were also pushed forward east of Monument Wood; the remainder of the 3rd Brigade brought its teams up to positions of assembly close to the guns.

The advance was continued east of Bapaume on the 30th; Fremicourt and the ridge east of it being seized, as well as Bancourt. The 5th Division was to have co-operated by taking

Beugny, further to the north, but their attack did not meet with success, and Beugny was not finally taken by them until the 2nd of September. Artillery support for the New Zealand Division was given by the 1st and 3rd New Zealand Brigades, acting in direct co-operation with infantry commanders. The 2nd Brigade assisted the barrage to beyond Fremicourt, after which it passed into divisional reserve, moving its guns forward so as to be able to cover the front of the Division if required. These new positions, which were all in the neighbourhood of Beugnatre, were occupied a few hours after the attack opened, and though the move was made during the period of heavy shelling, the Brigade got safely through with few casualties.

Shortly after dawn on the closing day of the month the enemy delivered a fairly strong counter-attack on the front held by the Division. The attack was preceded by heavy shelling, and assisted by six German tanks. S.O.S. signals brought the guns into action, forward sections engaging the enemy over open sights; the attack was beaten off with loss to the enemy, who left two of his tanks in the hands of the New Zealanders. Later in the day, the 18-pr. batteries of the 3rd Brigade advanced east of Bapaume, and the 4th (Howitzer) Battery occupied a position east of Monument Wood.

In the closing days of August an important change was effected in the tactical control of the field artillery supporting the Division. To make for closer and more effective co-operation with the infantry it was decided that all the field artillery directly supporting any operation should form a single group, and that the group commander should attach himself to the headquarters of the infantry brigade in the line. At the time this was regarded as one of the most effective means of providing for that close co-operation between the two arms which the rapidity and sweeping character of the advance, with its ever-changing situations, made desirable. Batteries or brigades which were not included in the group of advanced guard artillery remained under the direct control of Divisional Artillery Headquarters, and constituted a divisional reserve. Occupying positions of readiness, they were able to fire at call should the enemy's resistance stiffen, or should there be a danger of a counter-attack. On those occasions when the enemy failed to offer a strong resistance to the advance, fire was seldom opened from these positions of readiness, and batteries limbered up and moved forward once more in the wake of the infantry.

The grouping and attachment of brigades was as follows:— 1st Brigade, N.Z.F.A., and 26th (Army) Brigade, R.F.A. (Lieut.-Colonel I. T. Standish), attached to the 1st Infantry Brigade; 2nd (Army) Brigade, N.Z.F.A., and 293rd (Army) Brigade, R.F.A. (Lieut.-Colonel N. S. Falla), attached to the 2nd Infantry Brigade; 3rd Brigade, N.Z.F.A., and 317th Brigade, R.F.A. (Lieut.-Colonel R. S. McQuarrie), attached to the 3rd (Rifle) Brigade.

The attack was taken up with vigour on the 1st of September, when the Division attacked under cover of a barrage at 4.55 a.m., and advanced the line to the high ground east of Bancourt and Fremicourt. By 5 p.m. all batteries of the 2nd Brigade had moved forward to positions which had been reconnoitred on the previous day, midway between Bapaume and Fremicourt. The 4th and 12th Batteries of the 3rd Brigade also moved forward during the evening and carried out a programme of harassing fire. The day was remarkable for the heavy casualties amongst officers. Two forward observing officers from the 1st Brigade, Lieutenant Dean (1st Battery), and 2nd Lieutenant Russell (7th Battery), and three officers from the 3rd Brigade were killed, those from the 3rd Brigade being Captain F. V. Brown (11th Battery), 2nd Lieutenant A. J. Priestley (13th Battery), and Lieutenant J. M. Watkins (4th Battery). During the night battery areas and the eastern outskirts of Bapaume were heavily bombed and there was also a good deal of intermittent shelling.

In the operations planned for September 2nd the 42nd Division on the right was to take Villers-au-Flos and the spur in front with exploitation towards Barastre and Haplincourt Wood as a second objective. The New Zealand Division co-operated with the 5th Division on the left, which was attacking Beugny and Delsaux Farm, and the high ground east of Beugny. The New Zealand infantry were directly supported by the 2nd Brigade group artillery, which for the occasion included the 3rd Brigade. The 1st Brigade and the 123rd

Brigade, R.F.A., supported the 42nd Division, and the 317th Brigade, R.F.A., attached to the New Zealand Division, supported the 5th Division. The barrage opened up at 5.15 a.m., and the enemy replied about five minutes later with a heavy counter-barrage. The 3rd Brigade area was heavily shelled, and the 12th Battery sustained a good many casualties.

Strong resistance was encountered on the front of the Division; and, though the enemy was thrown back all along the line, the advance was for a time held up by heavy machine gun fire from some huts near the cross roads west of Haplincourt. A heavy concentration of fire was put down on this area at 1 p.m., and the infantry were able to push on again. The advance suffered another check in the afternoon, mainly owing to machine gun fire; and the procedure adopted earlier in the day was successfully repeated. The area was swept with a heavy barrage, the infantry following on and materially increasing their total captures of prisoners and machine guns for the day. The G.O.C., 2nd Infantry Brigade, expressed his thanks for the assistance given to the infantry by artillery observers, who had sent back to batteries and group a great deal of valuable and timely information. A forward observing officer from the 13th Battery effectively engaged two enemy field batteries and one anti-aircraft battery, and shelled another battery while it was in the act of effecting a retirement. During the forenoon the 1st Brigade moved forward to positions in front of Riencourt, the guns being in action in the new area about 1 p.m.

CHAPTER X.

THE ENEMY IN RETREAT.

On the 2nd of September the front occupied by the Division extended from a point west of Haplincourt, in the south, to the Fremicourt-Le Bucquiere Road, near Delsaux Farm, in the north. The results of the Battles of Amiens, Bapaume, and the Scarpe rapidly declared themselves, and during the night of September 2nd the enemy fell back rapidly along the whole front of the Third Army and the right of the First Army. By the close of the day he had taken up positions along the general line of the Canal du Nord from Peronne to Ytres, and thence east of Hermies, Inchy-en-Artois, and Eaucourt St. Quentin to the Sensee, east of Lecluse. Plans had been made overnight for the 3rd Brigade and the 317th Brigade, R.F.A., to assist in supporting the 5th Division in an attack to be made shortly after dawn on September 3rd on Delsaux Farm and the high ground east of Beugny, but shortly after the time fixed for the opening of the attack, word was received that the 5th Division had lost touch with the enemy. Practically the same position obtained on the front of the New Zealand Division. Fires were observed behind the enemy's lines during the night and infantry patrols found in the morning that Haplincourt had been evacuated. The 2nd Brigade N.Z.F.A. was at once ordered to move forward, and keep in touch with the 2nd Infantry Brigade; the remaining artillery brigades reverted to the control of Divisional Artillery Headquarters.

The Commander of the 2nd Brigade, whose orders were to push as far forward with the infantry as possible, at once went forward with the infantry Brigade Commander to the latter's new headquarters at Bancourt. There word was received that the infantry had got into touch with the enemy at Bertincourt, and that the advance was temporarily held up by machine guns and 77mm. guns firing at point blank range from near the railway junction north of Ytres. Battery positions were at once reconnoitred, and the brigade, which had been awaiting orders at the rendezvous near Haplincourt, was brought into action in the valley north-west of Bertincourt. The guns were got forward and into action by 2 p.m. In the meantime, the 1st and 317th Brigades had been ordered, shortly after 1 p.m., to take up positions north and east of Haplincourt, and at 2 p.m. the 3rd Brigade was ordered to a position of readiness on the eastern outskirts of Fremicourt. The 123rd Brigade was ordered to rejoin its division. The 2nd Brigade was now covering the forward or outpost line, and the three remaining brigades covered the main line in depth. After the 2nd Brigade batteries had got into position it was found that the infantry had pushed the enemy back to the railway line east of Bertincourt and west of Ytres, and at once fire was brought to bear on this area, driving the enemy back into the village of Ruyaulcourt. As the advance was to be continued next day, arrangements were made overnight for the 2nd Brigade to continue in close support of the infantry, and for the 3rd Brigade to be in a position of assembly, and report to the group commander by 7 a.m. on the 4th. Batteries of the 1st and 317th Brigades were to remain in action, with teams ready at hand for a move.

The Division was now drawing near to Havrincourt Wood, where the close growth and dense foliage provided good cover for enemy machine guns and light field batteries. Havrincourt Wood lay west of the Canal du Nord, but the canal at this point did not offer any obstacle to the Division's progress. North of Ruyaulcourt it ran into a deep tunnel, and continued its course underground for a distance of about five thousand yards, breaking ground again at a point south of Ytres. It was decided that if opposition was met with in Havrincourt Wood it would be turned from the north and south by flanking divisions. The policy to be followed was to keep touch with and engage the enemy's rearguard with the Division's advance guard, but not to undertake any attack on a large scale if strong opposition was encountered. The infantry continued the advance at an early hour on September 4th, and passed through Ruyaulcourt after the guns had dealt with opposition which was encountered east of the village. At 11 a.m., the 3rd Brigade, which had been maintained in its position of assembly pending developments, moved slightly forward to its front and went into action near Bertincourt. The 2nd Brigade batteries effectively dealt with large numbers of the enemy seen advancing towards Neuville shortly after mid-day, as also with enemy machine guns and artillery in Havrincourt Wood. At 3.40 p.m. the enemy was reported to be coming from Havrincourt down into the wood, and the whole area was subjected to intense and searching fire from both field and heavy batteries. At 7.15 p.m. a concentrated barrage was put down on Neuville, and the place was cleared of the enemy.

The headquarters of artillery brigades and battery areas were heavily shelled during the night of September 4-5th, the enemy using high velocity guns and a great quantity of gas shell. Hostile fire remained fairly heavy and continuous throughout the following day. The New Zealand batteries confined their activities to ordinary forms of harassing fire until the evening, when, at the request of the infantry, a strong barrage was put down on the road running north and south on the western edge of Havrincourt Wood. Attacking in the wake of the barrage, the infantry cleared the road, and reached a line skirting the western edge of the wood. During the day all batteries of the 2nd Brigade moved into positions about the railway line south-east of Bertincourt, and the 7th Battery took up a position in front of Ytres.

At midnight on September 5th the IV. Corps front was readjusted to a two-division front, with the New Zealand Division on the right and the 37th Division on the left. The readjustment involved some change respecting the constitution of the Royal Field Artillery Brigades attached to the Division; when the change was completed the artillery supporting the Division consisted of the 1st, 2nd, and 3rd Brigades, N.Z.F.A.; the 210th and 211th Brigades of the 42nd Divisional Artillery; and the 223rd Brigade of the 63rd Divisional Artillery. The 56th Brigade R.G.A., consisting of three batteries of six-inch howitzers, and one battery of 9.2in. howitzers, was affiliated to the Division. The heavy guns of two other brigades which were primarily employed for counter-battery work and long range harassing fire, could also be called on for bombardment purposes. The 2nd, 3rd, and 210th Brigades, grouped under the 2nd Brigade Commander, covered the three battalions in line; the remaining three field artillery brigades were in divisional reserve, but were maintained in action for S.O.S. purposes, and were available for operations at an approximate range of 4,500 yards from S.O.S. lines.

On the morning of September 6th the Division pushed on to the edge of Havrincourt Wood, and the trench system to the south; a little later reports were received at Artillery Headquarters that the enemy was withdrawing. In the early afternoon the 2nd Brigade, which was acting advance-guard artillery, reported that the enemy was retiring over the high ground towards Metz-en-Couture. The remaining brigades were ordered to reconnoitre positions to cover the trench systems on the eastern outskirts of Havrincourt Wood, Metz and the roads along which the enemy was retiring being vigorously shelled meanwhile. There was practically no hostile fire on artillery areas throughout the day, the indications being that the enemy was making big efforts to get his guns safely away to the rear. Soon after midday, the 2nd Brigade batteries were in action west of Neuville, with an advanced section pushed out on the enemy's side of the village. The enemy appeared to be suffering a certain amount of demoralisation, and shortly before dark the roads north of Gouzeaucourt Wood were black with enemy troops and transport retreating under heavy fire from the corps heavy artillery and the 92nd Brigade, R.G.A. The 1st Brigade had carried out some useful shooting during the day from the positions near Ruyaulcourt which it had occupied early in the morning; by midnight the 3rd Brigade was in action in the neighbourhood of the village.

CHAPTER XI.

BREAKING THE HINDENBURG LINE.

By September 7th the Division had reached the outer defences of the famous Hindenburg Line, on which it was to be expected that the enemy divisions would make a strong effort to impose a check on the advance of the British Armies, and save themselves from the growing disorganisation which was making itself apparent in their ranks. A successful attack upon this line, the last and strongest of the enemy's prepared positions, would be far-reaching and momentous in its consequences. Failure to break through would seriously stay the advance, and would go far towards reviving the declining morale of the German Armies. The Hindenburg Line, which really consisted of a whole series of entrenchments and fortifications, extended in places to ten thousand yards in depth, and was so skilfully sited as to take the greatest possible advantage of the configuration of the country through which it ran.

A few hours after midnight on September 6th messages were received at artillery headquarters that both the New Zealand and 37th Divisions were well into the heart of Havrincourt Wood, and were approaching its eastern edge. The commander of the 2nd Brigade met his battery commanders at six o'clock in the morning and rode forward and reconnoitred positions between Metz and the wood. These were occupied by 9 a.m. Enemy shelling during the move caused some casualties in the Brigade, which also lost about a dozen horses. Beyond some shelling at the 3rd Brigade waggon lines, enemy batteries did not display much activity during the day. Both the 3rd Brigade and the 210th Brigade advanced their guns after the 2nd Brigade had completed its move, but the 210th Brigade could not get all its guns up during daylight, as the positions were overlooked from the high ground south-east of Gouzeaucourt; individual sections were got on to the position, however, the remainder of the guns going in under cover of darkness.

Some effective shooting was carried out on parties of the enemy which were seen to be moving freely about Trescault and the country to the immediate south. On completion of the relief of the 2nd Infantry Brigade by the 3rd (Rifle) Brigade, Lieut.-Colonel R. S. McQuarrie assumed command of the group comprising the 3rd and 2nd Brigades, N.Z.F.A., and the 210th Brigade, R.F.A. The 1st and 223rd Brigades remained superimposed.

On September 8th the forward movement was continued, and Gouzeaucourt Wood was cleared. Although there was a good deal of intermittent shelling about some battery positions, the day was quiet so far as the artillery were concerned. Preparations were made for an operation to be carried out at 4 a.m., on the 9th by the New Zealand Division, acting in conjunction with the 17th Division. The objective of the New Zealand Division was the high ground east of Gouzeaucourt Wood and along the Trescault Ridge. This attack did not meet with complete success, however, and after the barrage had advanced through its various stages batteries continued firing on their final line to enable the infantry to dig in where they stood.

The enemy was now back on to a very strong line of defence. North of Havrincourt he had taken shelter behind the Canal du Nord. From the neighbourhood of Havrincourt southwards his main line of resistance was the Hindenburg line, which after passing through the village of Havrincourt ran south-east across the Beaucamp, La Vacquerie, and Bonavis Ridges to the Scheldt Canal at Bantouzelle, whence it followed the line of the canal to St. Quentin. Strong German forces held formidable positions about Havrincourt and Epehy, which had to be taken before the attack on the Hindenburg Line could be launched. Plans were therefore laid for an attack on September 12th, by the IV. and VI. Corps of the Third Army, on a front of about five miles in the Havrincourt sector, employing troops of the New Zealand, 37th, 62nd, and 2nd Divisions. This attack was originally planned for September 11th, but was postponed for twenty-four hours. During the two or three days preceding the attack, batteries were busy getting their guns forward for the assault, and stocking the new positions with ammunition up to five hundred rounds per gun for the 18-pr. batteries, and four hundred rounds for the howitzers. The 1st Brigade positions in or near Havrincourt Wood were occupied on the evening of the 9th, and as batteries were to remain silent until the opening of the attack, a gun guard only was maintained on the position. This lessened the risk of casualties, in addition to affording the gunners some brief respite from the guns. The New Zealand Division, with Trescault Spur as its objective, was supported by six field artillery brigades, three batteries of six-inch howitzers and four six-inch trench mortars, which had been sent forward and placed at the disposal of the G.O.C. 3rd (Rifle) Brigade. The three brigades then in the line—the 210th, R.F.A., and the 2nd and 3rd Brigades, in that order from right to left—covered the whole divisional front on the opening barrage line; the remaining three brigades were superimposed. The attack opened up well at 5.25 a.m., and the first objectives were early reported in the hands of the infantry, but thereafter the enemy's resistance hardened, and further progress was achieved only by dint of hard fighting. Enemy artillery fire was heavy on the forward areas, but battery positions suffered only some spasmodic shelling.

Following on the relief of the 3rd (Rifle) Brigade by the 1st Infantry Brigade on the night after the attack, Lieut.-Colonel I. T. Standish assumed command of the advance guard artillery. The group consisted of the 211th Brigade R.F.A., and the 3rd and 1st Brigades, N.Z.F.A., each of which was affiliated to a battalion in the line. The 2nd Brigade, with the remaining two R.F.A. Brigades was superimposed. On the following evening, however, the 210th and 211th Brigades were withdrawn from the Division, and were replaced by the 27th Brigade, R.F.A., only. The New Zealand Division, less artillery, was relieved by the 5th Division on September 15th, and went into corps reserve. The New Zealand Artillery, with attached brigades of R.F.A., remained in the line under the command of the 5th Division, but orders were then received transferring the 2nd (Army) Brigade, N.Z.F.A., to another area under the V. Corps. The Brigade succeeded in withdrawing its guns from the line without casualties, in spite of very heavy bombing by enemy aeroplanes. The brigade had already suffered about thirty casualties as the result of a heavy gas-shell bombardment in the early hours of September 14th while batteries had been engaged in firing on S.O.S. The affected areas were temporarily evacuated where possible, and every precaution was taken; but the total casualties ran into big figures. The 1st Brigade suffered even more severely. In the 15th Battery the battery commander and three other officers and forty-one other ranks had to be evacuated, and in the 1st Battery there were about twenty cases. The German batteries continued very active all day, and for about two hours in the morning the 18-pr. batteries of the 2nd Brigade were shelled by 28 c.m. howitzers. A good deal of material damage was done about the positions, one gun being blown a distance of thirty yards. Fortunately no casualties were suffered.

During the three nights following the relief by the 5th Division enemy night bombers were particularly active over Havrincourt Wood and the neighbourhood. They did not inflict a great deal of damage, however, and were not permitted to go unscathed, two of them being brought down in one night by British aeroplanes. On September 18th the artillery supported an operation by the 5th Division, which was engaged in throwing out a defensive flank to cover an attack by the 38th Division on the right. The enemy replied to the barrage fire by shelling batteries with guns of all calibres, and further heavy concentrations of gas were put down during the afternoon.

The 1st Brigade and No. 1 Section of the Divisional Ammunition Column withdrew to their waggon lines after dark on September 19th, and came under the orders of the C.R.A., New Zealand Division. The following night the 3rd Brigade, less the 4th Battery, which remained in action attached to the 123rd Brigade, also withdrew to waggon lines. Both brigades remained in rest until a day or two before the launching of the Battle of Cambrai and the attack on the Hindenburg Line on September 27th. The time was devoted to cleaning up and overhauling clothing and equipment, all of which had become sadly in need of attention during the four weeks' fighting in which the artillery had been engaged without respite since

August 21st. On September 23rd these units commenced to make preparations for their return to the line. Positions were selected for the 1st Brigade batteries in Havrincourt Wood, and for those of the 3rd Brigade in the vicinity of Metz, most of them close to the road running from Metz through Havrincourt Wood. Until these positions were occupied on the night of September 25th-26th, batteries devoted their energies towards preparing emplacements, and getting ammunition forward, a great deal of it being lifted from the positions recently vacated behind Metz. For the attack on September 27th the 1st Brigade was attached to the 42nd Division, and the 3rd Brigade to the 5th Division. Each field artillery brigade was to superimpose one of its 18-pr. batteries on the front covered by the remaining two, the 4.5in. howitzer batteries to distribute their fire along each brigade front. In addition to forward observing officers, each group sent forward on the day of the attack a forward intelligence officer, who was given every possible facility for communicating with his group. Trench mortars were to engage in wire cutting and assist in the initial stages of the barrage.

The attack was launched behind a close barrage at 5.20 a.m. on September 27th. The 5th and 42nd Divisions made fairly substantial progress, but complete success was not achieved. A second attack the following morning gave better results, and both the 1st and 3rd Brigades were able to advance their guns, the 1st Brigade in the afternoon, and the 3rd Brigade in the evening. During the night, September 28th-29th, the New Zealand Division returned to the line again, and command of the artillery on the sector passed to Brigadier-General G. N. Johnston, C.R.A. of the Division.

At 3.30 a.m. on September 29th the 1st and 2nd New Zealand Infantry Brigades passed through the 42nd Division, and attacked in conjunction with the 5th Division on the right and the 62nd Division on the left. This attack was supported by six brigades of field artillery. The objectives were Welsh Ridge and Bon Avis Ridge, in the heart of the Hindenbury system. Welsh Ridge lay to the north of La Vacquerie, and Bon Avis Ridge to the east. The advance was rapid and decisive; both the ridges were captured, and La Vacquerie was also cleared of

New Zealand Artillery crossing the River Selle by a bridge constructed by the New Zealand Engineers under heavy shell-fire

[*Official Photo*]

the enemy. The infantry pressed forward towards the Canal de St. Quentin, one brigade from each group of artillery being ordered to support the advance by advancing its guns to the eastern side of the Villers Plouich-Marcoing Road. At noon the 1st Brigade, N.Z.F.A., went forward to positions in the La Vacquerie Valley, and the 7th Battery moved up in close support of the infantry. Late in the afternoon the left group was ordered to place one brigade forward of the sunken road running northeast from La Vacquerie. All this country was intersected with a perfect maze of trenches, and was generally broken and battered by the destructive shelling to which it had been subjected. Efforts were made to clear a track for the guns, which even then were able only slowly to pick their way forward. By the close of the day a very satisfactory advance had been registered, and in addition to some hundreds of prisoners, a number of field guns, trench mortars, and machine guns, and much material had been seized. In the evening orders were issued for the resumption of the attack on September 30th, with the object of securing the eastern bank of the canal between Crevecour and Vaucelles, establishing bridgeheads, and capturing Crevecour and Lesdain and the high ground east towards Esnes. An attempt was made to cross the canal during the night, but the enemy holding the eastern bank was very active with his machine guns, and the intense darkness did not facilitate the operation. Early on October 1st, however, posts were established on the eastern bank, and Crevecour was occupied.

The 3rd Brigade, supporting troops of the 5th Division, on the right, did not move forward on the 29th, as the extent of the 5th Division's advance did not necessitate a change of positions. Orders were actually received to move forward to the neighbourhood of La Vacquerie, but when Battery Commanders went forward to reconnoitre positions, they found this area still in occupation by the enemy. At noon the Brigade received orders to remain for the time being in the positions near Beaucamp. Waggons and limbers, which had been brought forward in anticipation of a move, were parked on the outskirts of Metz. When the brigade assisted in supporting a further attack by the

5th Division on September 30th better progress was made, and by evening the 18-pr. batteries were in action near La Vacquerie, and the 4th (Howitzer) Battery near Gonnelieu.

The early days of October were occupied with preparations for a resumption of the general advance on October 8th. In the meanwhile everything was kept in readiness to meet any possible change in the situation. Orders were issued for reconnaissances to be made as far forward as possible, and it was arranged that in the event of an advance one brigade of artillery was to follow closely in support of each infantry brigade, the remaining brigades advancing their batteries as the situation required. As advanced positions were selected they were to be stocked with ammunition, and made ready for occupation. The Divisional Trench Mortar Officer was ordered to get mortars into position on the night of October 2nd to cover the canal crossings. The positions selected by the 1st Brigade were in the bend of the canal, south-east of Masnieres. They were not occupied immediately, but the 7th Battery was so badly shelled on the afternoon of October 2nd, that it was moved to its forward position, and there remained silent. That night the 3rd Brigade took over the positions of the 123rd Brigade, R.F.A., situated about a mile north-east of La Vacquerie. On the night of October 3rd the 3rd (Rifle) Brigade relieved the 1st Infantry Brigade in the line, and command of the Left Group Artillery, consisting of the 1st Brigade and the 124th and 317th Brigades, R.F.A., passed to Lieut.-Colonel Standish, and of the Right Group, comprising the 3rd Brigade and the 210th and 211th Brigades, R.F.A., to Lieut.-Colonel McQuarrie.

A deliberate bombardment of the enemy's known positions was carried out during the afternoon of October 4th, with the object of destroying his personnel and damaging his morale. Attention was paid to all sunken roads, as well as trenches and machine gun posts, to the Esnes Torrent Ravine, and to the valley running north-east from Crevecour. The heavy artillery co-operated by shelling Bel Aise and Pelu Wood. Early the following morning there were indications of an enemy withdrawal on the front. When the enemy commenced to shell Vaucelles, and was seen to be retiring all batteries were ordered into their barrage positions. By the close of the day the 1st

Brigade was established in the positions which had been reconnoitred on October 1st, and the 3rd Brigade was getting into action immediately east of the main road to Cambrai. Shortly before midnight the Right Group, assisted by the 90th Brigade, R.G.A., carried out a heavy bombardment on Lesdain. A forward observing officer who had crossed the canal during the day usefully directed the fire of his group, using a loop wireless set for his communications, and sent back a good deal of valuable information. Observed shooting and harassing fire were carried out on the 6th, and on the 7th. On this latter day batteries of the 3rd Brigade went into action in fresh positions near the southern end of Cheneaux Wood.

It had been expected that the crossing of the canal at this point would entail a difficult and, perhaps, costly attack, and preparations for an attack were actually being made when the enemy so unexpectedly withdrew from his formidable positions. The Division was, therefore, able to cross the canal without any heavy losses, and it became possible to establish the batteries of the 3rd Brigade on the eastern bank of the canal before the launching of the attack on Esnes.

On October 8th the New Zealand Division in conjunction with the 37th Division on the right and the 3rd Division on the left, attacked at 4.30 a.m., with the aim of establishing itself on a line represented by the sunken road south-west of Esnes, le Grand Pont, Esnes Mill, and the Esnes-la Targette Road. If opportunity offered, success was to be exploited by securing Esnes and a line approximately one thousand yards east of the Esnes-la Targette Road. The night preceding the attack was wet, and rain was still falling when the guns opened the barrage. The advance of the infantry was so rapid that within a few hours of the opening of the attack the guns were going forward again, and by the early afternoon the great proportion of the field artillery supporting the Division was in action east of the canal, having crossed on bridges erected or repaired by the Engineers. In consequence of reports having been received that a fresh German division was marching south-west on Cattenieres, it was considered probable that the enemy might launch a counterattack from the north-east during the afternoon, and it was, therefore, decided not to move all the guns east of the canal.

The 317th Brigade remained west of the canal with S.O.S. lines east of la Targette. The 1st Brigade positions were some distance north-east of Crevecour, and those of the 3rd Brigade in the neighbourhood of Pelu Wood. The day had been a very successful one for the Division, and casualties were small in both artillery brigades, though the 1st Brigade unfortunately lost two officers killed.

When the advance was resumed at 5.20 a.m. on the 9th, the reply to the barrage fire of the guns was slight, and it was soon discovered that the enemy was withdrawing from his positions. The infantry pushed on as rapidly as the barrage would permit, and were soon moving forward east of the railway line, which ran west of Cattenieres and Fontaines-au-Pire. After finishing the barrage the 3rd Brigade reconnoitred positions north of Longsart. These were occupied at once, the 11th and 13th batteries sending out forward sections, which kept close up with the infantry, and materially assisted their advance. The 1st Brigade occupied positions of assembly south of Seranvillers, where batteries remained until the following morning. The infantry entered Fontaine on the afternoon of the 9th, and pressing determinedly on, had reached the long straight road from Cambrai to Le Cateau, and cleared Beauvois, by the early morning of October 10th.

On the 11th Briastre was taken, and the Division reached the line of the river Selle. The guns moved forward early in the morning, after reports had come through that the infantry were advancing and meeting with little opposition. After sending the 13th Battery forward in support of the infantry, the 3rd Brigade remained in positions of readiness until it went into action near Beauvois. The 1st Brigade also took up positions near Beauvois during the afternoon, and at dawn on the 11th relieved the 3rd Brigade as advanced guard artillery. In order to cover the crossings of the River Selle, and the country east of the river, the 1st Brigade moved forward again to Viesly, batteries being in action there by about 9 a.m.

It was in these two towns of Beauvois and Caudry that the New Zealanders encountered the first civilians liberated from the dominion of the enemy who had invaded their country. In the earlier stages of the great advance the enemy had made a practice of clearing each village of its inhabitants before it became involved in the fighting, and sending them to the rear. By the time the Division reached Caudry, the advance had become so swift that the enemy was apparently unable to follow this usual practice, and both in Beauvois and Caudry, he had grouped the civilian inhabitants in the rear or eastern portion of the town, the buildings in which they were sheltered being indicated by red cross flags which flew from the roof.

During the brief period that batteries remained in reserve in this locality they naturally saw a great deal of the overjoyed inhabitants, from whom they learnt much regarding the miseries which they had had to suffer during the long years their towns were occupied by the enemy.

The 1st and 3rd Brigades both enjoyed a brief respite from active fighting, from the 12th to the 18th of October, and in addition to giving the horses a much-needed rest, units were provided with an opportunity of overhauling their guns and equipment. The whole Division, with the exception of the Divisional Ammunition Column, was relieved by the 42nd Division. The 1st Brigade was relieved by the 210th Brigade, R.F.A., and with the 3rd Brigade, which was then in Divisional Reserve, occupied rest billets at Beauvois. The horses were given as much grazing as possible, and benefited considerably by the rest. A visit was paid to the lines on October 15th by the Prince of Wales. On this day also orders were received for the artillery to return to the line, under the orders of the 42nd Division. The weather was bad on October 16th, heavy rain falling in the morning, when Brigade and Battery Commanders from both brigades went forward to reconnoitre positions east of Viesly and south of Briastre. The 1st Battery selected a flank position for one gun, which was to harass the railway line running from Briastre to Solesmes, and the sunken road south of the latter town. With the 223rd Brigade, R.F.A., the two New Zealand brigades formed the Right Group of the artillery supporting the 42nd Division, the group being commanded by Lieut.-Colonel F. B. Sykes R.A. who formerly commanded the 2nd Brigade, N.Z.F.A. Three guns per battery were taken to the positions on the night of October 18th,. the remainder following next night, when the carting of ammunition was also completed. The 15th (Howitzer) Battery was so heavily shelled that it was found necessary to move the guns to another position near by.

On October 18th Lieut-Colonel I. T. Standish relinquished command of the 1st Brigade, in order to proceed to New Zealand, his place as Brigade Commander being taken by Major C. N. Newman.

On October 20th both brigades fired in support of the 42nd Division, which attacked from Briastre with the 5th Division on its right, and the 62nd Division of the VI. Corps on its left. The attack was supported by three batteries of six-inch howitzers, in addition to six brigades of field artillery. For forty-five minutes after zero, which was at 2 a.m., one 18-pr. battery of the 1st Brigade fired incendiary shells into the railway triangle south of Solesmes; the remaining two 18-pr. batteries fired a smoke screen, and the 15th (Howitzer) Battery shelled the railway triangle and the railways abounding it. After completing this phase the brigade remained superimposed, first on the Right Group front, and later on that of the Left Group. The barrage was maintained to its final stages, but the Division did not succeed in reaching its objectives. A further attack, made later in the day under cover of artillery fire, was somewhat more successful. Early in the afternoon both brigades fired on S.O.S., in response to an order from Group Headquarters, but it was ascertained later that this was designed as a form of counter-preparation to break up the massing of enemy troops.

On October 21st the 2nd Brigade rejoined the Divisional Artillery, and Lieut.-Colonel Falla took command of a group consisting of the three New Zealand Brigades and two Brigades of the 42nd Divisional Artillery. The 2nd Brigade batteries, which had been ordered to rendezvous west of Rieux in the morning, went into action east of the river Selle, to the south of Solesmes. The 1st and 3rd Brigades advanced their batteries to positions about a mile beyond Belle Vue. The 1st Brigade had been allotted an area further to the east, but this was found to be under both observation and heavy machine gun fire from the neighbourhood of Beaurain, and was unapproachable by daylight. The weather continued unfavourable, and hostile fire being heavy during the afternoon and night, the work of occupying the positions and stocking them with ammunition was completed under difficulties. Casualties were suffered in every brigade, and at the 12th Battery waggon lines about a dozen horses were killed and as many more wounded by shell fire.

Preparations were now being made for an attack on October 23rd, to be made by troops of the Third and Fourth Armies, on a front of about fifteen miles, with the object of obtaining a line running from the Sambre Canal along the edge of Mormal Forest, to the neighbourhood of Valenciennes. During the first phase of the attack on the IV. Corps front the New Zealand brigades of artillery were to assist in the support of the 42nd Division, which was attacking with the 5th Division on its right and the 3rd Division of the VI. Corps on its left. The first objective for the 5th and 42nd Divisions was the ridge west of Beaurain; the 3rd Division was to attack Romries, north-east of Solesmes. An hour later the 5th and 42nd Divisions were to advance on a line running east of Beaurain. The attack was then to be taken up by the New Zealand and 37th Divisions, which were to pass through the foremost troops of the IV. Corps, and continue the advance in a north-easterly direction in conjunction with the 3rd Division on the left. In addition to the field artillery available for the support of the attack, three batteries of six-inch howitzers were employed to deal with sunken roads and ravines on the front of the Division. In dealing with villages in the line of the advance, shrapnel and smoke shell only were to be used by the field artillery, in order to conserve the safety of the French inhabitants as far as was possible.

Hostile fire was fairly heavy all along the front in the hours preceding the attack, the unfavourable weather conditions which prevailed having seriously interfered with counter-battery work. Areas in which the New Zealand batteries were situated were violently shelled during October 22nd, the enemy using a great number of gas and shells up to eight-inch calibre. The 3rd Battery had two guns disabled, but by taking parts from one to repair the other the battery was able to keep five guns in action. The barrage opened up splendidly at zero hour, 2 a.m. on October 23rd, and though the enemy's reply was fairly violent, little of it fell about the batteries. Rapid and substantial success was achieved along the whole front, and by 7 a.m. all batteries of the 2nd Brigade were on the move to new positions east of Solesmes. The brigade completed its move while the remaining brigades were supporting the advance of the 2nd New Zealand Infantry Brigade, which had taken up the attack after passing through the 42nd Division. That Division having completed its task, command of the artillery on the sector passed to Brigadier-General G. N. Johnston; the Left Group, consisting of the 2nd Brigade and the 210th and 211th Brigades, R.F.A., was commanded by Lieut.-Colonel Falla, and the 1st and 3rd Brigades of the Right Group by Lieut.-Colonel McQuarrie. The 2nd Brigade succeeded in getting 375 rounds per gun on to its forward positions by twelve noon, in time for the barrage to cover the advance to the final objective. A "shell storm" which fell on the brigade area caused a number of casualties, but the barrage was put down punctually at twelve minutes past twelve, and the New Zealand Infantry, who had already captured Vertigneul, and crossed the River Harpies in their first advance, continued the north-easterly movement, and finally entered Beaudignies after night had fallen, and secured the crossings of the river Escaillon, which flowed through the town. Thus they completed an advance for the day of over four miles.

The 211th Brigade, R.F.A., had been ordered to advance when the barrage reached the protective line for the Division's first objective, making every endeavour to get its guns forward in time to fire in the final barrage. The brigade did not succeed in this endeavour, however, and the barrage was therefore fired by the 2nd Brigade alone and was somewhat weak in consequence. The bridges over the Escaillon River having been reported fit to take field guns, the 1st and 3rd Brigades crossed the river during the afternoon, and occupied positions east and south-east of Vertigneul. While Brigade and Battery Commanders were reconnoitring these positions about midday, they were caught in the enemy's counter-barrage, and Major E. Gardner, Commanding 4th (Howitzer) Battery, was wounded.

There were no civilians in Beaudignies when the artillery entered the town, but evidences of their hasty departure were on every hand. An abundance of vegetables grew in the gardens, and while the artillerymen remained in the town or its neighbourhood, they made the most of this opportunity of supplementing their fare.

So far as the artillery were concerned, a period of abstention from active operations ensued until the close of October, when preparations were commenced for the great attack on November 4th, which was to prove a decisive blow for the disorganised and rapidly weakening German Armies. It was by no means a period of rest, however, for there were frequent changes of battery positions, and the enemy's artillery, despite the heavy losses and severe punishment which it had just suffered in the Battle of the Selle River, displayed a marked degree of activity, destructively shelling the villages in the area from which he had just been driven, and both gun and waggon line positions. On October 24th, when losses were fairly heavy in all three brigades, the 1st Battery suffered about a dozen casualties, in addition to the loss of about forty horses; while the 15th Battery had one of its howitzers put out of action by shell fire. As the 7th Battery had been withdrawn from the line to attend the Third Army Artillery School as demonstration battery, and the brigade was in a weak state, it was decided to place it in reserve, and the guns were withdrawn to the waggon lines. A position of readiness was selected for the 2nd Brigade on the north of the Pont a Pierres-Beaudignies Road, and while moving forward, viâ Pont a Pierres, the 6th Battery was caught in a shell storm, and had three men and several horses killed. The enemy continued to shell the area of the St. George's River, compelling the brigade to send its teams to the rear, with the exception of those of the 9th Battery, which moved its guns forward to the vicinity of La Haute Borne, north of Beaudignies. After remaining in a position of readiness throughout the day of the 24th, the 3rd Brigade moved forward the following day to the south-western outskirts of Beaudignies. Batteries remained in those positions only twenty-four hours, after which they crossed the Escaillon River, and went into action on the eastern side of the Baudignies-Ruesnes Road.

Following on the relief of the 2nd Infantry Brigade by the 3rd (Rifle) Brigade Lieut.-Colonel McQuarrie assumed command of the artillery in the line, consisting of the 3rd Brigade, and the 210th Brigade, R.F.A. The 2nd Brigade, in support, was superimposed on the group front, and the 211th Brigade was withdrawn to its waggon lines. As the 2nd Brigade was required for S.O.S. purposes only, gun crews were reduced to a minimum. In view of the fact that there was to be no attempt at a general advance in the meantime, it was decided on October 27th to withdraw the field artillery on the Divisional front to defensive positions, and keep all waggon lines west of Le Trousse Minou. Leaving a section per battery in the forward positions, the 3rd Brigade withdrew to the south-west of Beaudignies, and the 9th Battery vacated its forward positions and rejoined the 2nd Brigade, which remained superimposed on the front of the 3rd Brigade. Of two batteries of medium trench mortars which had gone forward to dig positions, one was withdrawn and the other remained in action. On the last night of the month the 3rd Brigade and the 210th Brigade, R.F.A., went into rest positions on relief by the 1st Brigade and the 211th Brigade, R.F.A.

Included in those who were casualtied as a result of the vigorous daily shelling to which the artillery areas were subjected in the closing days of the month, was Major J. M. Richmond, D.S.O., M.C., who was killed by a shell on October 27th outside the headquarters of the 2nd Artillery Brigade. Leaving New Zealand with the Main Body, Major Richmond served first as Adjutant of the Field Artillery Brigade, and later, when the force was reorganised, as Brigade Major of the Divisional Artillery. In this capacity he displayed ability of a very high order, the operation and other orders prepared by him being always remarkable for their lucidity and conciseness. After having been in command of the 9th Battery for two months Major Richmond had taken command of the 2nd Brigade on the day of his death, *vice* Lieut.-Colonel Falla, who proceeded to England at the close of the month to take command of the Artillery Reserve Depôt. Major Richmond was buried in the cemetery at Solesmes, the funeral being attended by the G.O.C. Division, Major-General A. H. Russell, Brigadier-General

Johnston, and a number of Officers from the Divisional Artillery. Command of the 2nd Brigade passed to Major C. N. Newman, and Lieut.-Colonel Symon reassumed command of the 1st Brigade on rejoining the Division.

A Diversion.

The 2nd (Army) Brigade was withdrawn from the front of the New Zealand Division on September 15th, in consequence of orders having been received the previous day instructing the Brigade to be prepared to move to a new area under the V. Corps. The Brigade was on the march on the 16th, moving during the afternoon to new waggon lines which had been reconnoitred that morning south of Equancourt. Batteries were settled down in their new quarters by 6 p.m., but the night was disturbed by heavy enemy bombing and shelling. One man was killed, and about twenty others were either wounded or gassed. Orders had been received that the brigade was to be grouped in action with the 95th Brigade, R.F.A., and so on the morning of September 17th, gun positions were selected south-east of Heudecourt. As these positions were within plain view of the enemy in his trenches only five hundred yards away, arrangements were made to move the batteries in under cover of darkness. The guns were got up, and positions were stocked before dawn with 300 rounds per gun and 250 rounds per howitzer. Operation orders had been received detailing the part to be played by the brigade in assisting to support an attack to be made on the morning of the 18th by the 21st Division, and final preparations for this attack were completed in the early hours of the morning. Meanwhile battery positions were being heavily shelled with gas and high explosive, the 2nd and 5th Batteries suffering most severely. The brigade fired in the barrage, behind which the infantry advanced and took all their objectives, and spent the remainder of the day in harassing various points on the enemy's front. The following day an observing officer was sent forward to the infantry holding the line in front of Villers-Guislain, with permission to employ the fire of the whole brigade, if necessary. Observation was good, and there was a tremendous amount of movement behind the enemy's front. This was engaged with brigade fire throughout the day, and though a great deal of ammunition was expended, its effect was such as to evoke enthusiastic comment from the infantry commander whose troops the brigade was supporting. Batteries withdrew to their waggon lines the same evening, and spent September 20th in cleaning up equipment and vehicles.

On September 21st, at 2.30 p.m., the Brigade was ordered to move northwards into the Lagnicourt area under the XVII. Corps, where it would be attached to the 40th Divisional Artillery. The column moved out about 7 p.m., and marching viâ Bus, Beugny, and Morchies arrived at its waggon lines in the new area north of Lagnicourt about daybreak. The Brigade was attached to the 57th Division for administration, but was tactically under the command of Headquarters, 40th Divisional Artillery. Positions were reconnoitred and stocked with ammunition, but were not occupied until the evening of September 25th. The brigade was to support an attack by the 57th Division on September 27th, and as it was required to advance its guns during the course of the barrage, forward positions were selected immediately in rear of the front line. After dawn on the 25th, all batteries essayed to get two hundred rounds per battery on to these forward positions, but when a total of six hundred rounds had been dumped the enemy attacked under cover of a heavy barrage, and teams had to get clear of the area at the gallop. They returned at dusk, however, and succeeded in dumping 1,800 rounds on to the position, a performance which was regarded with a great deal of satisfaction, as the ammunition had to be taken almost to the front line.

Zero hour on the 27th was at 5.20 a.m., and after firing in the barrage until 5.50 a.m., one section from each battery moved forward, the remaining guns increasing their rate of fire. The route over which the guns had to advance was being heavily shelled, and before the sections had got into action one man had been killed and eight wounded. Notwithstanding this, the four sections were in action by 6.30 a.m., and as soon as they opened fire the remainder of the brigade advanced at the trot. Heavy hostile shelling still persisted, but by 7.50 a.m. the whole brigade was in action, and firing in the barrage of the second phase of the attack. The infantry were held up on the Canal du Nord by heavy machine gun fire, so the engineers were not able to commence the cutting of passages for the advance of the artillery until about 3 o'clock in the afternoon. The Brigade Commander, accompanied by his battery commanders, reconnoitred positions west of Anneux, several thousand yards east of the Canal, but orders were received that in the meantime the brigade would remain in its positions in defence of the Canal. Shortly before midnight orders were received that the brigade would rendezvous east of the Canal on the following morning.

The brigade was early on the move next morning, and by 6 o'clock was at its rendezvous east of the Canal. Instructions were then received that the brigade was attached to the 89th Infantry Brigade of the 63rd Division, which was to pass through the troops of the 57th Division after they had gained their objective by crossing the Escault Canal. Two officers of the brigade were sent out to reconnoitre the route forward, and, if possible, report on the Canal crossings. At 8.30 a.m. word was received from the reconnaissance party that the infantry had not succeeded in crossing the Canal. After a conference of infantry and artillery Brigade Commanders with the G.O.C. 63rd Division, the brigade was ordered to rendezvous west of Anneux, and very shortly after got into action in the valley south of Fontaine-Notre-Dame. The 63rd Division, however, whose attack the brigade was to support, found that the 57th Division had not taken the Escault Canal, and therefore decided to await developments. Meanwhile the Brigade Commander endeavoured to obtain permission to open fire on the eastern side of the Canal, and drive the enemy from his positions, but the brigade was not allowed to fire. Later in the afternoon the 5th Battery got two guns into action, and engaged enemy movement on the Cambrai-Masnieres Road. Shortly afterwards the brigade received orders to bring its guns into action in the valley south of Fontaine-Notre-Dame, and a barrage was put down just east of the canal; this barrage was repeated after a brief interval, but the infantry were unable to force the passage of the Canal.

The Canal was eventually crossed under cover of barrage fire at half-past six the following morning, and some hours later the infantry were observed making their way up the slopes towards the Cambrai-Masnieres Road. The 9th Battery sent one gun forward to engage any fleeting targets, and carried out some effective shooting. The bridge across the Canal was badly damaged, and was still being bombed and shelled by the enemy; the Brigade Commander crossed the Canal to reconnoitre positions for the batteries, but was driven back by machine gun fire after having advanced a short distance on the eastern banks. Two battery commanders were wounded during the day—Major R. A. Wilson, 6th Battery, and Major A. B. Williams, 5th Battery. Command of the 6th Battery passed to Captain L. Gardner, and of the 5th Battery to Captain W. H. Jones.

The advance did not progress very rapidly on the 30th; the artillery carried out heavy harassing fire during the day, and fired a barrage at 5.30 p.m., but the infantry were unable to make any headway. The brigade moved its guns forward about a thousand yards during the afternoon, and brought 250 rounds per gun on to the new positions.

On October 1st the brigade was transferred to the 57th Division which took over the line from the 63rd Division. By evening only four guns, from the 40th Divisional Artillery, had been moved forward across the Canal, but ultimately they were withdrawn, as no positions could be found for them where they could clear the steep crest which flanked the Canal banks on the eastern side. The brigade carried out normal shooting during following days, and at dawn on October 5th withdrew to the rest area in the valley east of Louverval. Some casualties had been suffered the previous day by heavy shelling of gun and waggon lines, extending throughout the afternoon and late into the night, and necessitating the withdrawal of the waggon lines to the Sugar Factory on the main Cambrai Road.

The brigade's rest was of the briefest possible description; twelve hours after the guns had been withdrawn from the line, orders were received for the support of an attack by the 63rd Division on October 7th. On the 6th, positions were selected just east of the Canal, north-east of Noyelles, and these were occupied and stocked with ammunition by 6 p.m. Word was then received from 57th Divisional Artillery Headquarters, under which the brigade was grouped, that the attack had been postponed for twenty-four hours. The 9th Battery had been heavily shelled, and had lost one gun, and as the shelling of batteries became general, all the personnel at the guns, except one man per gun and one officer per battery, were sent back to the waggon lines for the night. The day before the attack was spent in improving the positions. Hostile artillery was consistently active, and every night enemy aeroplanes came over and bombed the whole area.

The 63rd Division's final objective in the attack was Niergnies, a small village about two miles south of Cambrai, and the road to the east. Zero hour was at 4.30 a.m. on October 8th; the enemy's reply to the barrage was light, and the infantry made good progress, Niergnies being reported taken within a few hours of the opening of the advance. Beyond that point the advance was held up by heavy machine gun fire. The enemy counter-attacked towards Niergnies about 11 a.m., using some captured British tanks, but the attack was met by artillery fire and stopped. At noon batteries were ordered to move forward east of the Noyelles-Cambrai road, in order to take part in a barrage to cover an attack on Awingt at 3 p.m. The move was carried out without delay, and all preparations made for the barrage, but the attack was postponed.

The brigade moved into a position of readiness the following morning, waggon lines were established on the eastern bank of the Canal, and headquarters was located at Rumilly. The brigade was now attached to the 57th Divisional Artillery, in support of the 19th Division. On October 10th, while the brigade was still in its position of readiness, it was ordered to move to the south-east of Cambrai. This move was carried out on the 10th, and the two following days were devoted to cleaning up the harness and equipment, and giving the horses as much grazing as could be obtained. Positions of readiness were occupied south-west of Rieux on the 13th, where batteries remained for almost a week, making the most of the precious opportunity of resting the horses and overhauling equipment.

On October 19th batteries went into action east of St. Aubert, in order to fire a barrage at 2 a.m. on the 20th, to assist the 19th and 24th Divisions in an attack on Haussy. After firing in the barrage, orders were received to withdraw the guns to the waggon lines in readiness to move to the IV. Corps on October 21st, when the brigade was to rejoin the New Zealand Division.

THE GUNS GOING FORWARD

[Official Photo

CHAPTER XI.

LE QUESNOY.

By the end of October, it had become apparent that the German Armies were in such desperate plight that one strong determined blow, struck in a vital quarter, would go far towards completing their utter disorganisation. Already they reeled from the effects of the rapid succession of heavy blows which they had sustained at the hands of the Allied Armies since the defensive had been first definitely assumed in the early days of August. The German soldiers had fought bravely, and their retreat had been conducted with skill, but their losses in artillery, machine guns, and material of every description had been enormous, and their reserves were exhausted. Now Germany was to be left alone to face the final issue. Bulgaria and Turkey had capitulated, and Austria was on the imminent verge of collapse. Confronted with conditions of such an utterly dispiriting character it is not surprising that the morale of the enemy troops was fast weakening, while the confidence of the Allied soldiers grew as they passed from success to success, and their belief in final victory became invincible. The day of victory was already beginning to dawn at the moment, when plans were laid for the last great British attack on November 4th. This was to be delivered by the Third, Fourth, and First Armies, on a front of about thirty miles from the Sambre, north of Oisy, to Valenciennes. The capture of Valenciennes was regarded as a necessary preliminary to the main advance, and this was satisfactorily accomplished in an attack which was launched on the morning of November 1st.

In the advance on November 4th the New Zealand Division was to attack with the 37th Division on its right, and the 62nd Division on its left and establish itself on the line Franc a Lour-Herbignies-Tous Vents. If opportunity offered, success was to be exploited by advancing through the Mormal Forest, and towards the Sambre. Le Quesnoy, fortified by a double moat and the high sheer walls of its ramparts, stood directly in the path of the Division; beyond, to the east, lay the large mass of the Mormal Forest. The field artillery supporting the Division was divided into Right and Left Groups, the former commanded by Lieut.-Colonel Symon, and the latter by Lieut.-Colonel McQuarrie. Right Group consisted of the 1st and 2nd Brigades, and the 211th Brigade R.F.A., and Left Group of the 3rd Brigade and the 210th and 72nd Brigades, R.F.A., and the 14th (Army) Brigade, R.H.A. Three batteries of six-inch howitzers were also to support the attack, while "X" and "Y" Trench Mortar Batteries were placed at the disposal of the G.O.C., 3rd (Rifle) Brigade. The barrage was to be carried forward to a depth of six thousand yards, and in order to accomplish this it was necessary to advance four out of the six brigades while the barrage was actually being fired. Brigades were to advance one battery at a time, the remaining batteries of the brigades distributing their fire over the brigade front during the move, and increasing their rate of fire. Routes were to be reconnoitred in advance, and ammunition dumped as far forward as possible, in order to maintain the supply during the barrage. The fullest use was to be made of the greater range of guns equipped with air recuperator buffers, and such guns were to be the last to move forward in every case. A section of 4.5in. howitzers from the 1st Brigade, and a section of 18-prs. from each of the 2nd and 3rd Brigades, were detailed for independent work in close co-operation with the infantry. These sections were to be responsible for engaging hostile tanks as well as movement, and in addition every battery was to be prepared to run one gun forward to engage enemy tanks over open sights. By the night of November 3rd all guns were east and north-east of Beaudignies, in their positions for the attack.

This was the last occasion on which the New Zealand Artillery paved the way for the advance of their infantry in a major operation, and from the complicated nature of the barrage and the masterly precision with which it advanced through all its stages, it may be regarded as a fitting climax to the work of the guns in supporting the infantry in attack. It was known that there was a large number of civilians in Le Quesnoy, and it was therefore decided that the barrage should sweep the ramparts garrisoned by the enemy, and as it moved forward completely encircle the town, but that no fire should fall within the limits of the town itself. This called for accurate calculation and planning in preparing the barrage table, and for extreme accuracy of fire at the guns. From its opening line at zero hour the barrage advanced in even lifts until it swept on to the western ramparts of the town. It then divided and continued eastwards, encircling the town as it went, and deluging the ramparts on the north and south with sharpnel and smoke shell, in order to protect the advance of the infantry on each flank. Having arrived on the eastern outskirts of the town it advanced again in a straight unbroken line, until it had reached a depth of six thousand yards from the starting point.

The battle which was about to open was destined to be the last of the long series of desperate combats, in which the Division had figured since that distant April morning, when the New Zealanders had first leapt from their boats on to the shores of Gallipoli and climbed the hills to grapple with the Turk. If their arms had not achieved invariable success, each successive engagement had added fresh lustre to the laurels which the New Zealanders had won for themselves in, the Gallipoli campaign; and disappointments had been endured with the same calm in which the soldiers viewed their victories.

The morning of November 4th dawned fine, but visibility was lessened by a mist which rose up from the ground after sunrise. Zero hour was at 5.30 a.m., and the barrage came down promptly and with practised precision. The enemy's fire was comparatively feeble, but a good deal of hostile fire fell on battery areas. The 9th Battery had two guns put out of action, and "D" Battery of the 211th Brigade had five guns destroyed in succession, and practically the whole of its personnel casualtied. Heavy shelling was also experienced at the waggon lines of the 11th Battery, more than fifty horses having been killed and wounded. The success of the infantry was rapid and complete, and at an early hour they were encircling Le Quesnoy, the garrison of which still held out, on the north and south. While troops of the 3rd (Rifle) Brigade were endeavouring to effect an entrance into the town, other battalions of the Rifle Brigade and the 1st Infantry Brigade swept round to the north and south and completely enclosed it. The advance, which was now due east, was continued to the line Villereau-Potelle-Jolimetz, and on towards the Forest de Mormal.

At 9.30 a.m. a reconnoitring party from the 2nd Brigade, consisting of the Brigade and Battery Commanders, moved forward and crossed the railway line about a mile north-west of Le Quesnoy, but was then held up by machine gun fire from the ramparts. A detour was made to the north, through Ramponeau and Villereau, battery positions eventually being chosen in the vicinity of St. Sepulchre about midday. Batteries were ordered up from their rendezvous near L'Orgnies, and the first battery was in action in the new area within a couple of hours. Reconnaissance parties went forward from the 1st and 3rd Brigades very shortly after the batteries of the 2nd Brigade had commenced to move. The 1st Brigade party was held up by machine gun fire on the northern outskirts of the town, and made a detour round to the south. Batteries of this brigade eventually occupied positions near Potelle; 3rd Brigade batteries went into action in the vicinity of St. Sepulchre. The advanced guard artillery now consisted of the three New Zealand Brigades under Lieut.-Colonel McQuarrie.

By the afternoon the infantry had reached Herbignies. Pressing determinedly on they crossed the road that skirted the western edge of the Forest de Mormal, and entered the tangled undergrowth of the Forest itself. By midnight they had penetrated deep into its heart. Le Quesnoy was not entered by the New Zealanders until the afternoon. The garrison at first refused to surrender, and ignored messages, explaining their hopeless situation, which were dropped into the town by low-flying aeroplanes. In the afternoon an officer of the Division, accompanied by a captured German officer, attempted to enter the town to explain the situation to the garrison, but they were fired on from the ramparts. Later in the day the garrison surrendered, and the New Zealanders entered the town to the wild delight of the civilian inhabitants. The Division had achieved a memorable and striking success in its last battle, making an advance of about six miles in depth, capturing the towns of Le Quesnoy, Rompaneau, Villereau, Potelle, and Herbignies, about two thousand prisoners, sixty field guns, and hundreds of machine guns. Included in the captures of field guns were complete batteries, with their gun crews, and teams and drivers.

Persistent rain fell on November 5th, rendering doubly difficult the advance through the dense and tangled undergrowth of the forest. Moving forward behind the barrage the infantry encountered little opposition until they reached Forrester's House, considerably more than half way through the forest. This was strongly held by machine guns, but was eventually taken under cover of artillery fire. At 9 a.m. the 3rd Brigade moved forward into positions of readiness near Rue Haute; the 12th Battery was detached from the brigade and went forward in support of the infantry. The 2nd Brigade moved up through Herbignies, and along the western edge of the forest until it reached the 3rd Brigade area. Batteries were in this neighbourhood by 5 p.m., but did not fire that night. The road along the western edge of the forest was in very bad condition, which was rapidly being made worse by the heavy rain. The 1st Battery of the 1st Brigade advanced in support of the infantry, the 3rd and 15th Batteries bivouacking on the edge of the forest. By evening the infantry had gone right through the forest, and reached their final objective on the eastern outskirts. That night the New Zealand Division, less artillery, was relieved in the line by the 42nd Division. The artillery came under the command of the C.R.A., 42nd Division.

On the following morning, November 6th, certain batteries fired a barrage in support of an attack by the 42nd Division, which was to make an effort to advance from the eastern edge of the Forest. The attack, however, was not successful. The 2nd Brigade, which was advanced guard artillery for the day, had its teams at the gun positions, ready for a move, at 7 a.m.; but a reconnaissance showed that the roads through the forest were quite impassable. The enemy had blown up bridges, and made the roads of little use to wheeled transport by mining cross-roads and other important points. Until bridges were erected it was almost an impossibility for the guns to cross the forest, in which few, if any, positions could be found for batteries; but it was imperative that the guns should go forward. A working party was, therefore, dispatched to make an endeavour to erect a temporary bridge over one stream, whilst the track running south-east through the forest to the north of the road was reconnoitred, and an advanced section of the 2nd Battery was got through and into action half way through the forest. A section of the 6th (Howitzer) Battery also got into action a little further to the north. About midday an attempt was made to get the remaining guns of the 6th Battery across the temporary bridge which had been constructed. It was a risky business; but the guns and vehicles were got safely over with the loss of one waggon, which went over the side into the stream, rendering the bridge unsafe for further traffic. As a demand had been made for some howitzers and 18-prs. to support a small operation by the 42nd Division, a section of the 5th Battery was sent forward over the forest track, the 9th Battery following the route taken by the advanced section of the 6th Battery, and going into action in the same locality.

The bridge having been repaired again, with the assistance of some Pioneers of the 42nd Division, the remainder of the guns and waggons of the Brigade were got across by dark, with the exception of two waggons which went over the side, but four others which had attempted to advance through the cross roads on the northern edge of the forest found the way blocked by mine craters. With the exception of the 9th Battery, and one section of the 6th Battery, which were on the northern edge of the forest, the whole of the 2nd Brigade had succeeded in getting into action near la Corne by 7 p.m.

Rain was still falling on November 7th, and conditions on the roads and tracks became steadily worse. The day was quiet, the enemy offering little opposition to the advance of the 42nd Division, which attacked at 8.45 a.m., under cover of a barrage fired by the 2nd Brigade. The 1st Brigade moved forward during the afternoon to the south of Hargnies and Vieux-Mesnil, and the 2nd Brigade became reserve brigade. The 3rd Brigade, less the 12th Battery, which went back to billets, also advanced to the eastern edge of the forest, and occupied positions of readiness. The 9th Battery, having got out of touch with its Group, pushed forward and got as far as the outskirts of Hautmont, where it got into action, and effectively engaged a variety of targets. The battery returned to the brigade area about dusk.

The New Zealand Artillery was in action for the last time on November 8th, when the 1st and 3rd Brigades carried out a little harassing fire. The enemy, now completely disorganised, was still retiring, and in the afternoon both these Brigades moved forward to the vicinity of Boussieres. The following day all batteries were relieved by the 42nd Divisional Artillery, and orders were issued for the three brigades and the Divisional Ammunition Column to march to Quievy, to rejoin the Division. This move was to be carried out on the 11th and 12th, the intervening night being spent in billets at Villereau.

The decisive nature of the results produced by the complete success of the great battle launched on November 4th speedily became apparent. The enemy's resistance was virtually broken. At odd points in the long battle line he still clung tenaciously to his positions and defended them with skill and courage. But the vast and complex machine of the German Army was rapidly going to pieces as a result of the incessant and irresistible blows of the French and British Armies, and the disintegrating influences which preceded from the unrest and bitter discontent which permeated the whole Empire. The Allies continued their steady advance eastwards, and on November 9th the enemy was in retreat along the whole of the British Front and all semblance of resistance was rapidly disappearing. To save its armies from the complete disaster which threatened to overwhelm them at any moment the German Supreme Command appealed for an Armistice. This was granted, but in its unconditional terms it represented for Germany nothing less than complete surrender.

The Armistice took effect from 11 a.m. on November 11th. The official intimation to this effect, announcing that hostilities would cease at 11 a.m., was received by units of the Divisional Artillery when they were on the march to Quievy or preparing to take the road. The announcement was received calmly, with no cheering, no demonstration. For these men, tired in body and mind and fresh from the tragic fields of battle, this momentous intelligence was too vast in its consequences to be appreciated in a single thought.

The brilliant nature of the work performed by the New Zealand Division during the period it was in the 4th Corps, and particularly during the last great series of battles, is sufficiently well indicated by the following letter which was sent to the Division by Lieut.-General Sir G. M. Harper, K.C.B., D.S.O., Commanding IV. Corps:—

"As the New Zealand Division is leaving the IV. Corps, I desire to place on record my appreciation of the valuable services they have rendered, and to thank all ranks for the magnificent fighting qualities which they have invariably displayed.

"The Division joined the IV. Corps at a critical time on the 26th March, 1918, when it completely checked the enemy's advance on Beaumont Hamel and Colincamps, and thus closed the gap between the IV. and V. Corps. By a brilliant stroke it drove the enemy from the commanding ground at La Signy Farm, and gained observation over the enemy's lines which greatly assisted in his defeat on the 5th April, 1918, when he made his last and final effort to break our front. Throughout the summer the Division held portions of the Corps front with but a short interval of rest. During this period I never had the least anxiety about the security of this portion of the front; on the other hand, by carefully conceived and well executed raids, the enemy was given little respite, and identifications were procured whenever required—in this connection I deplore the loss of that brave man, Sergeant Travis, V.C.

"It was the ascendancy gained by this Division over the enemy that compelled him to evacuate the ground about Rossignol Wood.

"At the commencement of the great attack on the 21st August, 1918, only a minor part was allotted to the Division, but subsequently on the night of the 24th August the Division was ordered to attack, and swept the enemy from Grevillers, Loupart Wood, and Biefvillers, and gained the outskirts of Bapaume. Stubborn fighting was experienced around Bapaume, but eventually the enemy was overcome and pushed back to the east.

OPEN FIGHTING

Official Photo

"From 24th August till 14th September the Division was constantly engaged, and drove the enemy back from Bapaume to the high ground west of Gouzeaucourt, where very heavy fighting occurred at African Trench.

"After a short period of rest the Division was put in again on 29th September to complete the capture of Welsh Ridge, and to gain the crossings over the Canal de l'Escaut. A night advance over difficult country, intersected by the trenches and wire of the Hindenburg Line, was brilliantly carried out and entirely successful, and resulted in the capture of over 1000 prisoners and over 40 guns. On the 1st October the Division captured Crevecour against strong opposition, and held it in spite of heavy shelling and several counter-attacks throughout the subsequent days until the great attack on 8th October, when the Division broke through the northern portion of the strongly organised Masnieres Line and penetrated far into the enemy's line at Esnes and Hancourt.

"Going out to rest on 12th October the Division was again in the line on 23rd October and drove the enemy back from the outskirts of Romeries to Le Quesnoy. Finally, on the 4th November, the Division, by an attack which did much to decide the finish of the war, forced the surrender of the fortress of Le Quesnoy and drove the enemy back through the Forest of Mormal, the total captures by the IV. Corps on that day amounting to 3,500 prisoners and some 70 guns.

"During the period the New Zealand Division has been in the IV. Corps they have captured from the enemy 287 officers, and 8,745 other ranks, 145 guns, 1,419 machine-guns and three tanks, besides much other material.

"The continuous successes enumerated above constitute a record of which the Division may well be proud. It is a record which I may safely say has been unsurpassed in the final series of attacks which led to the enemy's sueing for peace.

"I send every man of the Division my heartfelt good wishes for the future."

The Division might well entertain a justifiable feeling of pride in the unbroken record of success which it had achieved since the opening of the offensive on August 21st. Within a period of less than three months it had advanced to a depth of fifty miles, had captured many thousands of prisoners, seized enormous quantities of guns and booty of every description, and inflicted decisive defeats on the enemy in a series of battles in some of which, at least, the fighting was of as determined a character as had been experienced during the whole course of the war. In no arm of the service had the radical and complete change in the character of the fighting been more strongly exemplified than in the artillery. From the moment the offensive was fully under way, and the Division, having broken through the enemy's first organised system of defence, began to move eastward with increasing momentum, the guns were on the move almost every day. They fought in the open fields with only the sky above them, and often in positions which were under direct observation from the enemy's lines.

The constant movement imposed a heavy burden on batteries, falling more heavily on the drivers and their horses. In addition to moving the guns forward, they had to stock each fresh position with ammunition, generally to the extent of six or seven hundred rounds per gun. Beyond those stretches traversed by the enemy's first defensive systems and by the broad system of entrenchments which constituted the Hindenburg Line, the country elsewhere was well roaded and did not present any very serious obstacles to wheeled traffic. At the commencement of the offensive, batteries had rid themselves of all gear and stores that were not absolutely essential for fighting purposes, and the men's surplus kit had been stored in a dump located in one of the villages in rear of the old line.

After passing through the enemy's trenches near Puisieux, the Division, in its advance on Bapaume, crossed the old Somme Battlefields, and the ground over which the enemy had retreated in the winter of 1916-17. East of Bapaume, and until Havrincourt Wood and the Hindenburg Line were reached, the fighting was on open rolling country, all of which was admirably suited for artillery operations. For a depth of more than five miles beyond Havrincourt Wood very different conditions were encountered. Besides being somewhat broken in itself, this country was intersected with the wide network of trenches and defensive works which formed the Hindenburg Line. In breaking through the advanced system of this deep and formidable line the Division experienced some desperately hard fighting, and during the struggles for Gouzeaucourt Ridge and at Dead Man's Corner, four brigades of Field Artillery alone fired a total of 60,000 rounds. Beyond the thick belt of enemy wire on the eastern banks of the Canal de l'Escaut, near Cheneaux Wood, the guns fought over absolutely open country, and so far as they were concerned, the war became one of movement to a constantly increasing degree.

Batteries and even brigades frequently carried out their moves forward, and went into action in the new positions on the orthodox lines laid down in the Manual of Field Artillery Training. Ever since their arrival in France the Artillery Brigades had had but little respite from active duties in the line, as batteries seldom accompanied the Division when it was withdrawn for rest or training, but remained in action covering the troops of some other Division. The few spells of any duration which they had been afforded had generally been devoted to training for some impending operations, such as the first Battle of the Somme or the Battle of Messines, or had been devoted to rest and refitting after an exhausting period of severe fighting, such as was experienced at Passchendaele. It followed, therefore, that there had been little opportunity of indulging in any thorough training for moving warfare. The readiness and ease with which all ranks were able to adapt themselves to the altered conditions, however, proved that the years of trench warfare, often in elaborately constructed positions and served by secure and well-established systems of communication, had not induced any decay in those qualities of initiative and boldness in conception and execution which play so large a part in operations of a more active nature.

The fullest use was made of mobile sections of 18-prs., which were sent forward under the command of a subaltern who acted in direct co-operation with battalion commanders. These sections performed useful and often brilliant work, and even their presence so far forward was a cheering sight for the infantry. Sometimes, when the latter were waiting for the barrage to come down and take them forward, one of the mobile sections would come clattering right up to the front line, and there await its opportunity to go forward into action behind the advancing infantry. Wherever the enemy's resistance was inclined to stiffen, or where the advance was held up by enemy machine guns, they directed their fire, and their active support came to be invaluable to the infantry. Sometimes under direct fire from enemy machine guns, harassed from the air, and the target for the enemy's light field guns, they played their part with such resolution and skill as to win the highest praise from responsible infantry commanders. The gunners, on their part, enjoyed the experience on many occasions of laying on to their targets over open sights, and observing the effect of their own shells. While the guns were in action teams were always kept close at hand in charge of the senior non-commissioned officer. Ammunition was carried in the limbers and the firing battery waggon, each gun, therefore, having a total of about 100 rounds.

All battery positions were harassed a good deal by low-flying enemy aeroplanes; their only defence was the Lewis machine guns with which batteries had been equipped for defensive purposes while in the Ypres salient, and the gunners who had been trained in their use fought many exciting duels with the German airmen. Although they never succeeded in disabling any of the aeroplanes, it is certain that they saved many casualties by preventing the line of guns being swept by machine gun fire.

Great numbers of enemy guns of all calibres were captured during the advance; on one occasion at least a field battery was seized with its teams hooked in and drivers mounted as it was in the act of effecting a retirement. There was a plentiful supply of ammunition, and gunners took a particular pleasure in shelling the enemy with his own guns. They had no difficulty in mastering the details of the mechanism or the sights, and guns were always given a generous elevation in order that there should be no risk of the shells landing on the wrong side of the line. Light German field pieces were often run into position for use as anti-tank guns should occasion arise, thus obviating the necessity of detaching any of the Division's own 18-prs.

The original batteries which left New Zealand in 1914 and 1915 were equipped with the most modern type of gun and howitzer then in use by the British Army, and these were never superseded by any more modern or improved pattern guns during the War. In the winter of 1917-18, however, the Division was issued with a very few 18-prs. which had been fitted with a new type of buffer. The function of the buffer, of course, is to absorb the recoil of the gun, and the more efficiently this is done, the steadier and more accurate the shooting of the gun becomes. In the new air recuperator buffer, as it was known, air and oil inside the buffer replaced the springs and oil which had been used in the old type of buffer. In addition to being very steady in action, air recuperator guns had an increased range of about three thousand yards, their maximum range being 9,600 yards, as against 6,600 yards possessed by guns fitted with the spring buffer.

When the New Zealand batteries first went into action at Gallipoli, the 18-prs. used shrapnel only, and the 4.5in. howitzers both shrapnel and high explosive. About August, 1915, high explosive shells were issued in very limited quantities to the 18-pr. batteries, and from the time the Division went into the line in France, the use of shrapnel by howitzer batteries was discontinued altogether. A great variety of new types of shell was introduced during the course of the War; on the Somme in 1916, the howitzers were first issued with gas shell, both lethal and lachrymatory. The 18-pr. batteries were later issued with smoke shell, which was used a good deal in barrage work for screening the advancing infantry from the eyes of the enemy; and thermite, an incediary shell, for use against occupied buildings and similar targets. Thermite, which was first used by the 2nd (Army) Brigade, N.Z.F.A., in the retreat from Messines, was frequently used in barrages as a "beacon" to indicate some point or boundary to the infantry. Bursting low down in the air, it emitted a vivid sheet of flame, which was conspicuous even in the haze of the barrage.

Generally speaking, there were three distinct types of fuze, in addition to the time fuze, which was used for securing air bursts. These were the non-delay; the delay action, in which the disruptive effect of the explosive was heightened by allowing the shell to bury itself some distance in the ground before bursting; and an instantaneous fuze known as the 106 fuze. This fuze was remarkable at once for its simplicity and its deadly effectiveness. It secured an absolutely instantaneous burst at the moment of impact, and against personnel in the open, hight explosive shell fitted with these fuzes were quite as effective as shrapnel. In barrage fire 18-prs. normally used 50 per cent. shrapnel and 50 per cent. high explosive, and generally the latter had the 106 fuze. The fuze was first used by the New Zealand Artillery when it carried out its practice shoot at Calais when the Division first went to France, but it was not until the middle of 1917 that howitzer batteries were first issued with shell fitted with this fuze, its use being extended to 18-pr. shell some time later.

The flow of reinforcement drafts to replace casualties in the Artillery was always steady, and generally sufficient, but at all periods of heavy fighting, when casualties were abnormally high, batteries were a good deal under strength, and conditions in consequence became more trying. Up to November 12th, 1918, the total number of artillerymen who sailed from New Zealand was 132 officers and 5,441 other ranks, making a grand total of 5,573. To this total there must be added the numbers of men who were transferred to the artillery from other units, the majority of them drawn from the Mounted Rifle Regiments, which supplied a good percentage of the personnel which formed the batteries that were created at Moascar in 1916. The following table shows the total casualties to officers and other ranks during the whole period of the War:—

	Officers	Other Ranks	Total
Killed in Action	37	411	448
Died of Wounds	17	254	271
Died of other causes	6	129	135
Wounded	136	2,217	2,353
Totals	196	3,011	3,207

All drafts from New Zealand passed through the Artillery Reserve Depôt in England, whence after a period of further training they were dispatched to the Division as required through a base reinforcement camp in France. The

Reserve Artillery Depôt was first opened in England in June, 1916. It was then incorporated with the New Zealand Reserve Group at Sling Camp, on Salisbury Plain. It was commanded by Major Swaine, R.F.A., who was detached from his own regiment for this duty. On September 19th, 1916, Major F. G. Hume, of the New Zealand Divisional Artillery, assumed command of the Depôt, and a few months later two more officers were sent over from France to assist in the training of reinforcements. A few horses were available for training, but there was no equipment.

On January 8th, 1917, the Depôt moved to the Talavera Barracks, Aldershot, and came under the direct supervision of N.Z.E.F. Headquarters, London. While at Aldershot four complete sections were raised and trained and sent over to France to assist in completing the reorganisation of the Divisional Artillery on a six-gun basis. At the beginning of April, 1917, the Depôt transferred to Chadderton Camp, Royton, and remained there until August 13th, of the same year, when it was finally established at Ewshott Barracks, Fleet, in the Aldershot command, where it remained until the close of the War. Before moving from Chadderton, Major Hume had relinquished his command to Lieut.-Colonel I. T. Standish. For purposes of administration and training the Depôt was divided into two sections, known respectively as Headquarters and Battery. In the one were men below Class "A," who attended to all fatigues and camp duties; in the other were the fit men training for the front. The training was of a more comprehensive character than had hitherto been possible, owing to increased facilities and improved equipment. At various periods, visits of inspection were paid to the camp by his Majesty the King, accompanied by Princess Mary, Viscount French (at the time Commander-in-Chief of the Home Forces), and Lieut.-General Sir Archibald Murray, General Officer-in-Chief, Aldershot Command.

On July 1st, 1918, Lieut.-Colonel F. Symon assumed command of the Depôt and remained in charge until a week or two before the close of the war. A week after the Armistice Lieut.-Colonel Falla took charge of the Depôt, and remained in command until it was closed.

The March to Germany.

On November 13th, after the Artillery had rejoined the Division at Quievy, the announcement was made that the New Zealand Division was to form part of the Army of Occupation which was to march to Germany and occupy the bridgeheads on the Rhine. The following day an impressive Thanksgiving Service was held at a massed parade of the whole Division, after which the C.R.A., Brigadier-General G. N. Johnston, addressed each battery in turn regarding the march to Germany.

The Divisional Artillery remained at Quievy from the 13th until the 28th November, cleaning up and getting everything in readiness for the trek to Germany, which was all to be done by road. Horses that were lame or poor in condition were evacuated, and fresh horses were drawn from the remount depôt to bring batteries and ammunition columns up to their establishment. On the 28th November the whole Divisional Artillery set out for Escarmain—the first stage on the long trek to Cologne. The next day's march was from Escarmain to Tasmieres through Beaudignies and Le Quesnoy, over the country, across which the Division had fought its way but a little while before. The Forest de Mormal was avoided by making a detour to the north through Bavai. Units remained in billets in the Tasnieres area for two days; an inspection was to have been held at this place by his Majesty the King, but this did not eventually take place.

On December 3rd, the column marched to Ferriere-la-Grande and on the 4th to Fontaine-Valmont. On this second day the way lay through Marrpent and Jeumont, where the enemy had had an important railroad centre and big munition works. The railway yards were crowded with a heterogeneous collection of rolling stock, including French, Belgian, and German. There were many train loads of ammunition, and others loaded up with a wonderful variety of odds and ends salvaged from the battlefields, affording a striking illustration of the systematic manner in which the Germans converted all waste and scrap material to profitable use. Many of the buildings in the station yards, and much of the rolling stock had been wrecked and burned; and according at least to the statements of the civilian inhabitants, this destruction had been wrought by the Germans themselves on the declaration of the Armistice.

ONE OF THE MOBILE TRENCH MORTARS *Official Photo*

Designed by the Divisional Trench Mortars to meet the changed conditions of fighting in the last advance

A NEW ZEALAND BATTERY COMING INTO ACTION ON THE SITE OF A CAPTURED GERMAN BATTERY *[Official Photo*

The frontier having been crossed at Solre-sur-Sambre during the 4th, the route now lay through Belgium, and in every town and every village the New Zealanders were received with such enthusiasm that their march became almost a triumphal progress. Many of the inhabitants gave up their most comfortable rooms for the soldiers, and to have them billeted in the house was regarded as a privilege. On December 5th, the march was continued to Lobbes, and during the three days that units were billetted there, almost everyone visited Charleroi, some few miles off. The column marched through Charleroi and the thickly populated industrial district surrounding it on the 8th, when it moved from Lobbes to Lambusart. While in the Bothey-Bossiere area, which was reached on the 9th, arrangements were made for special trains to enable the men to visit Brussels. On the 12th the march was to Hauret-Harlue and next day to the Wanze area in the Meuse Valley, and near the famous waterway from which it takes its name. The wonderful old citadel at Huy was visited by nearly the whole of the Divisional Artillery. Of considerable interest also was the beet sugar factory, one of the largest in Europe. The night of the 17th was spent at Seraing, a densely populated suburb of Liege, and next day the trek was continued to the Chence-Chaud-Fontaine area.

The last night in billets in Belgian territory was spent at Verviers, where the enthusiasm of the population knew no bounds, their hospitality being more pressing and open-handed than anything that had hitherto been experienced. The following day, December 20th, the German frontier was crossed. Passing under the triumphal arch, decorated with evergreens and the flags of the Allied Nations, which marked the Belgian boundary, brigades marched down the slope and through the little village of Eupen, that stood just inside the German frontier. Had there been no other indication of the fact, the attitude of the civil population would have been sufficient to tell the soldiers that they, at last, were actually on German soil. When the first New Zealanders went through Eupen, the streets were absolutely deserted, and beyond a furtive lifting of blinds, there was no sign of life in the dwelling houses. The German population were evidently somewhat fearful of the consequences to themselves of the Allied occupation, but they soon recovered

U

from their initial fears, and exhibited a conciliatory attitude and a desire to please, which was no doubt prompted by self-interest. After entering Germany the column marched through a hilly and inhospitable countryside, until it reached the billetting area near the poor and scattered village of Rotgen. Before night fell and batteries had settled down in their quarters, hail and sleet had begun to fall, and the bitter cold made the draughty barns and outbuildings but a poor substitute for the comfortable billets which had been the rule in the march through France and Belgium.

On December 23rd, the march was resumed to the Hurtgen-Birgel area, and on the following day through Duren, where were located the headquarters of the 7th Brigade Army Corps, to the Blatzheim-Kerpen area. Christmas Day, cold and somewhat cheerless, was spent here, and on the following morning the final stage of the journey was commenced. Cologne was entered about midday; the remainder of the Division had preceded the Artillery, having gone on by train from Verviers. The long column marched through Cologne, and crossing the Rhine by the Hohenzollern Bridge, proceeded to their respective areas in Deutz and Kalk on the eastern banks of the river.

Divisional Artillery Headquarters was situated in the main thoroughfare in Deutz, the 1st Brigade and the D.A.C. were billetted in big school buildings, the 2nd Brigade in some exhibition grounds, and the 3rd Brigade in old Imperial Army Barracks. During the latter half of the trek, and until the units of the Divisional Artillery were demobilised, Lieut.-Colonel Symon acted as C.R.A. of the Division. Brigadier-General Johnston had proceeded on leave shortly after the declaration of the Armistice, and on his arrival in Cologne assumed command of the Division, following on the departure of the Divisional Commander.

In Cologne, batteries had only the ordinary routine to occupy their time and consequently after they had settled down in their quarters and removed the stains of travel from their vehicles and equipment all ranks had ample leisure and opportunity to go sight-seeing in the city itself or to make excursions to various places, attractive or interesting, along the banks of the Rhine

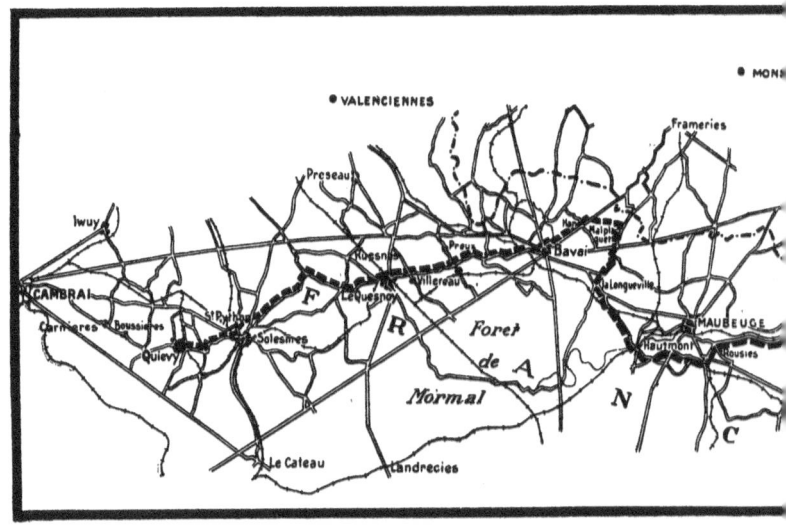

THE ROUTE TAKEN BY THE NEW ZEALAND ARTILLERY IN ITS MARCH TO COLOGN[E]

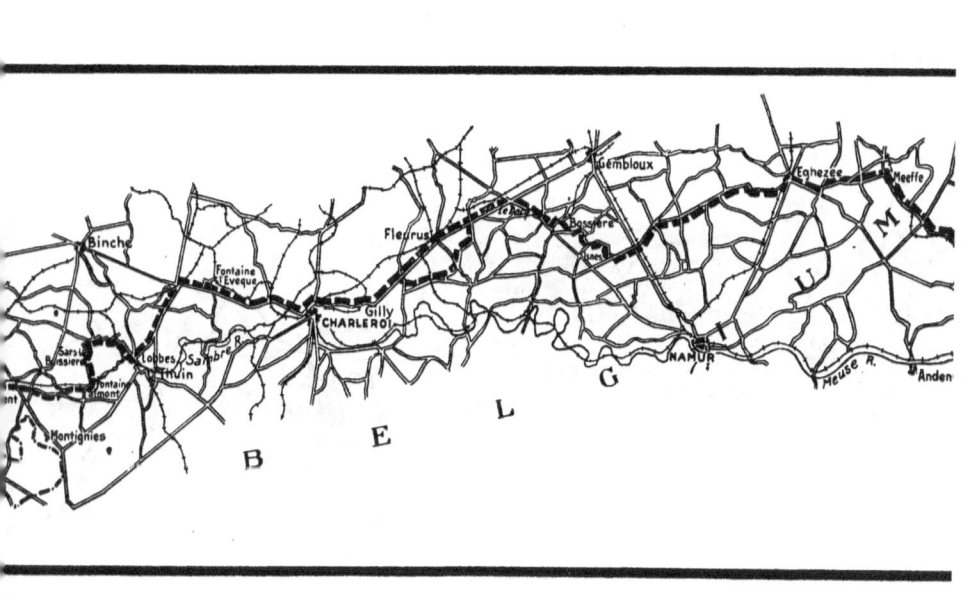

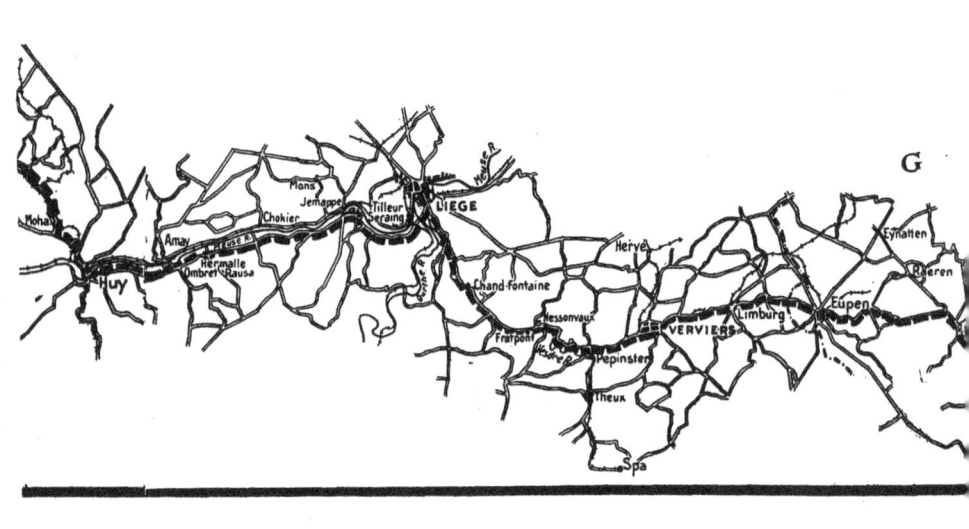

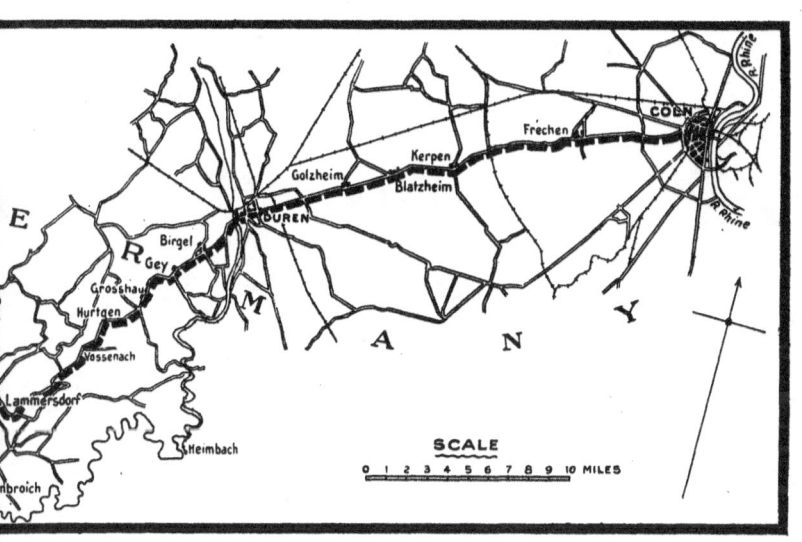

The inhabitants of the city probably realised that the presence of troops of the Army of Occupation was not without its advantages, as it secured them from the possibility of any disturbances and upheavals, such as were then taking place in other parts of Germany. At any rate the majority of them displayed a quite friendly attitude towards the British troops who were quartered in and about the city. The civilian population suffered a great many hardships as a result of the war conditions, and there was almost a total lack of many commodities which normally are regarded as indispensable. There was no lack of amusement or gaiety, however, and the cafes and places of entertainment were generally crowded each night; the strongest attraction for many of the soldiers being the "Opernhaus," where for a very modest charge they could hear operas produced by companies which generally attained a high standard of ability. They were produced in German, of course, but that circumstance did not seriously detract from their enjoyment.

A good deal of time was devoted to sport, principally football, and for all ranks the stay in Cologne will always have pleasant memories. A visit was paid to the Division by H.R.H. the Prince of Wales, and as it was of a purely informal character it was so much the more appreciated by the men of the Division.

The demobilisation of the Division commenced with the New Year. On January 1st, 1919, the first draft, consisting of 1914 men, left Cologne for England, *en route* to New Zealand. In the bitter cold of mid-winter the two days' train journey to the coast was tedious and uncomfortable in the extreme. On arrival in England drafts proceeded direct to one of the New Zealand Base Depôts, the majority of the artillerymen going to Sling Camp. From there, after a period of leave, and a longer period of waiting, they proceeded to the port of embarkation, and finally set out on their return to New Zealand.

Once under way, demobilisation proceeded rapidly. All stores, equipment, and guns were returned to the ordnance authorities, and the horses were disposed of after being divided into three main classes. A certain number of mares were selected for breeding purposes, others were marked for retention in the

Imperial Army, and the remainder were sold, either to be butchered or used for general purposes. By the end of January demobilisation was practically complete and the Divisional Artillery, as a unit, had ceased to exist.

APPENDIX.

HONOURS AND AWARDS.

* Denotes killed in action, or died of wounds or sickness.

Companion of St. Michael and St. George.

Lieut.-Col. N. S. Falla, D.S.O. Lieut.-Col. I. T. Standish, D.S.O.
Brig.-General G. N. Johnston, Lieut.-Col. F. Symon, D.S.O.
D.S.O., R.A.

Bar to Distinguished Service Order.

Major H. G. Wilding, D.S.O. †Lieut.-Col. F. B. Sykes, D.S.O., R.A.

Distinguished Service Order.

Major H. J. Daltry
Lieut.-Col. N S. Falla, C.M.G.
Major T. Farr, M.C.
Major D. E. Gardner.
Lieut.-Col. M. M. Gard'ner.
Major H. C. Glendining.
Brig.-Gen. G. N. Johnston, C.M.G.
Major C. McGilp.
Lieut.-Col. R. S. McQuarrie, M.C.
Major R. Miles, M.C.
Major R. S. Milligan.
Major C. N. Newman.

Major E. H. Northcroft.
*Major J. M. Richmond, M.C.
*Major V. Rogers.
Major C. Somerville.
Lieut.-Col. I. T. Standish, C.M.G.
Lieut.-Col. F. B. Sykes, R.A.
Lieut.-Col. F. Symon, C.M.G.
Major R. C. Wickens.
Major A. B. Williams.
Major H. G. Wilding, Bar to D.S.O.
Major R. A. Wilson, R.G.A.

Member Order of British Empire.

Captain G. H. Forsythe.

Bar to the Military Cross.

Lieutenant G. R. Park, M.C.

Military Cross.

2nd Lieut. R. E. Bennett.
2nd Lieut. C. Boswell.
2nd Lieut. G. Bridgeman.
2nd Lieut. A. C. Cameron.
Lieut. L. S. Carmichael.
'Captain G. E. Daniell.
Captain R. W. Dunn.
Captain W. E. Earnshaw.
Captain P. J. Ellis.
2nd Lieut. A. E. Esquilant.
Major T. Farr, D.S.O.

2nd Lieut. L. B. Foster.
Lieut. J. E. L. Gardner.
Lieut. W. McK. Geddes.
Lieut. C. T. Gillespie.
*Major A. E. Horwood.
Captain J. G. Jeffery.
Captain W. H. Johnson.
Major C. V. Leeming.
Lieut. G. Lyon.
Lieut. A. C. Macdonald.
2nd Lieut. C. R. McKenzie.

† Awarded while with the 63rd Division.

310   NEW ZEALAND ARTILLERY IN THE FIELD

*2nd Lieut. D. G. McMillan.
Lieut. R. McPherson.
Major R. S. McQuarrie, D.S.O.
Lieut. J. Mayer.
Captain R. Miles, D.S.O.
2nd Lieut. A. H. Miller.
Lieut. F. M. Mitchell.
2nd Lieut. R. Nelson.
2nd Lieut. H. C. Nolan.
Lieut. E. G. Norman.
2nd Lieut. G. R. Park, Bar to M.C.
2nd Lieut. L. R. Pulham.
*Major J. M. Richmond, D.S.O.
2nd Lieut. J. G. Rickleton.
Lieut. W. N. Sievers.
*2nd Lieut. L. Smith.
2nd Lieut. H. E. Speight.
Lieut. F. J. W. Stallard.
2nd Lieut. V. Stocker.
Lieut. B. A. Todd.
Captain F. M. Turner.
2nd Lieut. E. F. Tyson.
*2nd Lieut. J. M. Watkins.
Lieut. E. R. Winkler.

Bar to Distinguished Conduct Medal.
B.S.M. J. J. Riddett, D.C.M.

Distinguished Conduct Medal.

*Corporal A. N. Andrews.
B.S.M. A. Bailey.
B.S.M. G. R. Bain.
*Sergeant R. Birnie.
Fitter N. Clark.
Sergeant V. R. Davy.
Gunner A. S. Driver.
Lieut. C. J. K. Edwards.
Corporal A. Gapes.
Corporal W. B. Goile.
Sergeant F. Greig.
R.S.M. W. A. Gustafsen.
Sergeant J. F. Hill.
Sergeant F. N. Holder.
Lieut. W. Ibbotson.
Bdr.-Fitter D. C. Inglis.
B.S.M. J. P. Joyce.
B.S.M. P. D. McCrae.
Bdr. W. McQueen.
B.S.M. L. G. Morrison.
Corporal H. Muir.
Corporal G. W. Osbourne.
B.S.M. W. L. F. Porter.
B.S.M. J. J. Riddett, Bar to D.C.M.
Corporal T. W. Sharp.
Sergeant J. M. Stringer.
*Bdr. G. Syme.
Sergeant J. H. Taplin.
Bdr. J. P. Thompson.
B.S.M. G. Varrall.
Driver S. Wade.

Bar to Military Medal.
Bombdr. J. P. Alexander, M.M.
Cpl.-Fitter A. H. Bennie, M.M.
Bdr. J. I. Y. Cochran, M.M.
Sergeant F. Kennedy, M.M.
Sergeant F. W. Maindonald, M.M.
Bdr. R. D. Pattie, M.M.

Military Medal.
Bdr. T. Adams.
Gunner J. P. Alexander, Bar to M.M.
Bdr. E. F. Allan.
Bdr. A. Ashworth.
Sergeant F. S. Baddeley.
Bdr. J. N. Baxter.
Bdr. S. L. Beck.
Gunner L. D. Belton.
Cpl.-Fitter A. H. Bennie, Bar to M.M.
Bdr. A. W. Bird.
Cpl.-Fitter A. W. Bird.
Gunner C. M. Blackwell.
Sergeant R. M. Blackwell.
*Bdr. A. G. L. Bliss.
Driver G. H. Boag.
*Bdr. R. J. Bond.
Bdr. R. I. Brake.
Gunner W. Brown.
Gunner W. J. Brown.
Bdr. L. H. Buchanan.
Corporal T. F. Buchanan.
Corporal H. A. K. Burns.
Corporal J. M. Burt.
Sergeant O. C. H. Burt.

APPENDIX 311

'Bdr. A. Cadman.
Corporal E. H. Calder.
Bdr. C. H. Capper.
Corporal A. H. Carrington.
Gunner J V. Castles.
Bdr. J. I. Y. Cochran, Bar to M.M.
'Sergeant K. McI. Cole.
Bdr. A. C. Cooke.
Cpl. T. A. Cordell.
Sergeant A. J. Cossbrook.
'Gunner W. R. Costar.
Driver D. W. Couborough.
Driver F. Craig.
Bdr. N. E. Cross.
Corporal A. A. Currey.
'Corporal H. P. C. Davie.
Sergeant C. H. Davis.
Bdr. T. Dobson.
Gunner A. E. Dockery.
Gunner F. A. Dunstall.
'Driver P. Durward.
Sergeant W. B. Easton.
Driver A. E. Edmonds.
Driver C. Entwistle.
Gunner R. E. Everett.
Gunner R. I. Fleming.
Gunner C. Gibson.
Gunner G. C. Girdlestone.
Bdr. R. W. Girven.
Bdr. R. A. Grainger.
Bdr. R. McP. Grant.
'Sergt. H. B. Grave.
Corporal H. V. Green.
S.-Sergt. J. Gregson.
Sergeant W. J. Grubb.
Corporal H. Guise.
Bdr. A. H. Guthrie.
Gunner G. W. A. Gwilliam.
Sergeant A. C. Hall.
Gunner I. E. Hammond.
Driver G. H. Hansen.
Bdr. L. Hartman.
Gunner A. L. H. Henderson.
Driver G. E. Henry.
Sergeant F. T. Hicks.
Lieut. W. J. Hicks.
Sergeant W. R. Holder.
Corporal R. H. Horn.
Sergeant W. Hutchings.
Gunner D. J. F. Jeune.
Gunner F. W. Johnson.
Gunner A. H. Johnston.
Gunner W. A. Jones.
Sergeant F. Kennedy.
Driver F. W. Kennedy, Bar to M.M.

Gunner R. Kidd.
Corporal T. Kirton.
Bdr. J. R. H. Kuhtz.
Gunner J. C. H. Lloyd.
*Corporal J. A. Loffhogen.
Gunner J. Longmuir.
Corporal F. G. Lynch.
Corporal W. G. McClintock.
Gunner G. McConnell.
Gunner H. McDonald.
Gunner M. McDonald.
Gunner R. H. McDonald.
Corporal D. A. McGibbon.
*Sergeant J. A. Mackay.
Gunner J. R. MacLean.
Fitter L. D. McLean.
Gunner W. McMillan.
Bdr. K. MacMurray.
Corporal G. P. McNamara.
Sergeant D. McRae.
*Bdr. J. W. McRae.
Gunner F. W. Maindonald, Bar to M.M.
Bdr. C. E. Mains.
Corpl.-Fitter J. H. Mains.
Gunner D. Malone.
Gunner L. J. Mander.
Sergeant J. Martin.
Sergeant J. Martindale.
Sergeant A. J. Mason.
Driver S. Mason.
Bdr. W. Mawdsley.
Sergeant D. Mayall.
Gunner W. Millar.
Gunner J. McA. Mills.
Corporal L. W. G. Millward.
Bdr. H. P. Mole.
Bdr. E. W. Moore.
Bdr. W. A. Moore.
Sergeant L. G. Mortenson.
Bdr. E. Mowbray.
Sergeant E. A. Mulligan.
Gunner P. Murphy.
Bdr. E. F. Newman.
Bdr. W. C. Norman.
Corporal W. L. O'Connor.
Gunner W. W. Olliver.
Driver K. O'Neil.
Gunner H. K. Osmers.
Gunner E. A. Parr.
Gunner A. J. Paterson.
Bdr. R. D. Pattie, Bar to M.M.
Corporal W. C. Perry.
Gunner E. W. Philpott.
Fitter J. L. Pickford.
Corporal E. E. Pope.

Far.-Sergeant J. Potter.
Gunner E. I. Prime.
Driver A. Pringle.
*Bdr. E. P. Prisk.
Driver E. J. Pycroft.
Gunner E. J. Quinlan.
2nd Lieut. K. R. Rigby.
*Gunner F. S. Riley.
*Gunner W. C. Rimmer.
Gunner F. V. H. Robinson.
Bdr. K. J. Robinson.
Sergeant H. L. Ross.
Bdr. P. J. T. Roselli.
Gunner W. Sandison.
Sergeant W. Saunders.
Gunner P. Savigny.
Driver J. R. Scrimshaw.
*Fitter H. Selby.
Driver H. Sheerin.
Bdr. S. Shove.
Corporal W. A. Sinton.
Sergeant W. D. Smaill.
Bdr. H. P. Smith.
Driver D. P. Sperry.
Corporal R. W. Steele.
Sergeant A. Stewart.
Sergeant J. M. Stringer.

Gunner F. J. Sutton.
Gunner H. J. Thomas.
Gunner H. Thompson.
Bdr. C. W. Tomlinson.
Bdr. W. Trembath.
Corporal L. E. Tucker.
Bdr. J. Turkington.
Bdr. W. H. Turner.
Gunner P. W. Tyne.
*2nd Lieut. A. H. Vial.
Sergeant S. J. Vine.
Bdr. J. R. Voss.
Bdr. A. E. Warburton.
Corporal A. Watkins.
Corporal E. G. Watson.
Gunner E. A. T. White.
Gunner H. H. White.
Sergeant J. A. White.
*Bdr. W. C. White.
Gunner A. E. B. Wilkinson.
Sergeant S. A. Williams.
Gunner T. Williams.
Corporal J. F. Wilsher.
Sergeant H. F. Wilson.
Gunner R. P. Withell.
Corporal A. A. Wright.

Meritorious Service Medal.

S.-Sergeant C. L. W. Armitage.
Bdr. D. J. Alabaster.
R.S.M. C. Asher.
Bdr. W. Carrick.
Gunner R. D. Cochran.
S.S.M. F. S. Cooper.
Gunner C. Dent.
Corporal H. J. Dewsnap.
Sergeant A. J. Dumper.
B.Q.M.S. E. Dunstan.
Corporal S. W. Eustace.
Far.-Sergeant R. J. Hancock.
Sergeant A. B. Hudson.
Bdr. J. Lemon.
Driver W. M. Leitch.

S.-Sergeant J. R. McCardell.
Sergeant R. Macaulay.
Fitter L. D. McLean.
S.S.M. A. E. Manners.
Sergeant W. L. F. Porter.
Sergeant R. A. Ricketts.
Gunner W. T. Ritchie.
Gunner J. A. Rodgers.
S.S.M. H. W. Sinclair.
Gunner J. Slight.
Sergeant E. O. Spraggs.
Gunner H. Waugh.
*Gunner G. E. Whitfield.
Sergeant A. H. Youngman.

Mentioned in Despatches.

*Lieut. C. G. Adams.
Bdr. A. N. Andrews.
B.S.M. C. J. Atkins.
Corporal H. W. Auburn.
Gunner J. N. Baxter.
*Sergeant R. Birnie.
Sergeant R. M. Blackwell.
Captain S. Boscawen (2).
Corporal T. Buchanan.

*Gunner D. F. W. Bushell.
Fitter N. Clark.
Bdr. H. F. Cobb.
S.S.M. F. S. Cooper.
Sergeant A. J. Cosbrook.
Lieut. A. J. Coutts.
Captain D. M. Cuthbertson.
Major H. J. Daltry, D.S.O. (2).
*Lieut. F. Daly.

APPENDIX

Captain G. E. Daniell, M.C.
Captain H. V. Davies.
Lieut. J. M. T. Downey.
Corporal W. A. Duggan.
Sergeant E. Dunstan.
Captain W. E. Earnshaw.
Lieut. C. J. K. Edwards.
Captain P. J. Ellis, M.C.
Lieut.-Col. N. S. Falla, C.M.G., D.S.O. (4).
Major T. Farr, D.S.O., M.C. (2).
Q.M.S. Artificer W. E. Ford.
Major D. E. Gardner (2).
Major H. C. Glendining.
2nd Lieut. C. W. Greig.
Sergeant R. N. Hamlin.
Gunner W. H. Harris.
Lieut. W. J. Hicks (2).
Sergeant J. Hill.
Sergeant V. H. Hoare.
Corporal A. E. Hunt.
Lieut. W. Ibbotson.
Bdr. D. C. Inglis.
Captain R. Irvine.
Lieut. A. R. Jacobson.
Sergeant R. C. Jamieson.
Captain W. Janson.
Captain C. H. G. Joplin.
2nd Lieut. L. A. Johnson.
Captain D. G. Johnston.
Brig.-General G. N. Johnston, C.M.G., D.S.O. (7)
Corporal V. L. Jones.
Lieut. E. F. H. Knowles.
2nd Lieut. W. A. Knox.
Lieut. J. J. Kyne (2).
Bdr. D. H. Lilico.
Major C. McGilp, D.S.O. (2).
Captain J. G. McKenzie.
Lieut. R. McPherson, M.C.
Gunner L. J. Mander.
Major R. Miles, D.S.O., M.C.
Captain R. G. Milligan (3).
2nd Lieut. F. M. Mitchell.
*2nd Lieut. S. Moore.
Lieut. W. L. Moore.
Sergeant L. G. Morrison.
Lieut. C. H. Nelson.
Lieut. R. Nelson, M.C.
Captain E. G. Norman, M.C.
Gunner W. C. Norman.
Corporal H. W. Pascoe.
Lieut. W. Pollard.
*Major J. M. Richmond, D.S.O., M.C. (4).
*Major V. Rogers, D.S.O.
Sergeant B. J. Russell.
*Sergeant H R. Salmon.
Major C. Sommerville, D.S.O. (2).
Lieut.-Col. I. T. Standish, C.M.G., D.S.O. (2).
Corporal R. Stewart.
Lieut.-Col. F. B. Sykes, D.S.O. (4).
Lieut.-Col. F. Symon, C.M.G., D.S.O. (2).
Bdr. J. P. Thompson.
*Captain J. L. H. Turner, M.C.
2nd Lieut. S. V. Tyler.
2nd Lieut. R. G. Vernon.
2nd Lieut. R. F. Vial.
Lieut. H. N. Webster.
Major R. C. Wickens, D.S.O.
Major H. G. Wilding, D.S.O. (2).
Gunner S. A. Wilson.
Lieut. E. R. Winkler.
Sergeant A. H. Youngman.

FOREIGN DECORATIONS.
FRENCH.

Legion of Honour (Croix d'Officier).
Brig.-General G. N. Johnston, C.M.G., D.S.O.

Croix de Guerre.

S.S.M. F. S. Cooper.
Sergeant A. J. Cosbrook.
Major C. N. Newman, D.S.O.

Medaille Militaire.
Sergeant R. Stewart.

BELGIAN.
Belgian Croix de Guerre.

Gunner H. Armitage.
Sergeant A. C. M. Barker.
Sergeant J. D. Beattie.
Captain S. Boscawen.
Sergeant R. J. Cox.
Bdr. A. K. Greves.
Sergeant V. H. Hoare.

Gunner A. W. McLeod.
Sergeant H. Muir, D.C.M.
Bdr. R. G. Thackwell.
B.S.M. G. Varrell.
Sergeant A. E. Wixon.
Sergeant T. M. Woodrow.

SERBIAN.
Silver Medal.

Gunner J. M. Boocock.   Gunner W. C. White.

ROUMANIAN.
Medaille Barbatie si Credentia.

2nd Class—Sergt. R. N. Hamlin.   3rd Class—Driver V. Bockman.

www.ingramcontent.com/pod-product-compliance
Lightning Source LLC
Chambersburg PA
CBHW021827220426
43663CB00005B/155